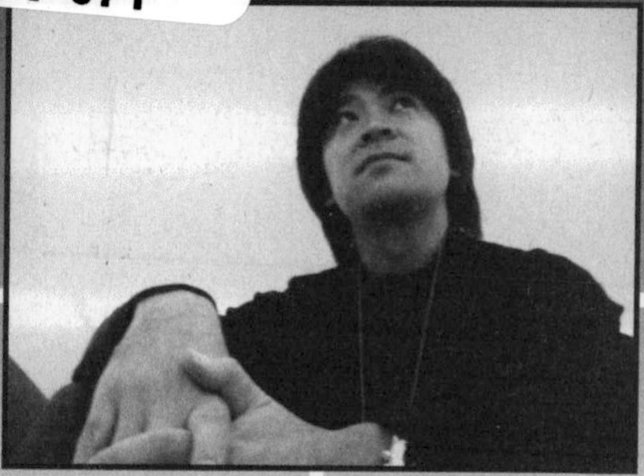

I finished writing the lyrics for the upcoming *Prince of Tennis* CD. I wasn't planning on singing on it, but somehow I wound up in the studio. The backup vocals with the assistants went well. We did about seventy takes, and when we were done we all felt a strange sense of unity.

— Takeshi Konomi, 2008

About Takeshi Konomi

Takeshi Konomi exploded onto the manga scene with the incredible **THE PRINCE OF TENNIS.** His refined art style and sleek character designs proved popular with **Weekly Shonen Jump** readers, and **THE PRINCE OF TENNIS** became the number one sports manga in Japan almost overnight. Its cast of fascinating male tennis players attracted legions of female readers even though it was originally intended to be a boys' comic. The manga continues to be a success in Japan and has inspired a hit anime series, as well as several video games and mountains of merchandise.

THE PRINCE OF TENNIS
VOL. 41
SHONEN JUMP Manga Edition

STORY AND ART BY
TAKESHI KONOMI

Translation/Joe Yamazaki
Touch-up Art & Lettering/Vanessa Satone
Design/Sam Elzway
Editor/Daniel Gillespie

Printed in Canada

Published by VIZ Media, LLC
P.O. Box 77010
San Francisco, CA 94107

10 9 8 7 6 5 4 3 2 1
First printing, April 2011

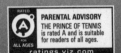

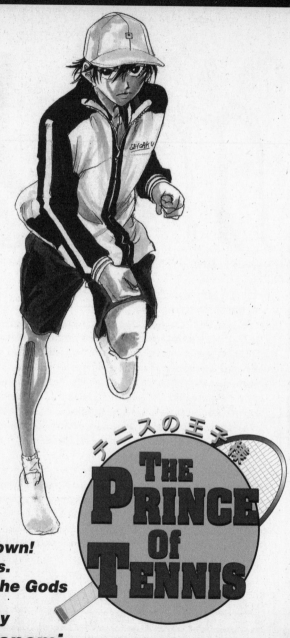

SHONEN JUMP Manga

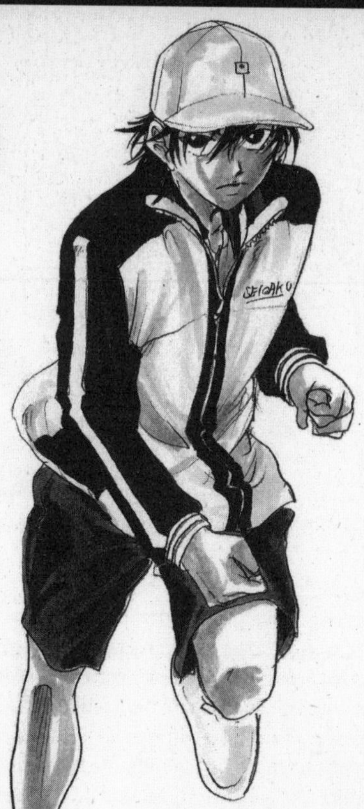

テニスの王子様

THE PRINCE OF TENNIS

VOL. 41

Final Showdown! The Prince vs. the Child of the Gods

Story & Art by
Takeshi Konomi

ENNIS CLUB

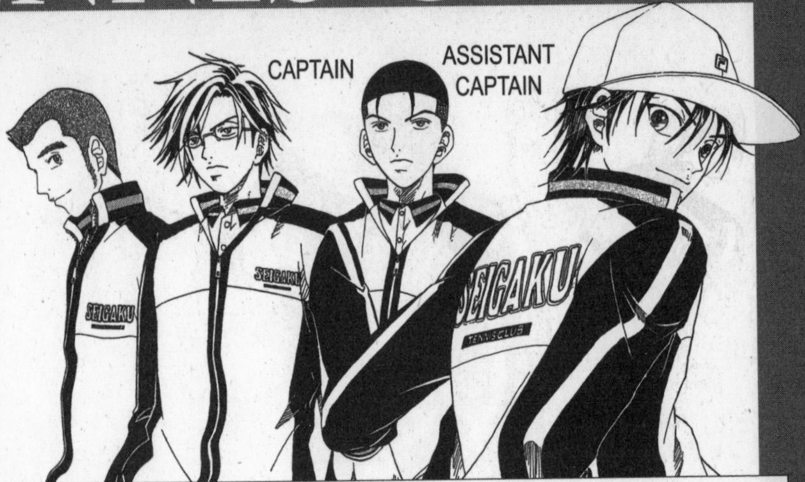
CAPTAIN
ASSISTANT CAPTAIN

• TAKASHI KAWAMURA • KUNIMITSU TEZUKA • SHUICHIRO OISHI • RYOMA ECHIZEN •

Seishun Academy student Ryoma Echizen is a tennis prodigy, with wins in four consecutive U.S. Junior Tennis Tournaments under his belt. He became a starter as a 7th grader and led his team to the District Preliminaires! Despite a few mishaps, Seishun won the Destrict Prelims and the City Tournament, and earned a ticket to the Kanto Tournament. The team came away victorious from its first-round matches, but captain Kunimitsu Tezuka injured his shoulder and went to Kyushu for treatment. Despite losing Kunimitsu and assistant captain Shuichiro to injury, Seishun pulled together as a team, winning the Kanto Tournament and earning a slot at the Nationals!

With Kunimitsu recovered and back on the team, Seishun enter the Nationals with their strongest lineup and defeat Okinawa's Higa Junior High in the opening round, Hyotei in the quarterfinals, and Shitenhoji in the semifinals. In the final round, they're up against Rikkai. After losing both Singles 3 and Doubles 2, Seishun's backs are against the wall. They send Fuji out to face the Nio, the con artist of the court! Fuji struggles against Nio's pitch-perfect simulation of Kunimitsu, but…?!

STORY &

HARACTERS

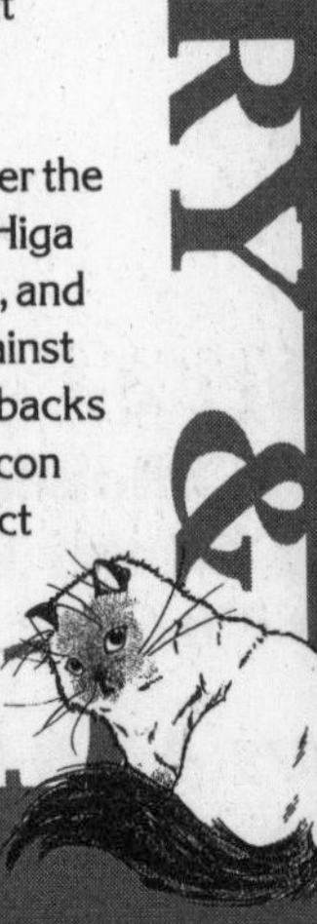

SEIGAKU T

KAORU KAIDO ● TAKESHI MOMOSHIRO ● SADAHARU INUI ● EIJI KIKUMARU ● SHUSUKE FUJI ●

SHITENHOJI

KINTARO TOYAMA

HYOTEI ACADEMY

KEIGO ATOBE

SEISHUN ACADEMY
TENNIS COACH

SUMIRE RYUZAKI

RIKKAI

BUNTA MARUI

RIKKAI

MASAHARU NIO

RIKKAI

SEIICHI YUKIMURA

RIKKAI

GENICHIRO SANADA

RIKKAI

JACKAL KUWAHARA

RIKKAI

AKAYA KIRIHARA

CONTENTS

Vol. 41
Final Showdown! The Prince vs. the Child of the Gods

Genius 362: Shusuke Fuji's Ultimate Struggle   7
~Second Best~

Genius 363: With Eyes Shut, I Think of You, I Feel You   25

Genius 364: Con   43

Genius 365: The Moment of Movement   61

Genius 366: Remember!!   79

Genius 367: One Piece of Memory   97

Genius 368: Bond   115

Genius 369: Connect to Ryoma   133

Genius 370: Reinforcements   151

Genius 371: Final Showdown!   169
The Prince vs. the Child of the Gods

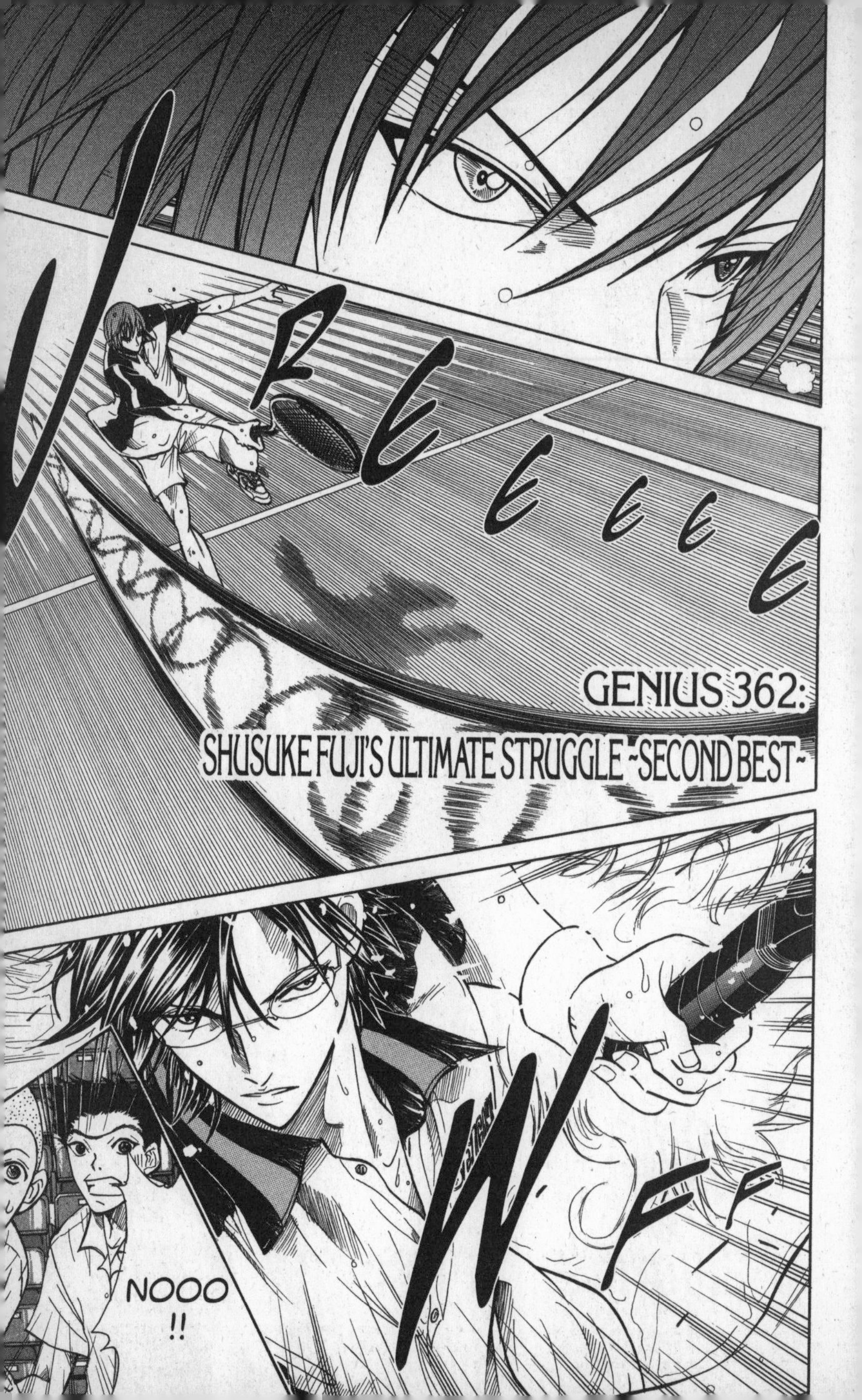
GENIUS 362:
SHUSUKE FUJI'S ULTIMATE STRUGGLE ~SECOND BEST~
WFFF
NOOO !!

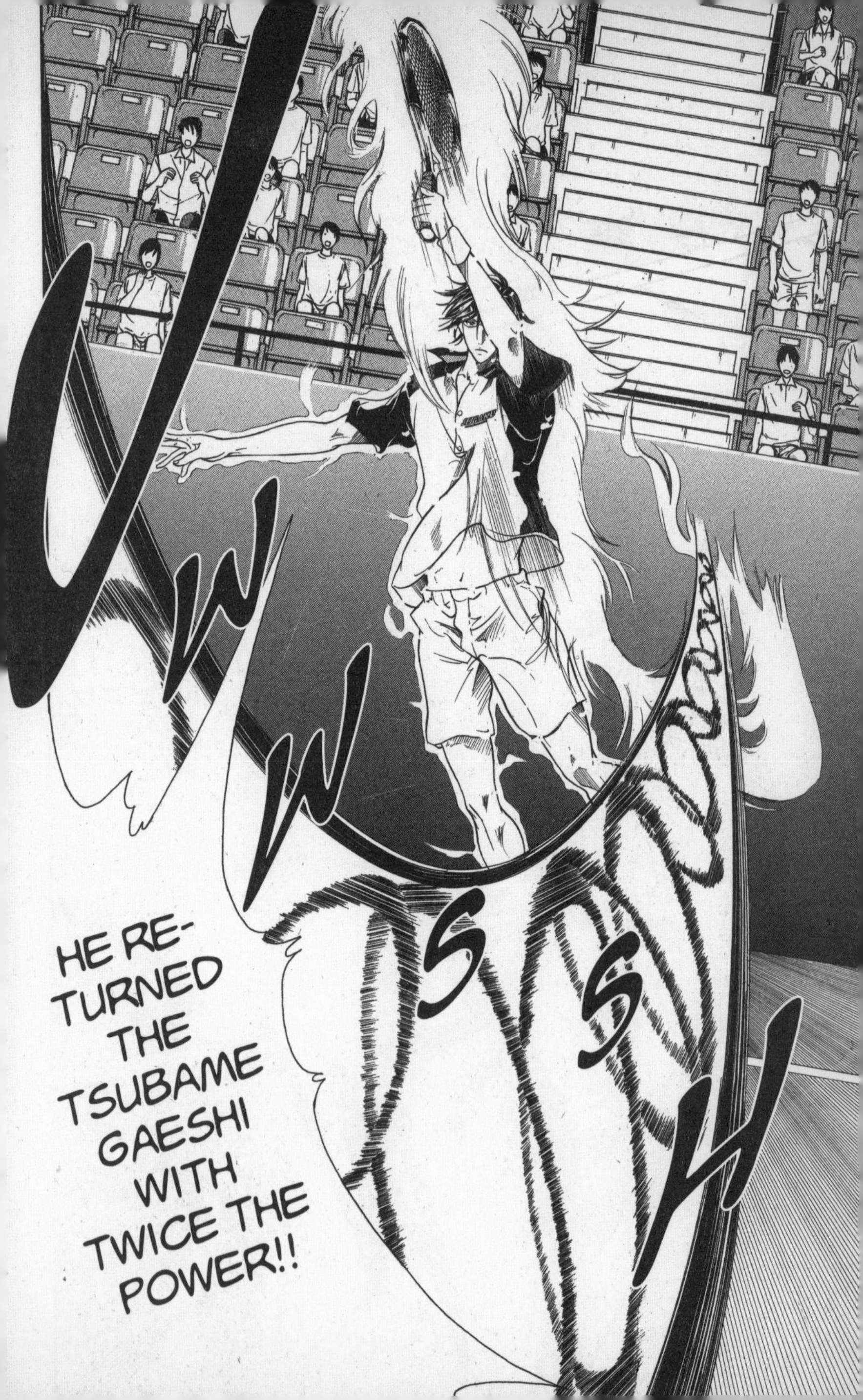
WWWSSH
HE RE-TURNED THE TSUBAME GAESHI WITH TWICE THE POWER!!

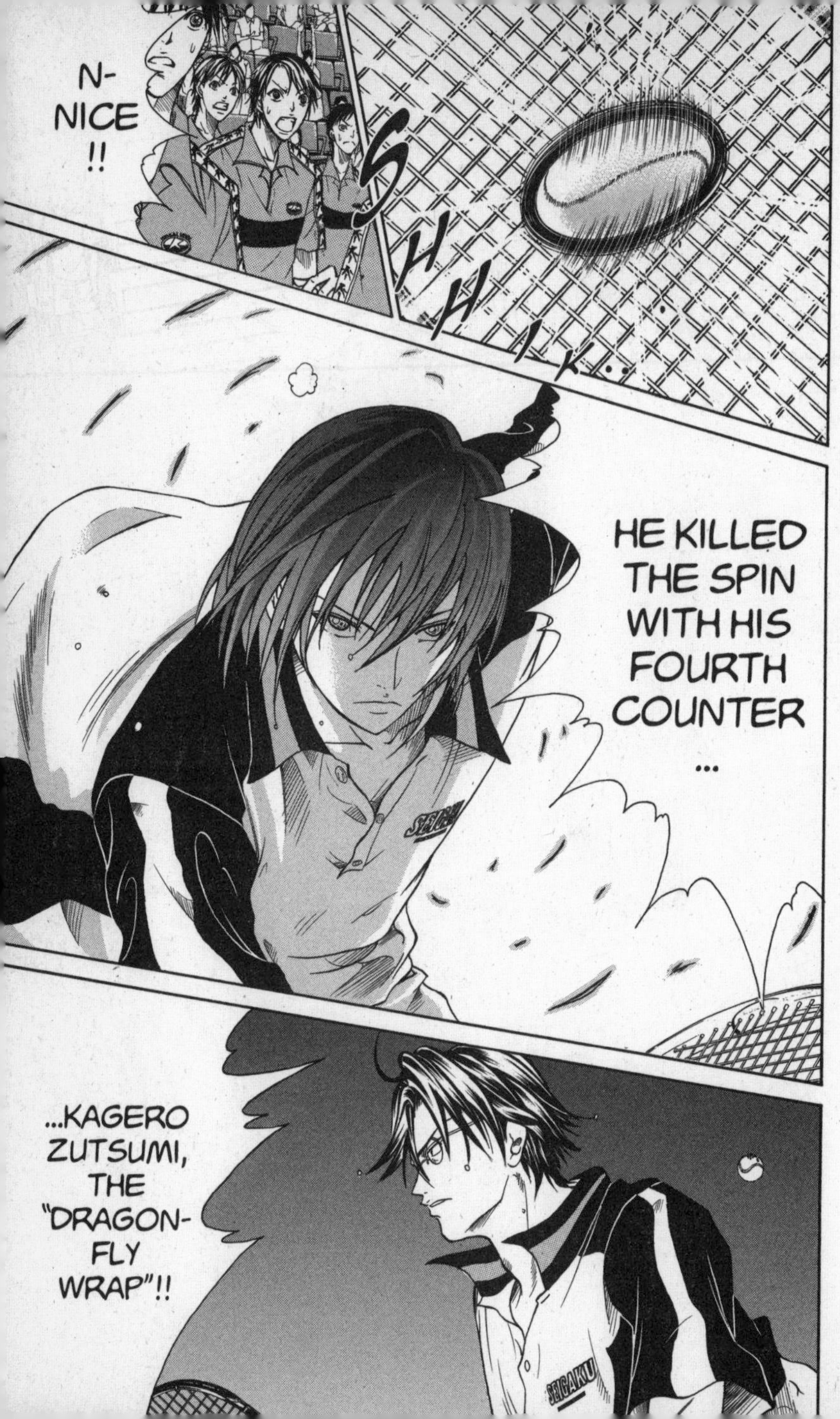
SHHIK...
N-NICE!!
HE KILLED THE SPIN WITH HIS FOURTH COUNTER...
...KAGERO ZUTSUMI, THE "DRAGON-FLY WRAP"!!
SEIGAKU

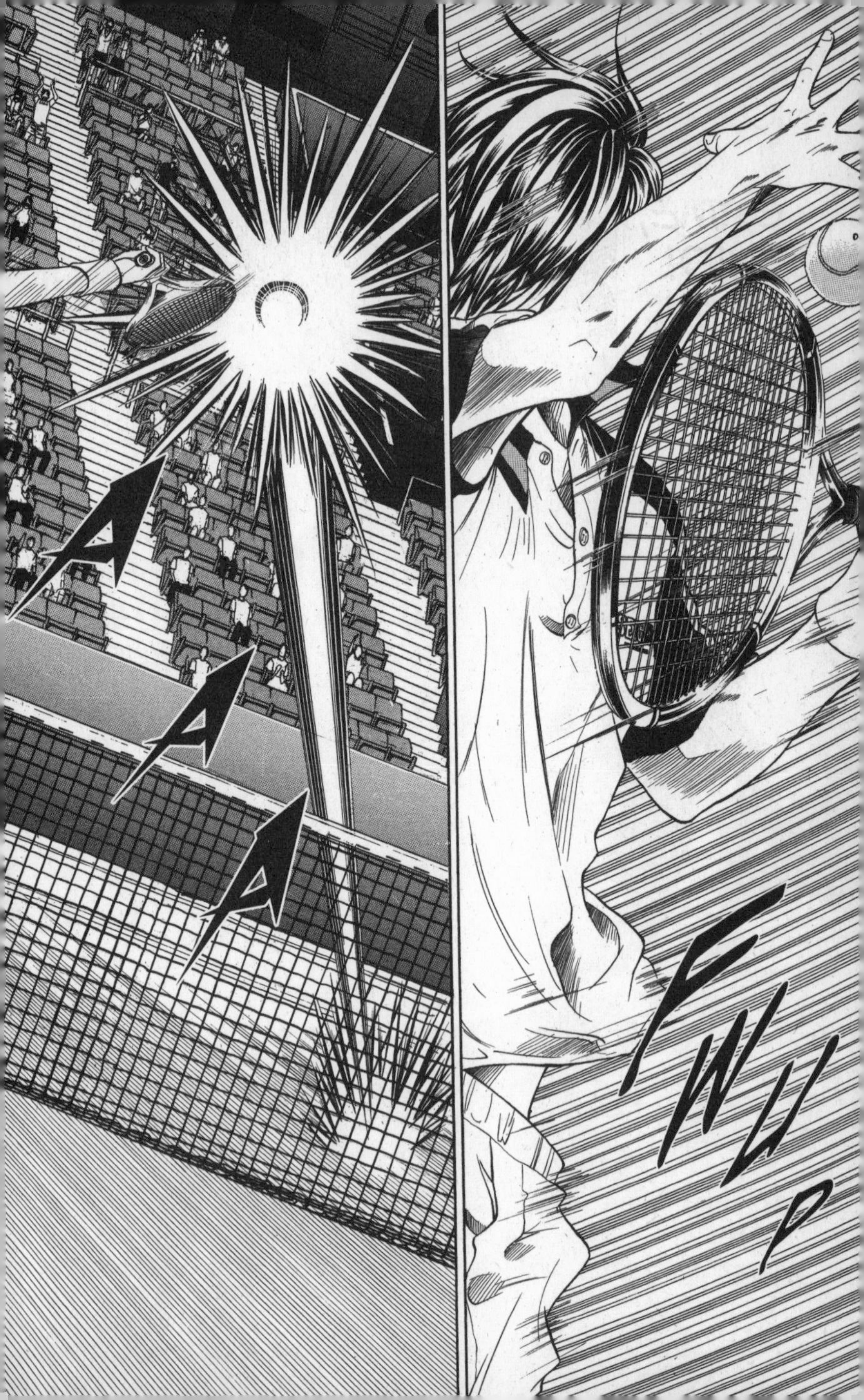
FWUP

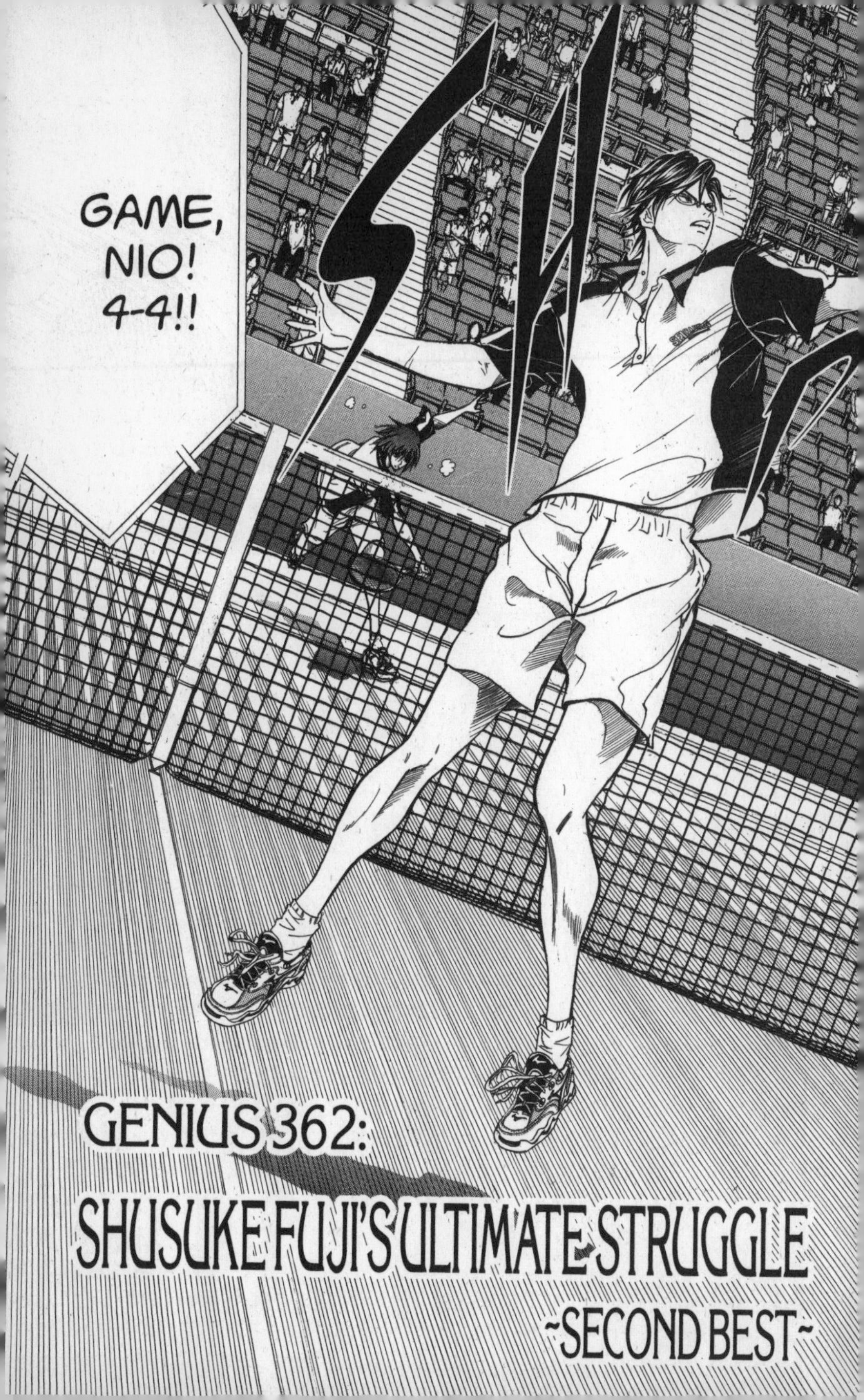
GAME, NIO! 4-4!!
GENIUS 362:
SHUSUKE FUJI'S ULTIMATE STRUGGLE
~SECOND BEST~

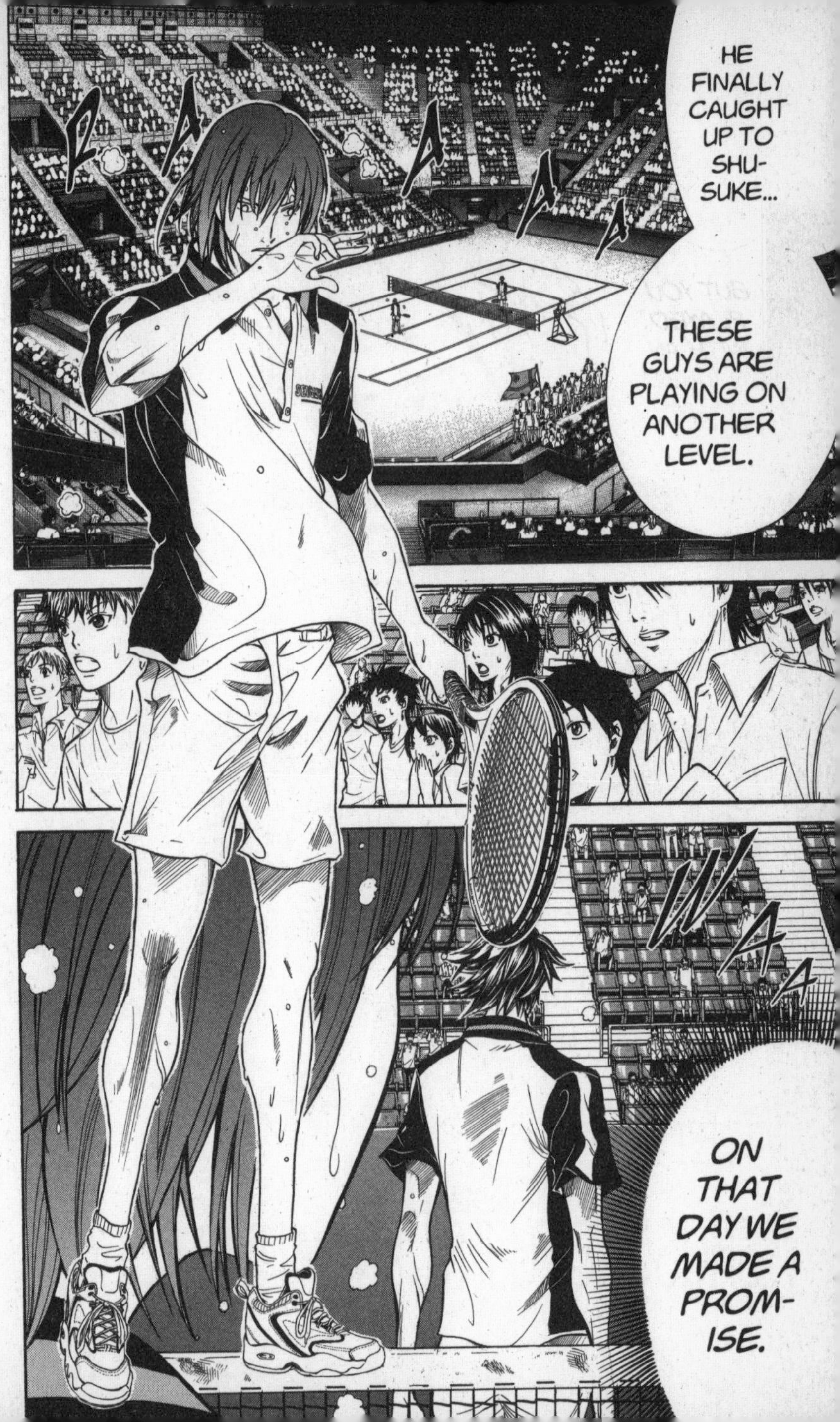
HE FINALLY CAUGHT UP TO SHU-SUKE...
THESE GUYS ARE PLAYING ON ANOTHER LEVEL.
ZAAAAA
WAAA
ON THAT DAY WE MADE A PROM-ISE.

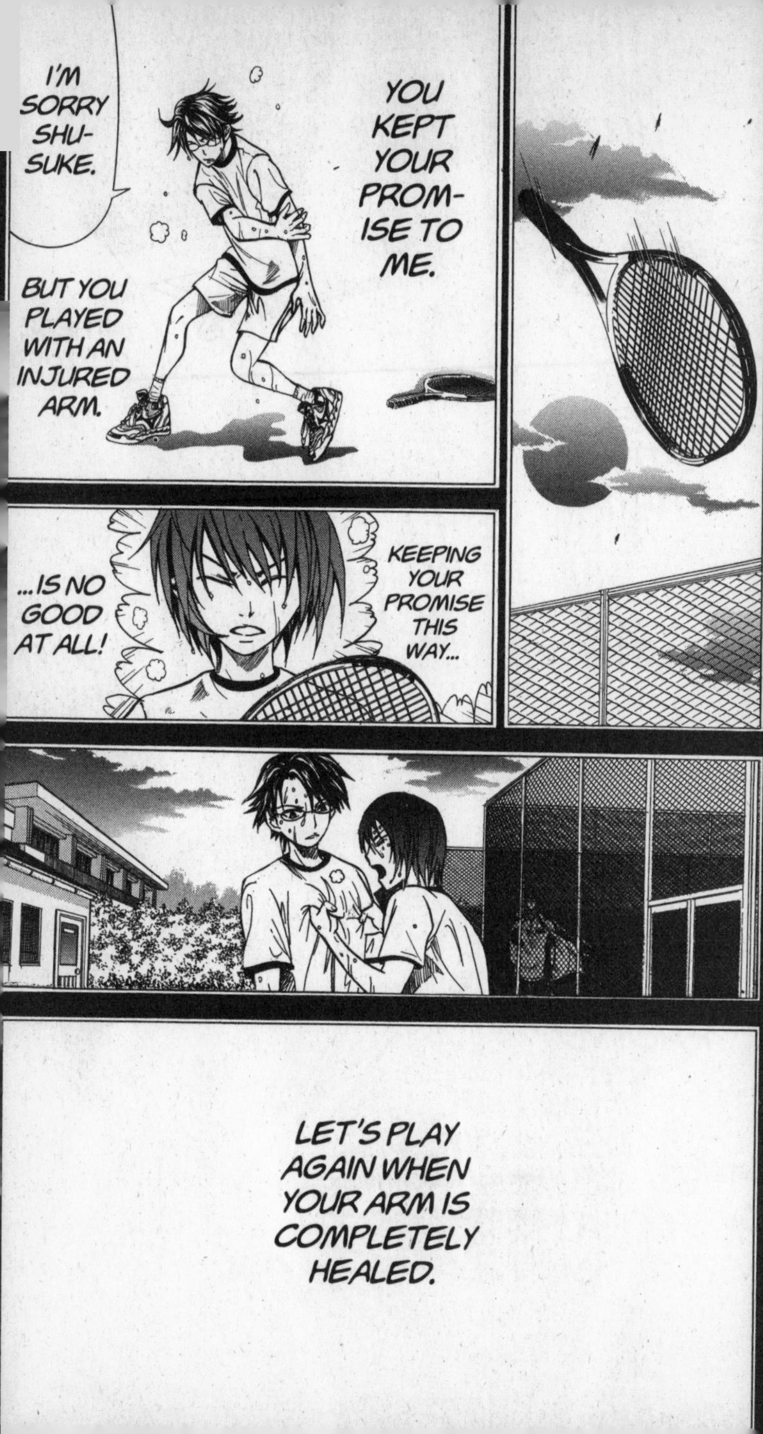
YOU KEPT YOUR PROMISE TO ME.
I'M SORRY SHUSUKE.
BUT YOU PLAYED WITH AN INJURED ARM.
KEEPING YOUR PROMISE THIS WAY...
...IS NO GOOD AT ALL!
LET'S PLAY AGAIN WHEN YOUR ARM IS COMPLETELY HEALED.

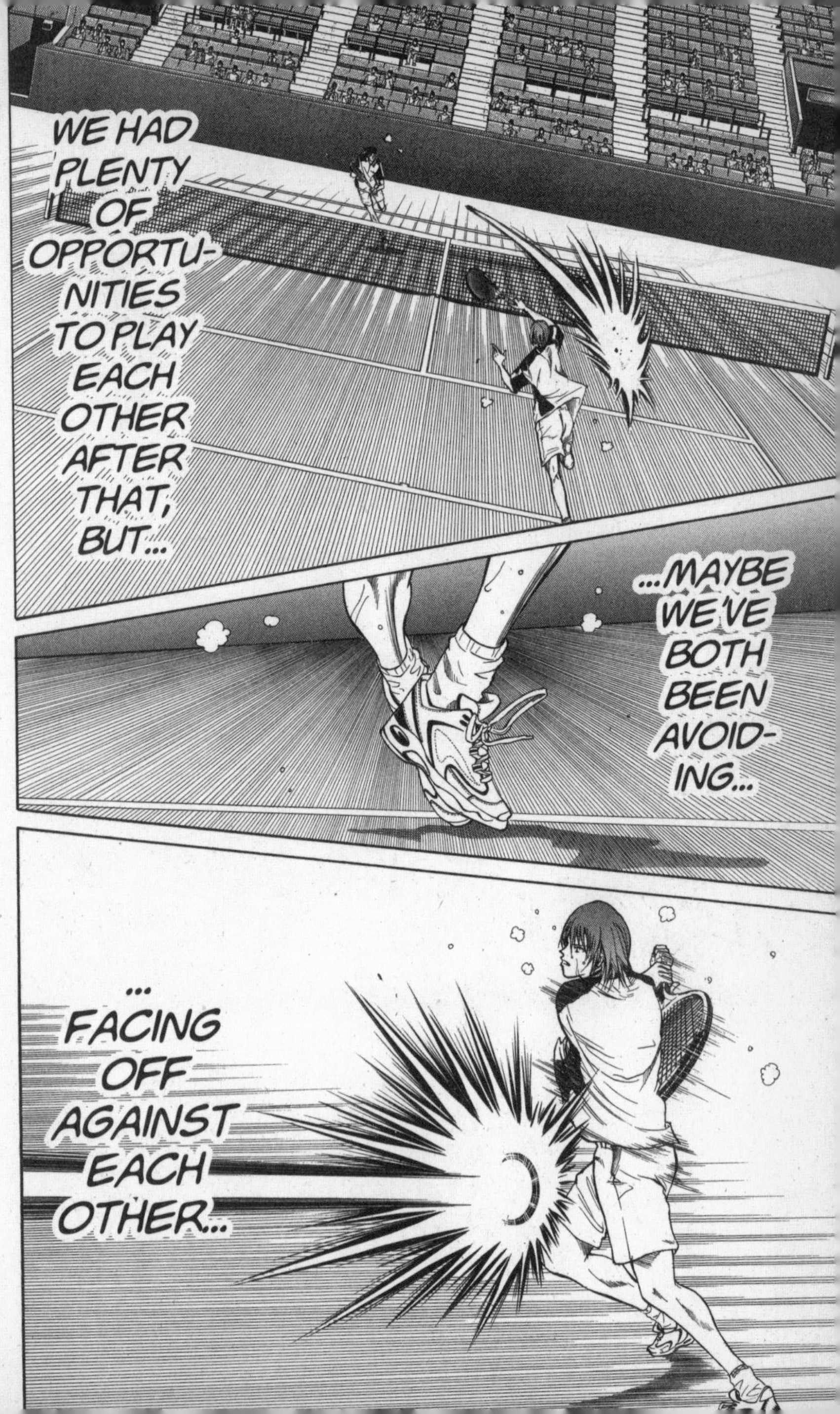
WE HAD PLENTY OF OPPORTUNITIES TO PLAY EACH OTHER AFTER THAT, BUT...
...MAYBE WE'VE BOTH BEEN AVOIDING...
... FACING OFF AGAINST EACH OTHER...

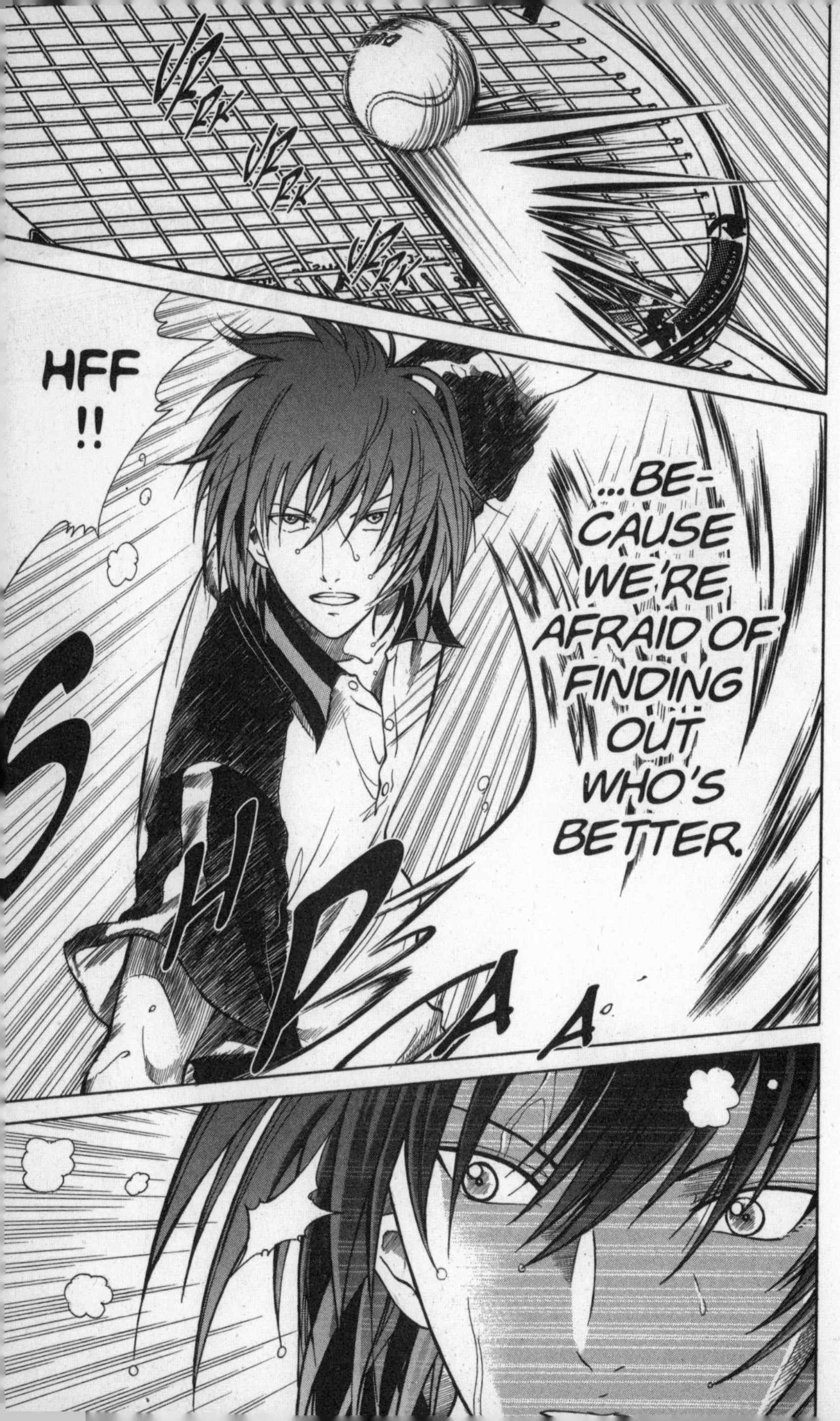
...BE-CAUSE WE'RE AFRAID OF FINDING OUT WHO'S BETTER.
HFF !!
SHPAA

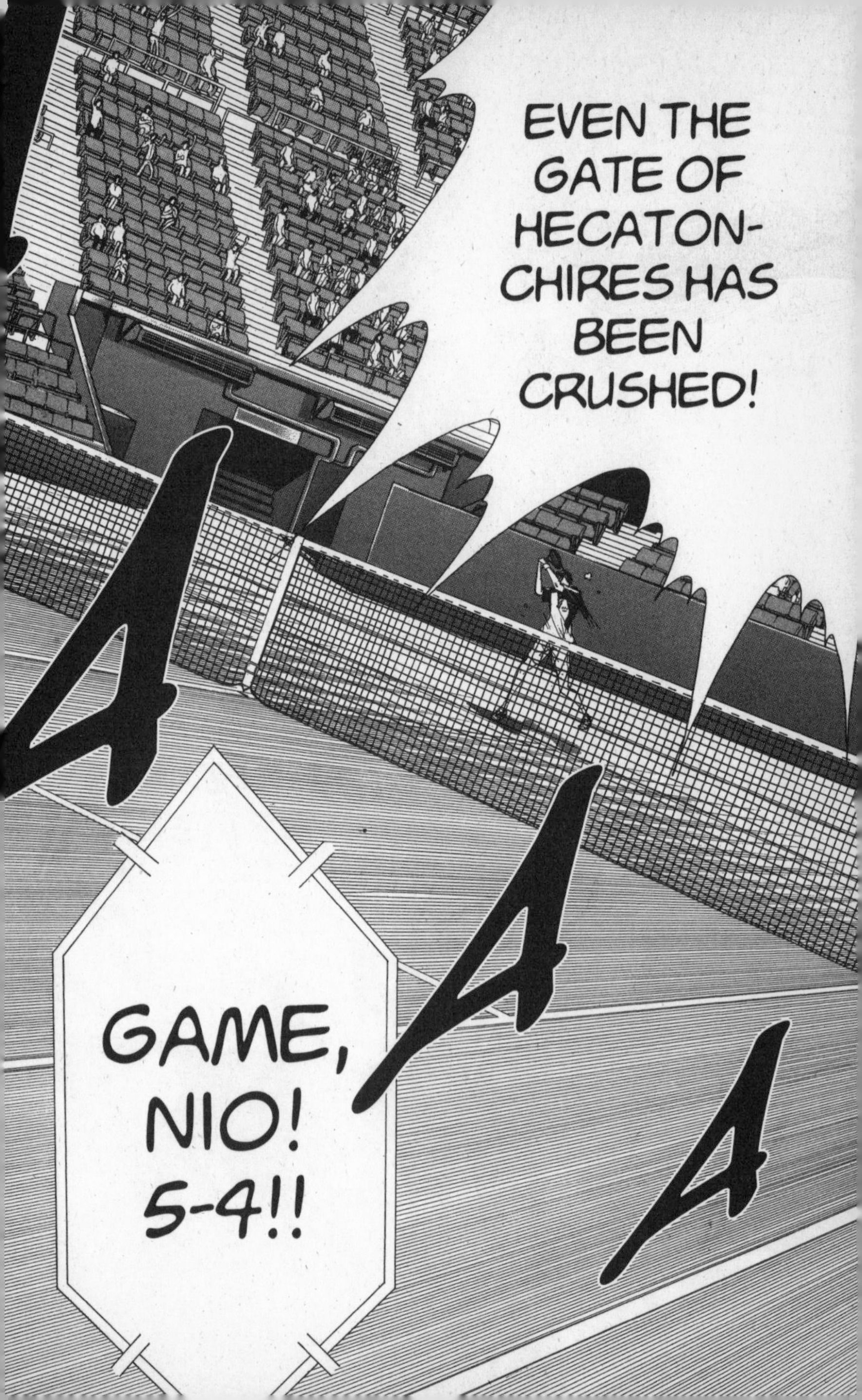
EVEN THE GATE OF HECATON-CHIRES HAS BEEN CRUSHED!
GAME, NIO! 5-4!!

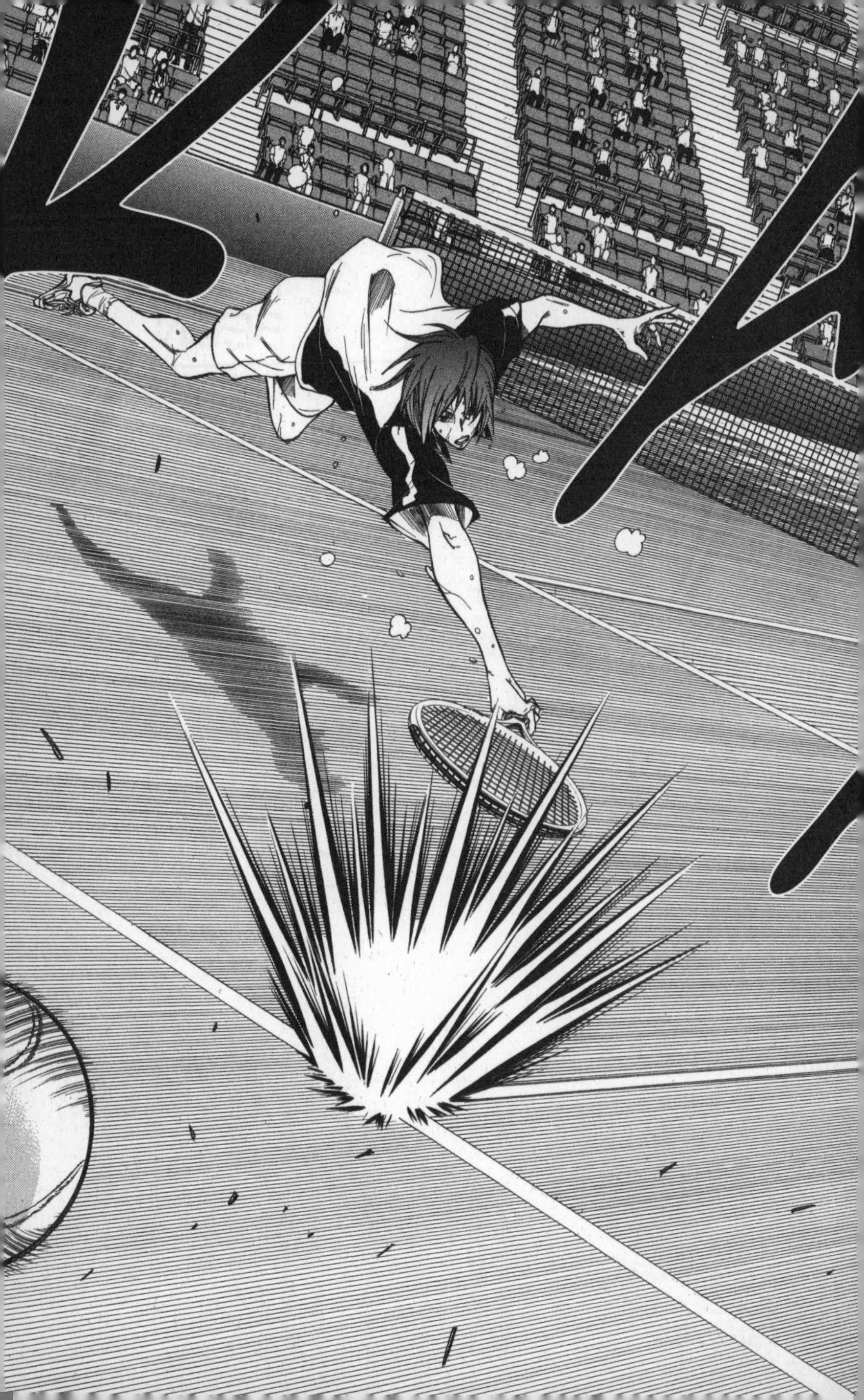

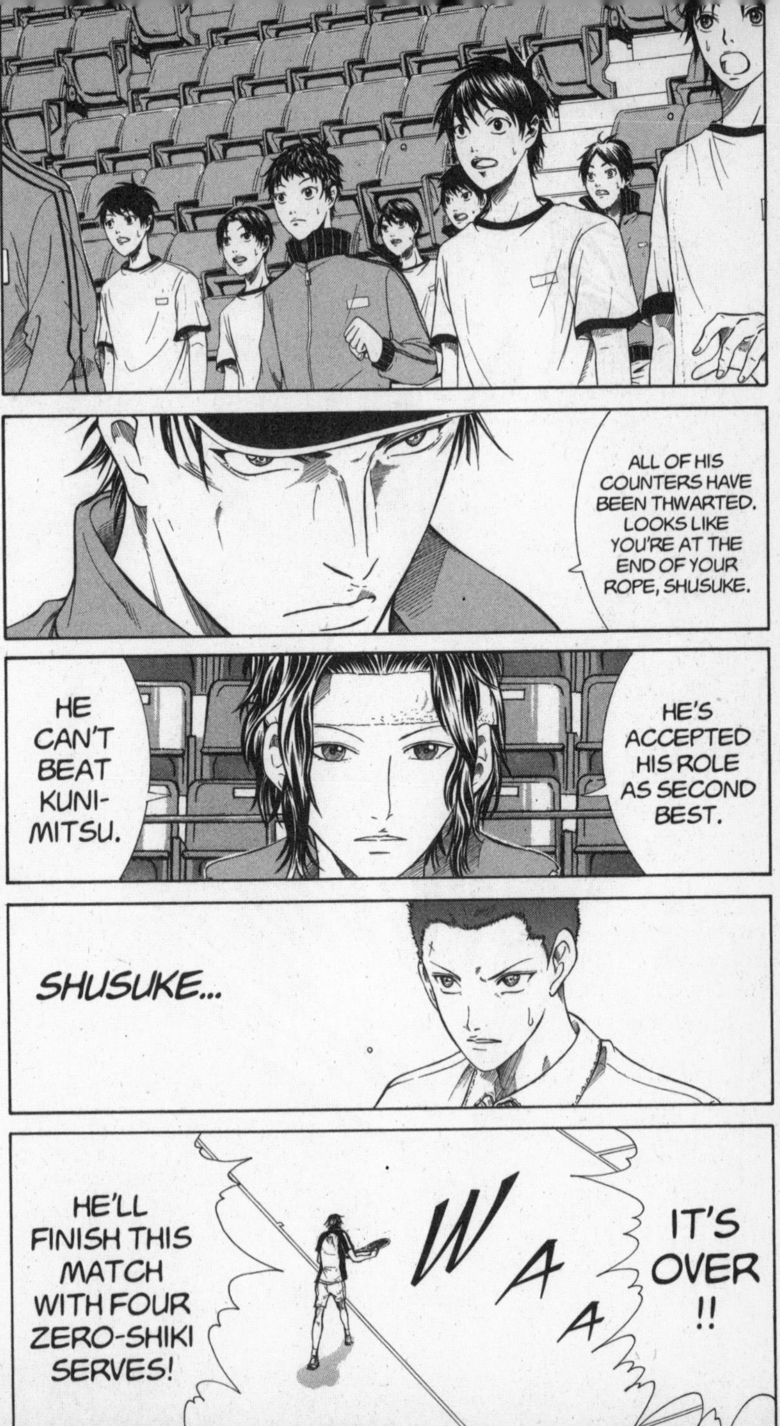
ALL OF HIS COUNTERS HAVE BEEN THWARTED. LOOKS LIKE YOU'RE AT THE END OF YOUR ROPE, SHUSUKE.
HE'S ACCEPTED HIS ROLE AS SECOND BEST.
HE CAN'T BEAT KUNI-MITSU.
SHUSUKE...
IT'S OVER!!
WAA
HE'LL FINISH THIS MATCH WITH FOUR ZERO-SHIKI SERVES!

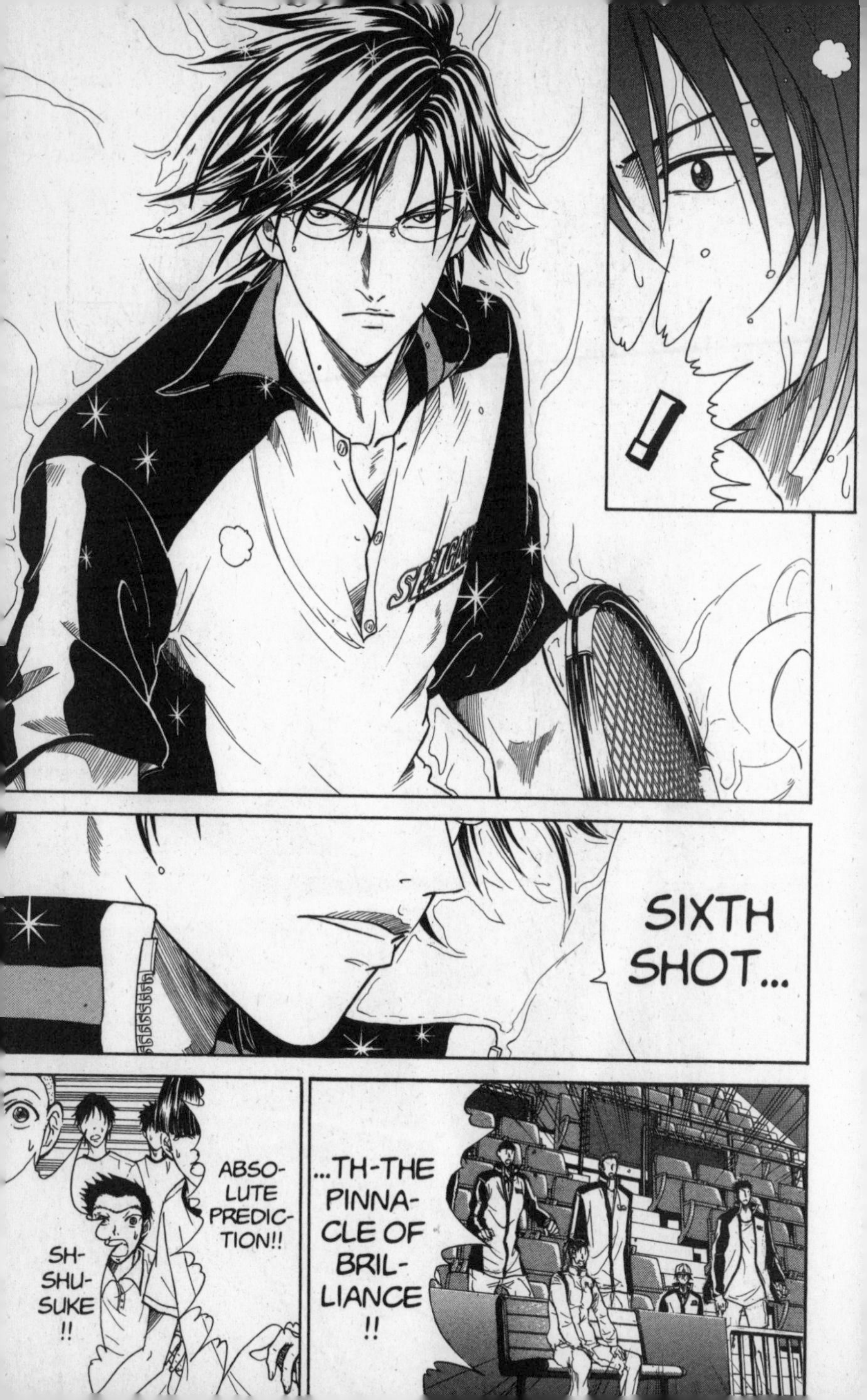
!
SIXTH SHOT...
...TH-THE PINNACLE OF BRILLIANCE!!
ABSOLUTE PREDICTION!!
SH-SHUSUKE!!

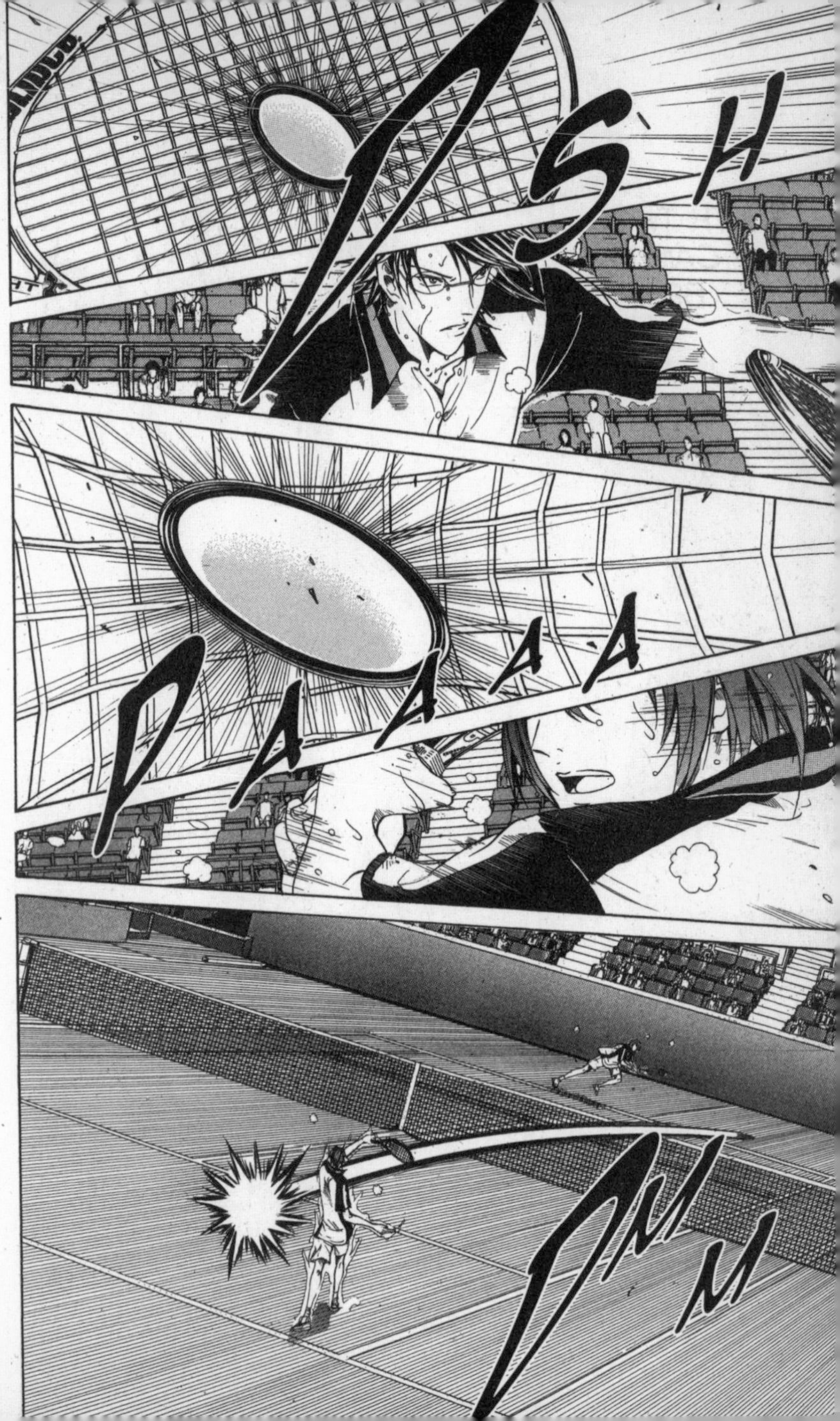

WHSH
DAAAA
DMM

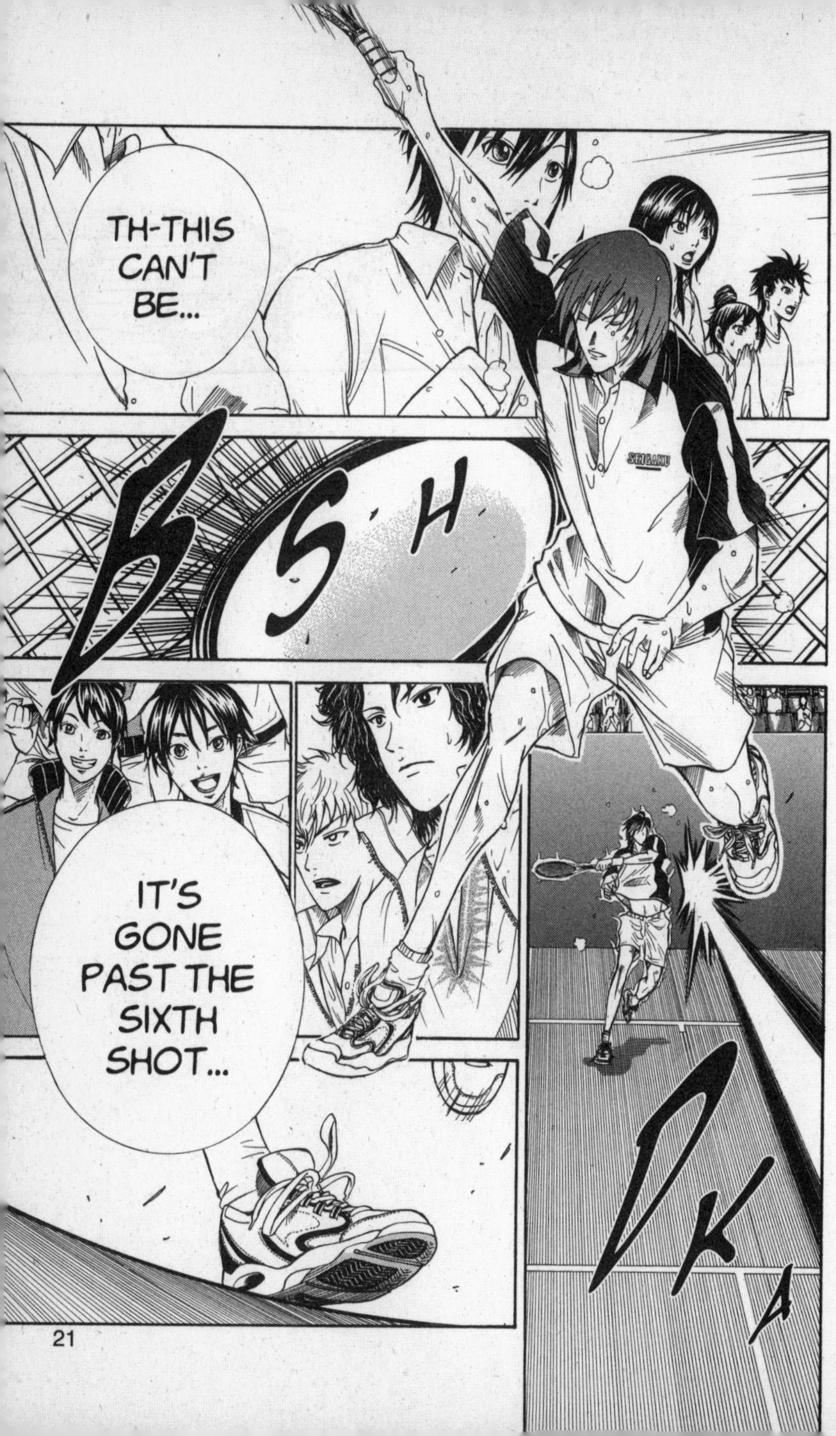
TH-THIS CAN'T BE...
BSH
IT'S GONE PAST THE SIXTH SHOT...
DKA

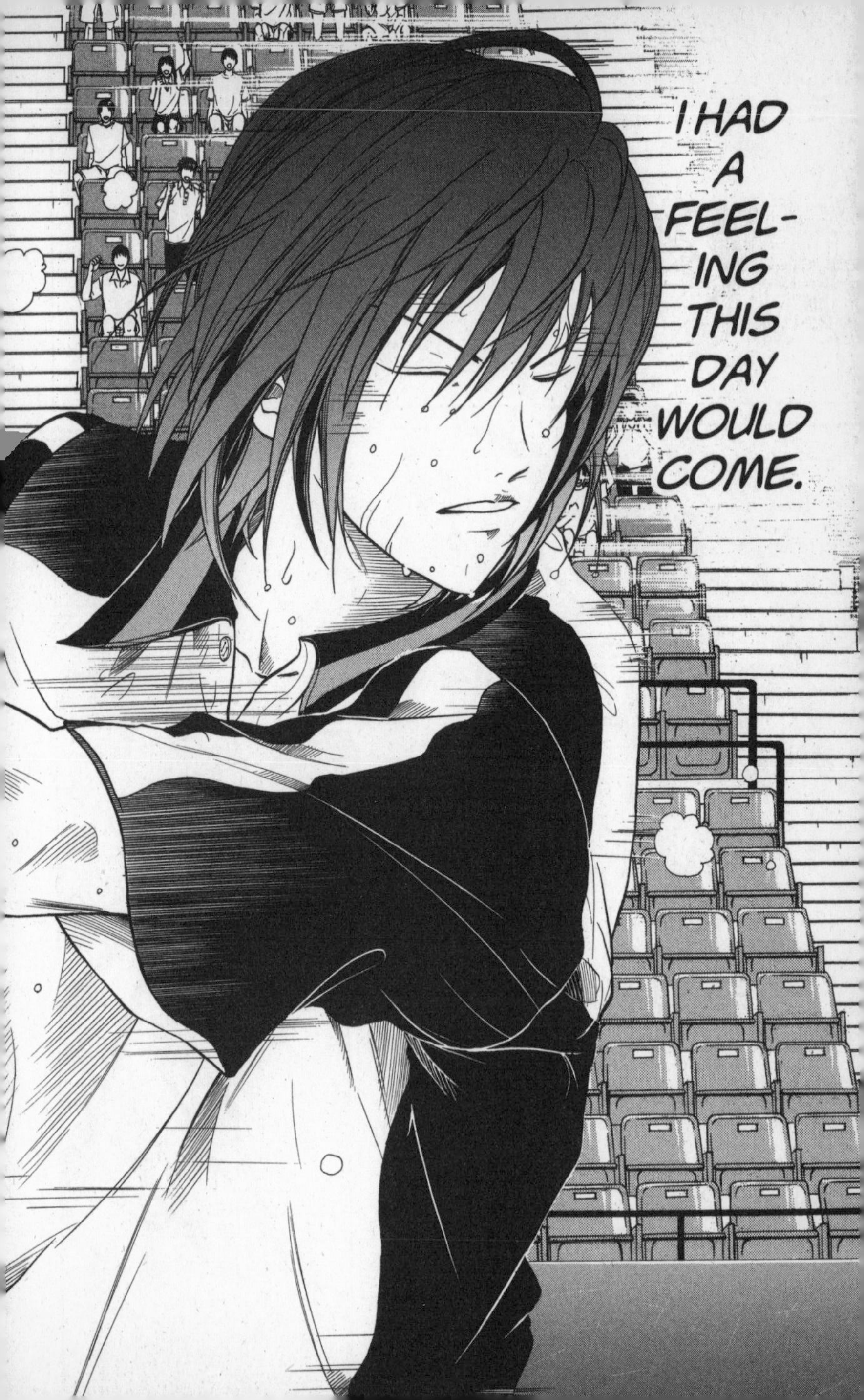
I HAD A FEELING THIS DAY WOULD COME.

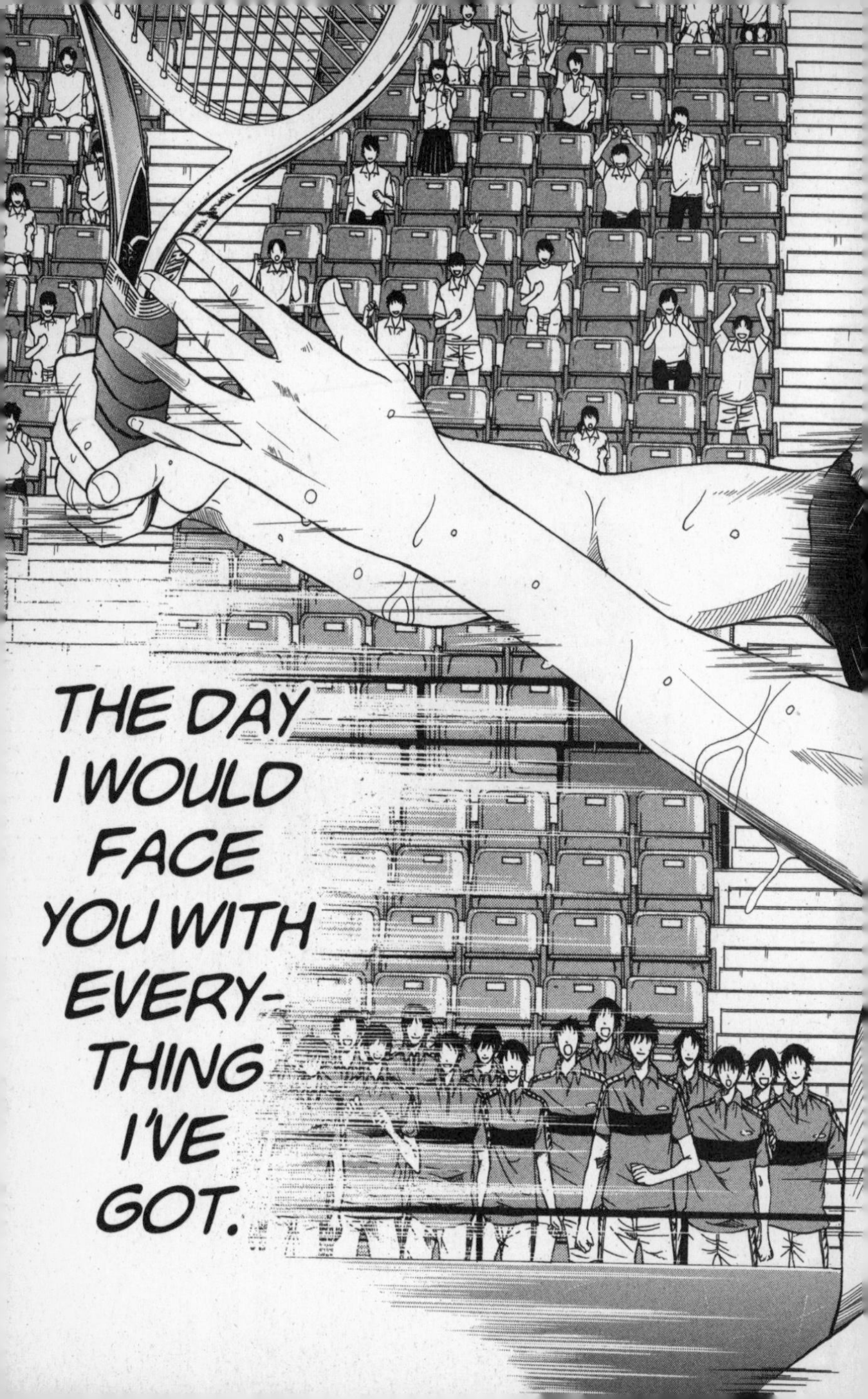
THE DAY I WOULD FACE YOU WITH EVERY-THING I'VE GOT.

テニスの王子様

THE PRINCE OF TENNIS

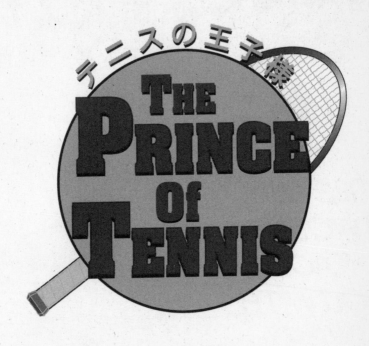

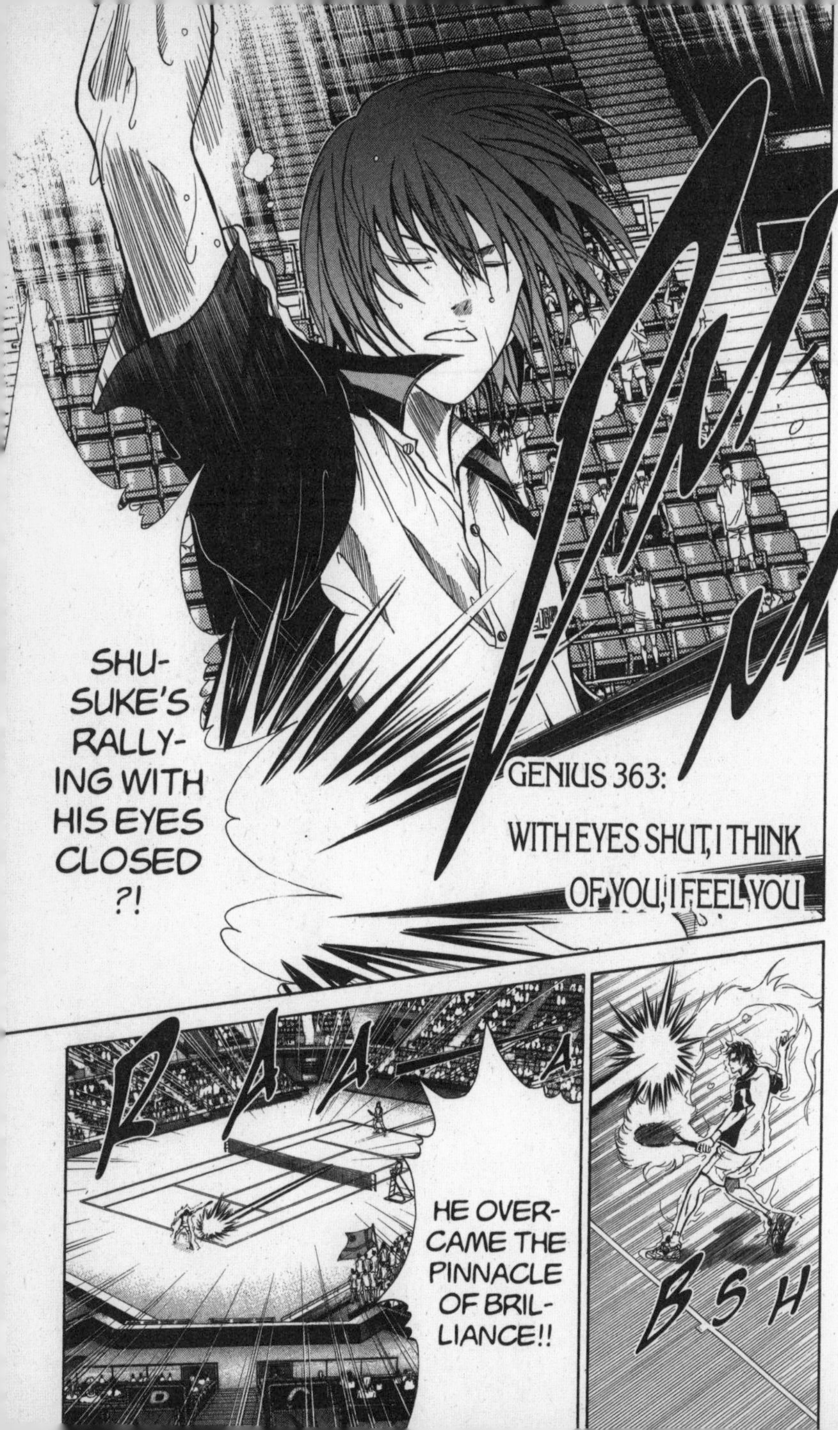
GENIUS 363:
WITH EYES SHUT, I THINK OF YOU, I FEEL YOU
SHUSUKE'S RALLYING WITH HIS EYES CLOSED ?!
BSH
RAAA-
HE OVERCAME THE PINNACLE OF BRILLIANCE!!

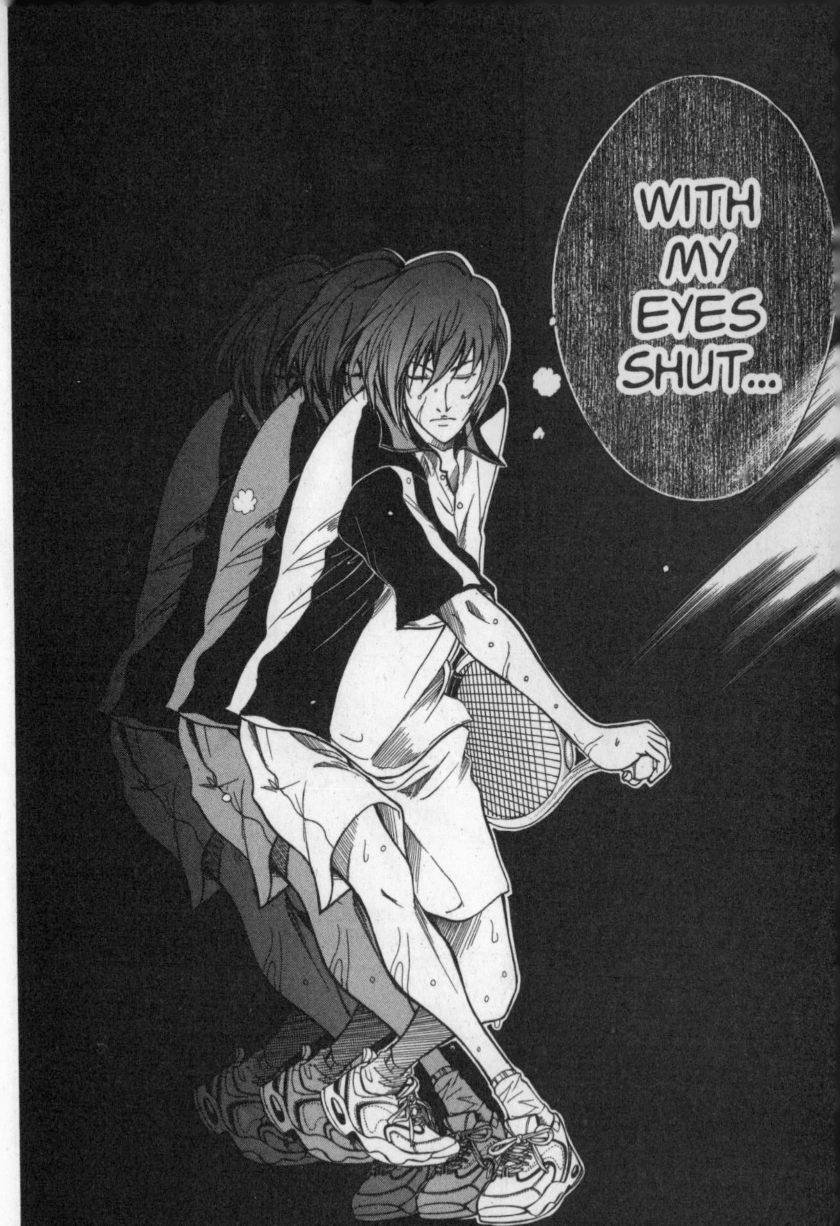
WITH MY EYES SHUT...

GENIUS 363:

WITH EYES SHUT, I THINK OF YOU, I FEEL YOU

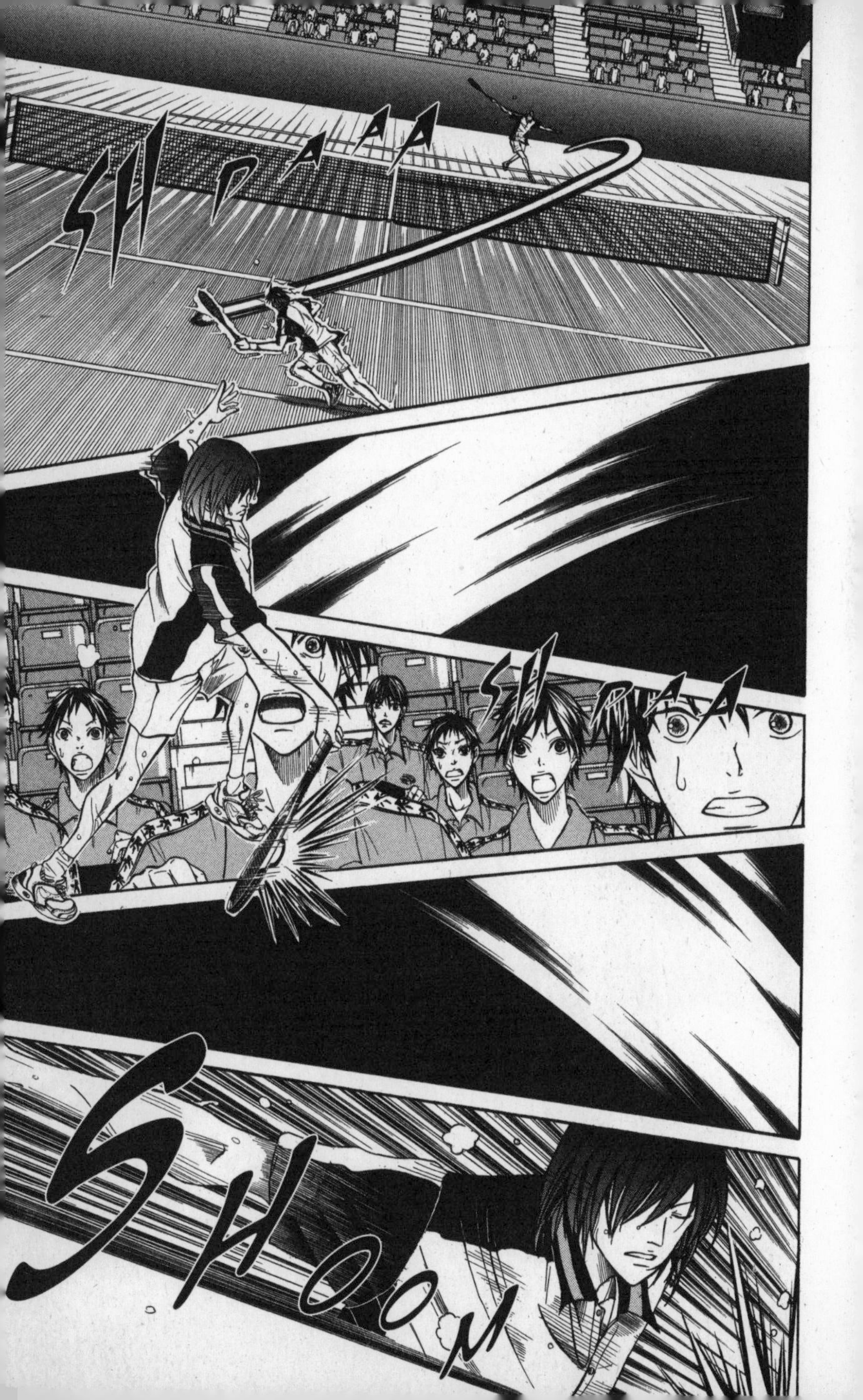
SHPAAA
SHPAA
SHOOM

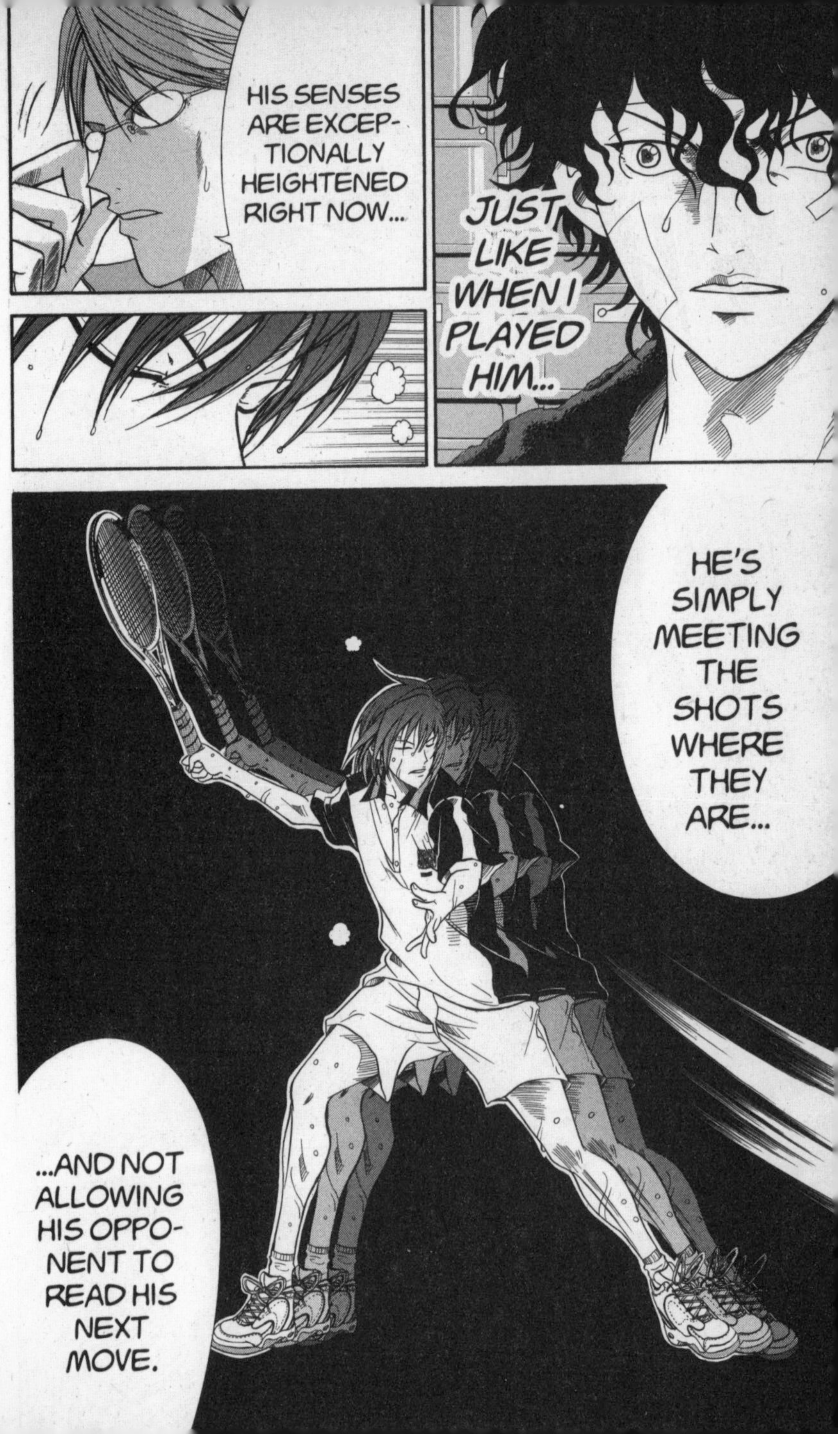
JUST LIKE WHEN I PLAYED HIM...
HIS SENSES ARE EXCEPTIONALLY HEIGHTENED RIGHT NOW...
HE'S SIMPLY MEETING THE SHOTS WHERE THEY ARE...
...AND NOT ALLOWING HIS OPPONENT TO READ HIS NEXT MOVE.

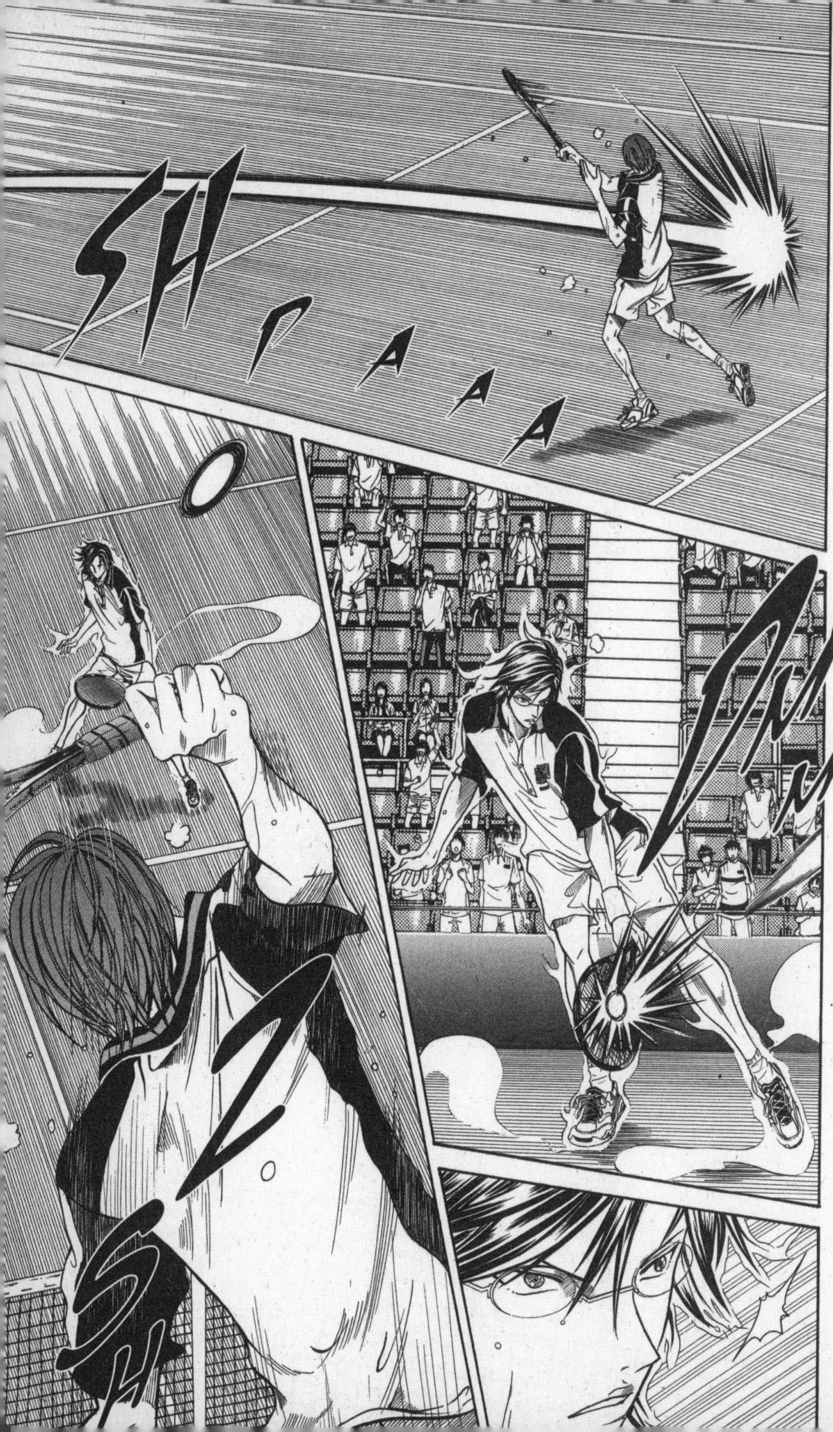
SHRAAA

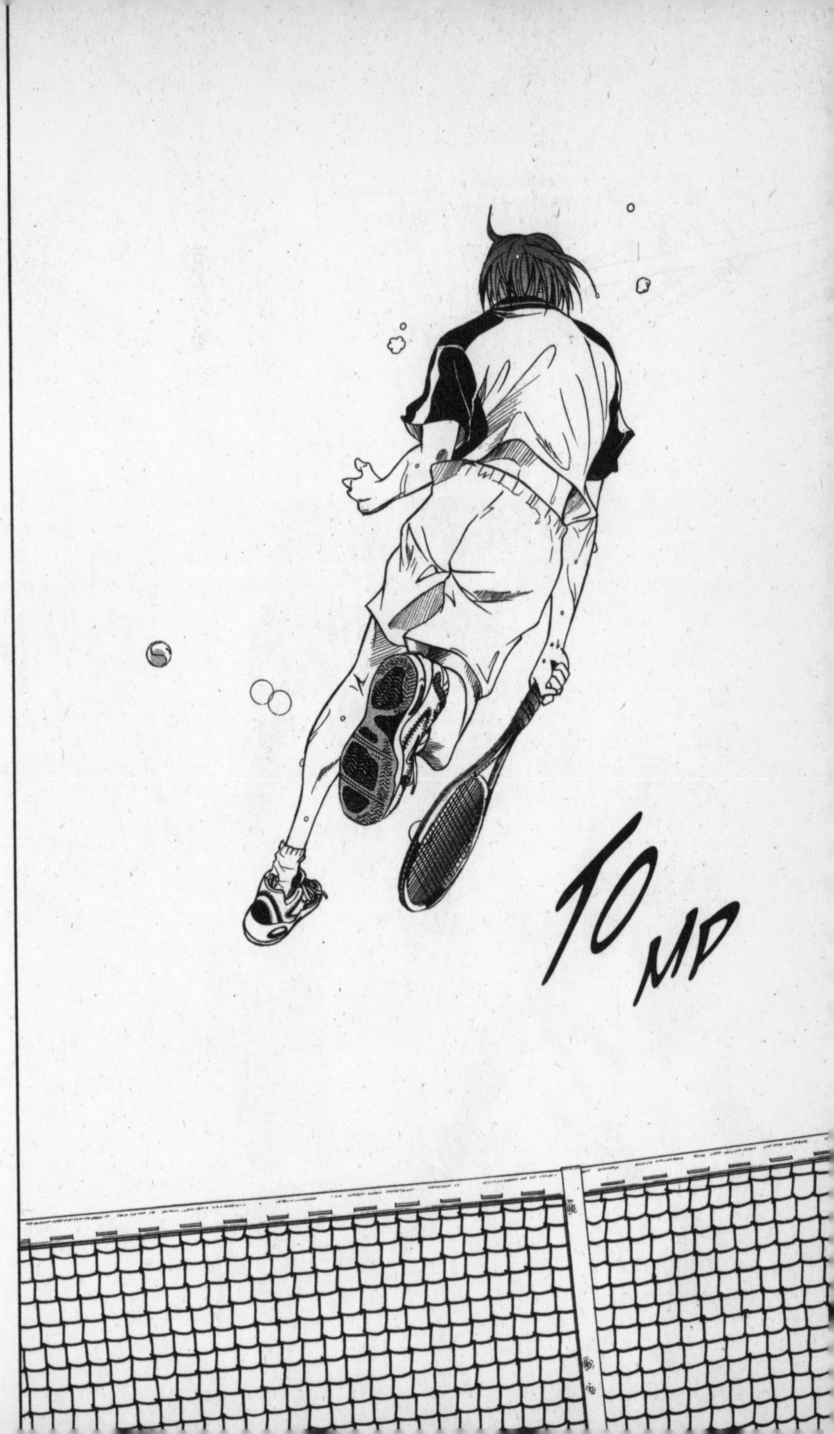
TOMP

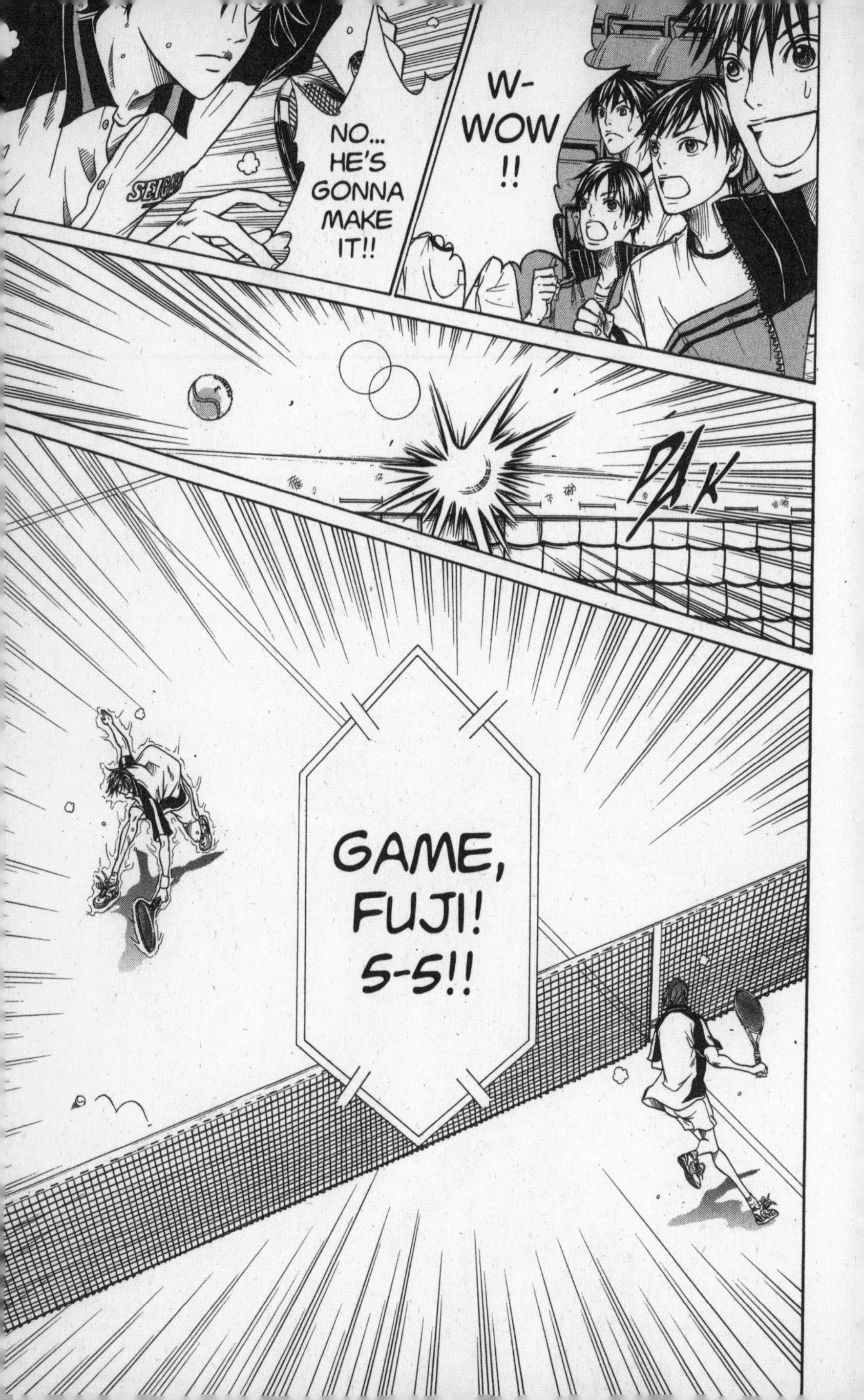
W-WOW!!
NO... HE'S GONNA MAKE IT!!
DAK
GAME, FUJI! 5-5!!

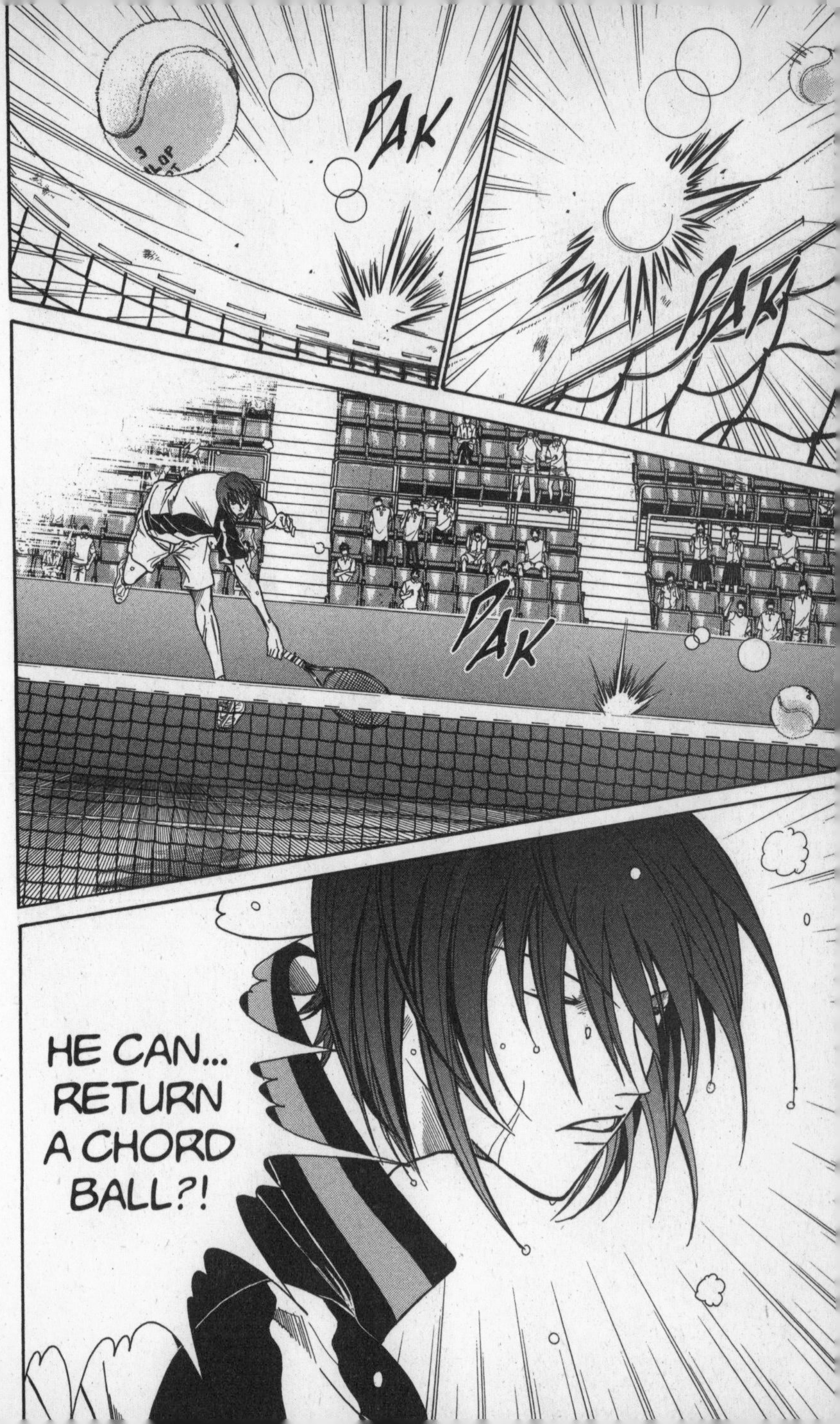
PAK
PAK
PAK
HE CAN... RETURN A CHORD BALL?!

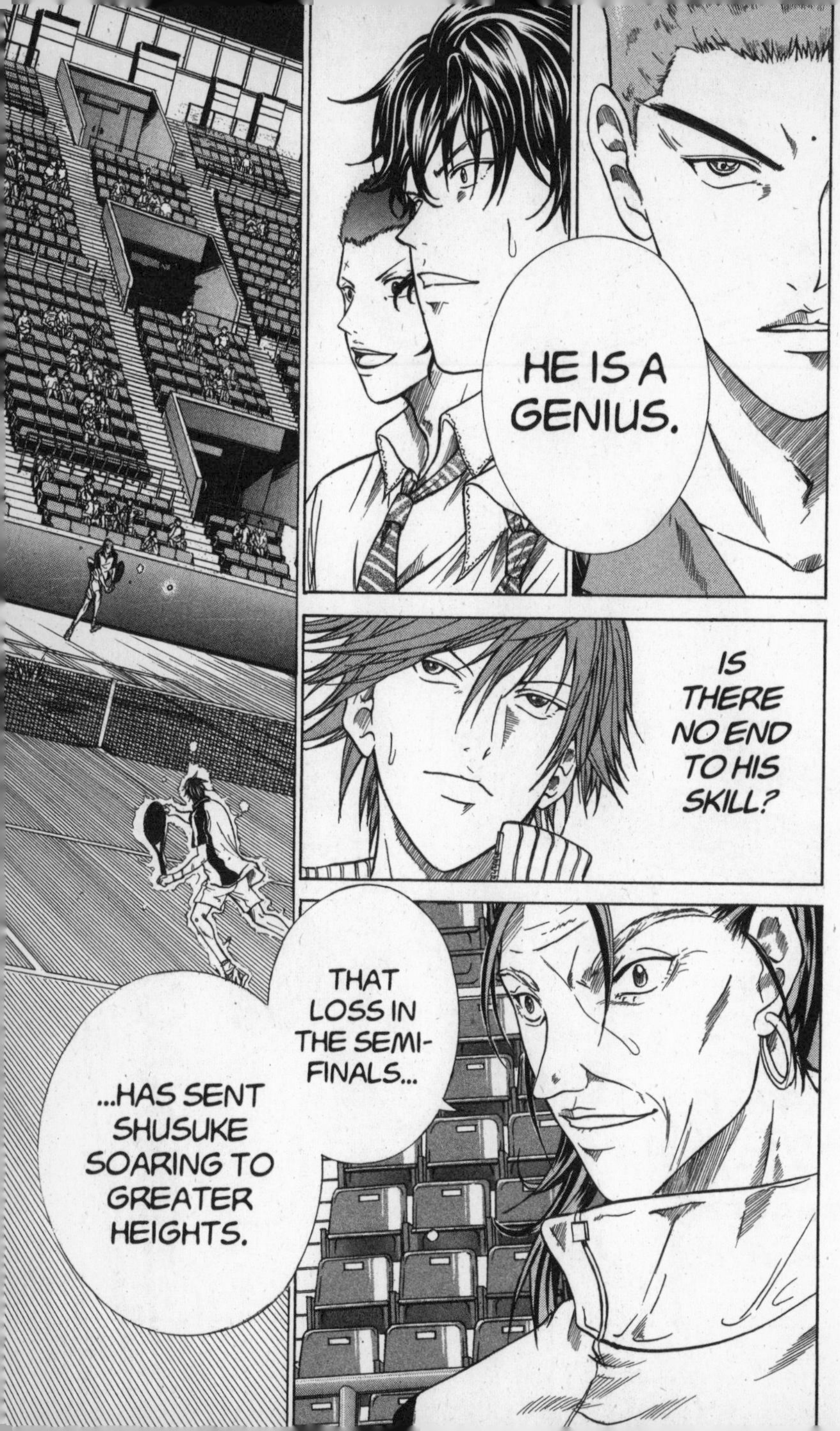
HE IS A GENIUS.
IS THERE NO END TO HIS SKILL?
THAT LOSS IN THE SEMI-FINALS...
...HAS SENT SHUSUKE SOARING TO GREATER HEIGHTS.

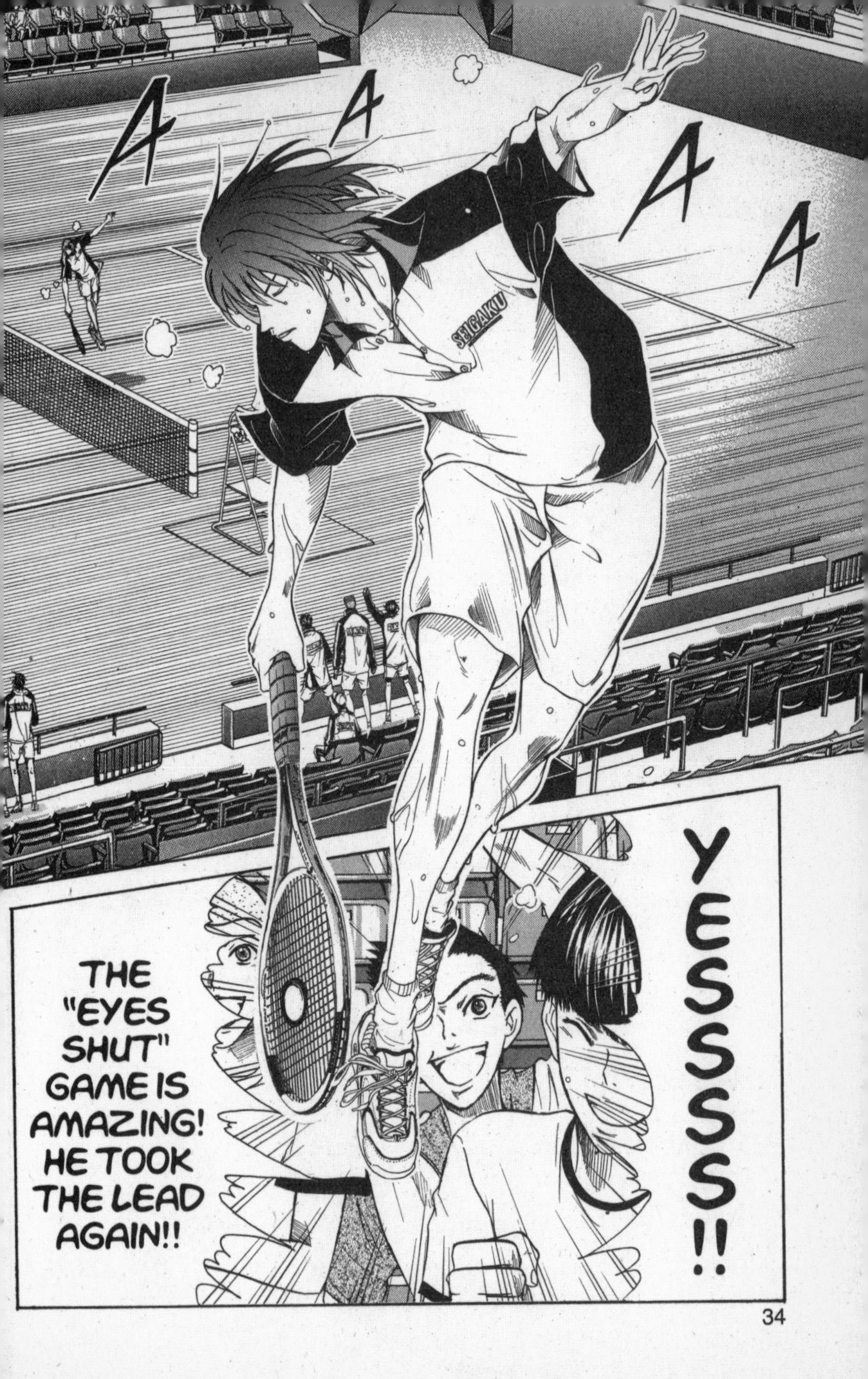
AAAAA
YESSSS!!
THE "EYES SHUT" GAME IS AMAZING! HE TOOK THE LEAD AGAIN!!

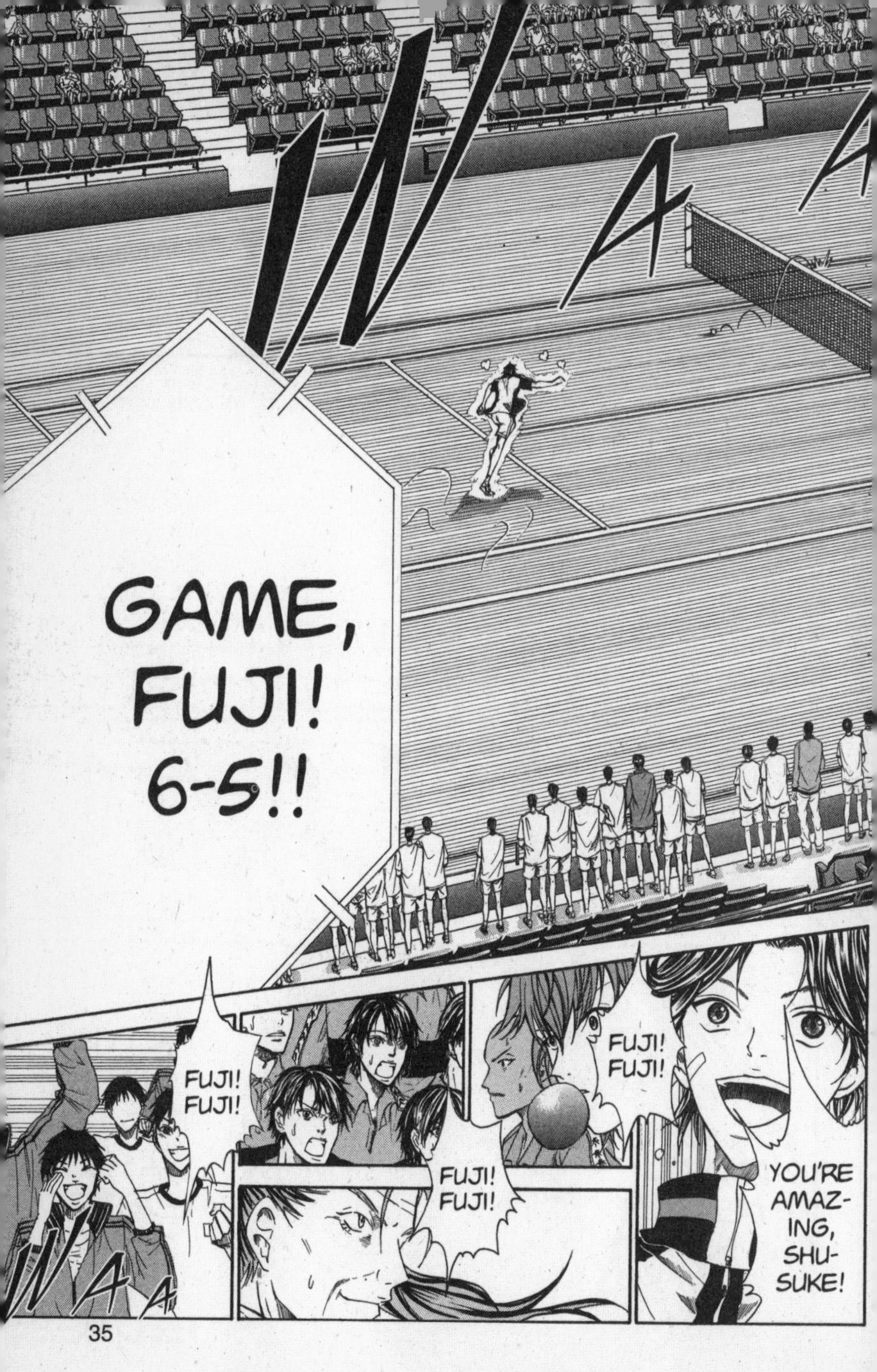
WAA
GAME, FUJI! 6-5!!
FUJI! FUJI!
YOU'RE AMAZ-ING, SHU-SUKE!
FUJI! FUJI!
FUJI! FUJI!
WAA

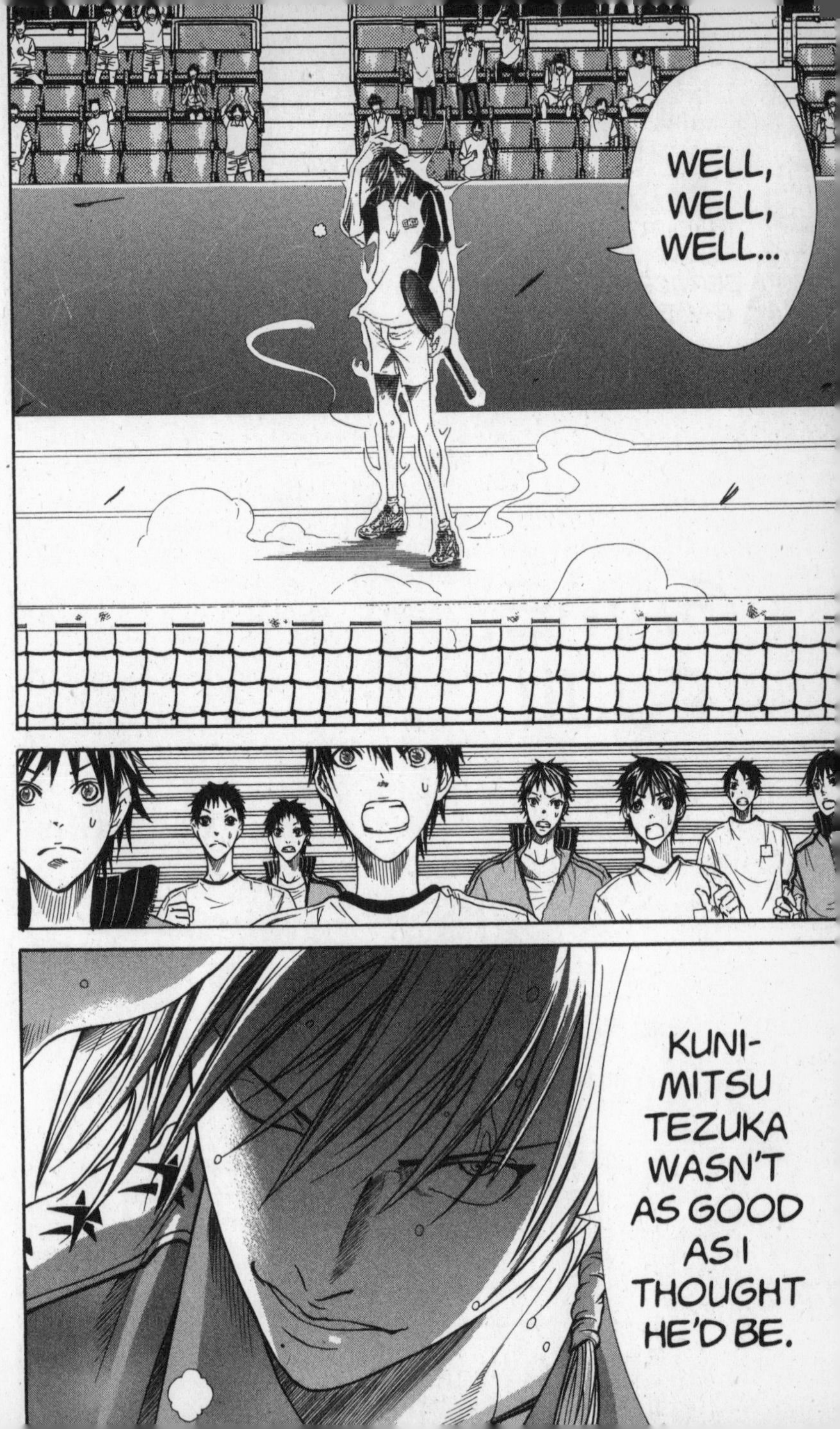
WELL, WELL, WELL...
KUNI-MITSU TEZUKA WASN'T AS GOOD AS I THOUGHT HE'D BE.

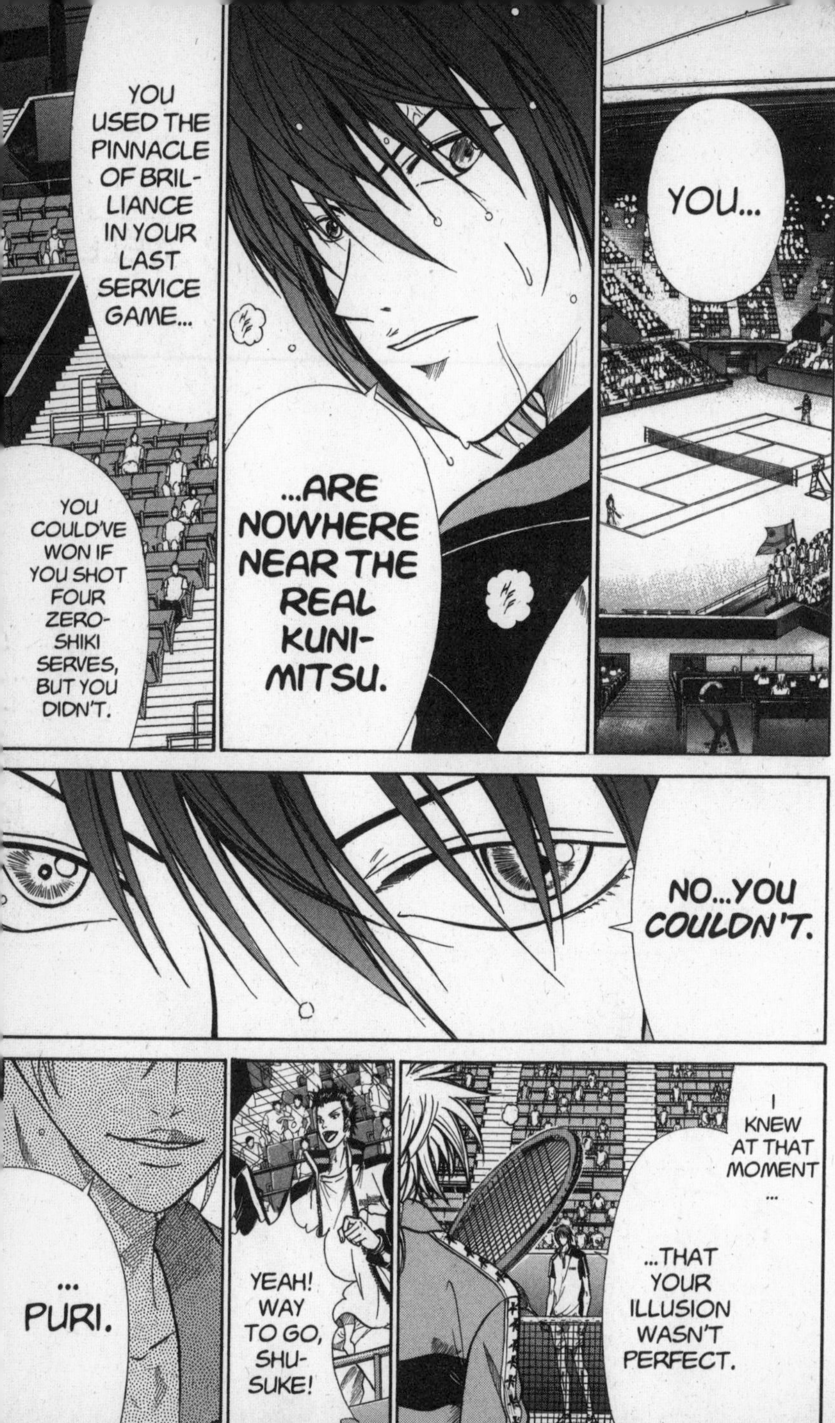
YOU...
...ARE NOWHERE NEAR THE REAL KUNIMITSU.
YOU USED THE PINNACLE OF BRILLIANCE IN YOUR LAST SERVICE GAME...
YOU COULD'VE WON IF YOU SHOT FOUR ZERO-SHIKI SERVES, BUT YOU DIDN'T.
NO...YOU COULDN'T.
I KNEW AT THAT MOMENT...
...THAT YOUR ILLUSION WASN'T PERFECT.
YEAH! WAY TO GO, SHUSUKE!
...PURI.

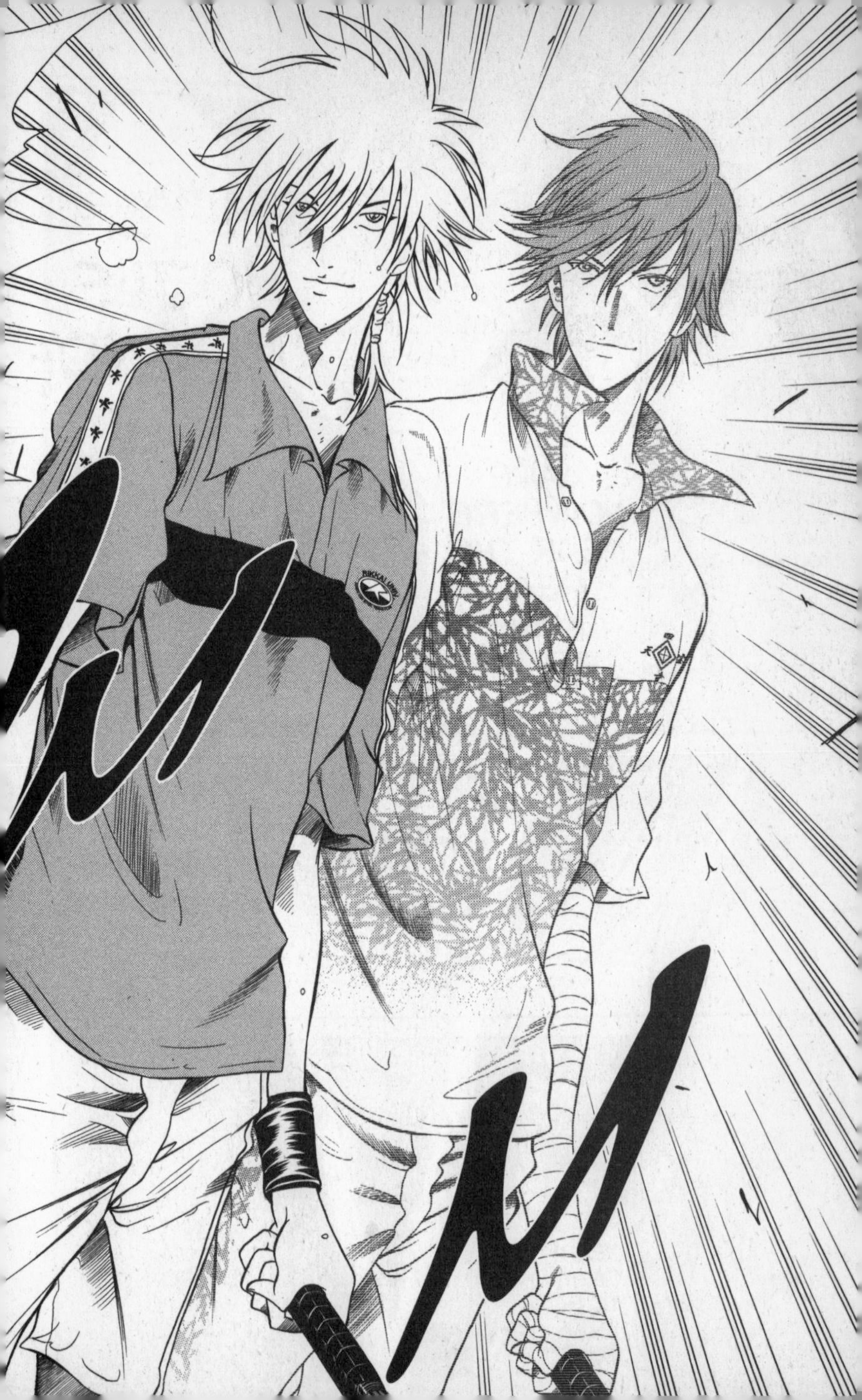

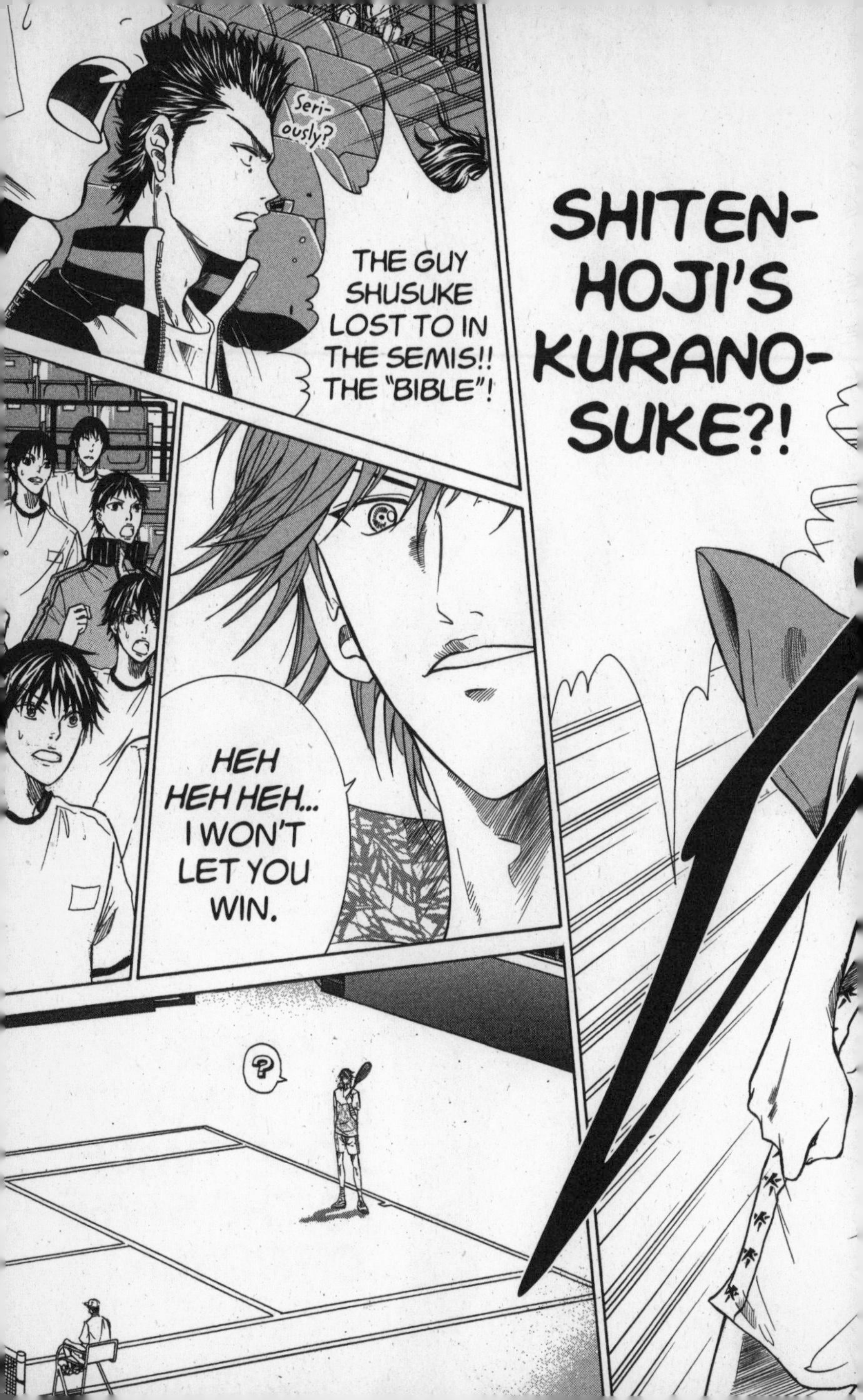
SHITEN-HOJI'S KURANO-SUKE?!
Seri-ously?
THE GUY SHUSUKE LOST TO IN THE SEMIS!! THE "BIBLE"!
HEH HEH HEH... I WON'T LET YOU WIN.
?

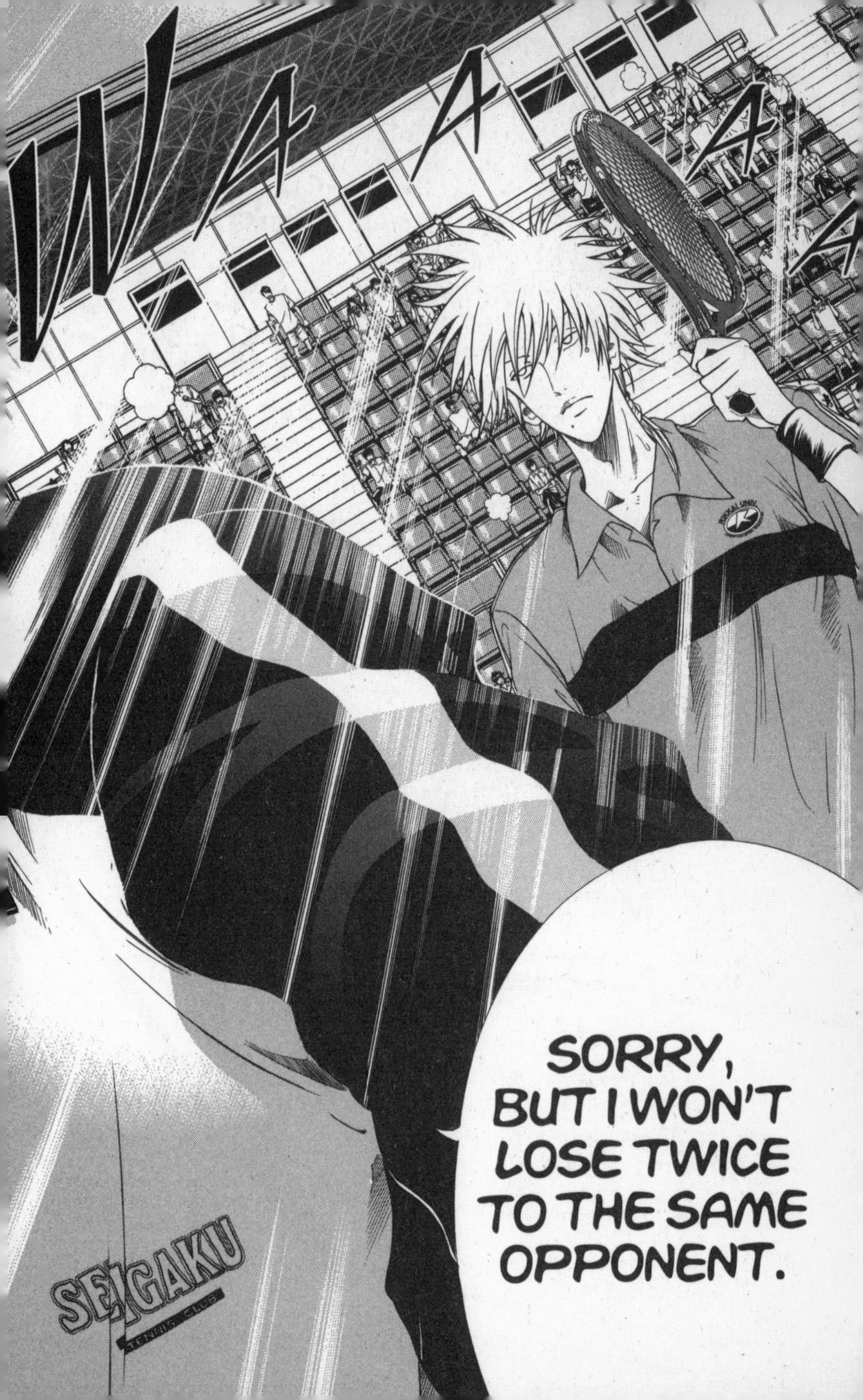
WAAAA
SORRY, BUT I WON'T LOSE TWICE TO THE SAME OPPONENT.
SEIGAKU

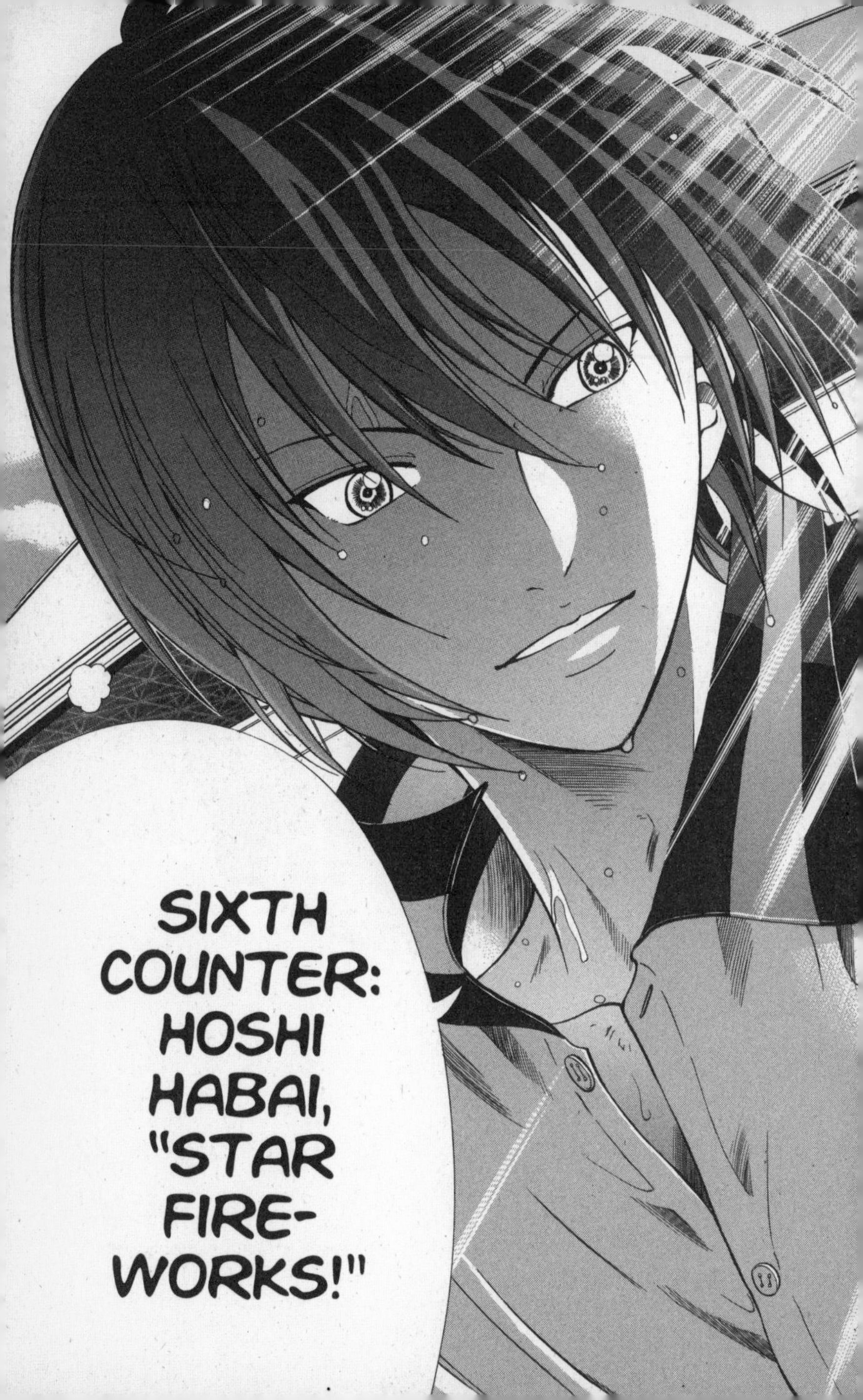
SIXTH COUNTER: HOSHI HABAI, "STAR FIRE-WORKS!"

テニスの王子様

THE PRINCE OF TENNIS

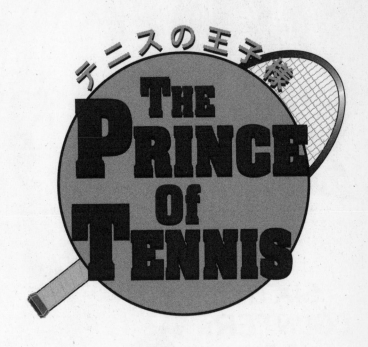

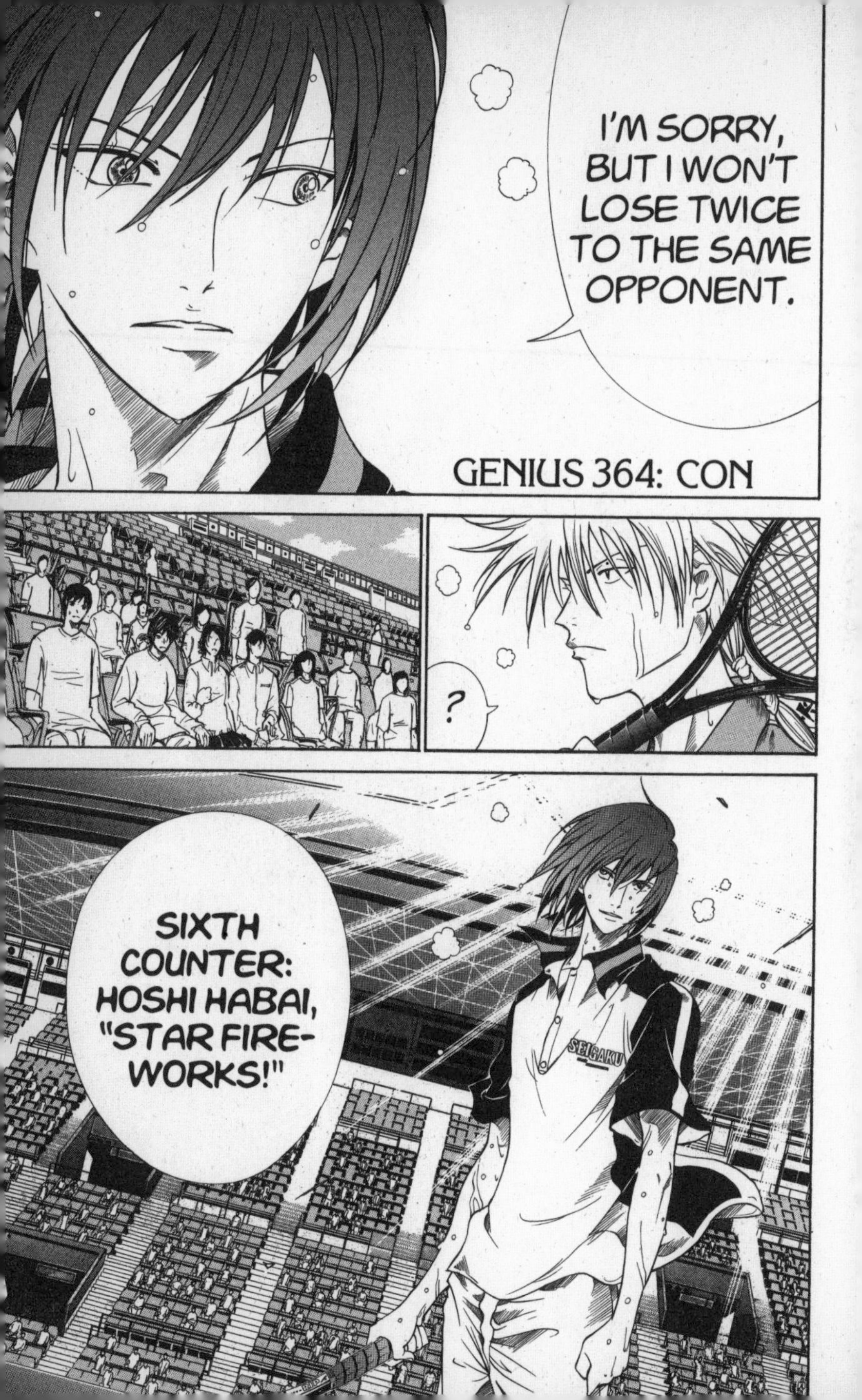
I'M SORRY, BUT I WON'T LOSE TWICE TO THE SAME OPPONENT.
GENIUS 364: CON
?
SIXTH COUNTER: HOSHI HABAI, "STAR FIRE-WORKS!"
SEIGAKU

GENIUS 364: CON

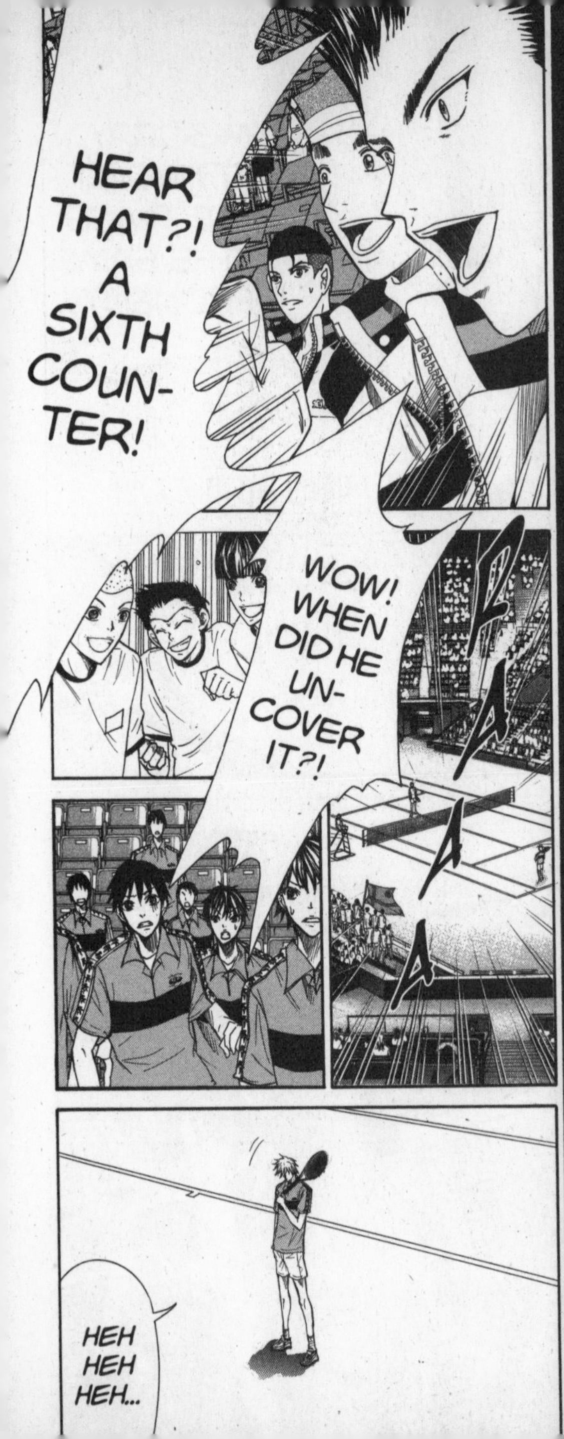

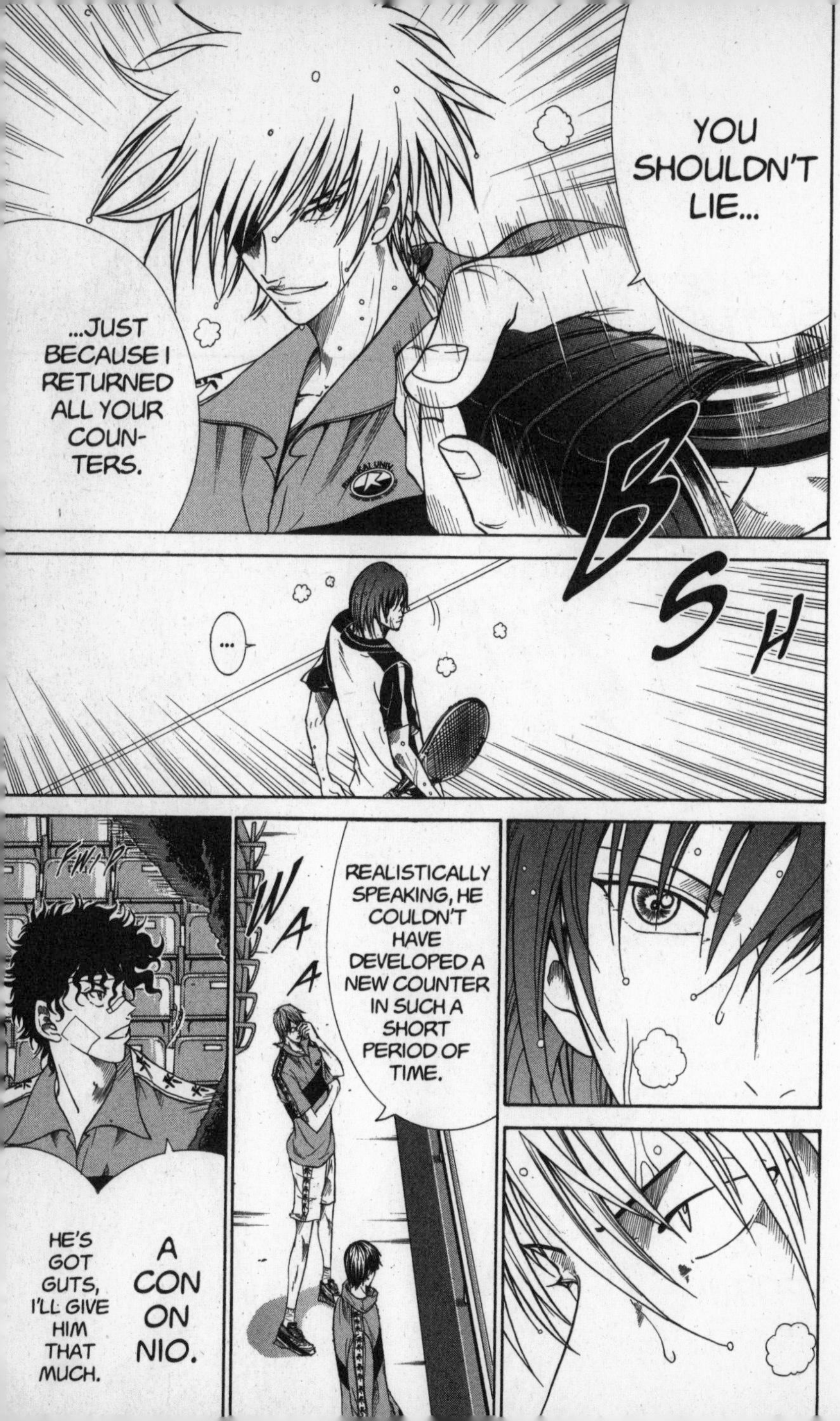
YOU SHOULDN'T LIE...
...JUST BECAUSE I RETURNED ALL YOUR COUNTERS.
BSH
...
WAA
REALISTICALLY SPEAKING, HE COULDN'T HAVE DEVELOPED A NEW COUNTER IN SUCH A SHORT PERIOD OF TIME.
FWIP
A CON ON NIO.
HE'S GOT GUTS, I'LL GIVE HIM THAT MUCH.

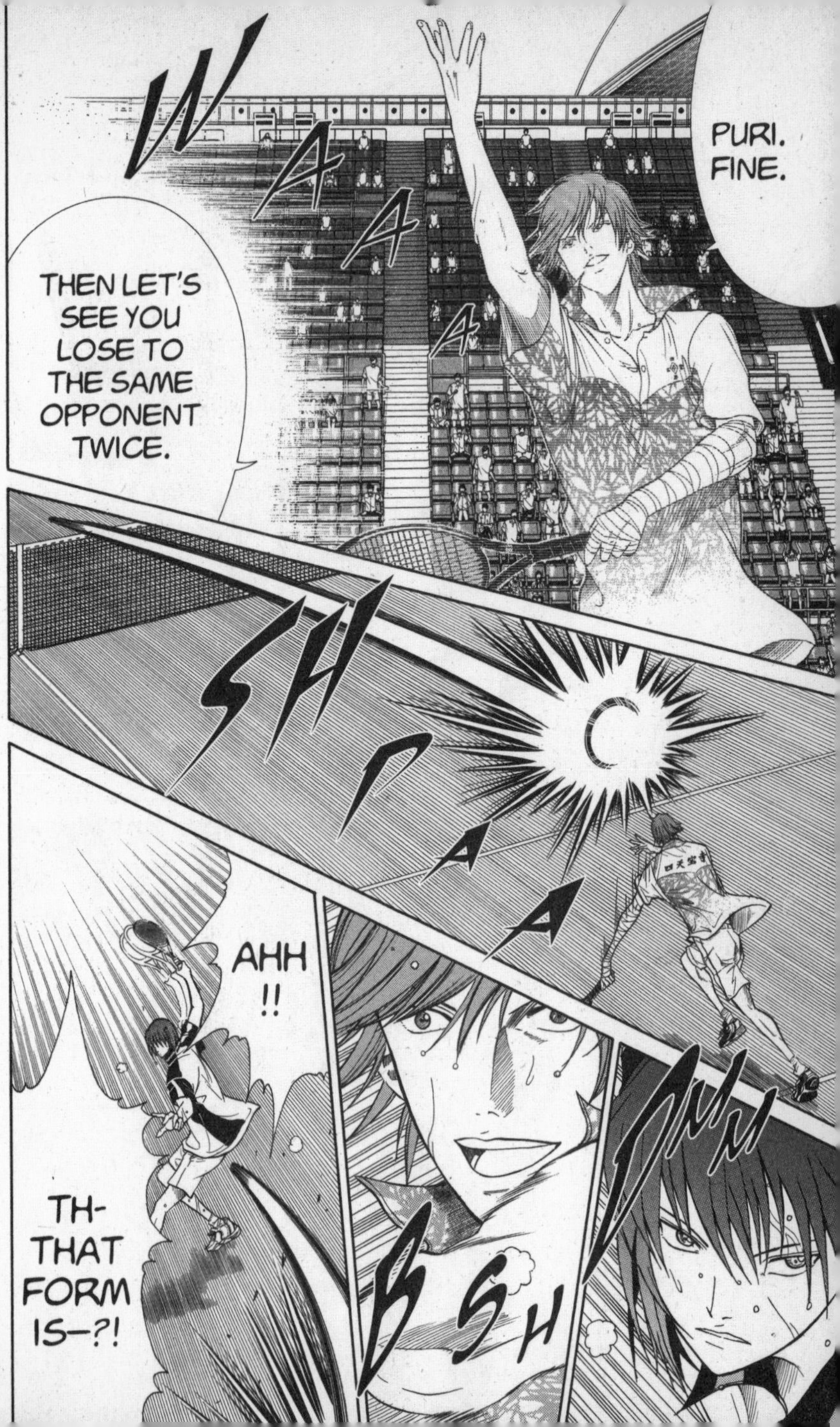
PURI. FINE.
WAAAA
THEN LET'S SEE YOU LOSE TO THE SAME OPPONENT TWICE.
SHIAAA
BSH
AHH !!
TH- THAT FORM IS—?!

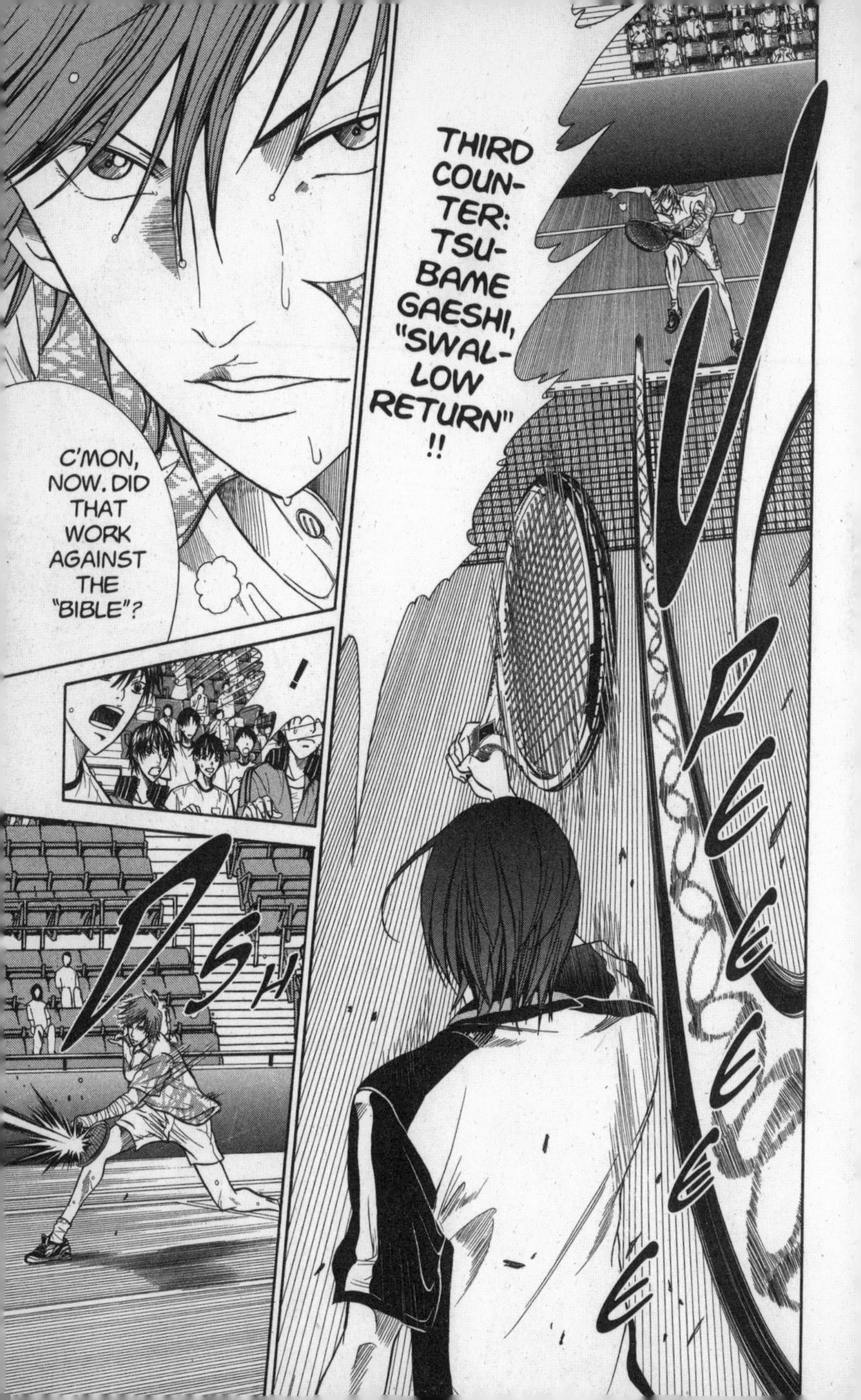
THIRD COUNTER: TSUBAME GAESHI, "SWALLOW RETURN"!!
C'MON, NOW. DID THAT WORK AGAINST THE "BIBLE"?
!

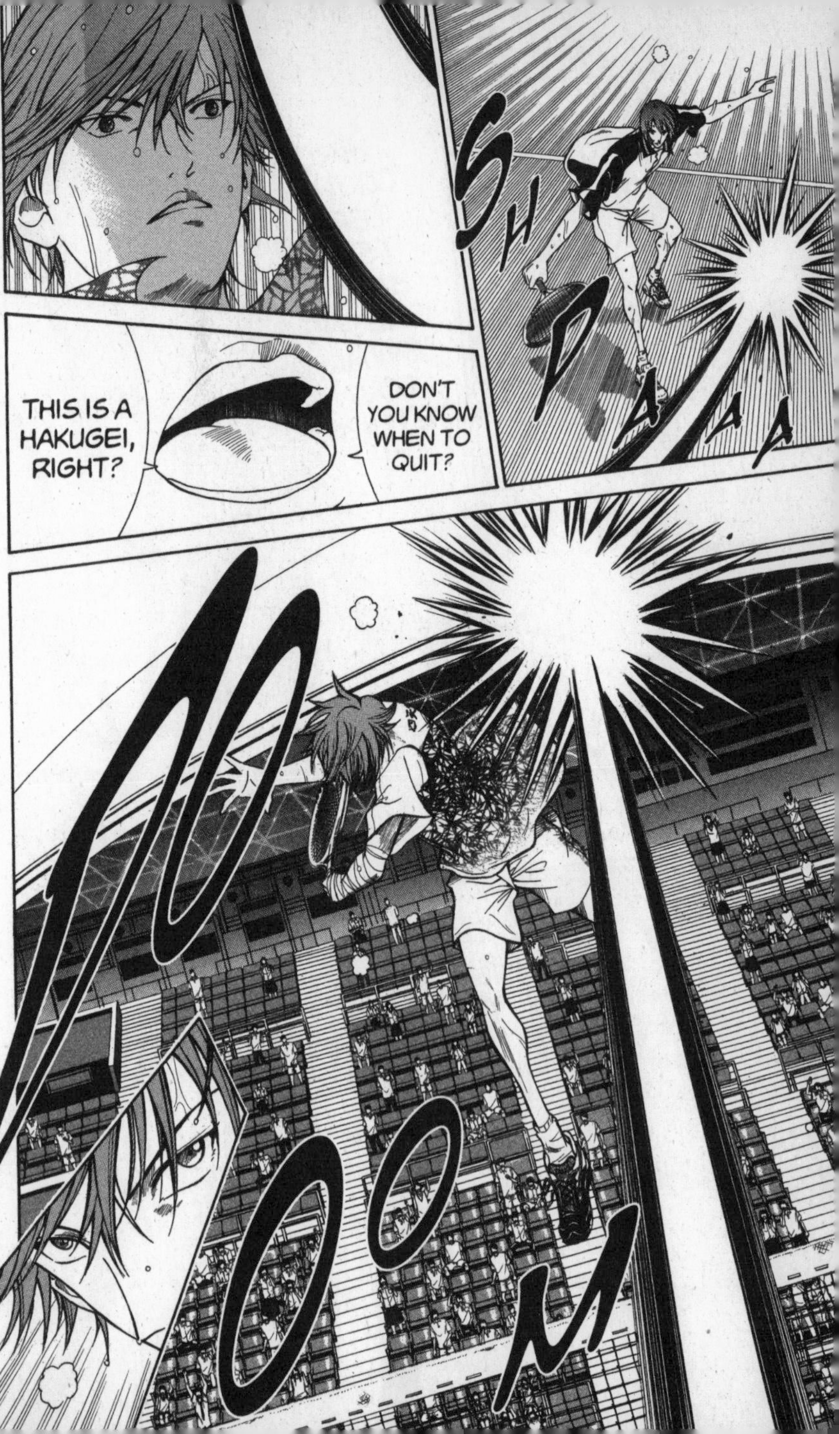
SHPAAA
DON'T YOU KNOW WHEN TO QUIT?
THIS IS A HAKUGEI, RIGHT?
VOOOOM

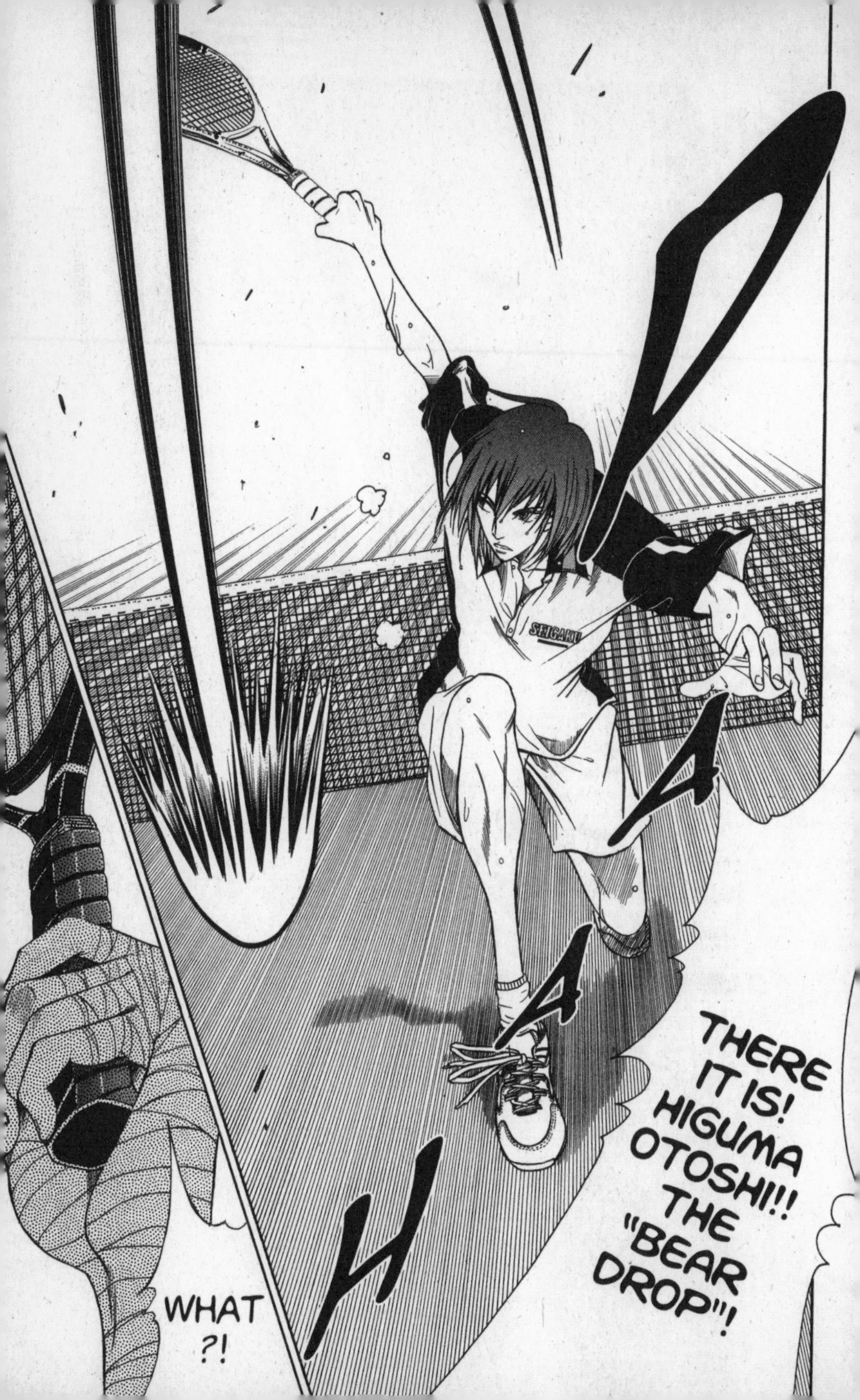
THERE IT IS! HIGUMA OTOSHI!! THE "BEAR DROP"!
WHAT ?!

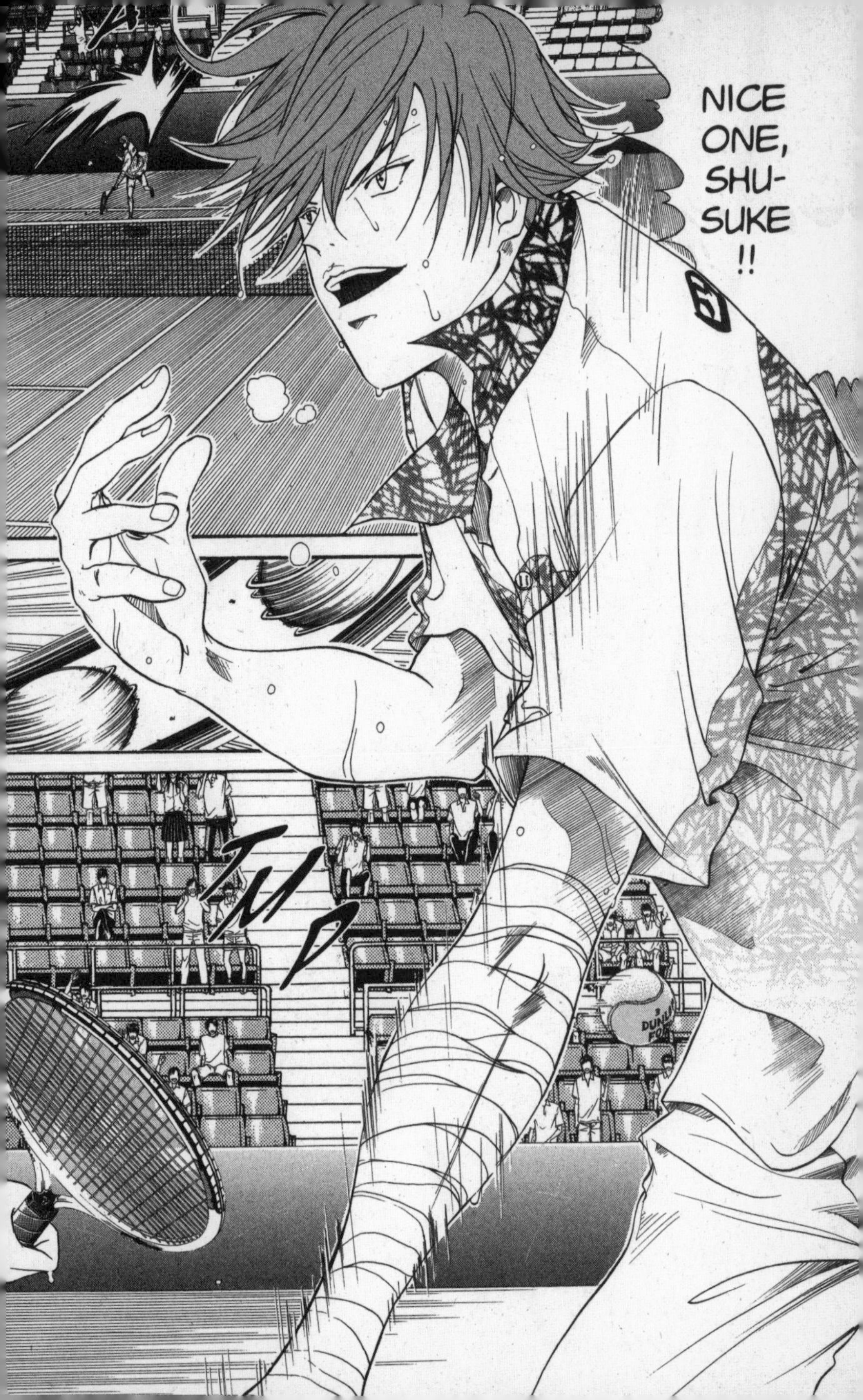
NICE ONE, SHUSUKE !!
TMP

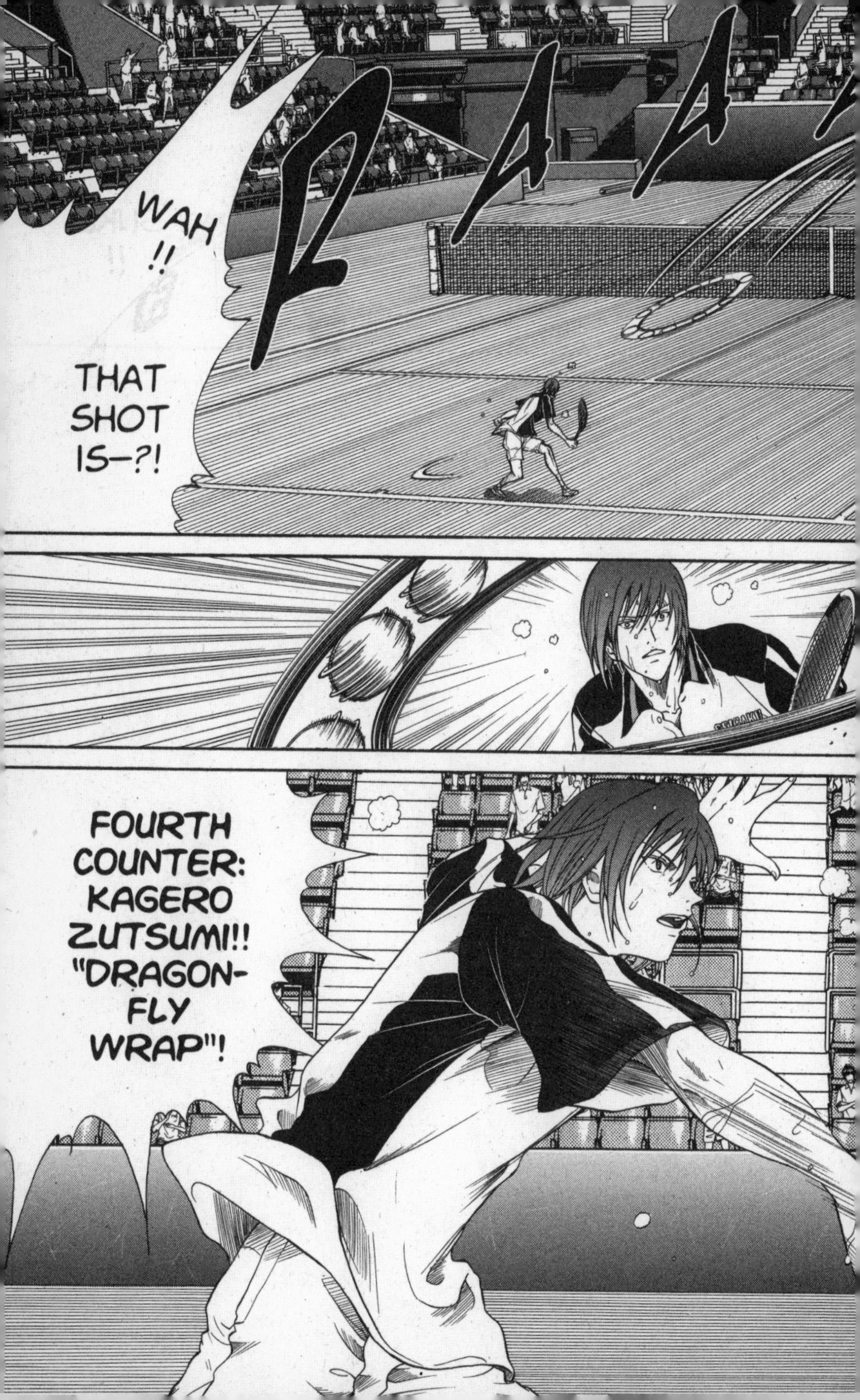
WAH!!
THAT SHOT IS—?!
FOURTH COUNTER: KAGERO ZUTSUMI!! "DRAGON-FLY WRAP"!

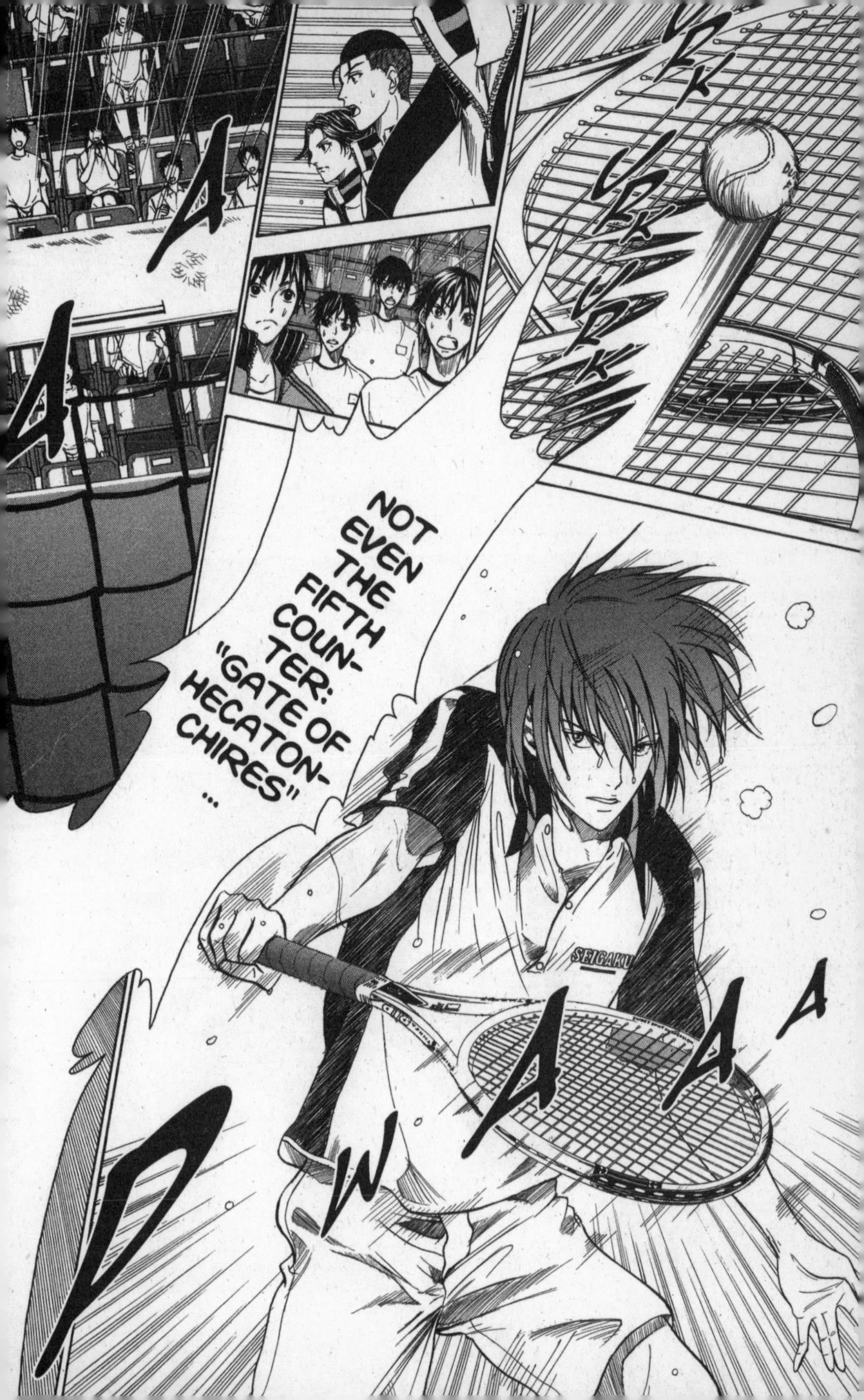
VRRRRRRRRR
NOT EVEN THE FIFTH COUNTER: "GATE OF HECATONCHIRES"...
SEIGAKU
WAAAA

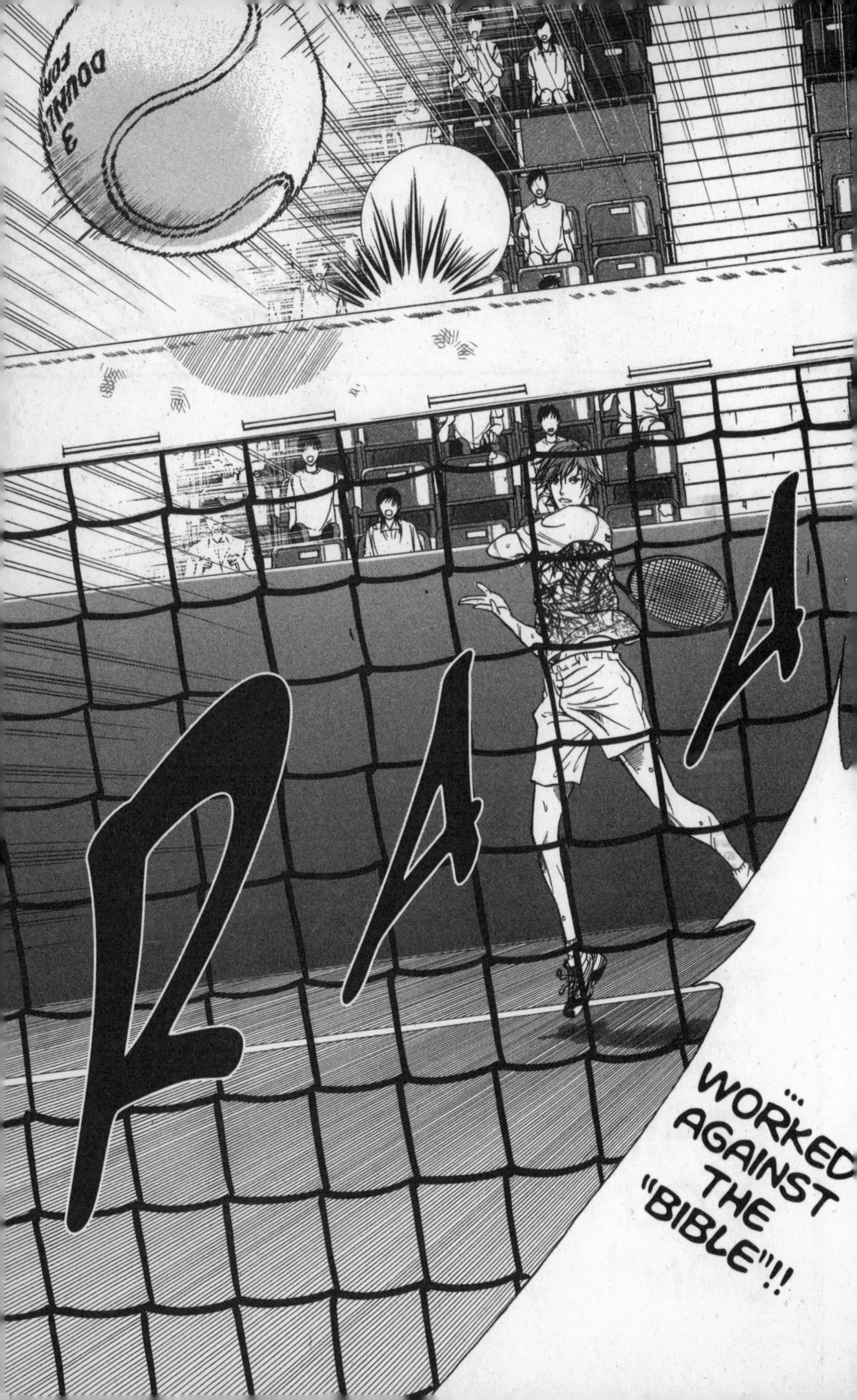
...WORKED AGAINST THE "BIBLE"!!

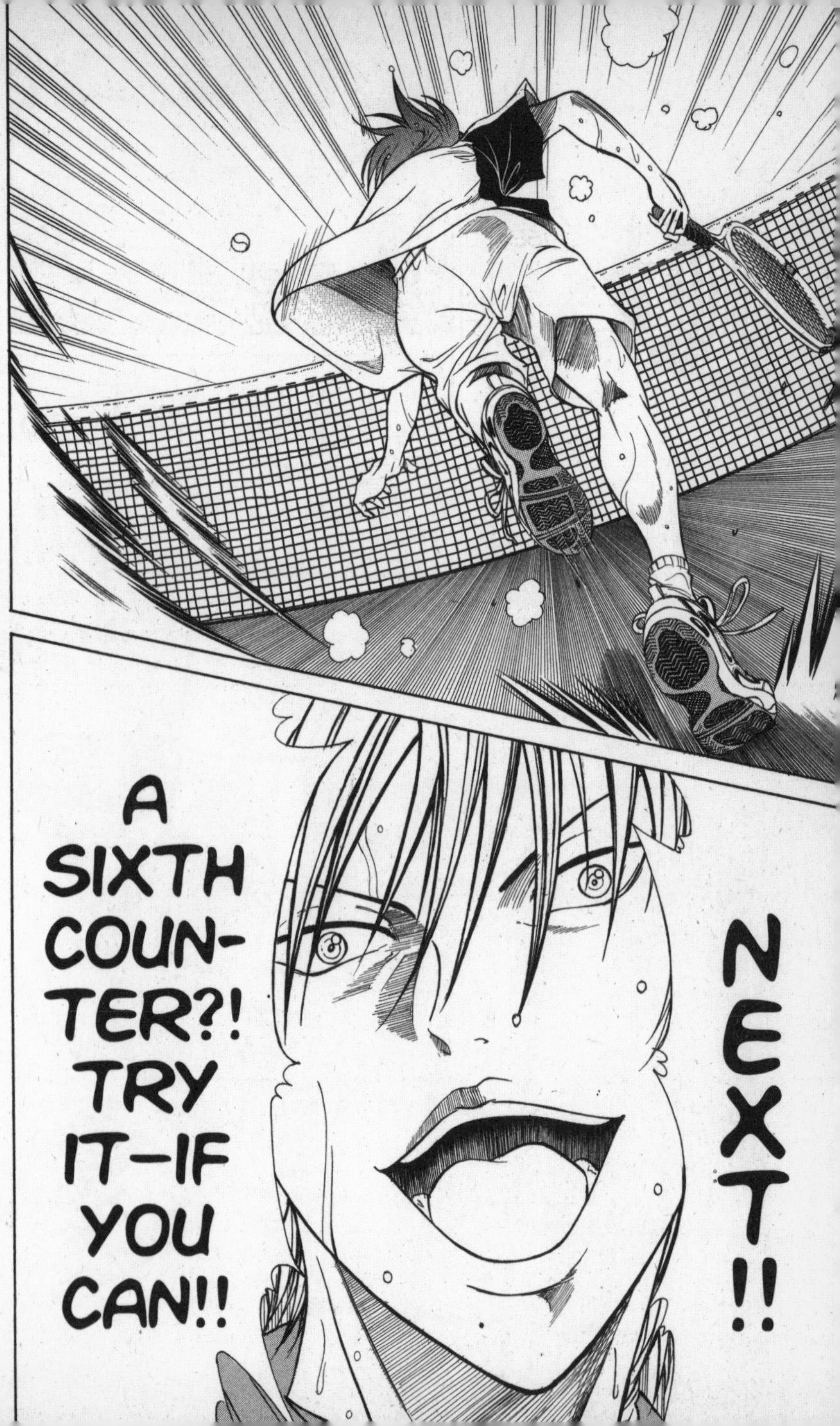
NEXT!!
A SIXTH COUNTER?! TRY IT—IF YOU CAN!!

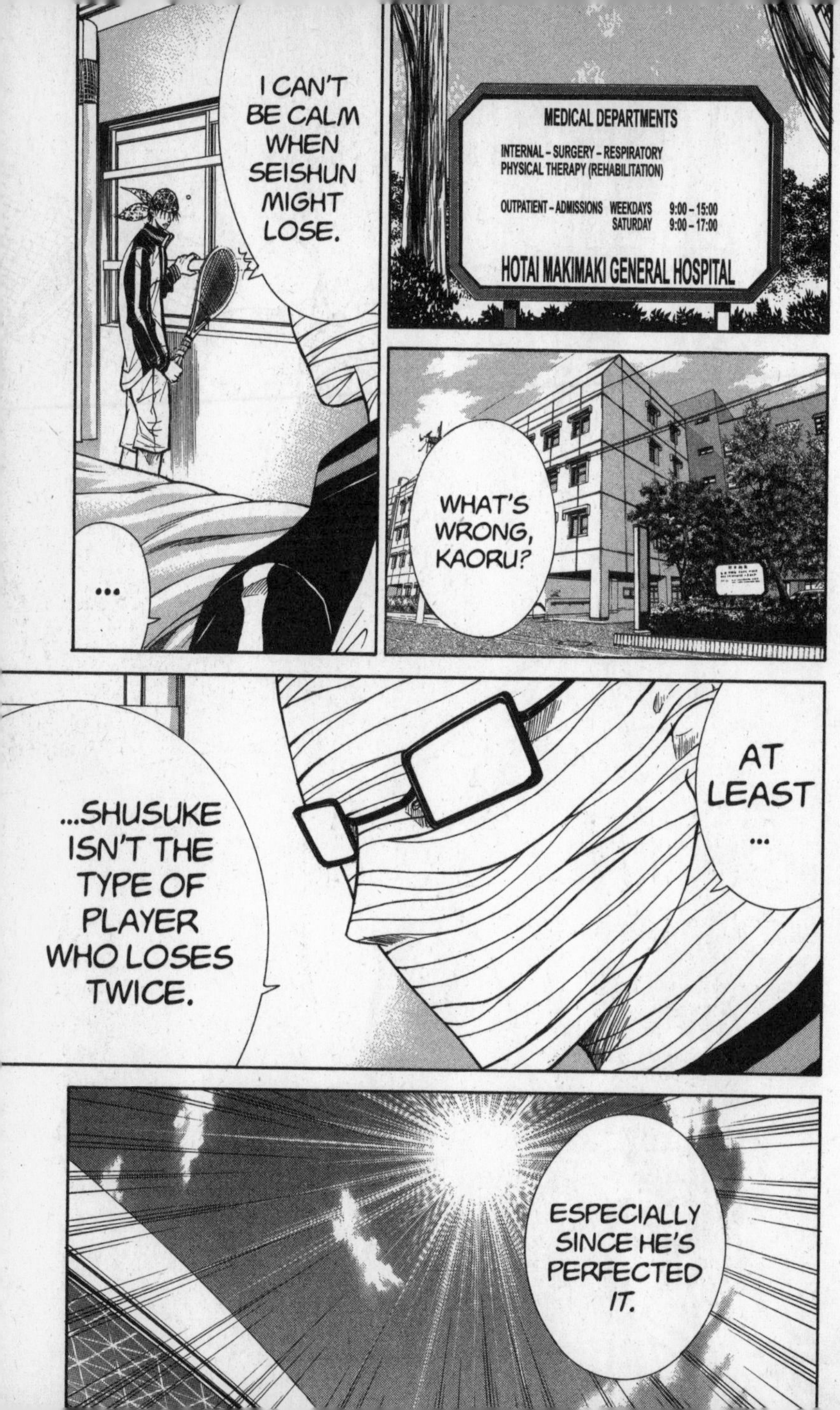
MEDICAL DEPARTMENTS
INTERNAL - SURGERY - RESPIRATORY
PHYSICAL THERAPY (REHABILITATION)
OUTPATIENT - ADMISSIONS WEEKDAYS 9:00 - 15:00
SATURDAY 9:00 - 17:00
HOTAI MAKIMAKI GENERAL HOSPITAL
WHAT'S WRONG, KAORU?
I CAN'T BE CALM WHEN SEISHUN MIGHT LOSE.
...
AT LEAST...
...SHUSUKE ISN'T THE TYPE OF PLAYER WHO LOSES TWICE.
ESPECIALLY SINCE HE'S PERFECTED IT.

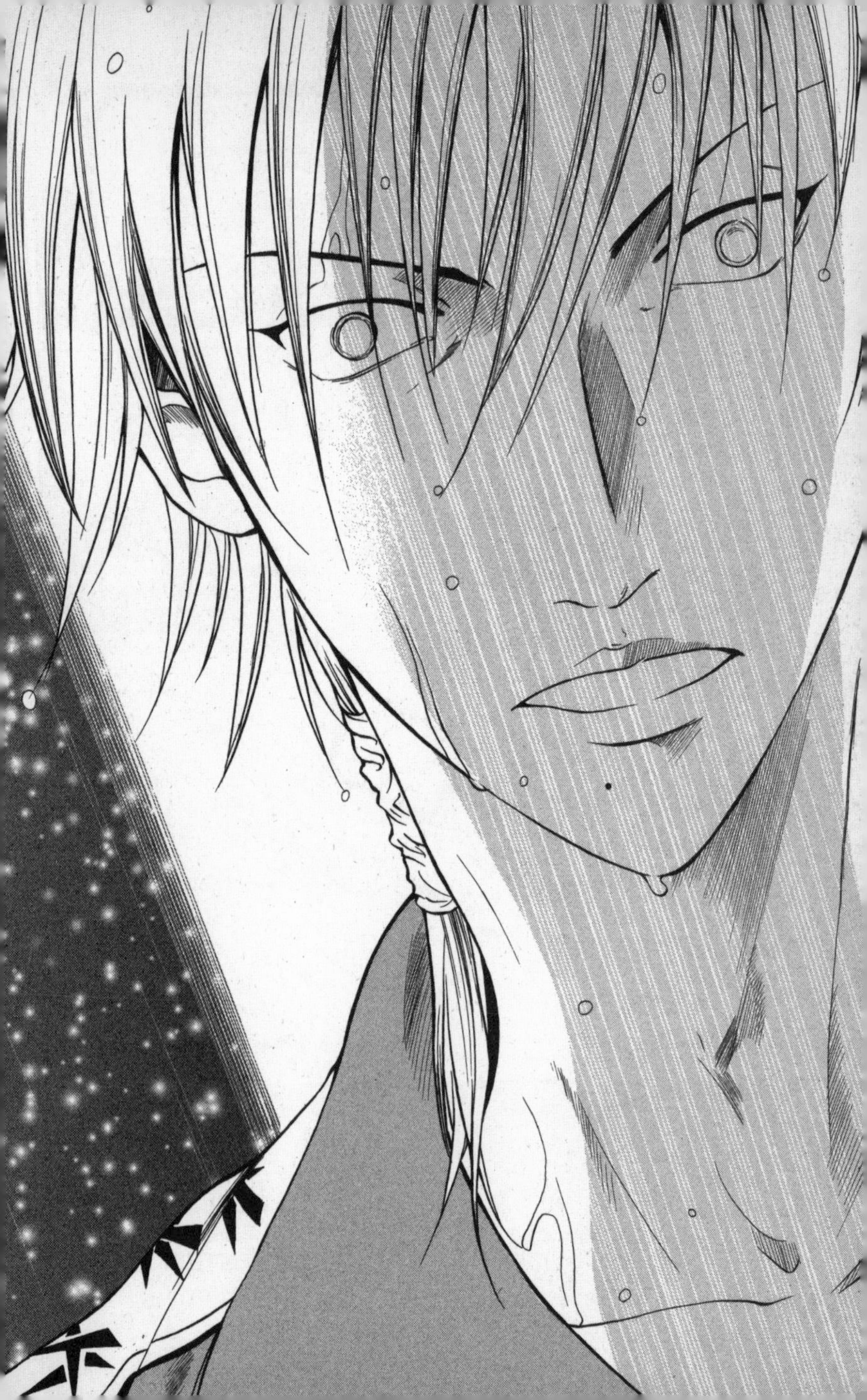

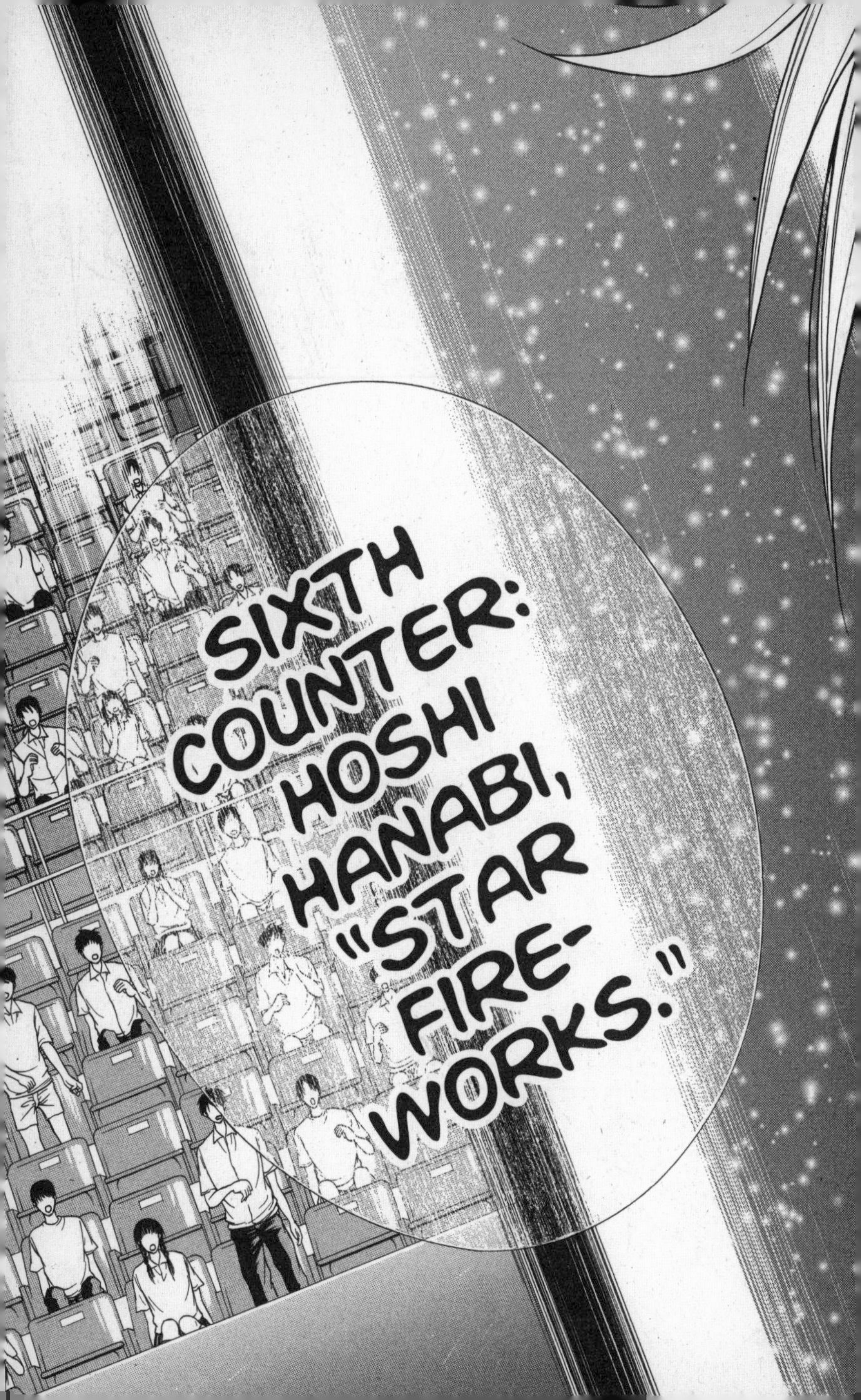
SIXTH COUNTER: HOSHI HANABI, "STAR FIRE-WORKS."

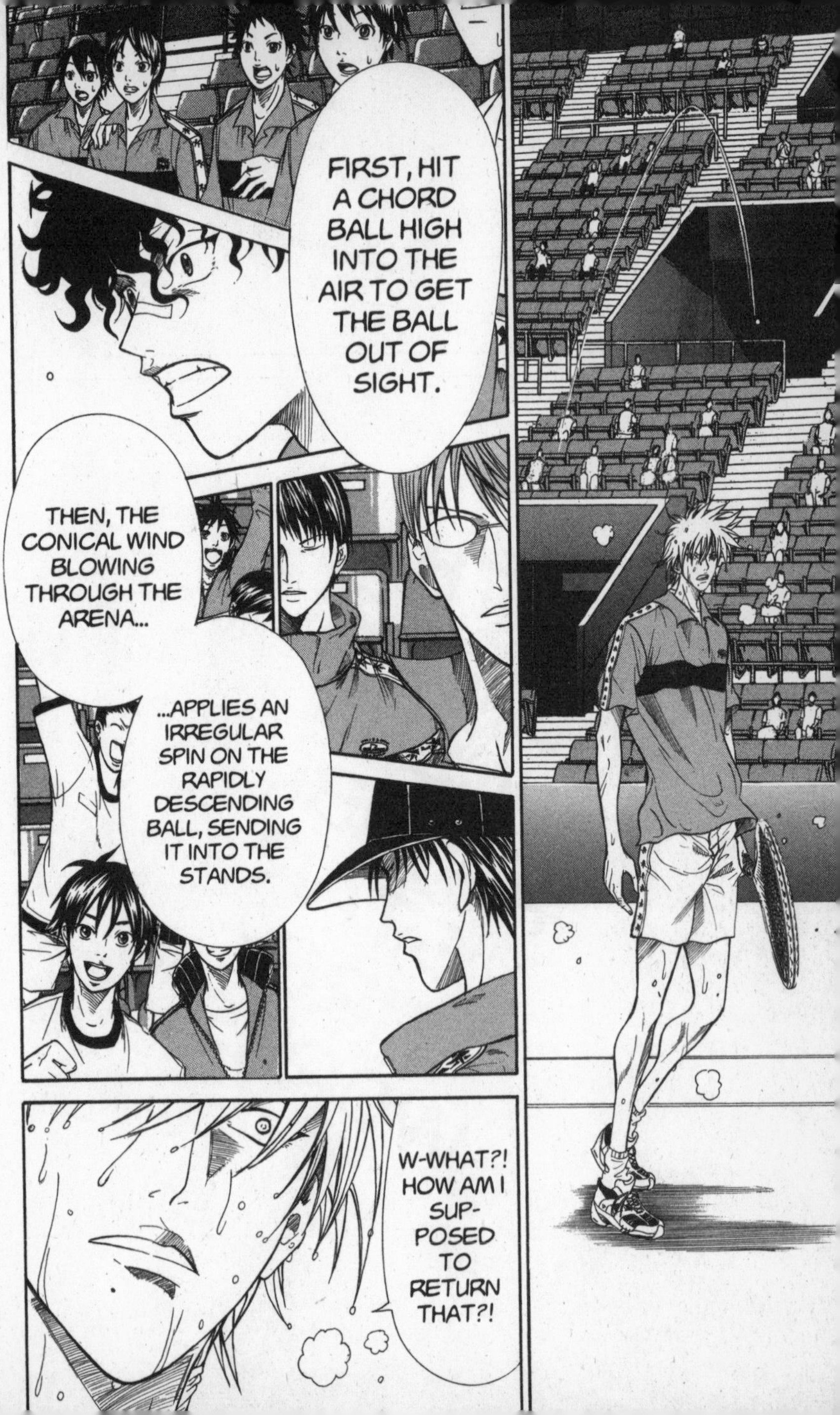
FIRST, HIT A CHORD BALL HIGH INTO THE AIR TO GET THE BALL OUT OF SIGHT.
THEN, THE CONICAL WIND BLOWING THROUGH THE ARENA...
...APPLIES AN IRREGULAR SPIN ON THE RAPIDLY DESCENDING BALL, SENDING IT INTO THE STANDS.
W-WHAT?! HOW AM I SUP-POSED TO RETURN THAT?!

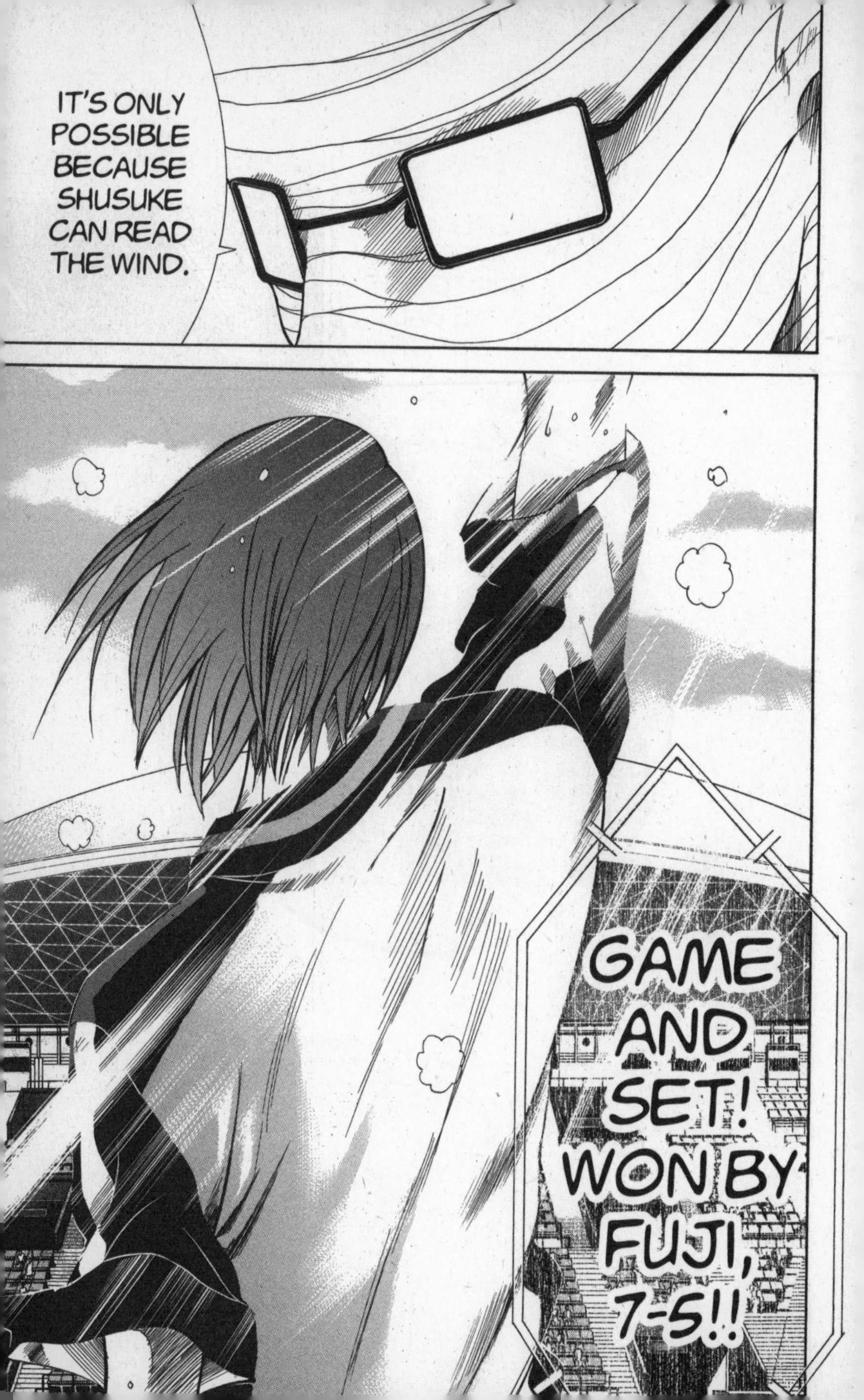
IT'S ONLY POSSIBLE BECAUSE SHUSUKE CAN READ THE WIND.
GAME AND SET! WON BY FUJI, 7-5!!

テニスの王子様

THE PRINCE OF TENNIS

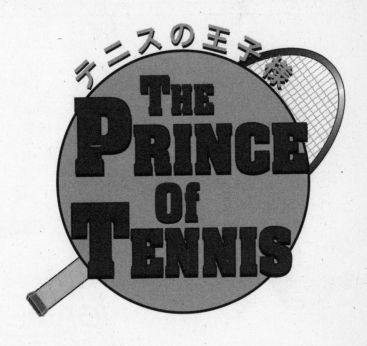

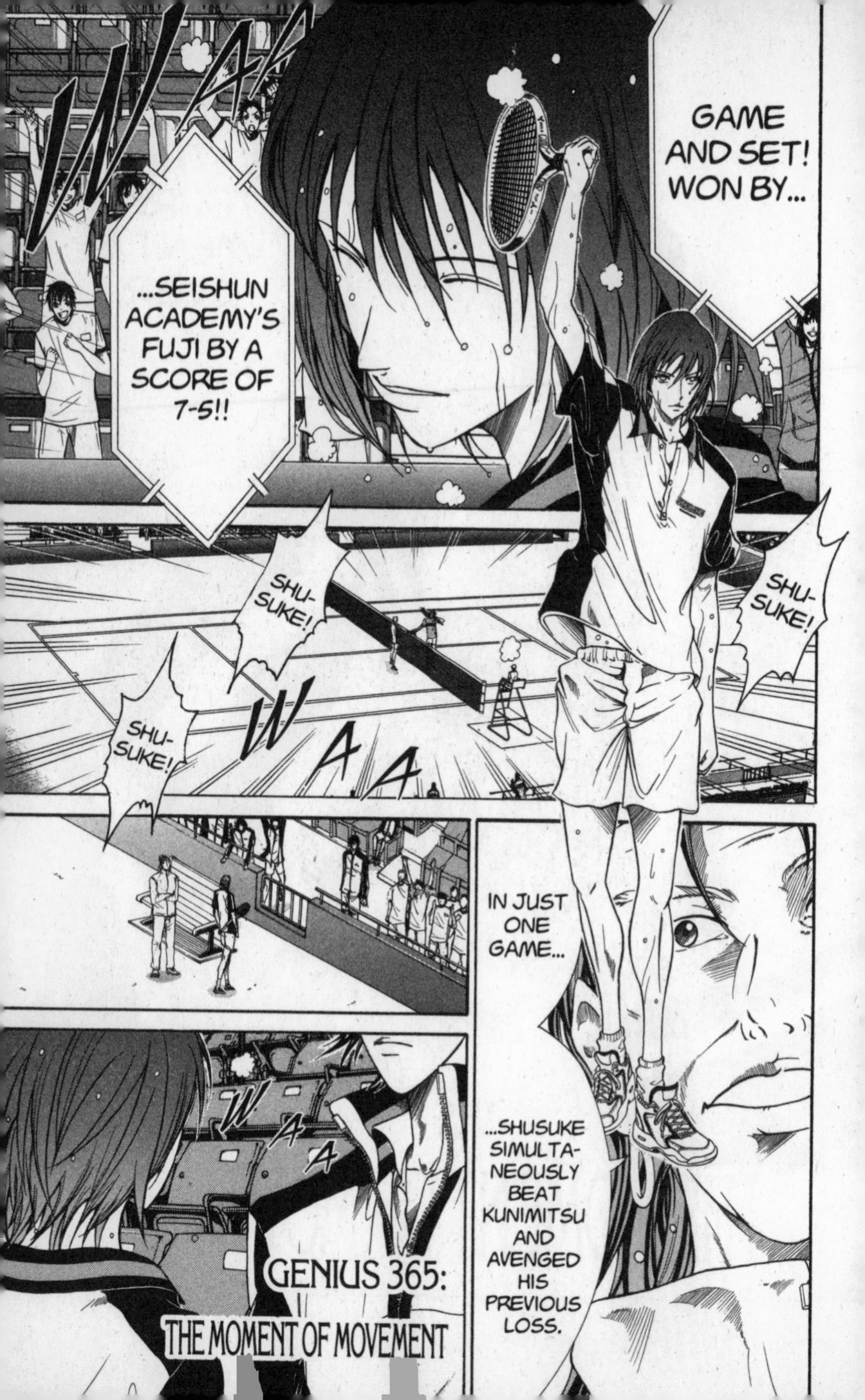
GAME AND SET! WON BY...
...SEISHUN ACADEMY'S FUJI BY A SCORE OF 7-5!!
WAA
SHU-SUKE!
SHU-SUKE!
SHU-SUKE!
WAA
IN JUST ONE GAME...
...SHUSUKE SIMULTANEOUSLY BEAT KUNIMITSU AND AVENGED HIS PREVIOUS LOSS.
WAA
GENIUS 365:
THE MOMENT OF MOVEMENT

WHEN THIS TOURNAMENT IS OVER...
GENIUS 365:
THE MOMENT OF MOVEMENT

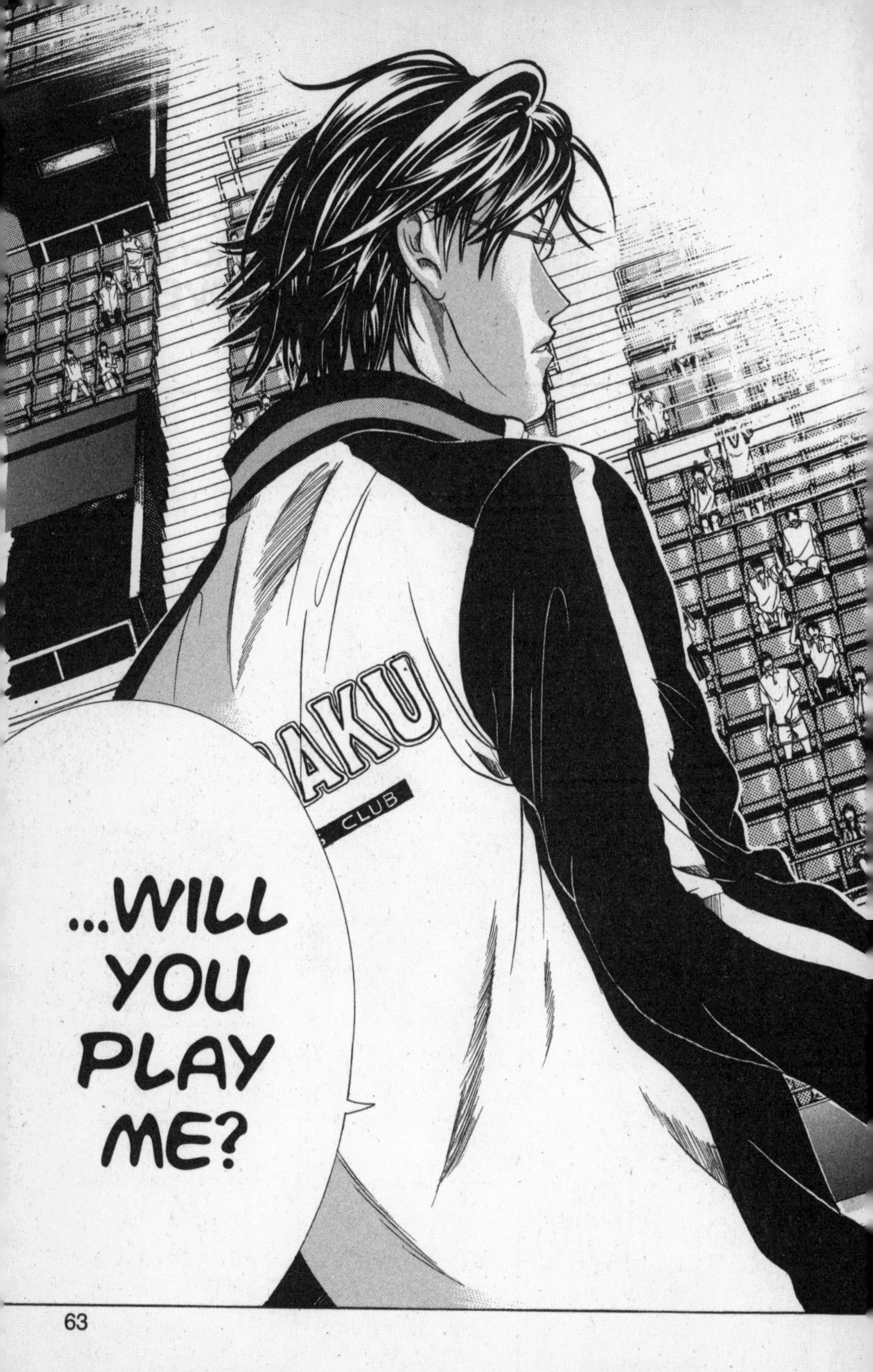
...WILL YOU PLAY ME?
AKU
CLUB

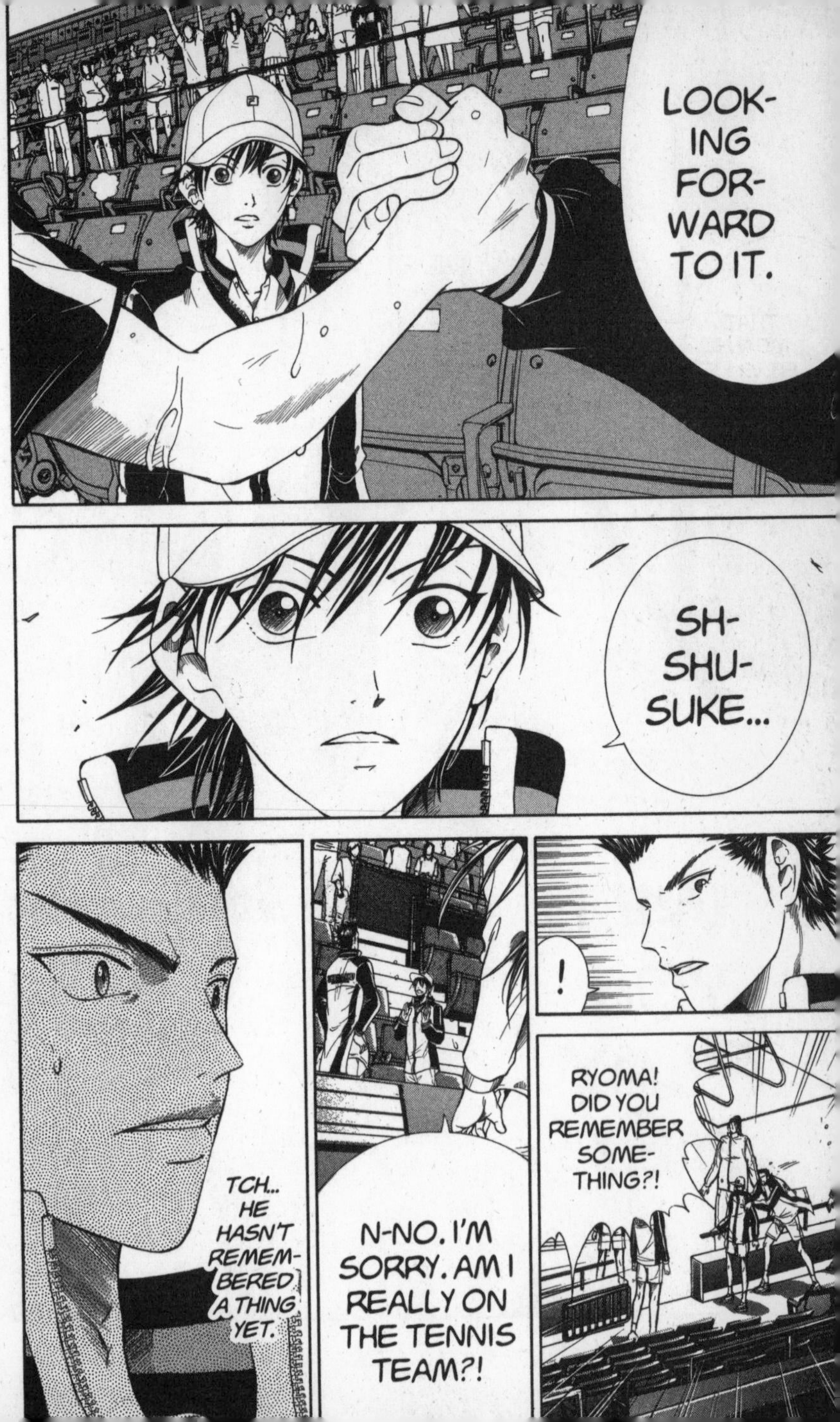
LOOKING FORWARD TO IT.
SH-SHUSUKE...
!
RYOMA! DID YOU REMEMBER SOMETHING?!
N-NO. I'M SORRY. AM I REALLY ON THE TENNIS TEAM?!
TCH... HE HASN'T REMEMBERED A THING YET.

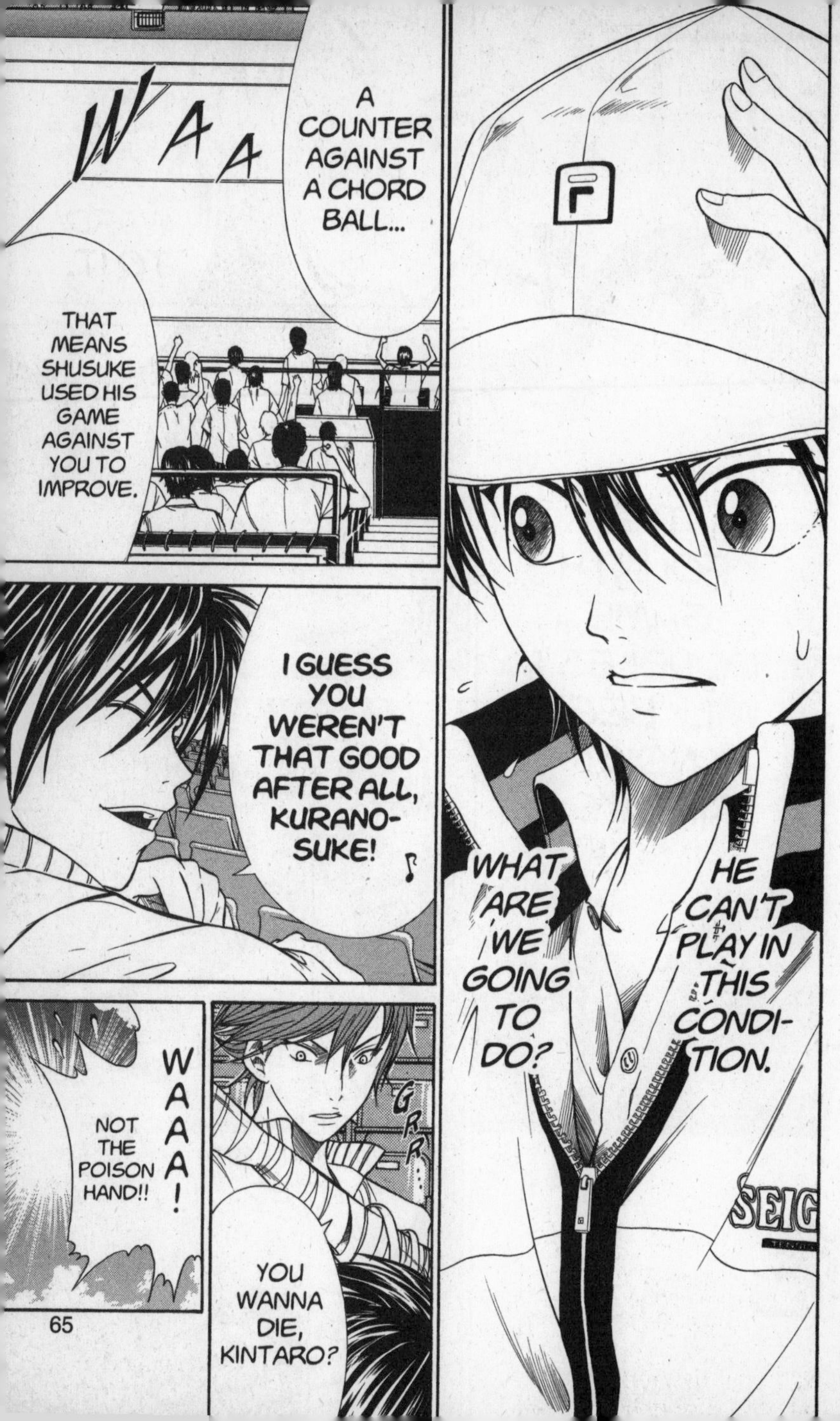

WAA
A COUNTER AGAINST A CHORD BALL...
THAT MEANS SHUSUKE USED HIS GAME AGAINST YOU TO IMPROVE.
I GUESS YOU WEREN'T THAT GOOD AFTER ALL, KURANO-SUKE! ♪
WAAAA!
NOT THE POISON HAND!!
GRR...
YOU WANNA DIE, KINTARO?
HE CAN'T PLAY IN THIS CONDI-TION.
WHAT ARE WE GOING TO DO?
SEIG

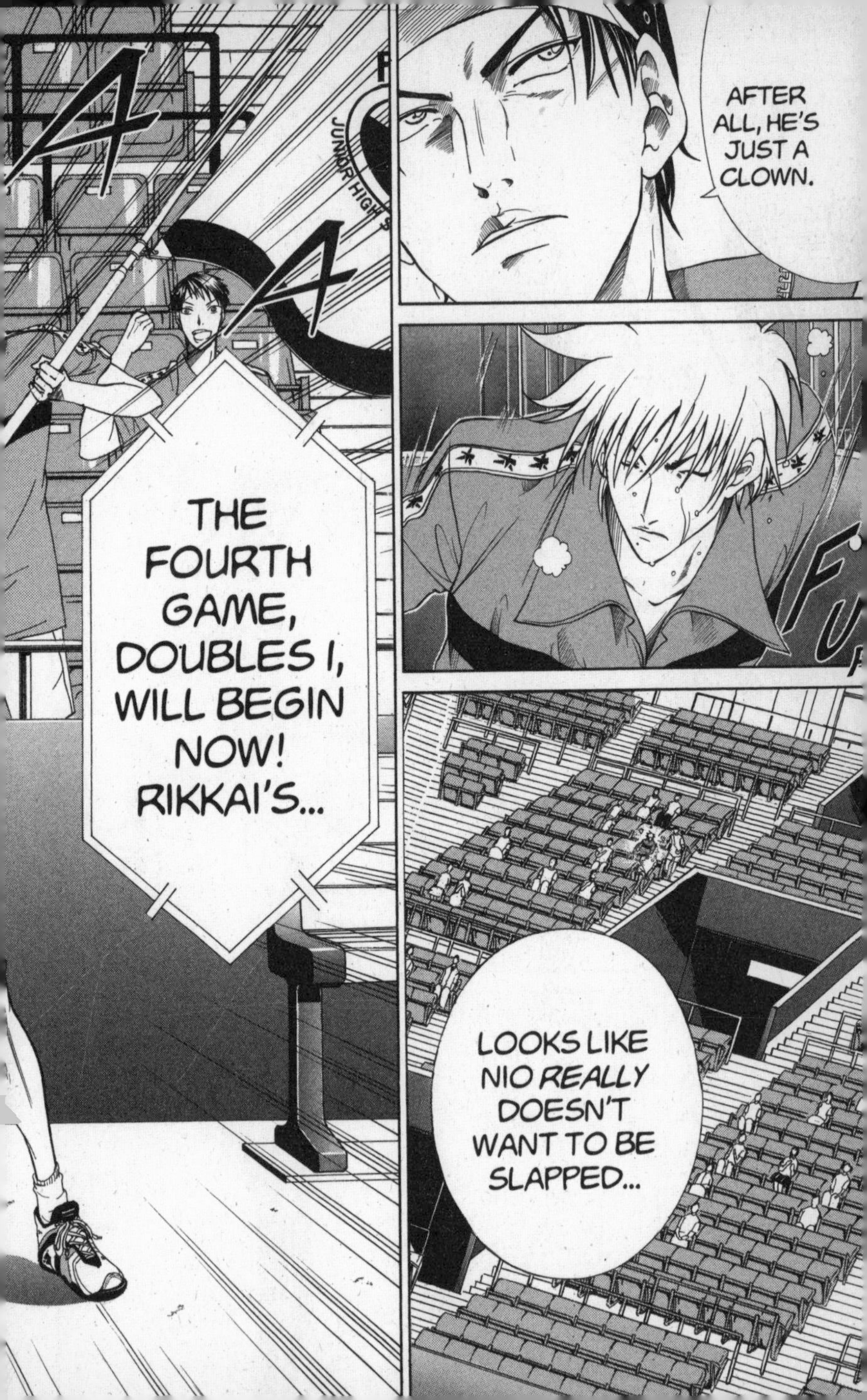
AFTER ALL, HE'S JUST A CLOWN.
LOOKS LIKE NIO REALLY DOESN'T WANT TO BE SLAPPED...
THE FOURTH GAME, DOUBLES 1, WILL BEGIN NOW! RIKKAI'S...

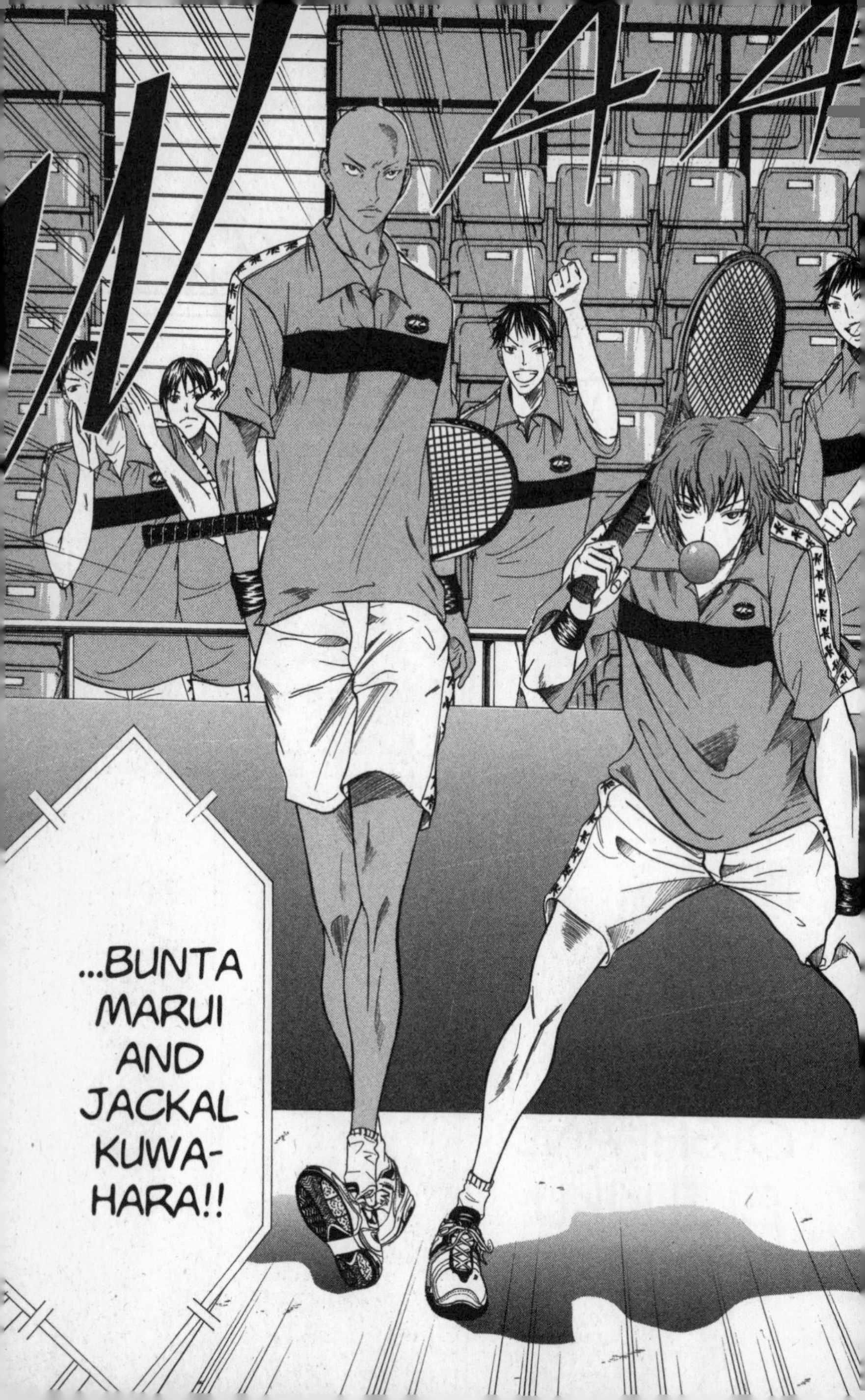
WAAA
...BUNTA MARUI AND JACKAL KUWA-HARA!!

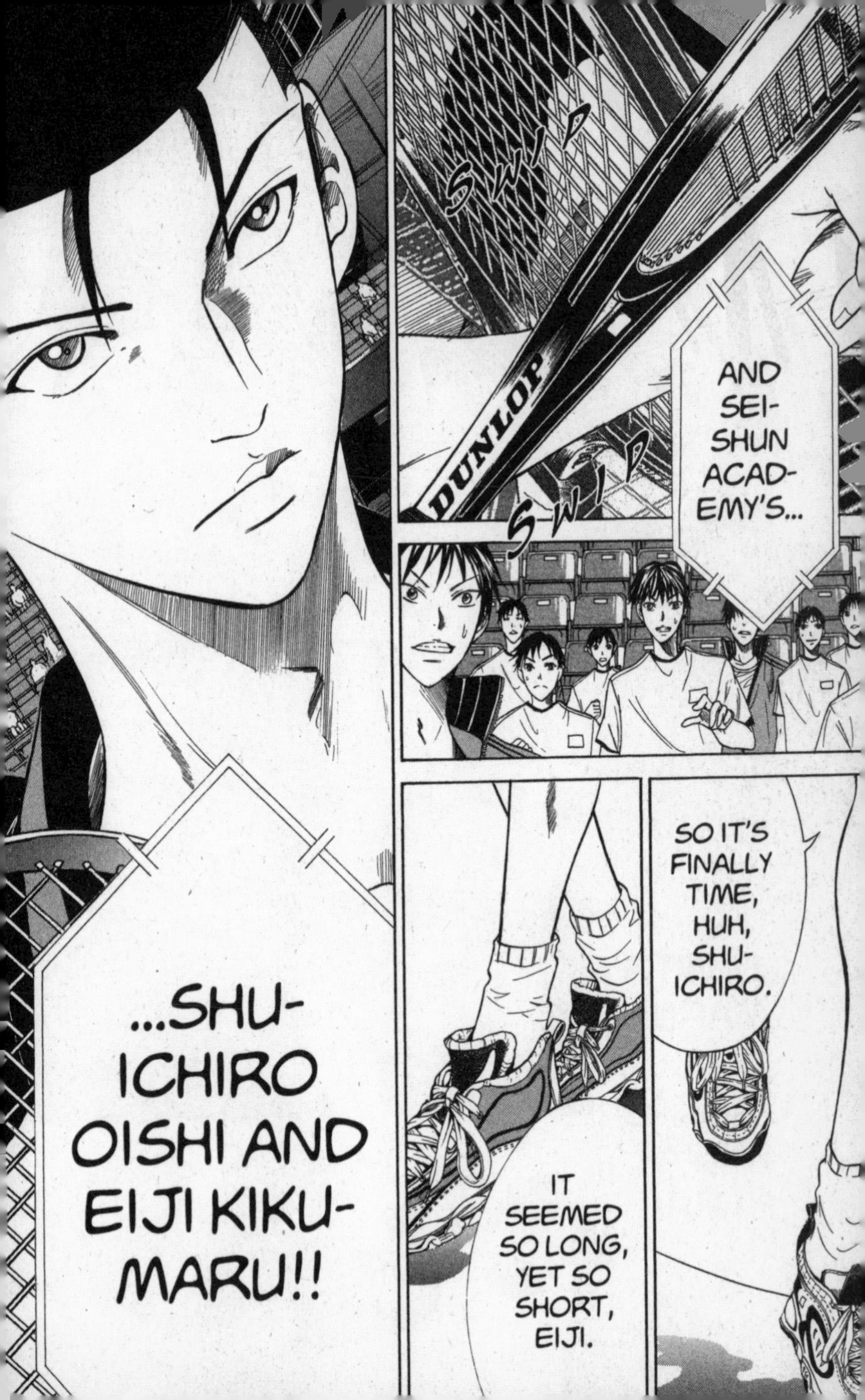
SWID
SWID
AND SEI-SHUN ACAD-EMY'S...
SO IT'S FINALLY TIME, HUH, SHU-ICHIRO.
IT SEEMED SO LONG, YET SO SHORT, EIJI.
...SHU-ICHIRO OISHI AND EIJI KIKU-MARU!!

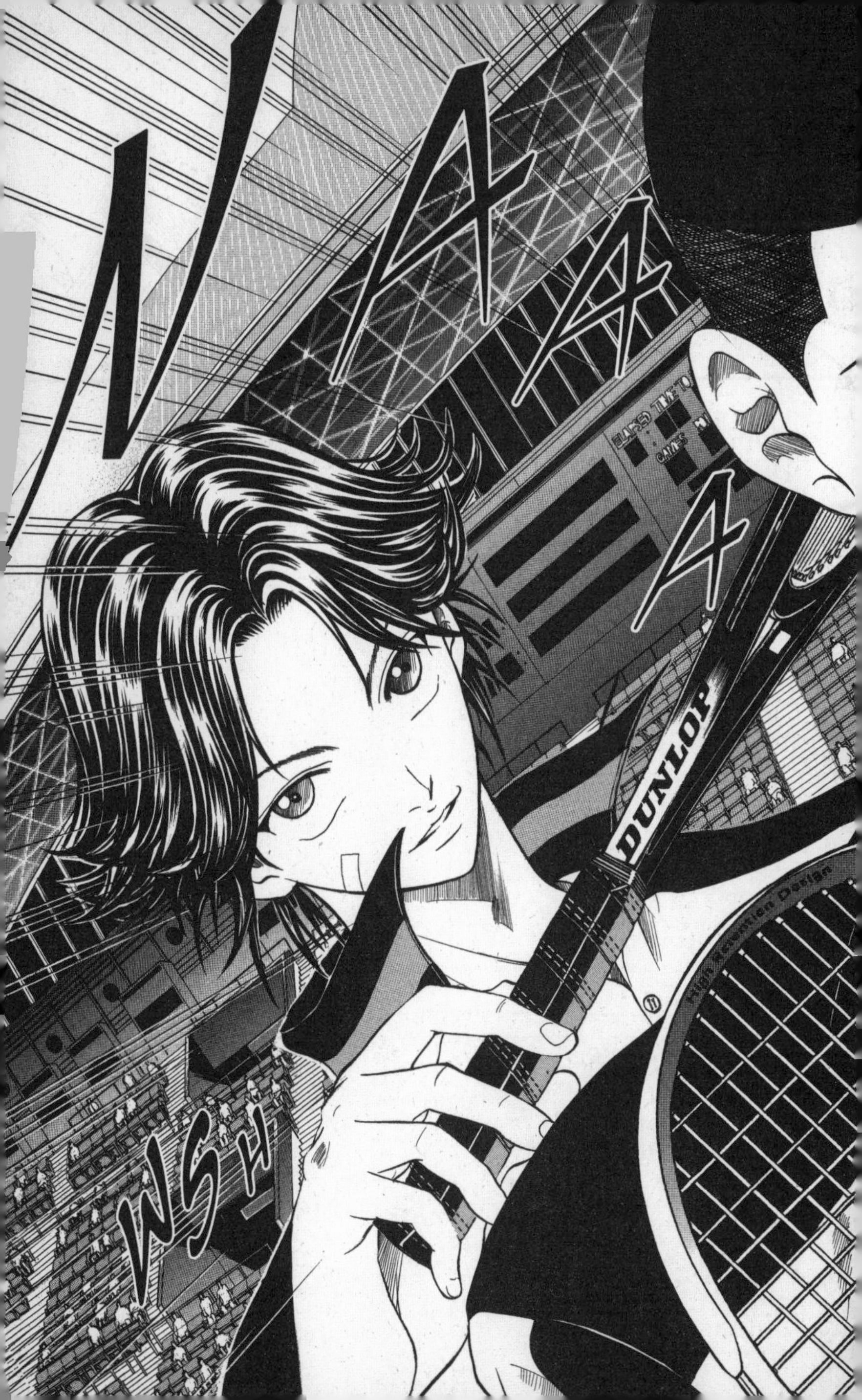
WAAAA
WSH
DUNLOP
High Retention Design

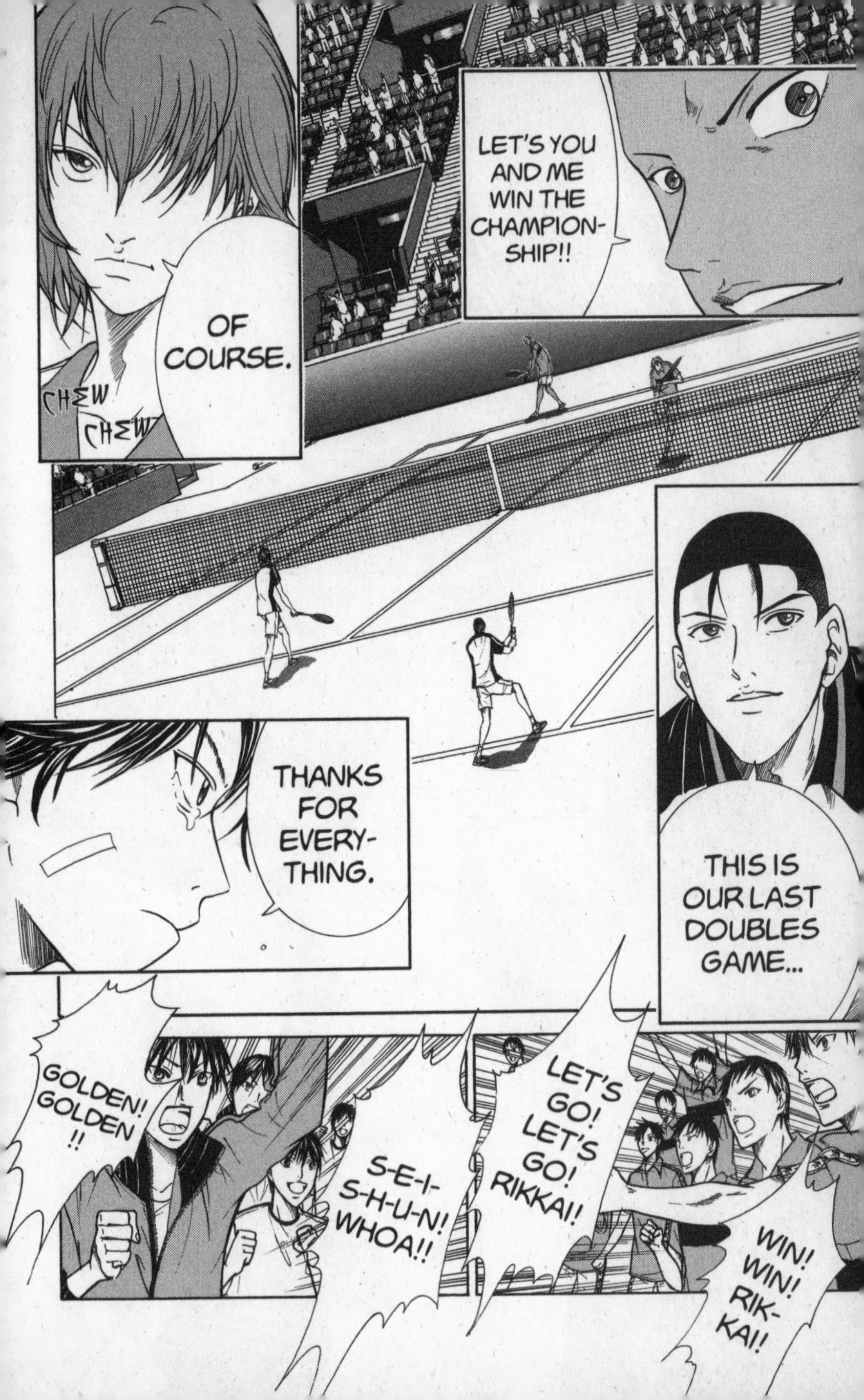
LET'S YOU AND ME WIN THE CHAMPION-SHIP!!
OF COURSE.
CHEW CHEW
THIS IS OUR LAST DOUBLES GAME...
THANKS FOR EVERY-THING.
WIN! WIN! RIK-KAI!!
LET'S GO! LET'S GO! RIKKAI!!
S-E-I-S-H-U-N! WHOA!!
GOLDEN! GOLDEN!!

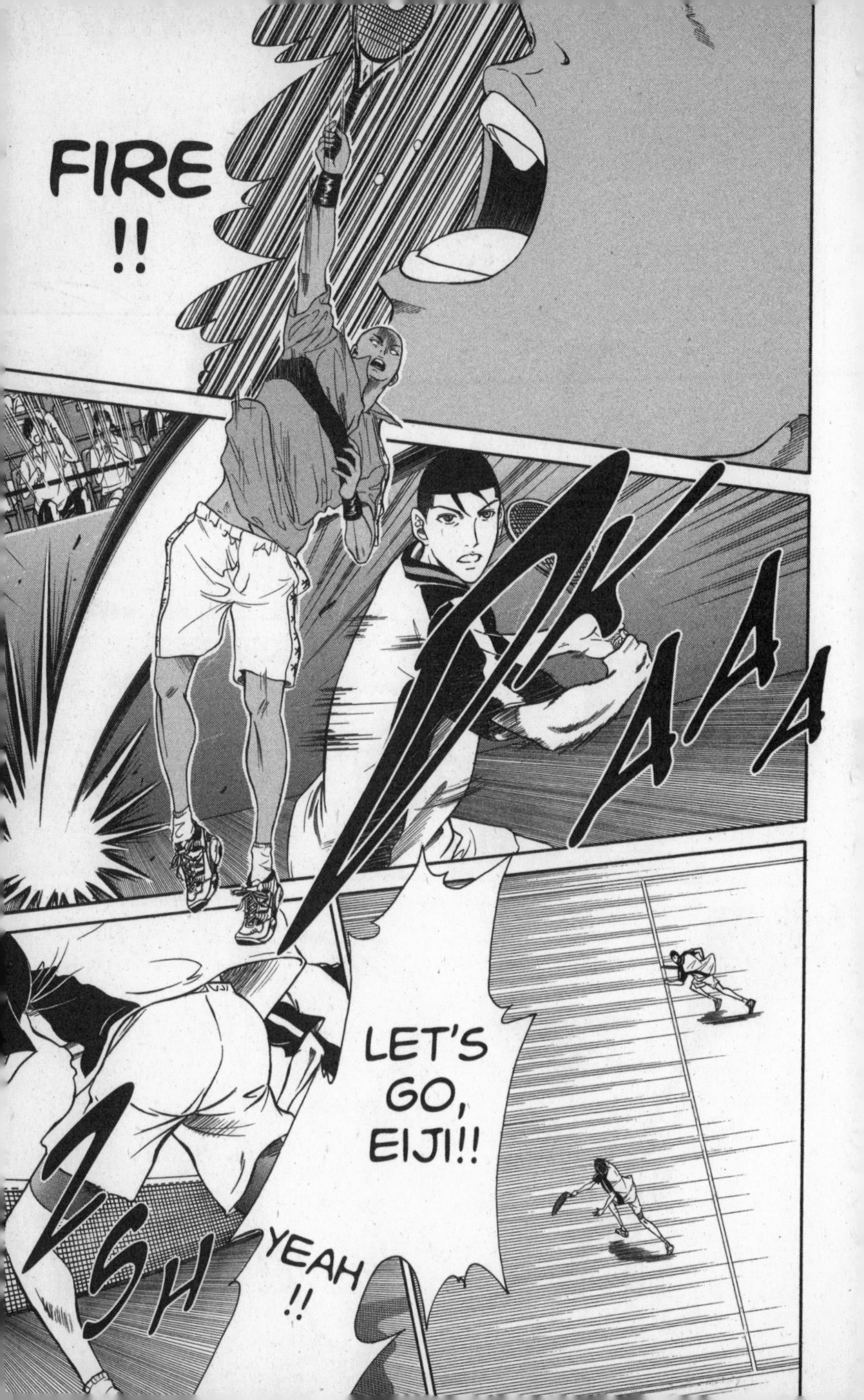
FIRE !!
WHAAA
LET'S GO, EIJI!!
YEAH !!
VSSH

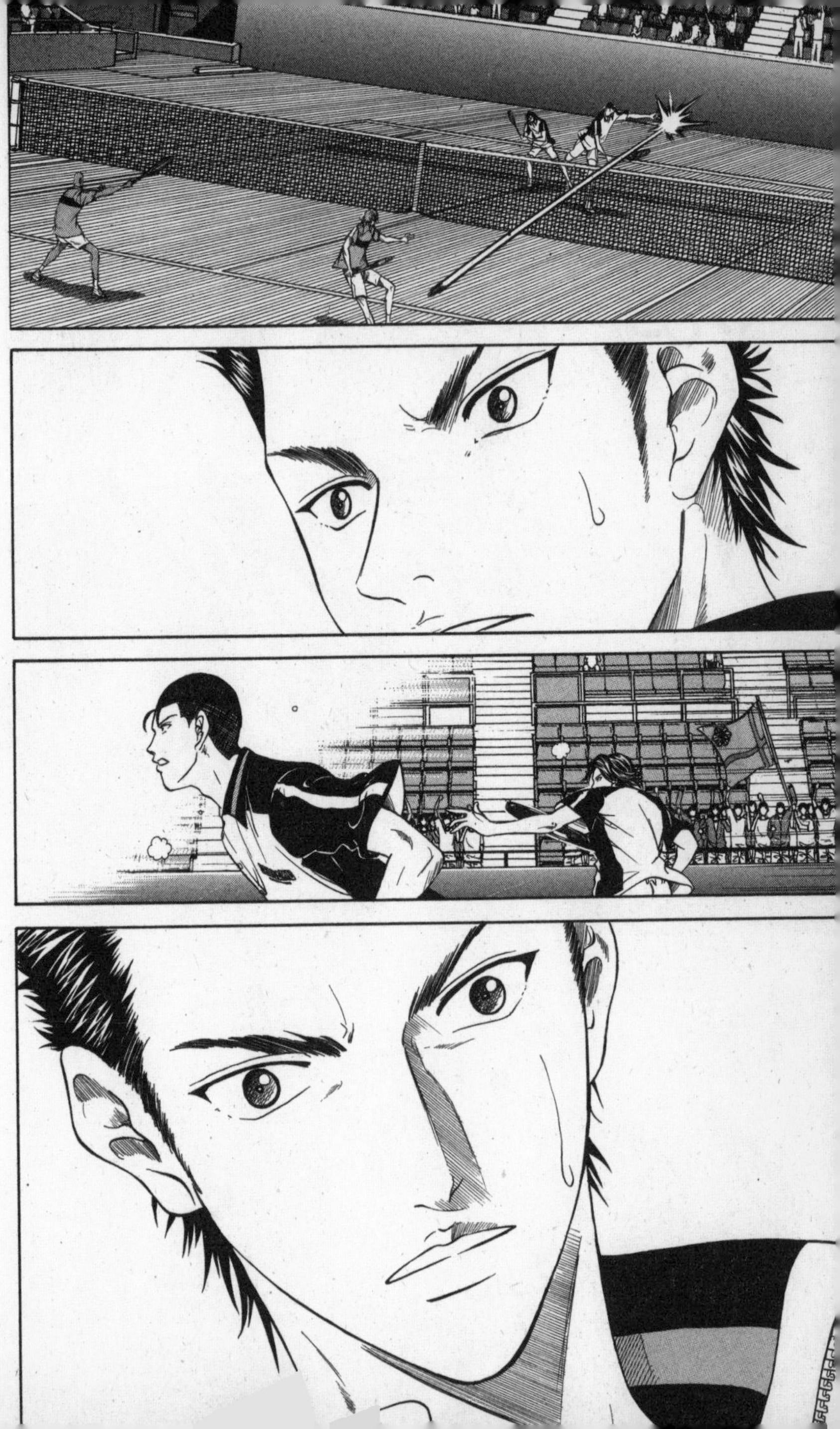

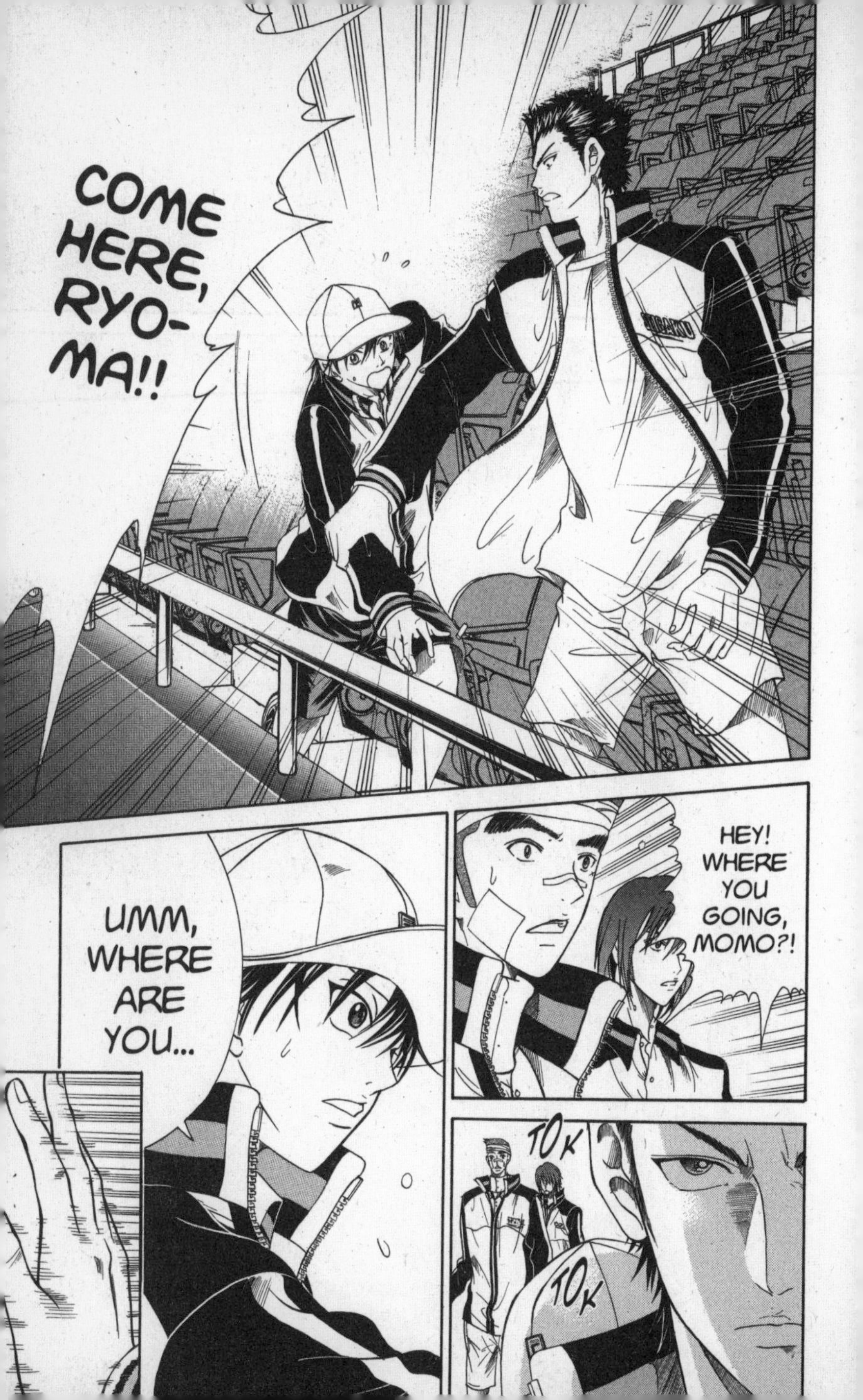
COME HERE, RYO-MA!!
HEY! WHERE YOU GOING, MOMO?!
UMM, WHERE ARE YOU...
TOK
TOK

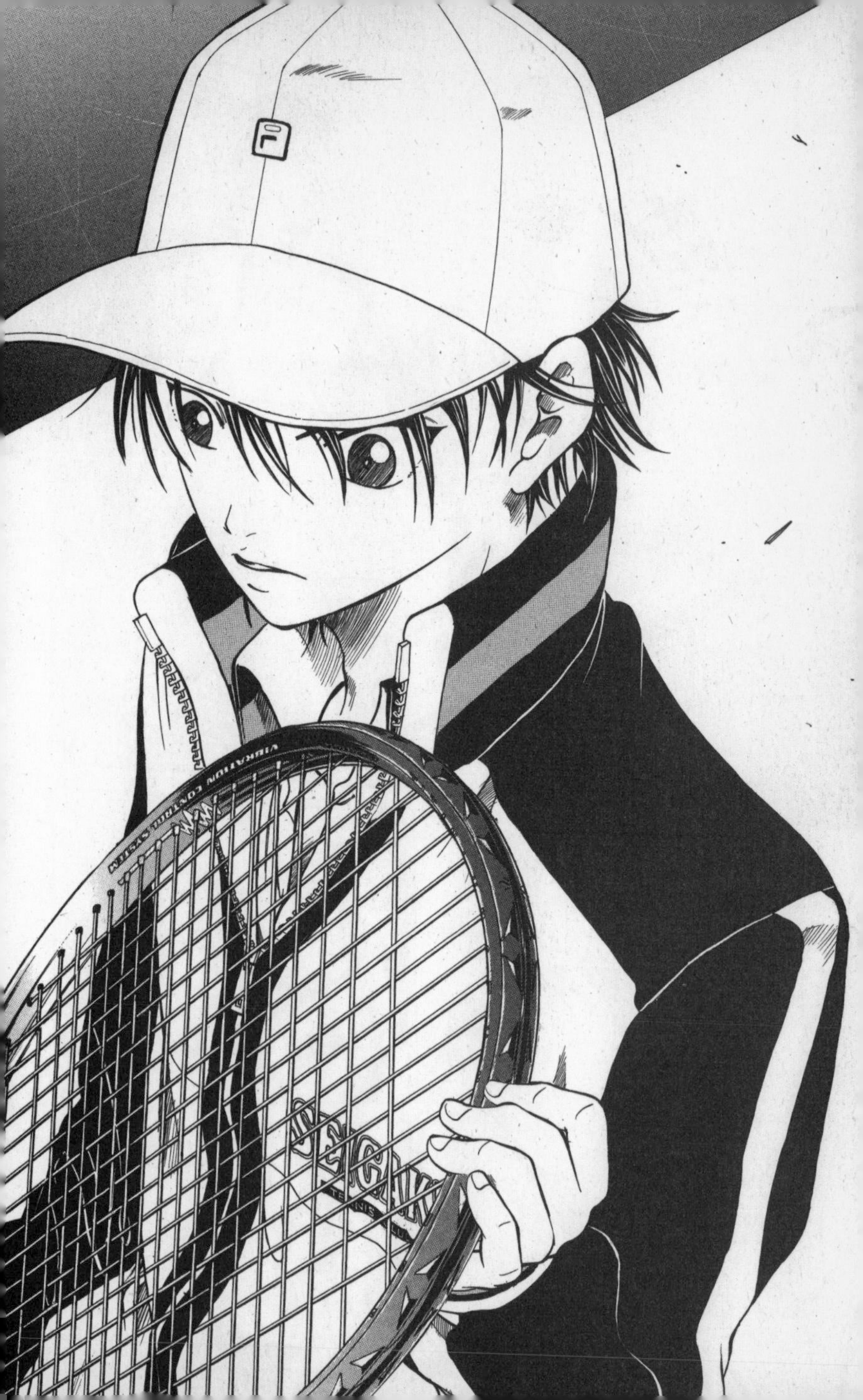

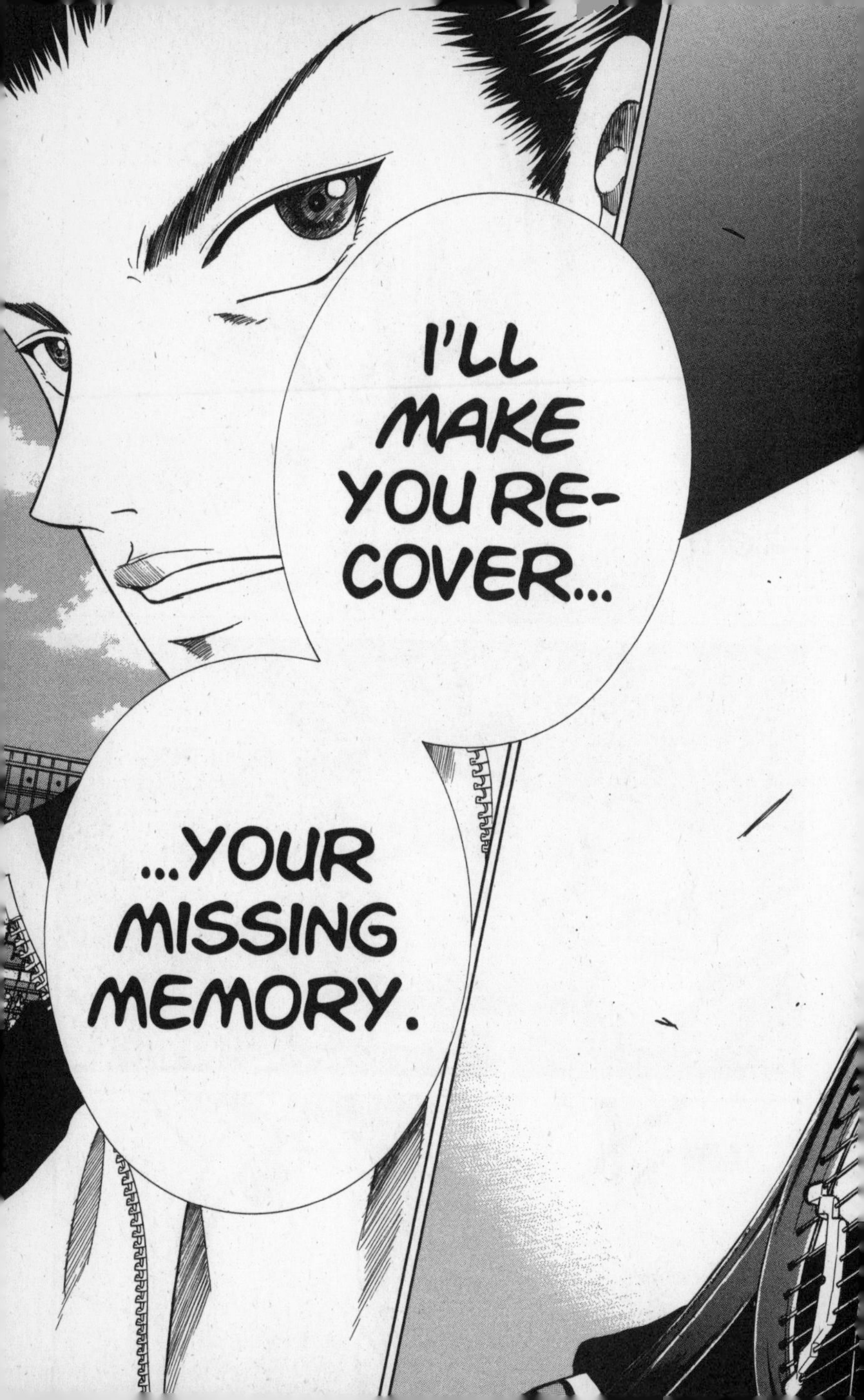
I'LL MAKE YOU RE-COVER...
...YOUR MISSING MEMORY.

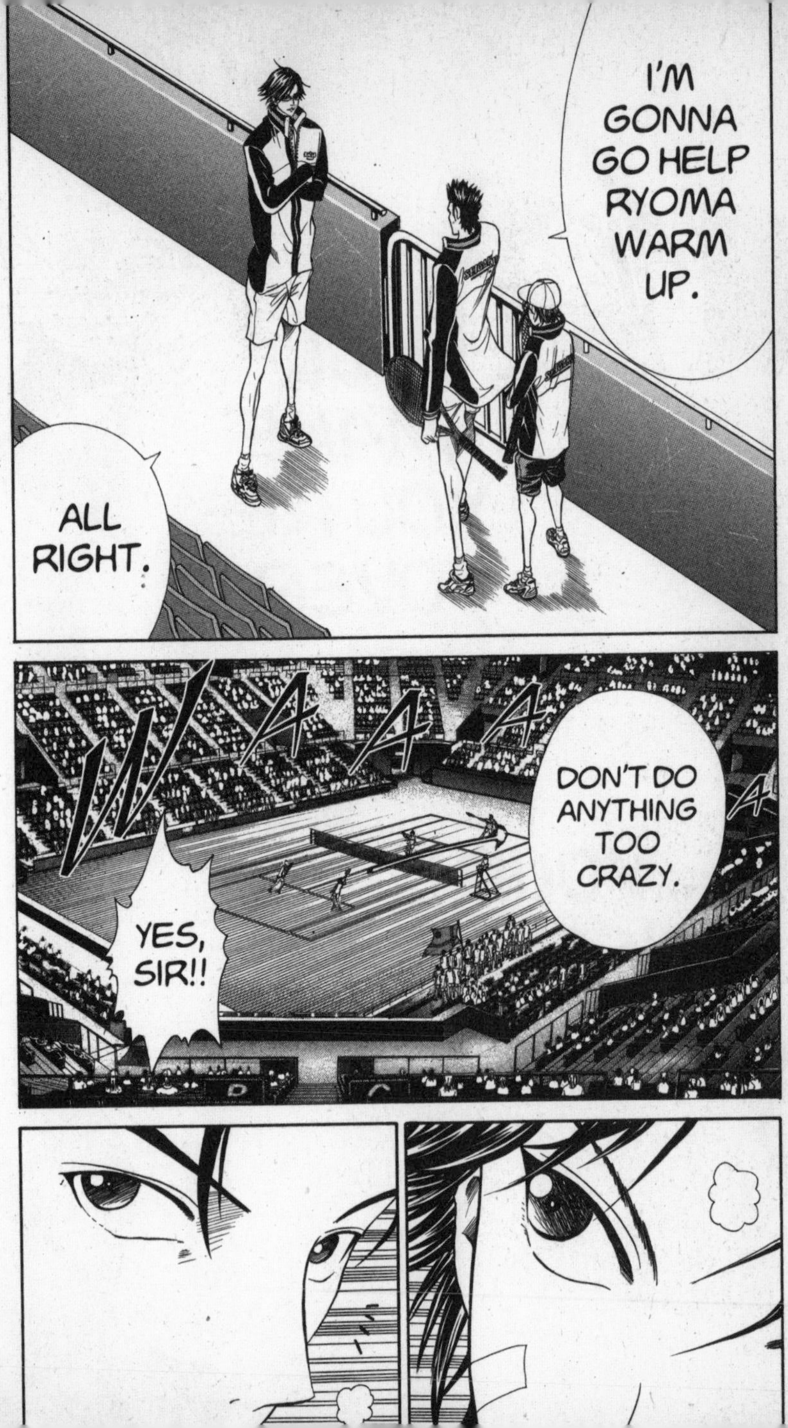
I'M GONNA GO HELP RYOMA WARM UP.
ALL RIGHT.
WAAAA
DON'T DO ANYTHING TOO CRAZY.
YES, SIR!!

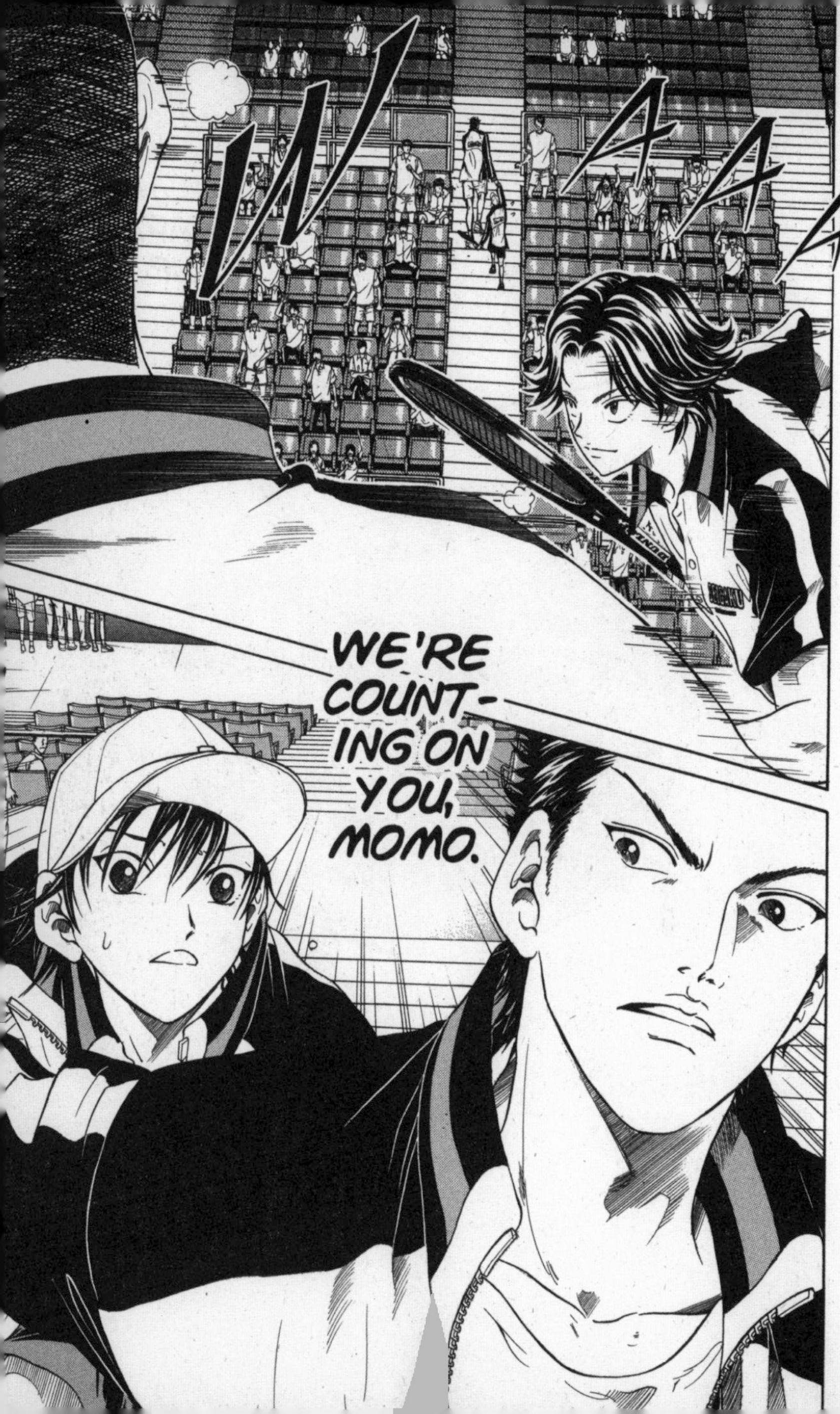
WAAAA
WE'RE COUNTING ON YOU, MOMO.

テニスの王子様

THE PRINCE OF TENNIS

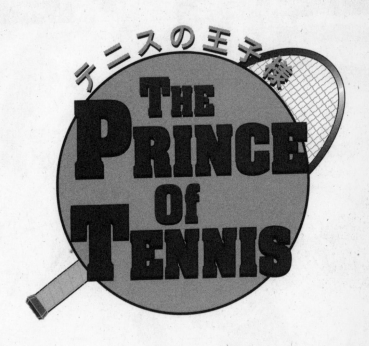

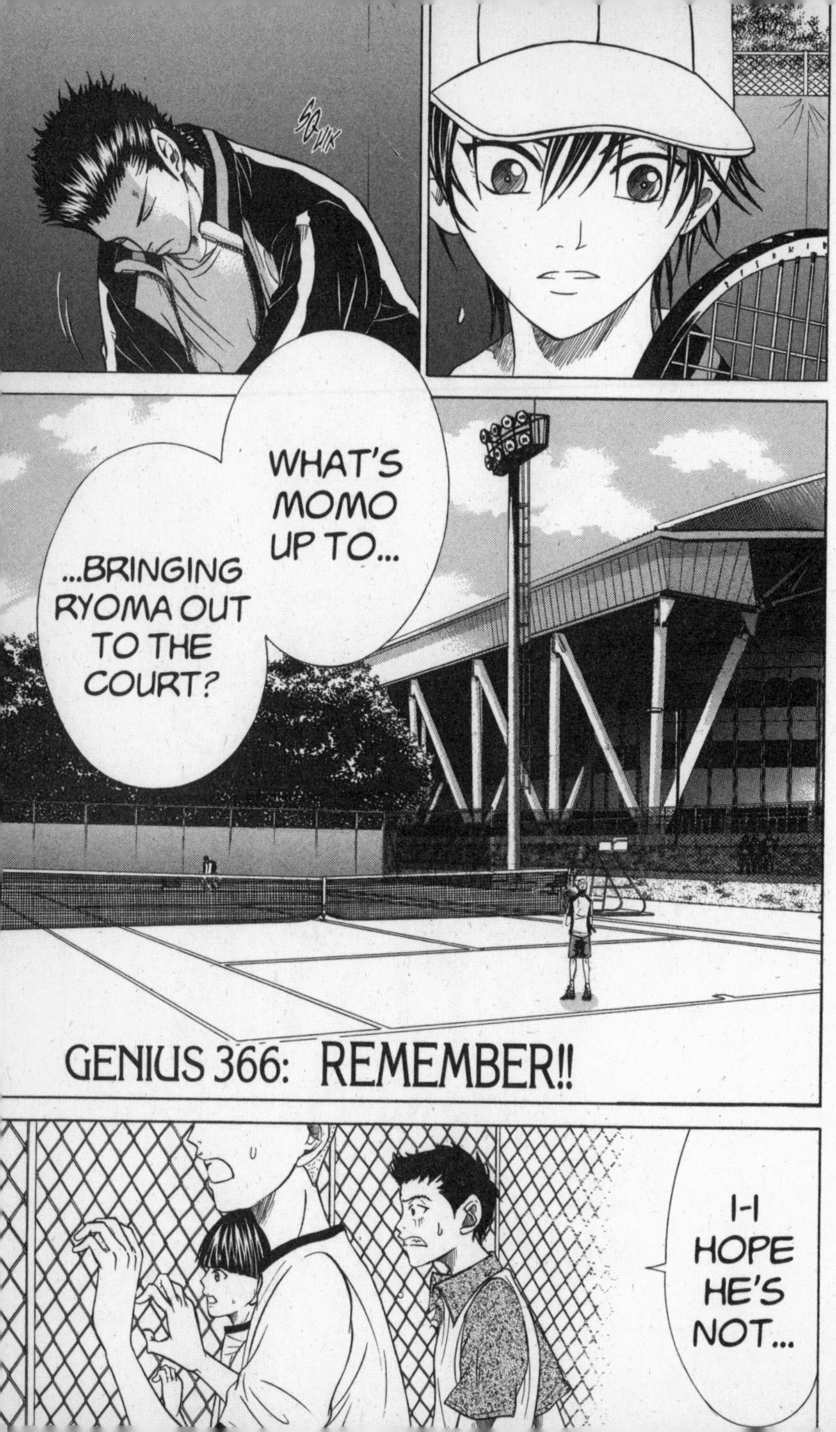
SQUIK
WHAT'S MOMO UP TO...
...BRINGING RYOMA OUT TO THE COURT?
GENIUS 366: REMEMBER!!
I-I HOPE HE'S NOT...

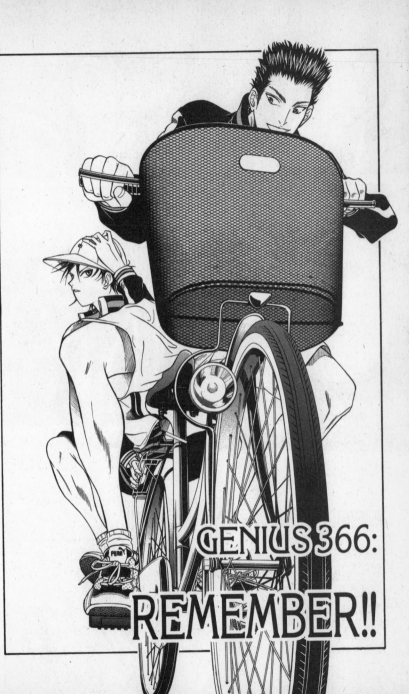

GENIUS 366:
REMEMBER!!

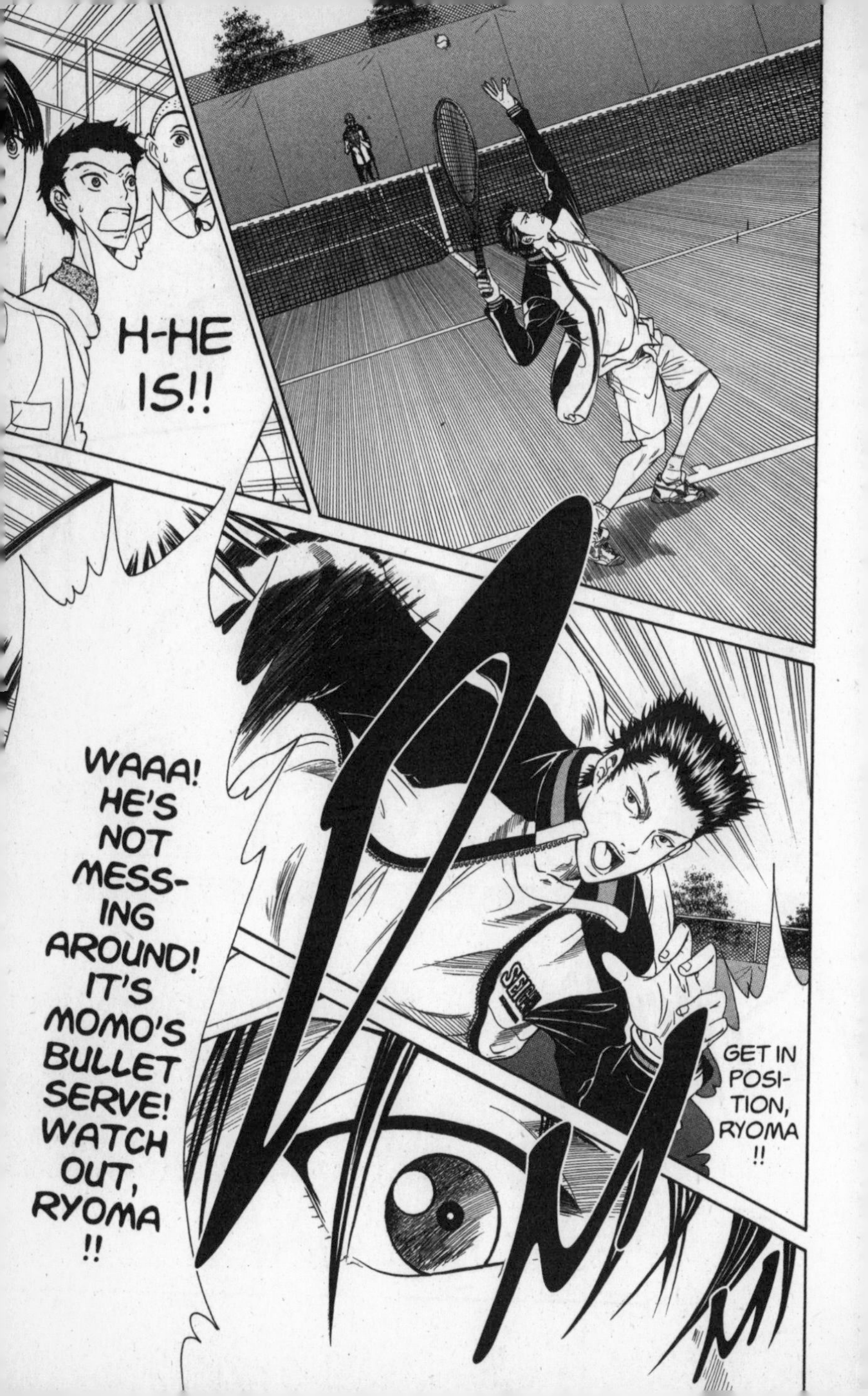
H-HE IS!!
GET IN POSI- TION, RYOMA !!
WAAA! HE'S NOT MESS- ING AROUND! IT'S MOMO'S BULLET SERVE! WATCH OUT, RYOMA !!

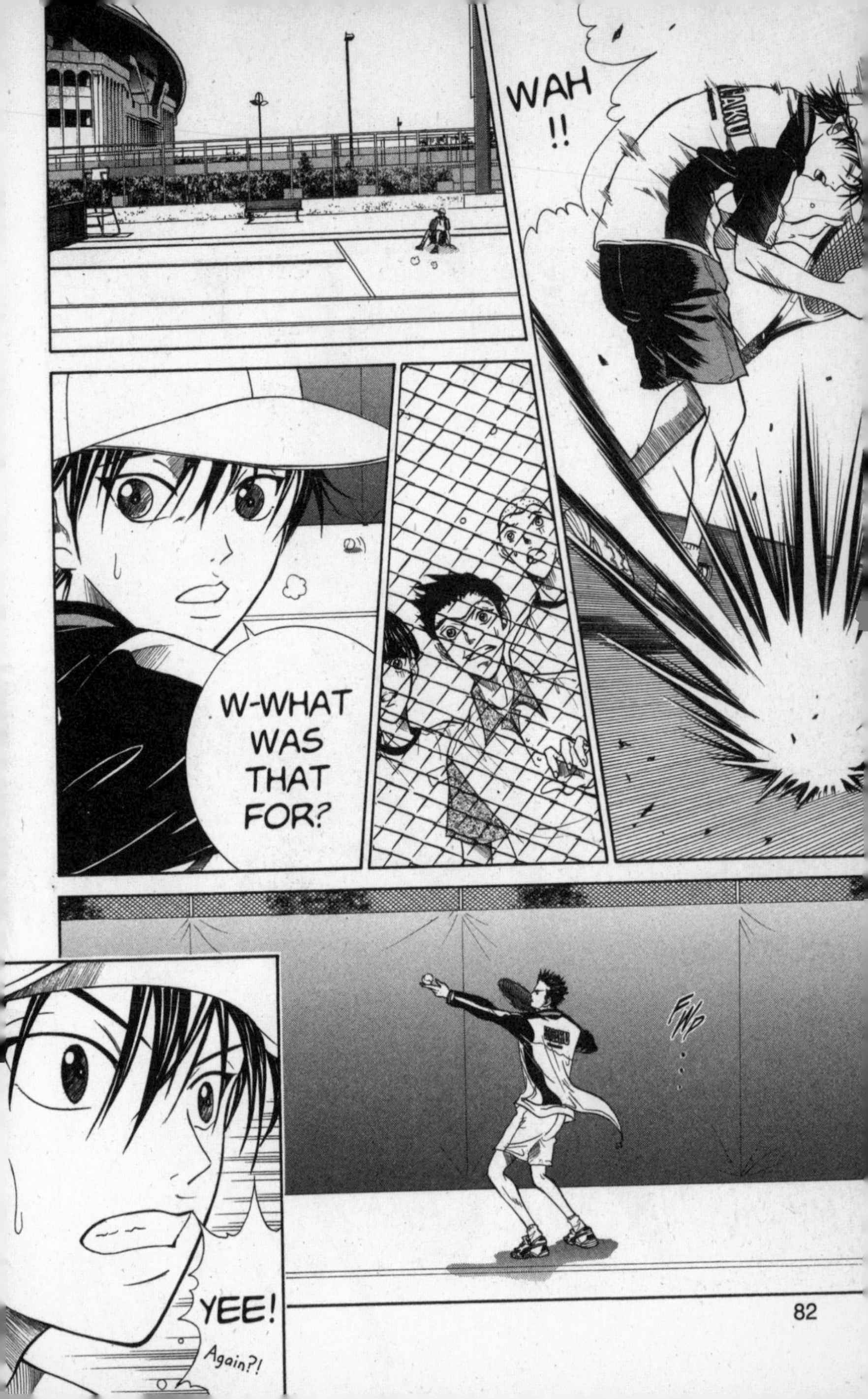
WAH !!
W-WHAT WAS THAT FOR?
FWP
YEE!
Again?!

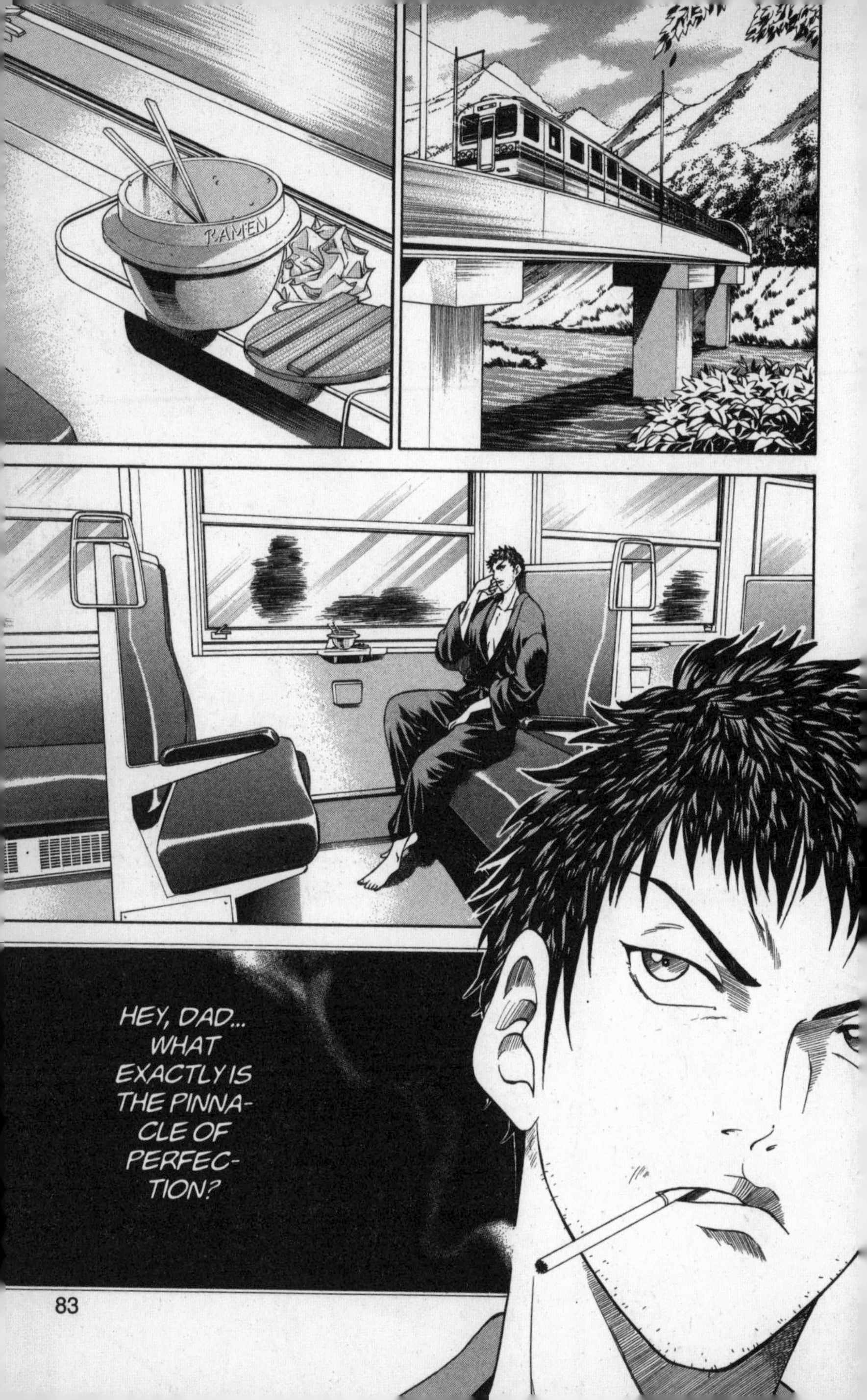
RAMEN
HEY, DAD... WHAT EXACTLY IS THE PINNA-CLE OF PERFEC-TION?

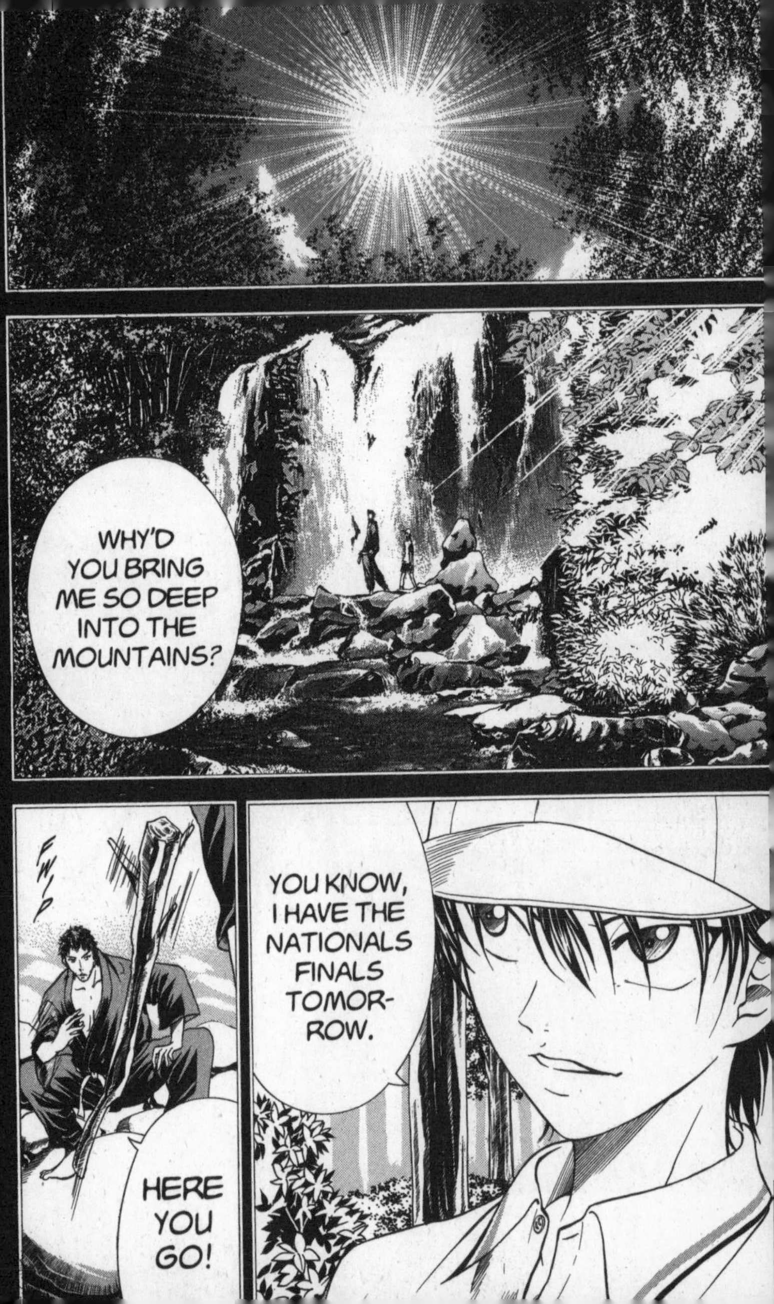
WHY'D YOU BRING ME SO DEEP INTO THE MOUNTAINS?
YOU KNOW, I HAVE THE NATIONALS FINALS TOMOR-ROW.
FWIP
HERE YOU GO!

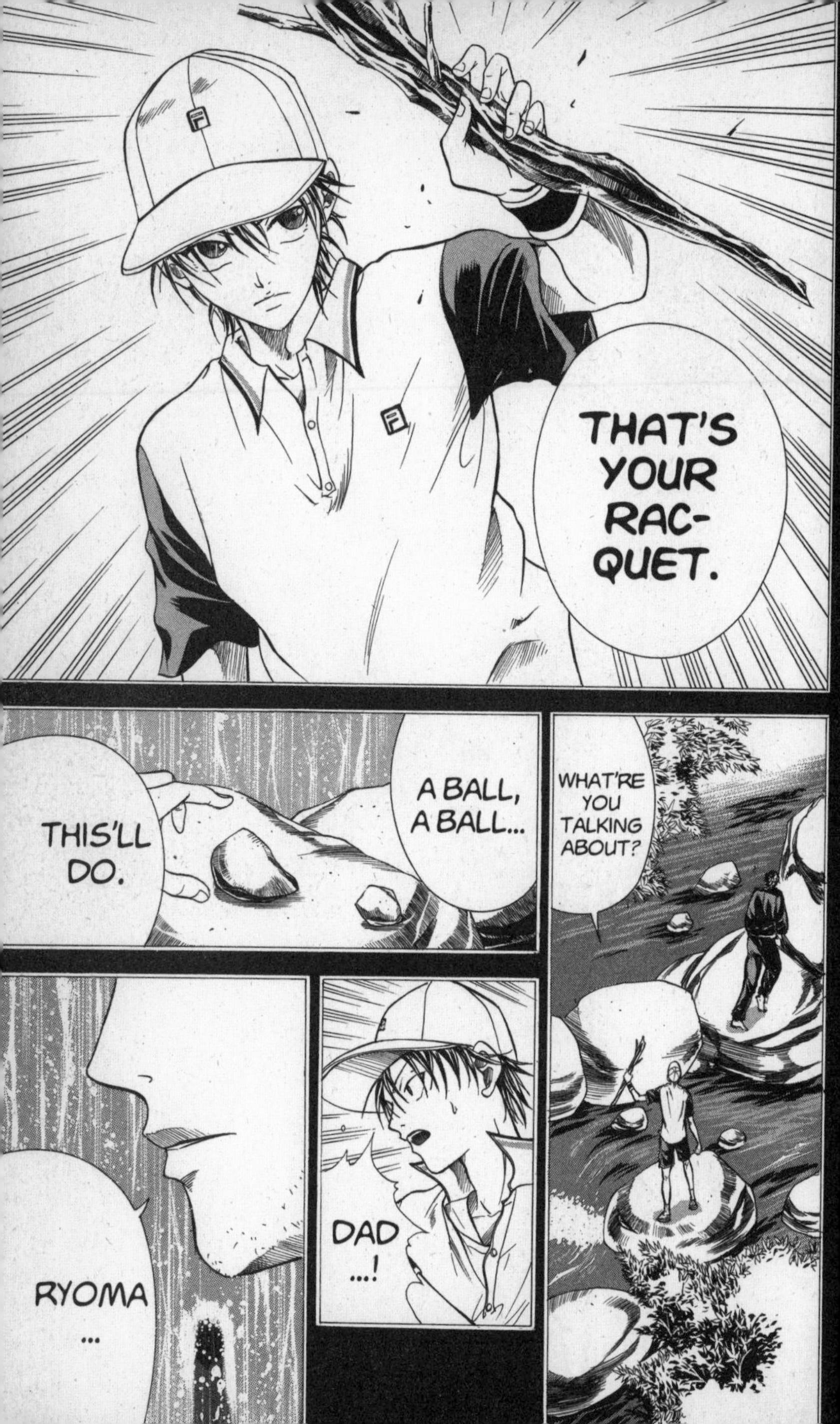
THAT'S YOUR RAC-QUET.
WHAT'RE YOU TALKING ABOUT?
A BALL, A BALL...
THIS'LL DO.
DAD ...!
RYOMA ...

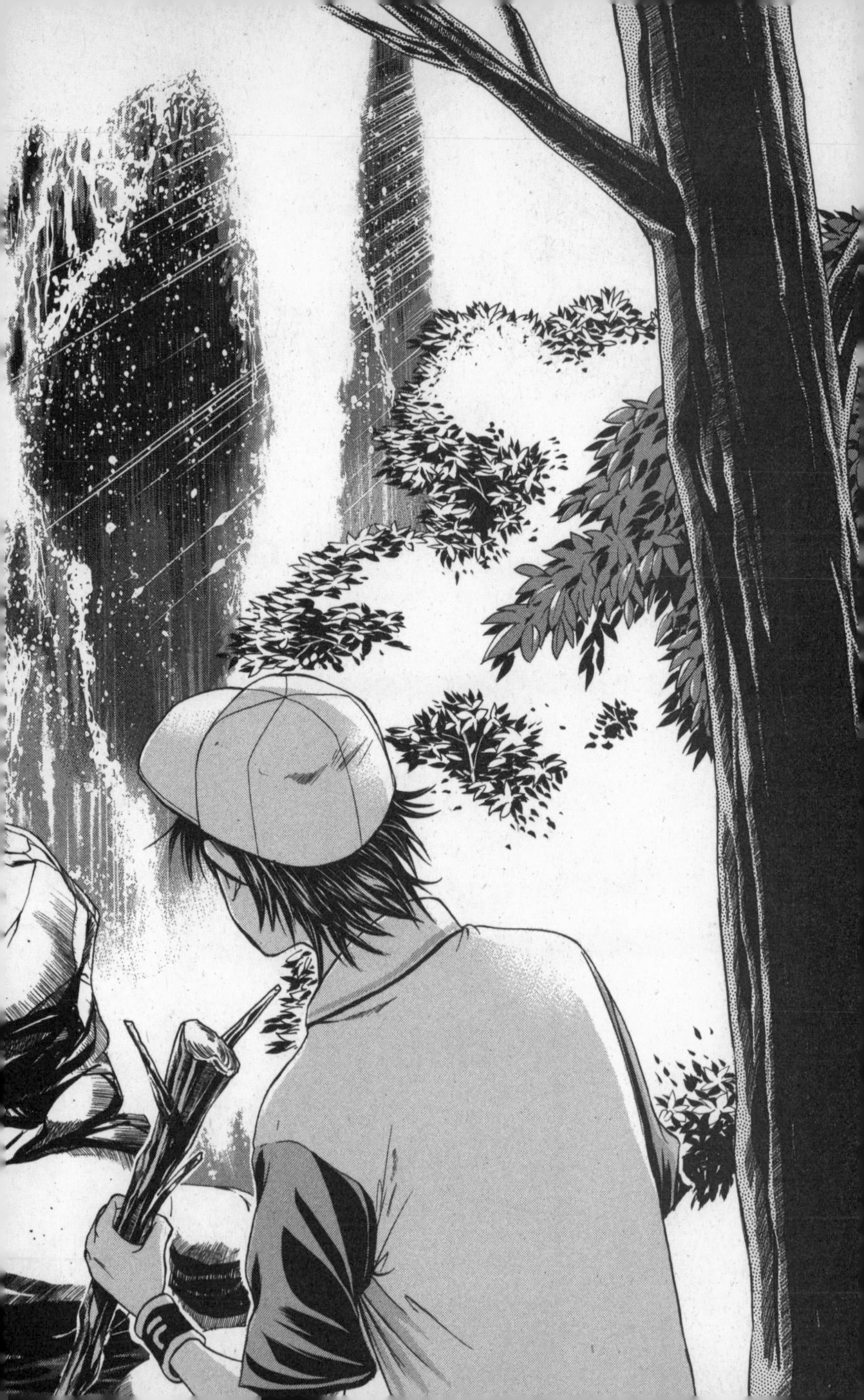

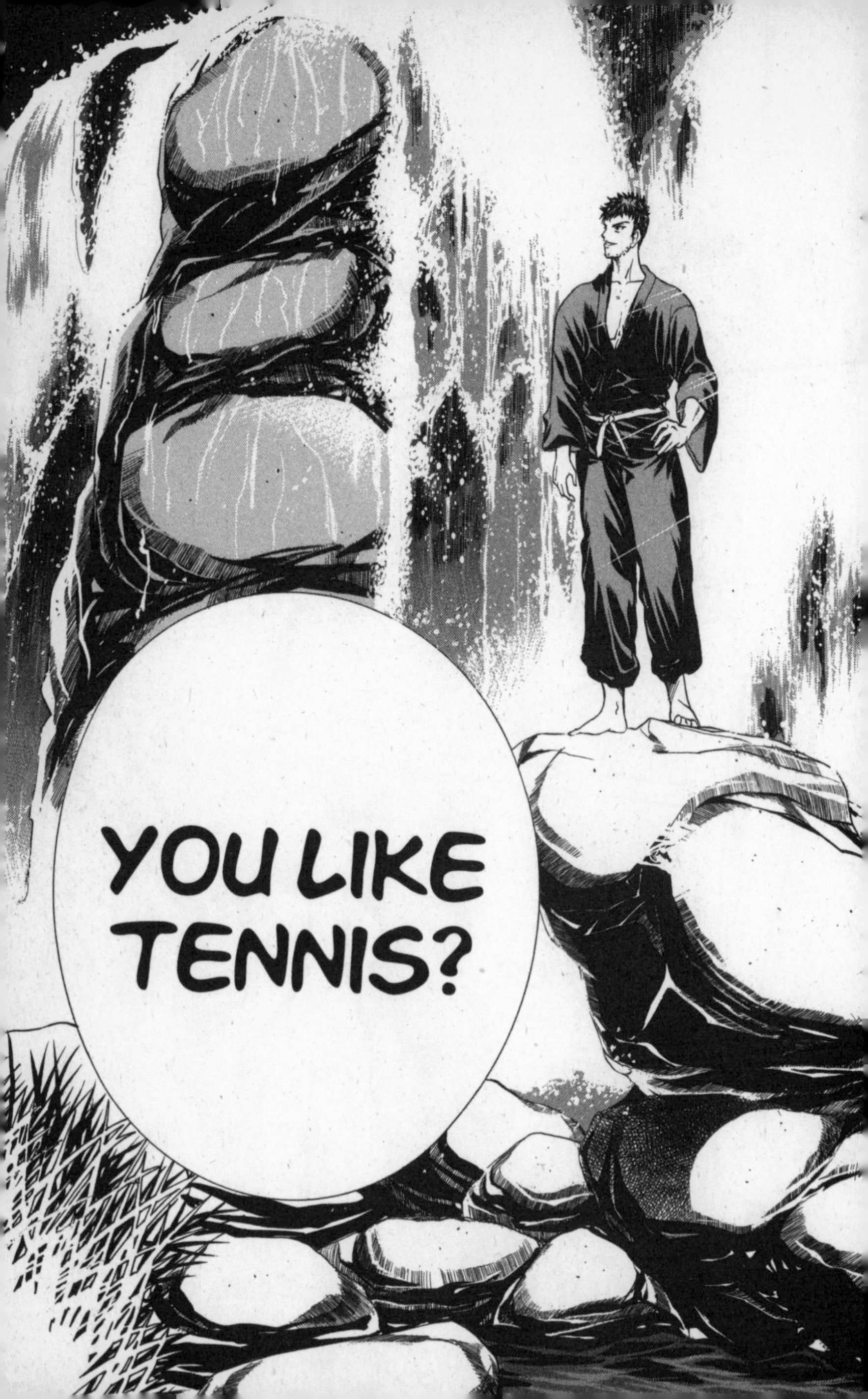
YOU LIKE TENNIS?

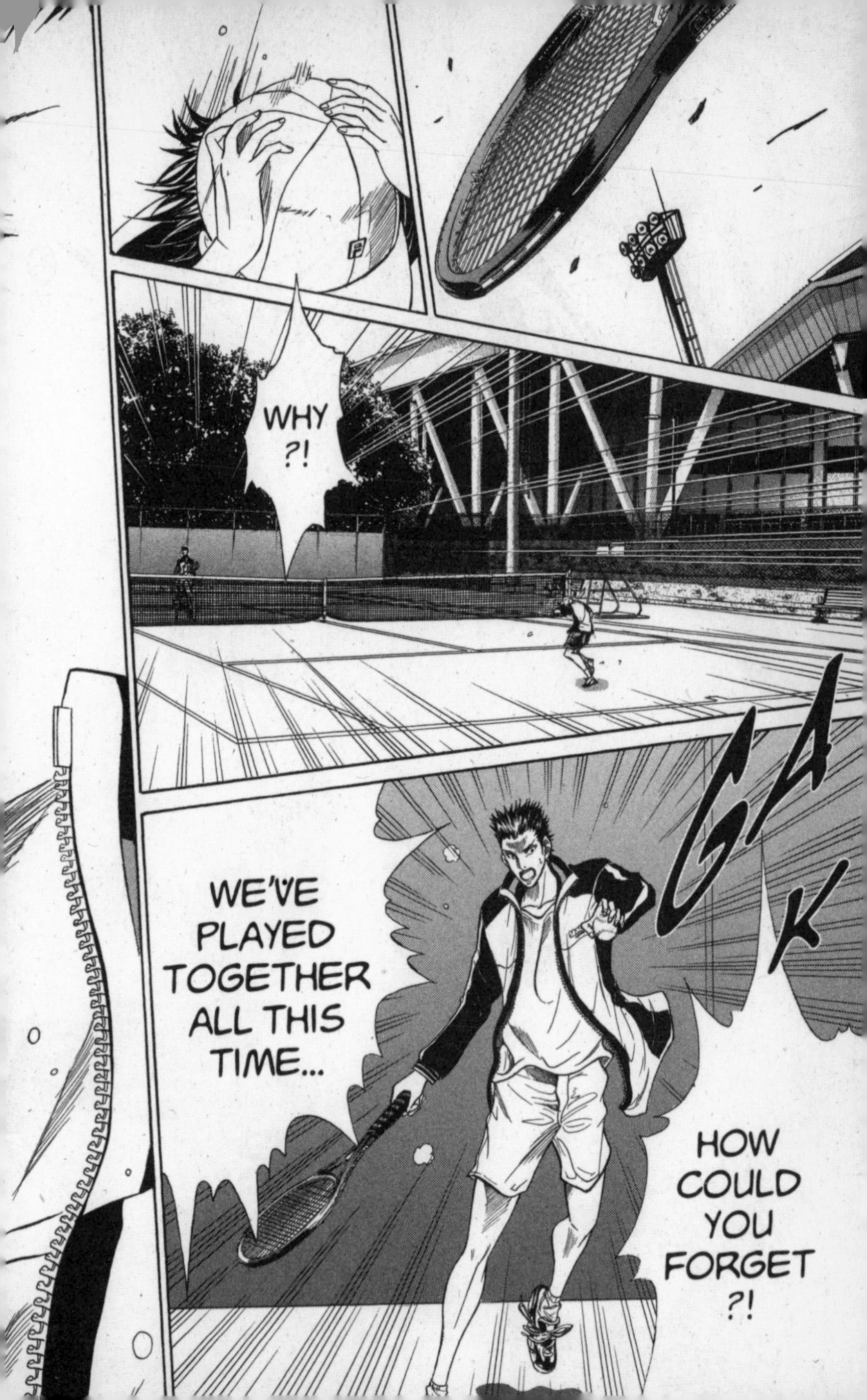
WHY ?!
GAK
WE'VE PLAYED TOGETHER ALL THIS TIME...
HOW COULD YOU FORGET ?!

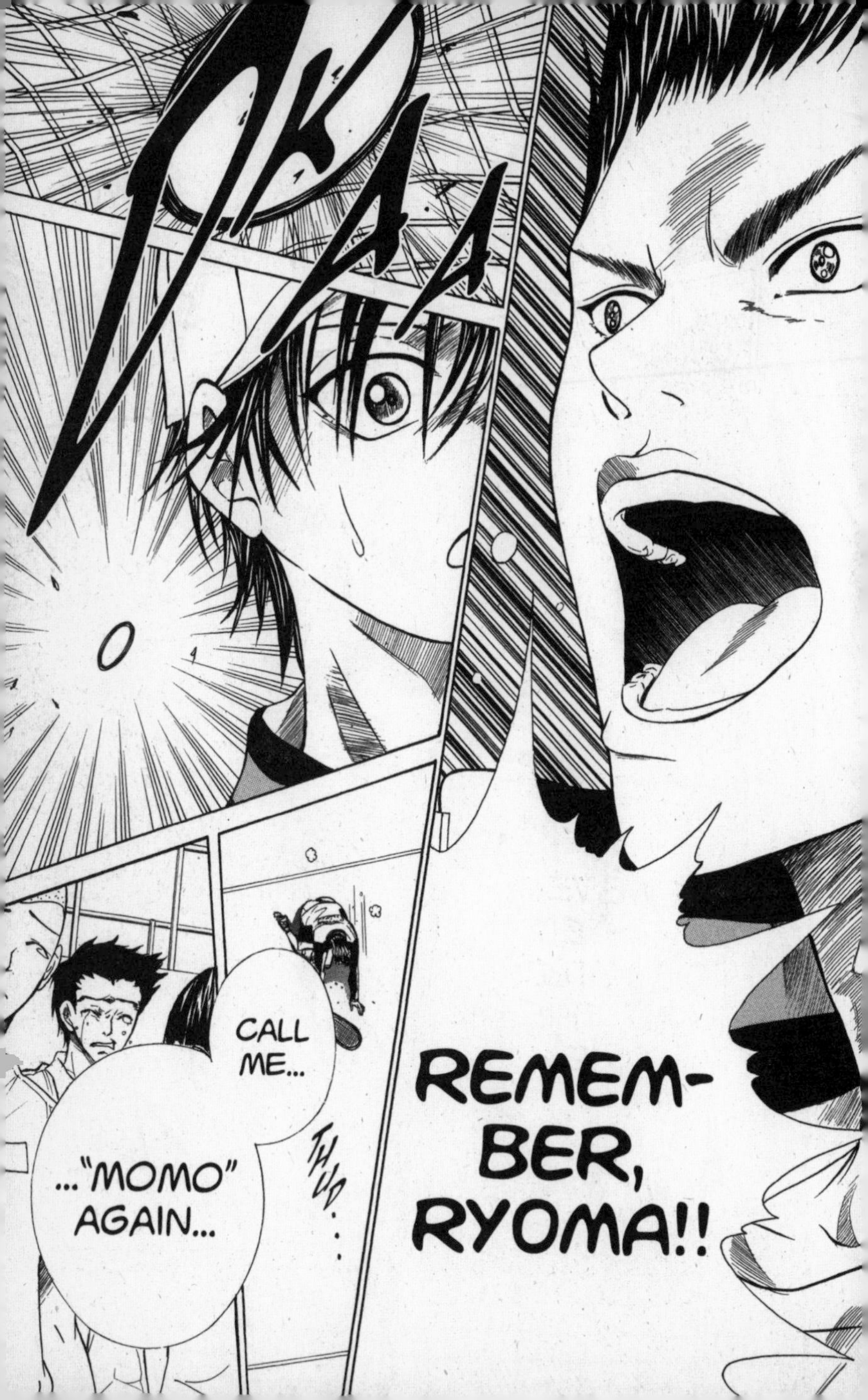
REMEM-
BER,
RYOMA!!
CALL ME...
..."MOMO" AGAIN...
THUD...

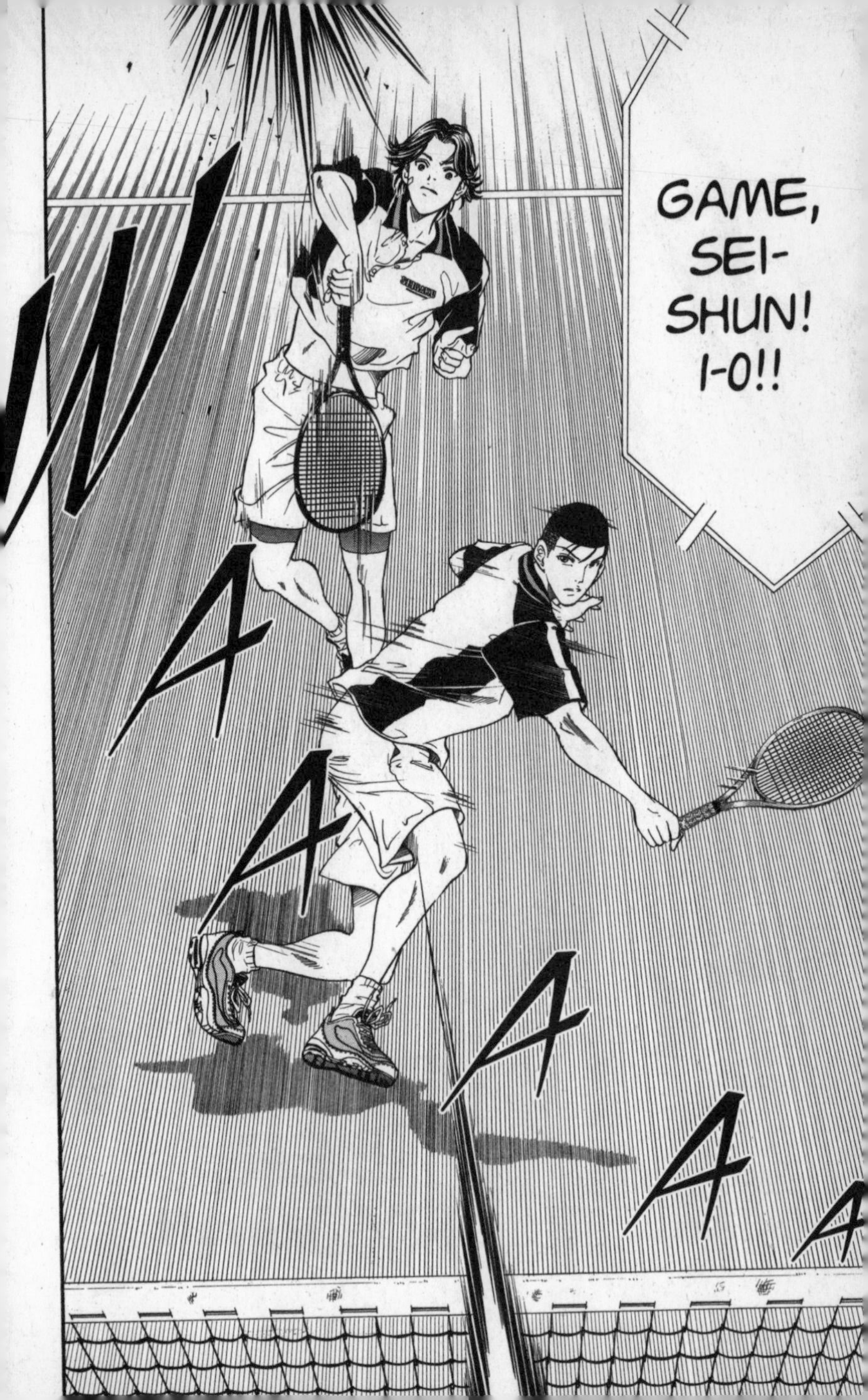
GAME, SEI-SHUN! 1-0!!
WAAAAAA

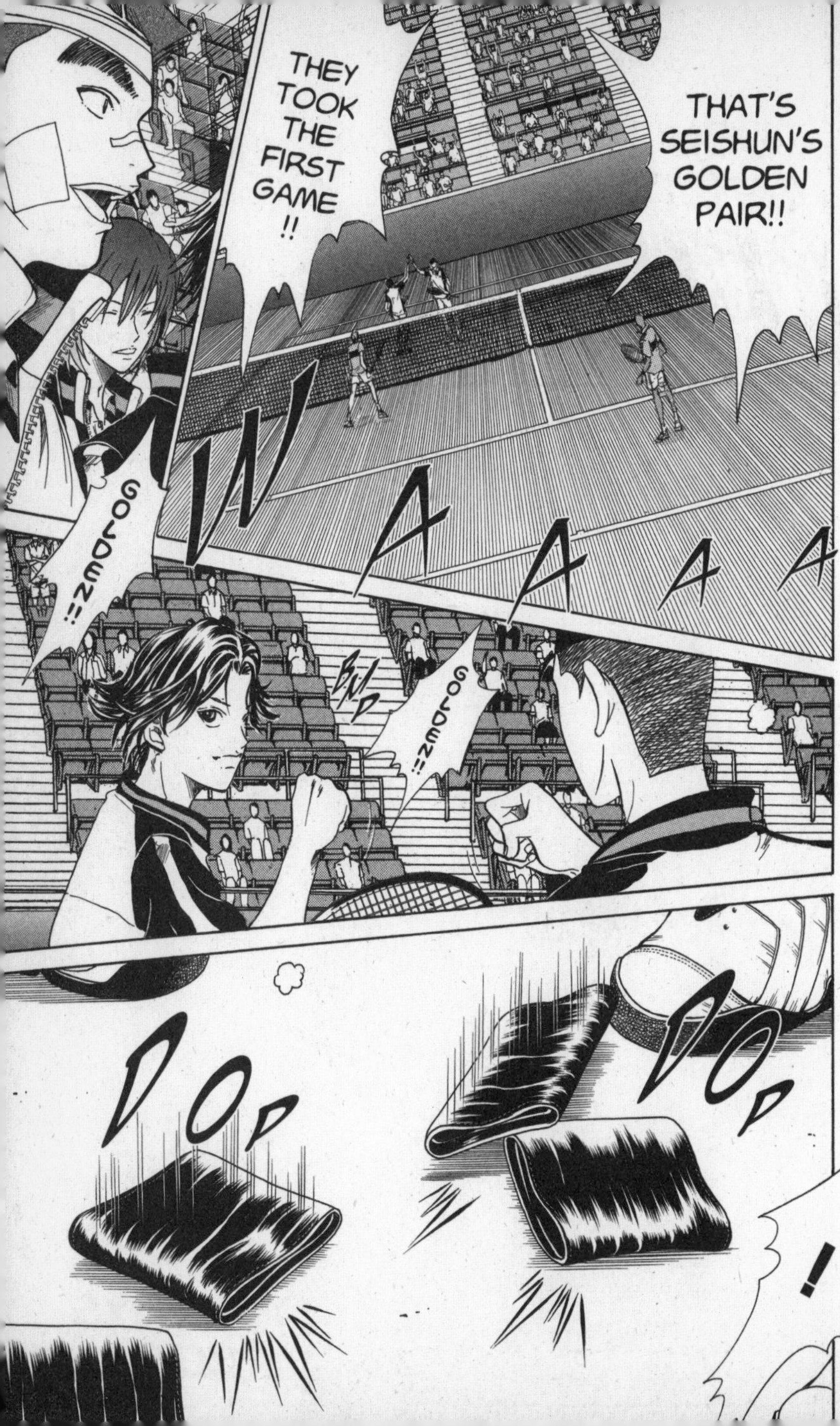
THAT'S SEISHUN'S GOLDEN PAIR!!
THEY TOOK THE FIRST GAME !!
WAAAA
GOLDEN!!
GOLDEN!!
DOP
DOP
!

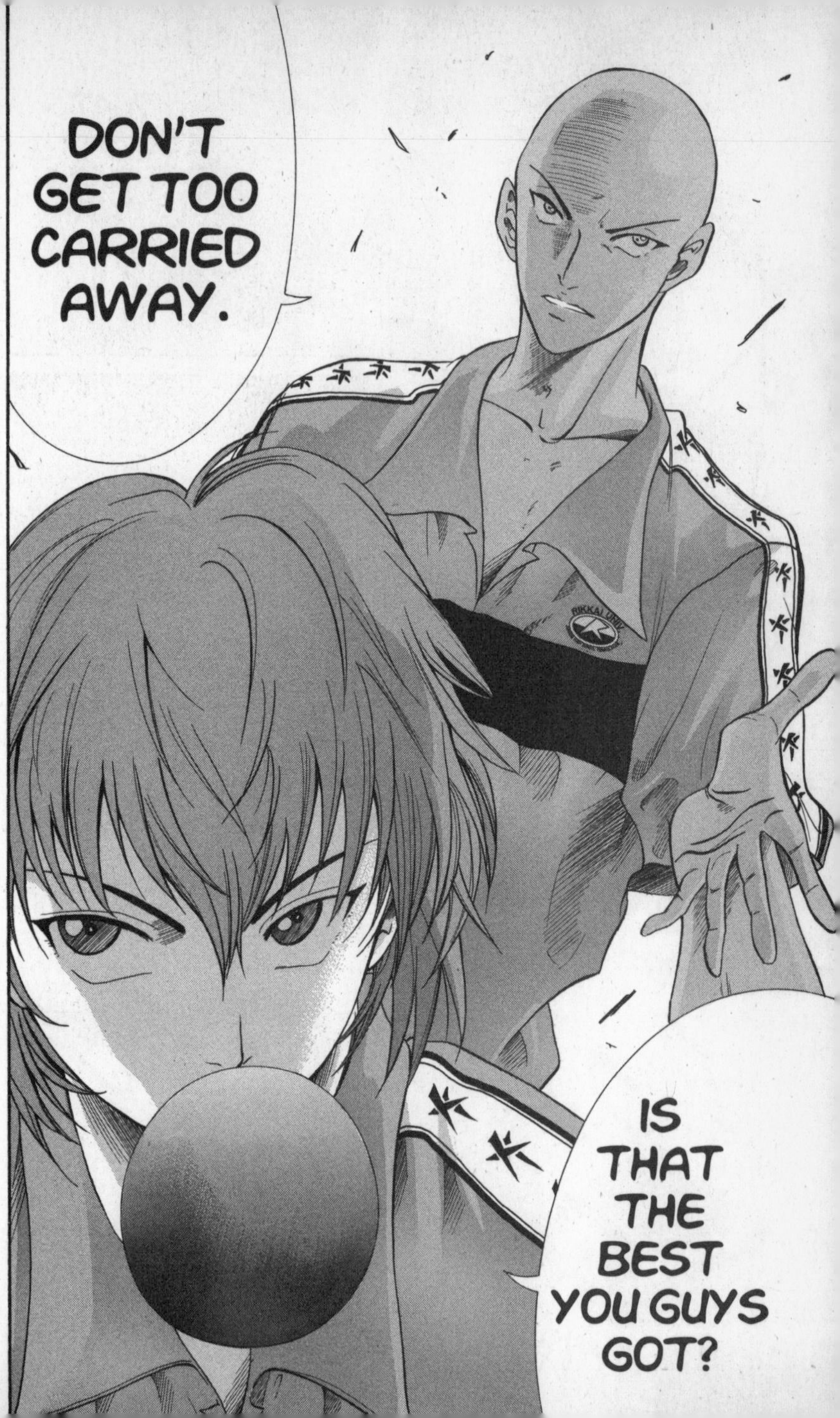
DON'T GET TOO CARRIED AWAY.
IS THAT THE BEST YOU GUYS GOT?

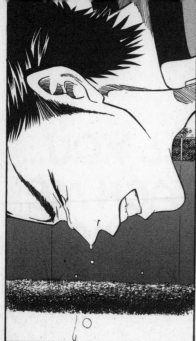

UMM...

ZSH...

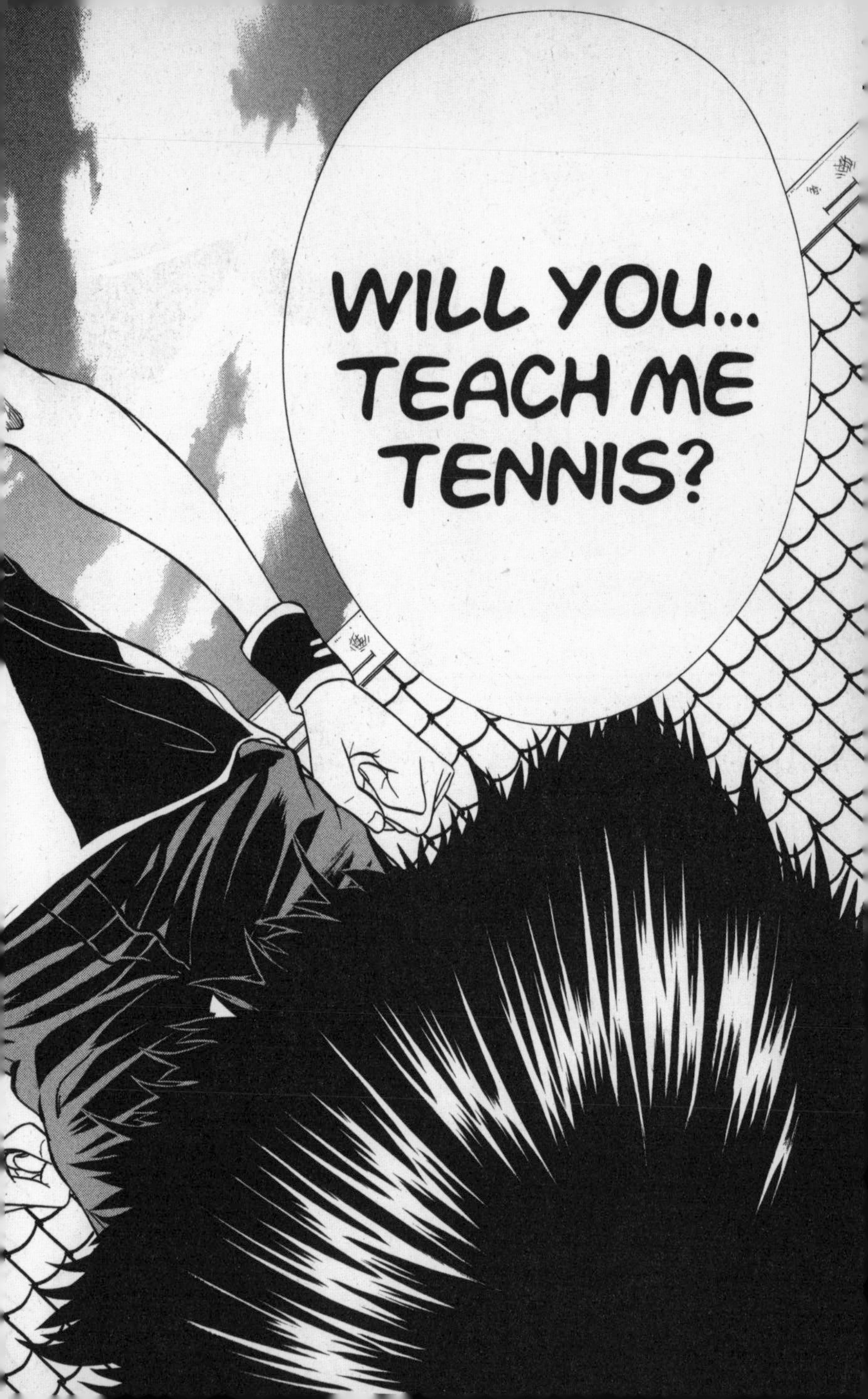
WILL YOU... TEACH ME TENNIS?

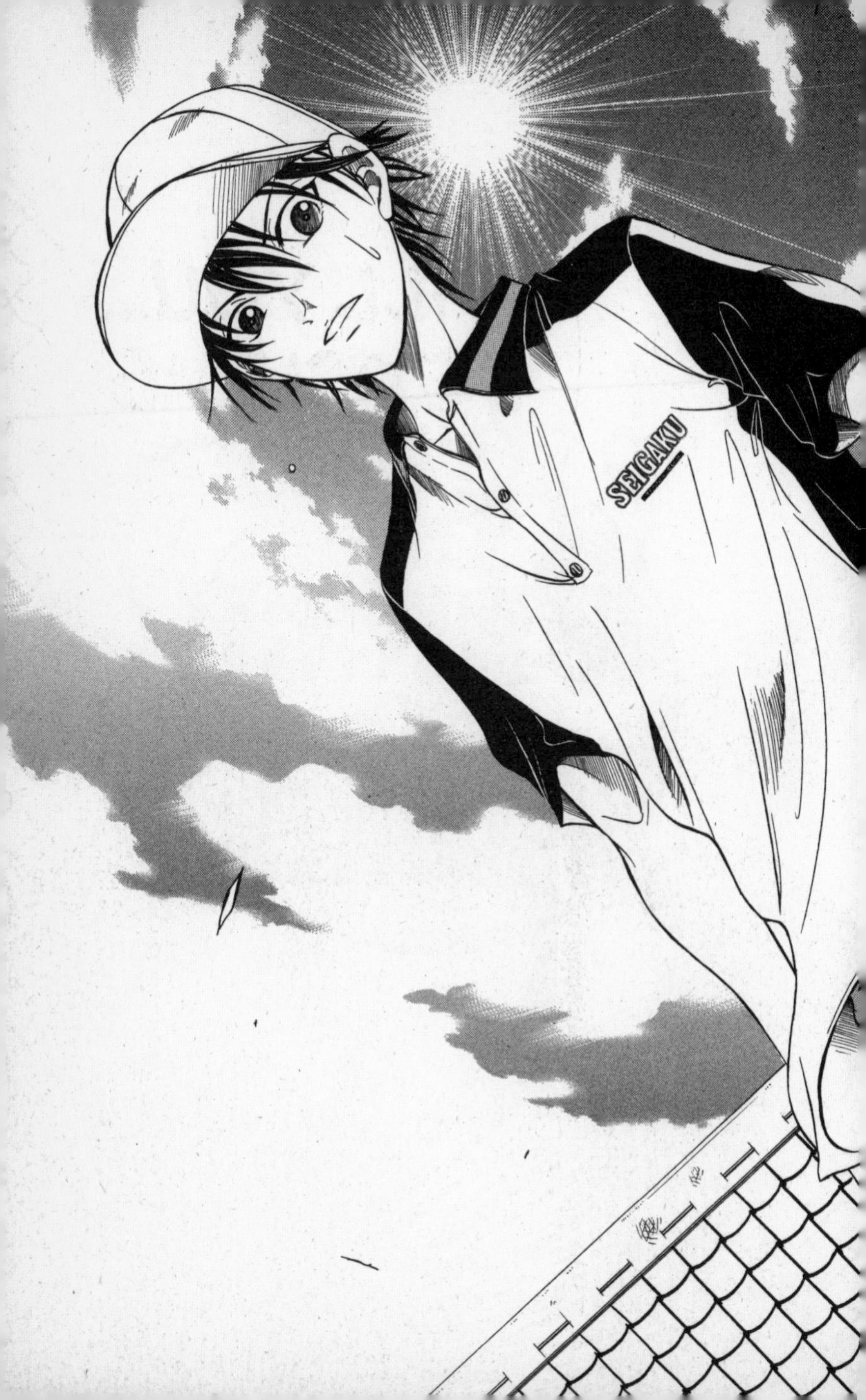
SEIGAKU

テニスの王子様

THE PRINCE OF TENNIS

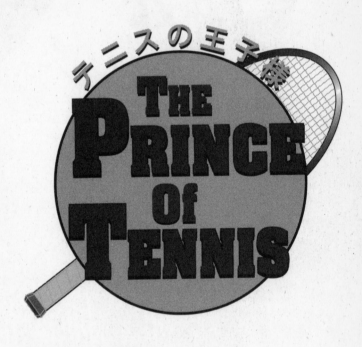

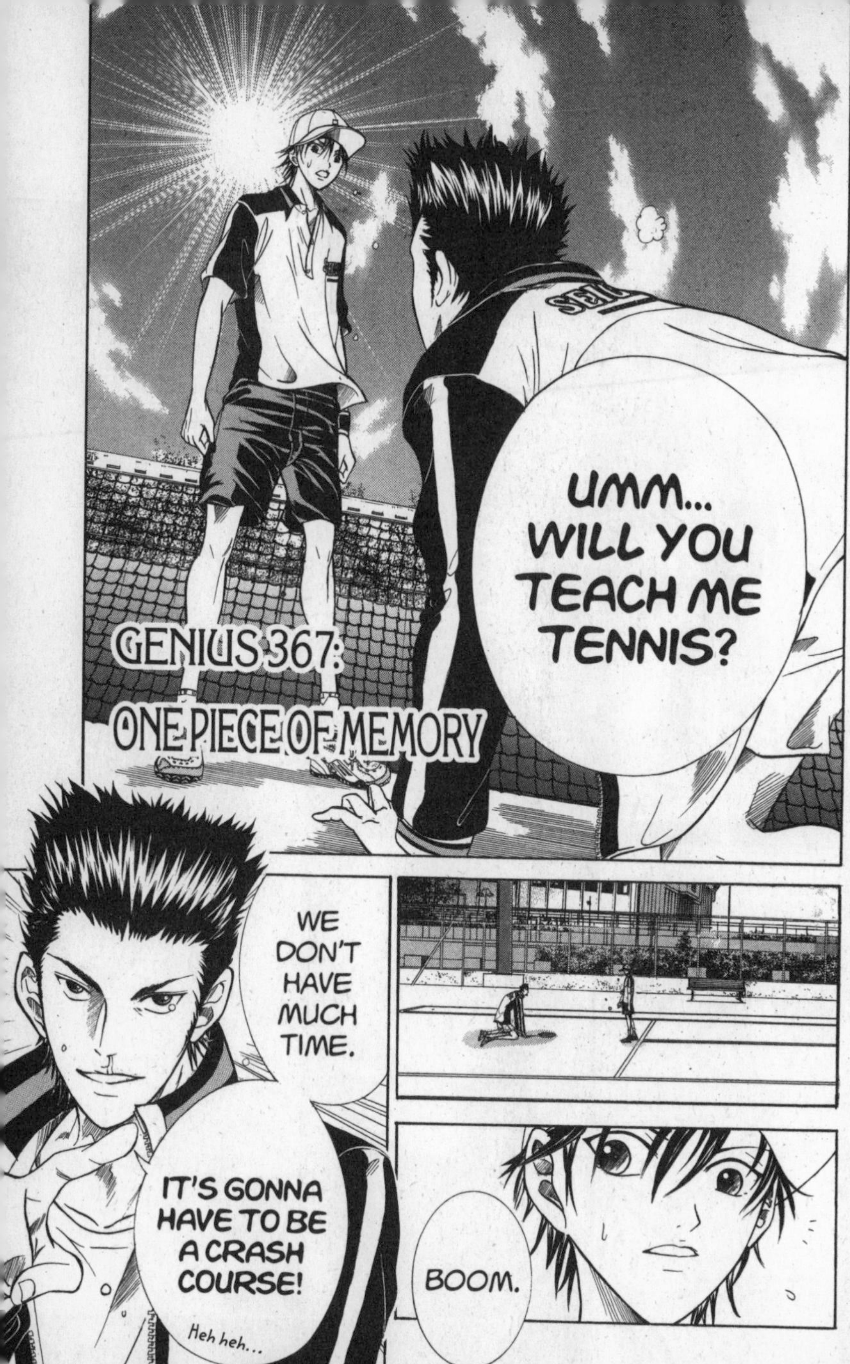
GENIUS 367:
ONE PIECE OF MEMORY
UMM... WILL YOU TEACH ME TENNIS?
BOOM.
WE DON'T HAVE MUCH TIME.
IT'S GONNA HAVE TO BE A CRASH COURSE!
Heh heh...

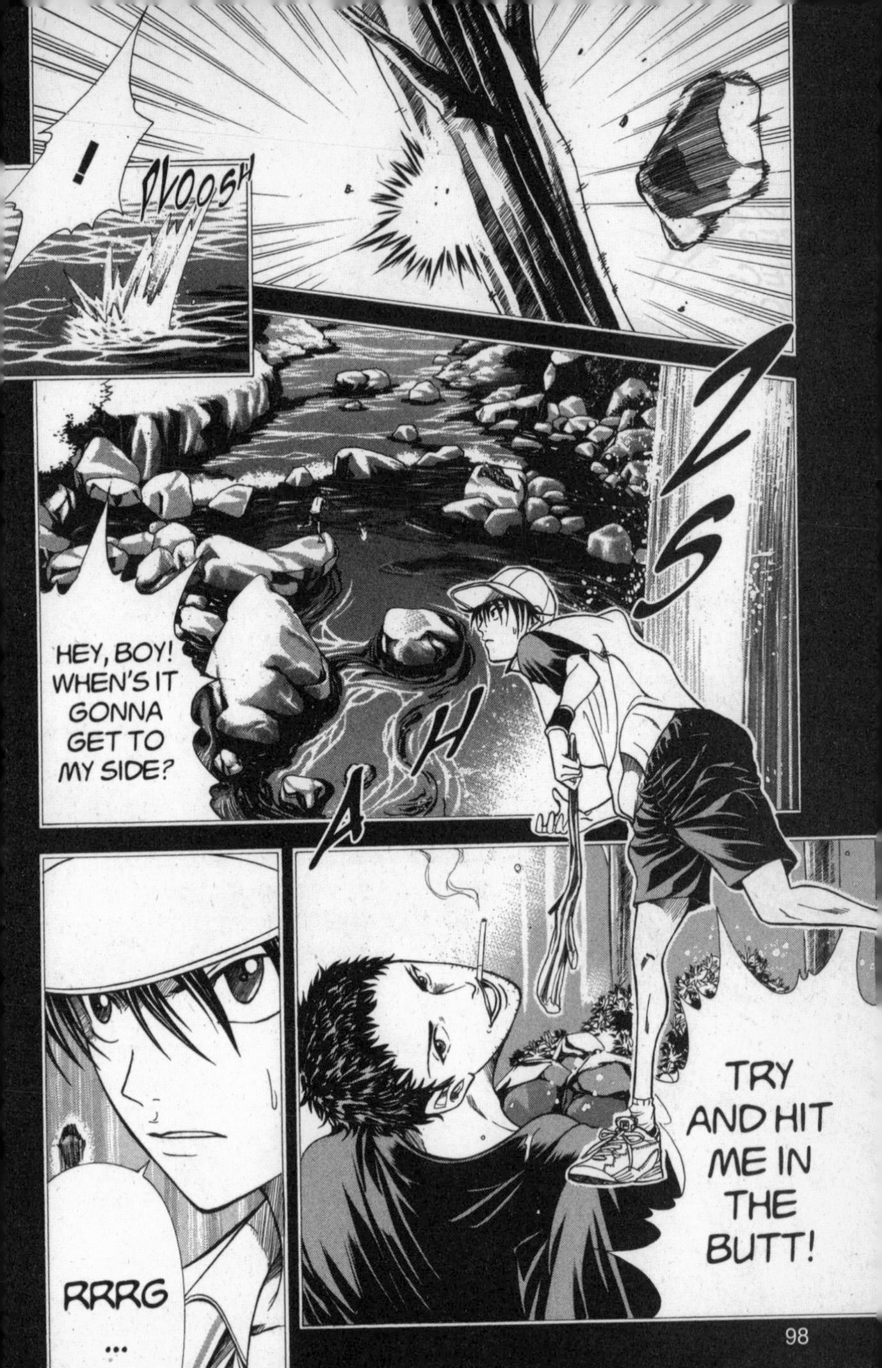
!
VOOSH
ZHSS
HEY, BOY! WHEN'S IT GONNA GET TO MY SIDE?
AH
TRY AND HIT ME IN THE BUTT!
RRRG ...

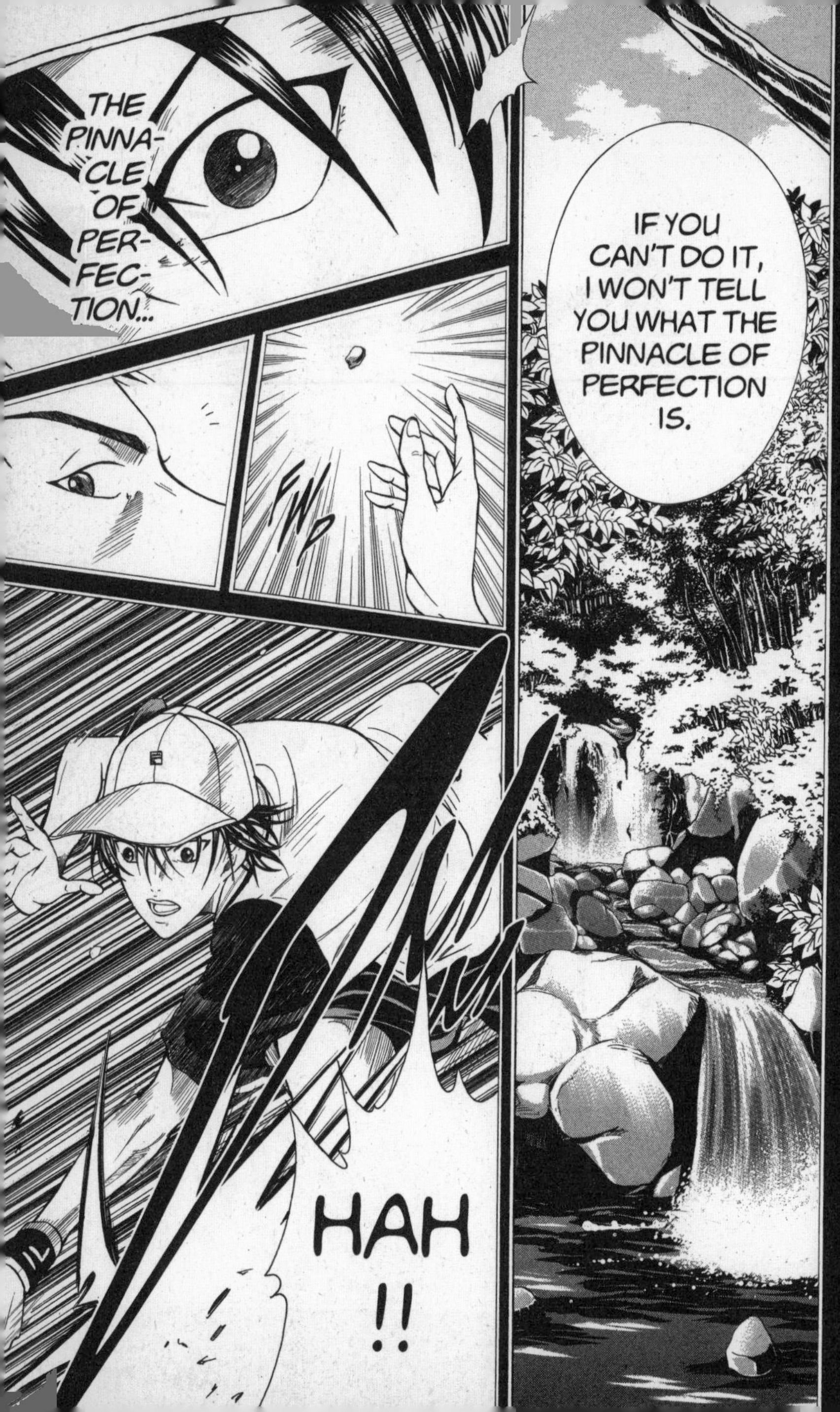
IF YOU CAN'T DO IT, I WON'T TELL YOU WHAT THE PINNACLE OF PERFECTION IS.
THE PINNACLE OF PERFECTION...
FWP
HAH !!

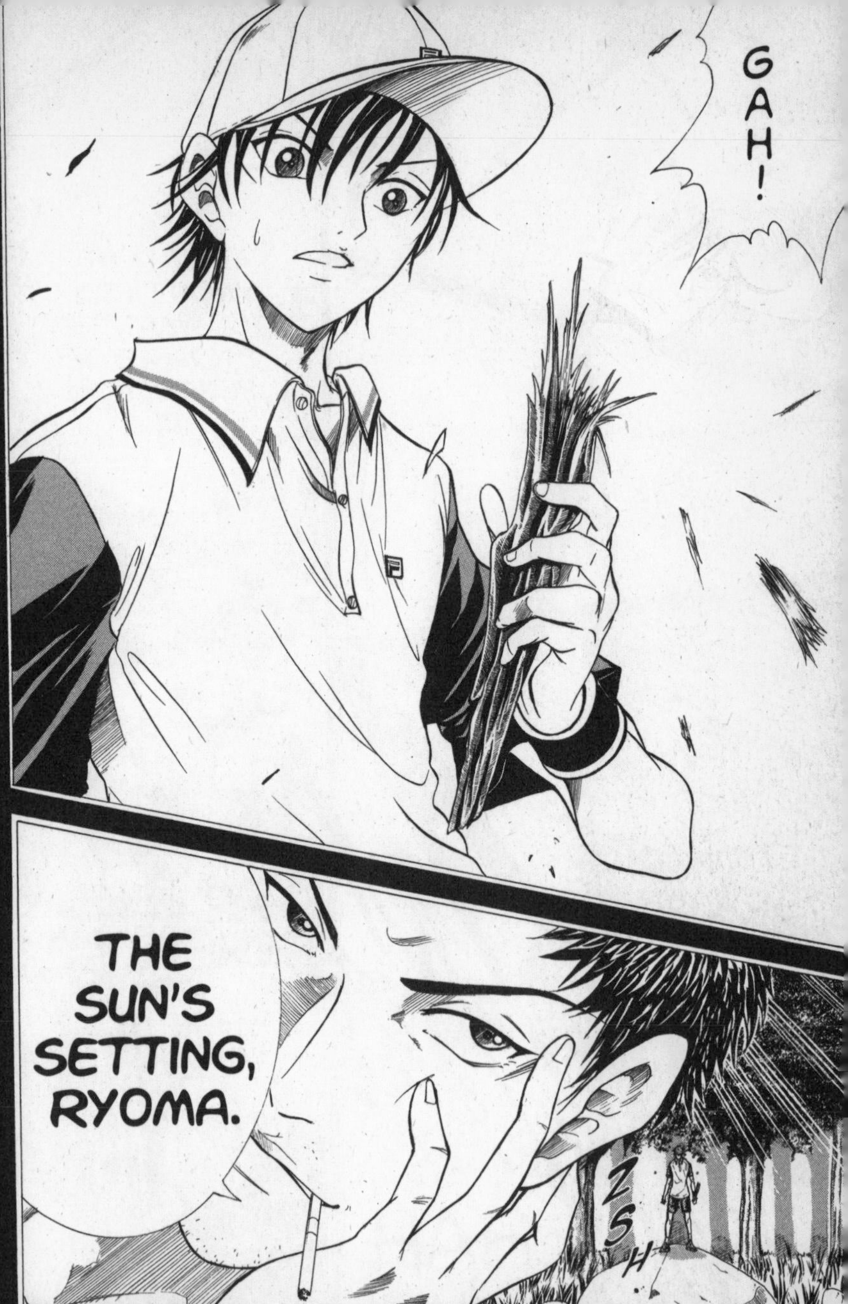
GAH!
THE SUN'S SETTING, RYOMA.
ZSH

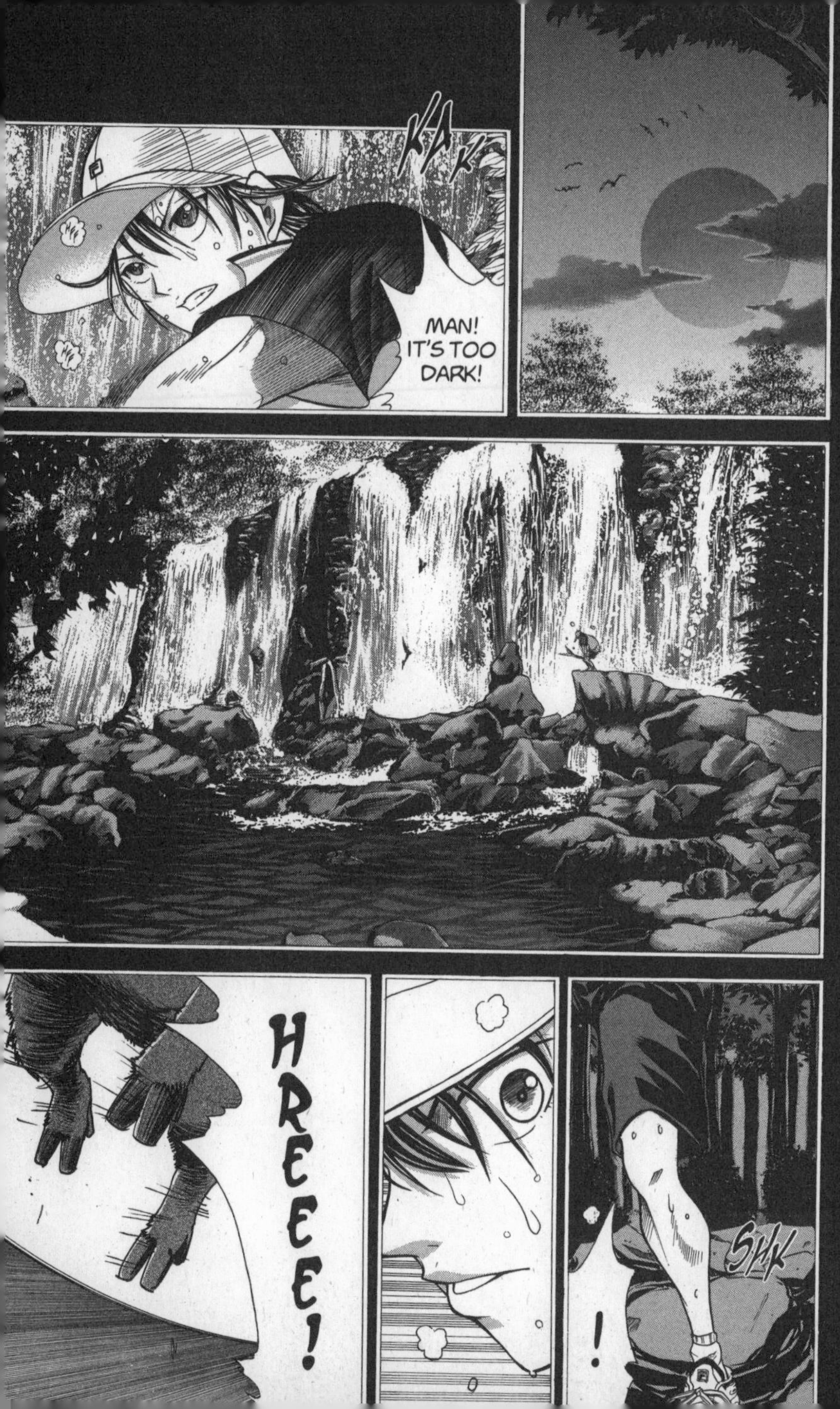
KAK
MAN! IT'S TOO DARK!
SHK
!
HREEE!

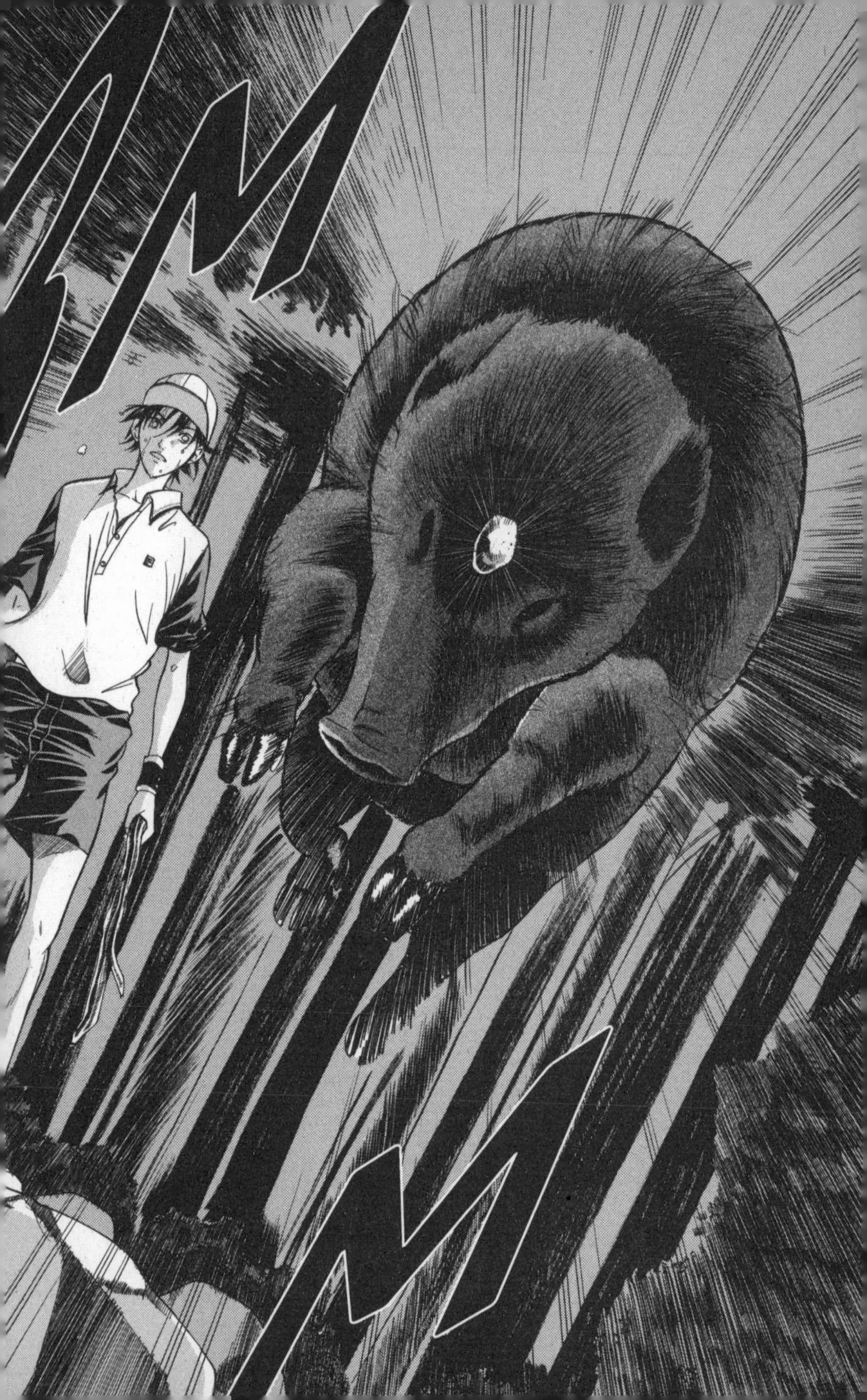

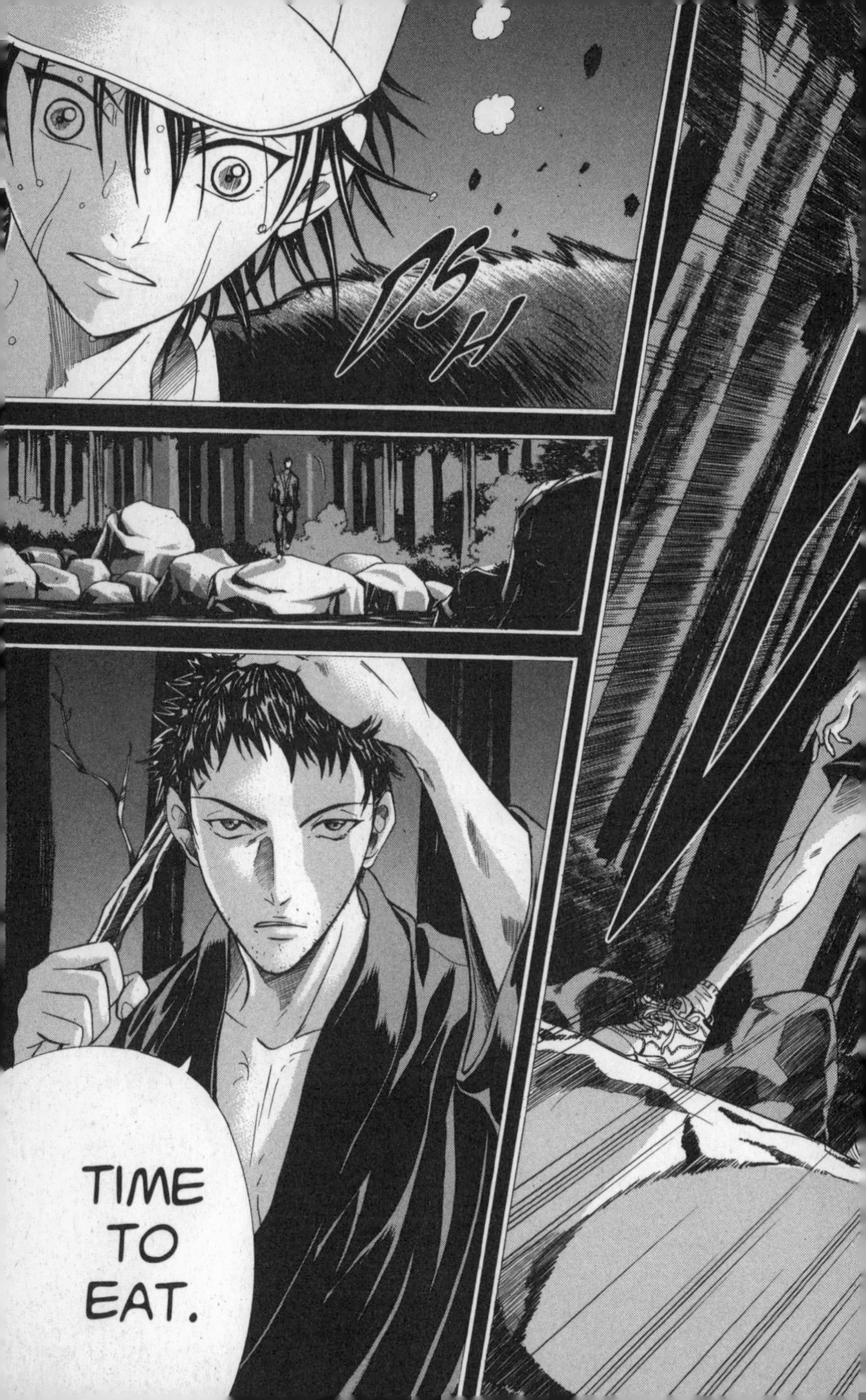

FSH
TIME TO EAT.

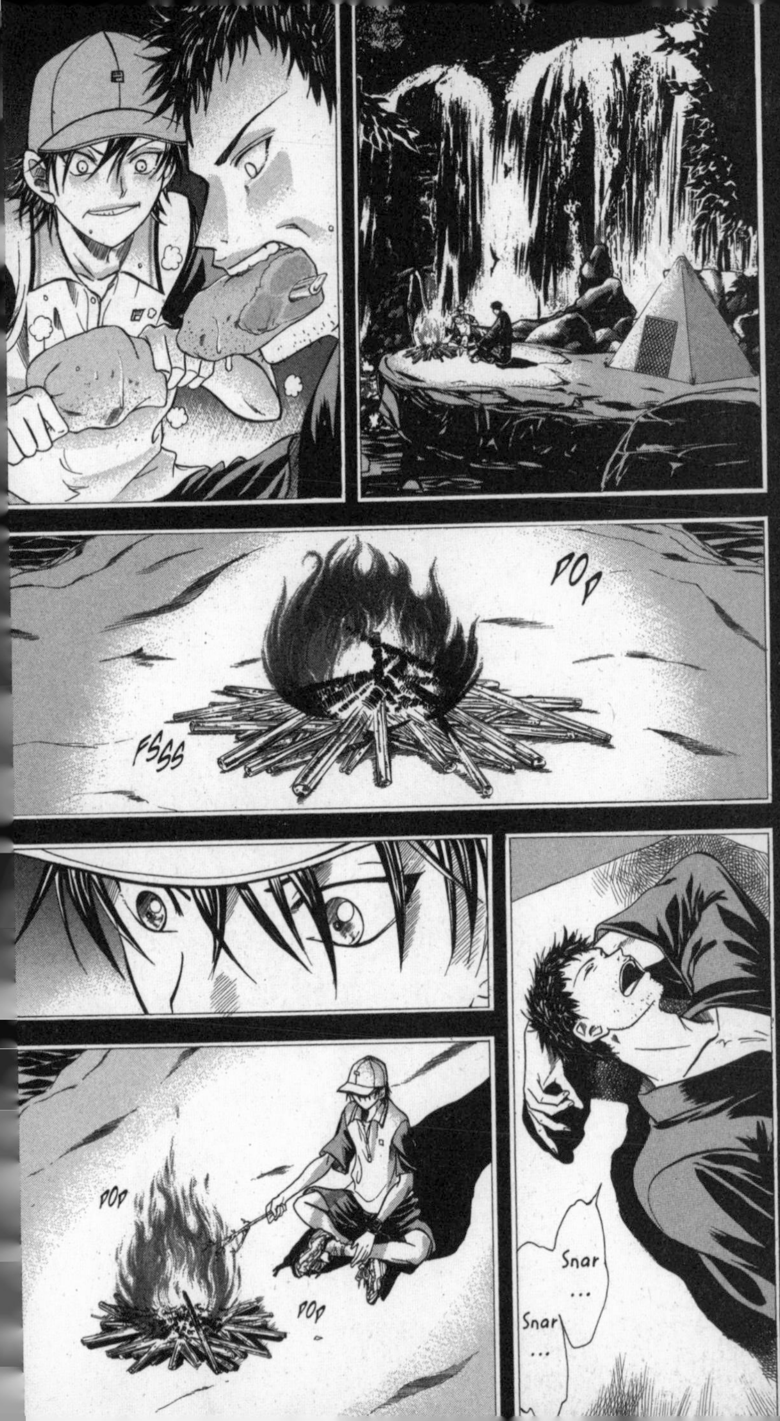
POP
FSSS
Snar...
Snar...
POP
POP

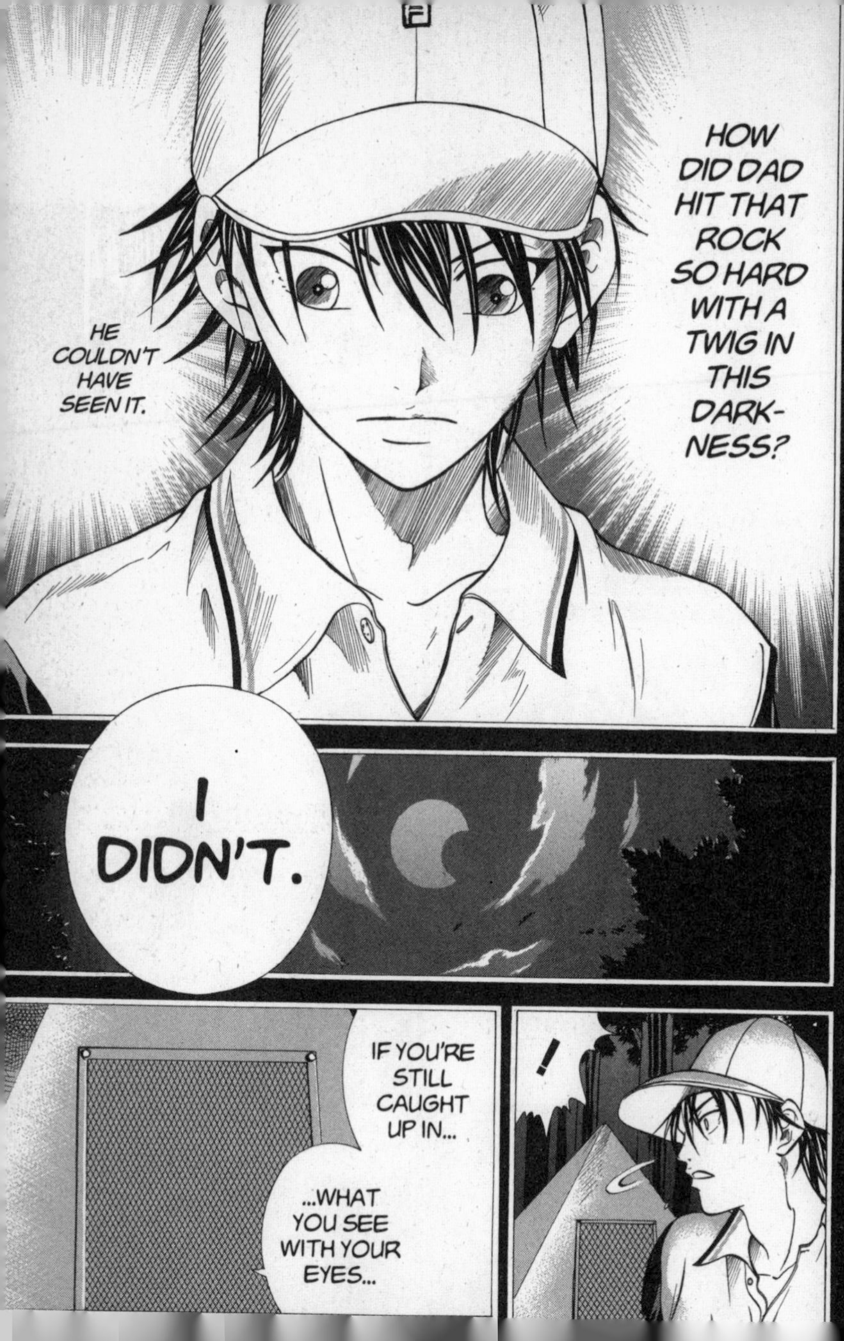
HOW DID DAD HIT THAT ROCK SO HARD WITH A TWIG IN THIS DARKNESS?
HE COULDN'T HAVE SEEN IT.
I DIDN'T.
!
IF YOU'RE STILL CAUGHT UP IN...
...WHAT YOU SEE WITH YOUR EYES...

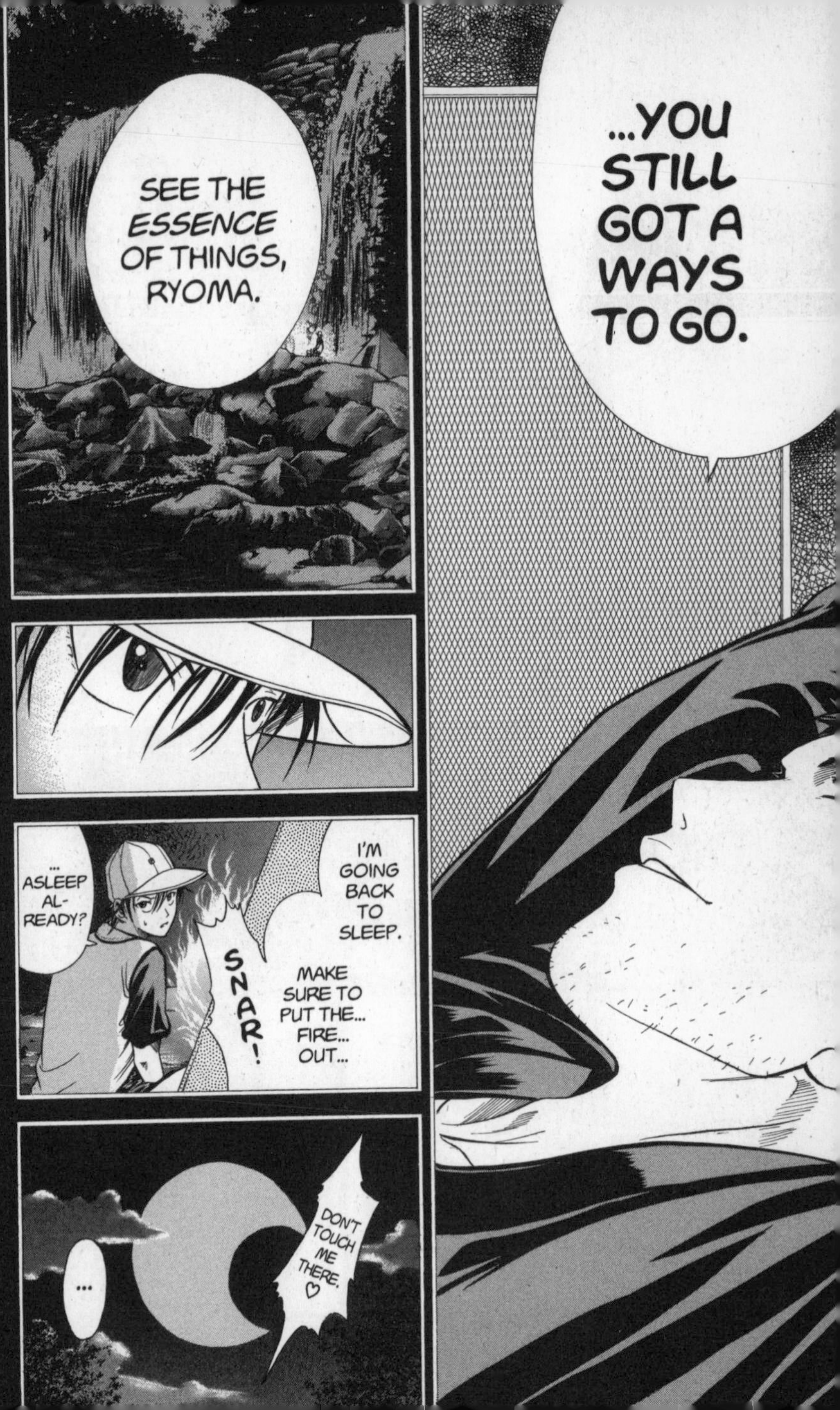
...YOU STILL GOT A WAYS TO GO.
SEE THE ESSENCE OF THINGS, RYOMA.
I'M GOING BACK TO SLEEP.
MAKE SURE TO PUT THE... FIRE... OUT...
SNAR!
...ASLEEP AL-READY?
DON'T TOUCH ME THERE. ♡
...

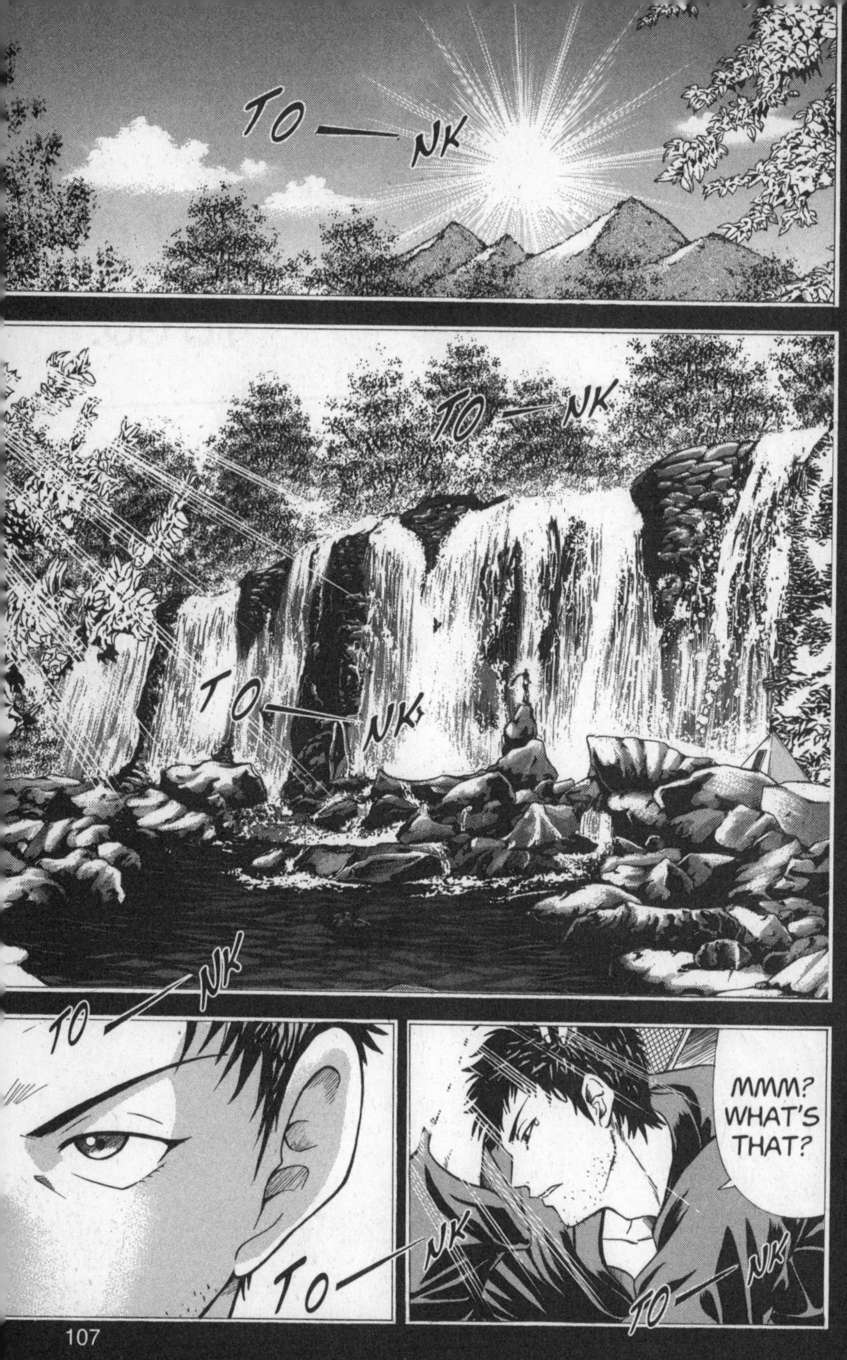
TO—NK
TO—NK
TO—NK
TO—NK
MMM? WHAT'S THAT?
TO—NK
TO—NK
TO—NK

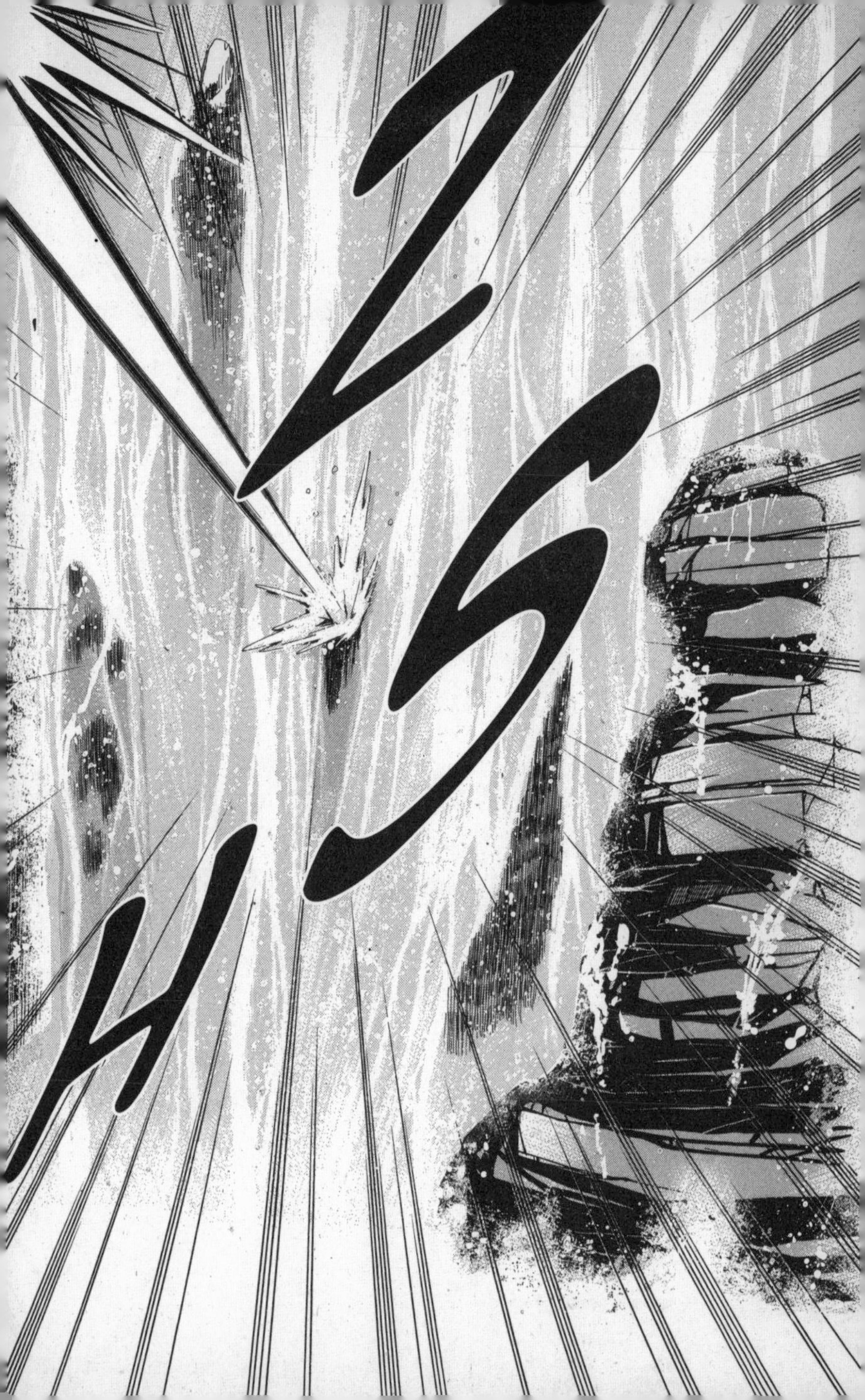

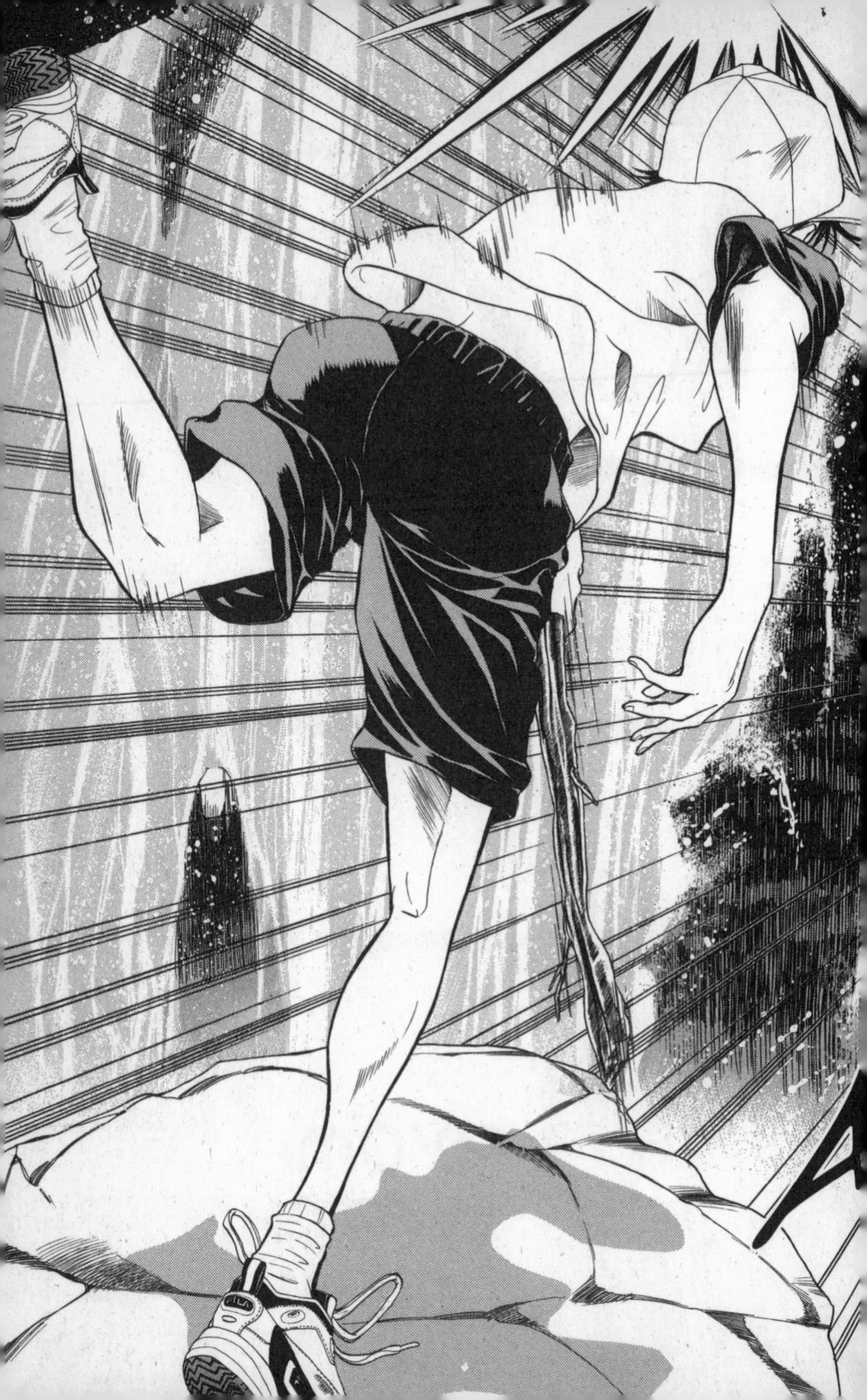

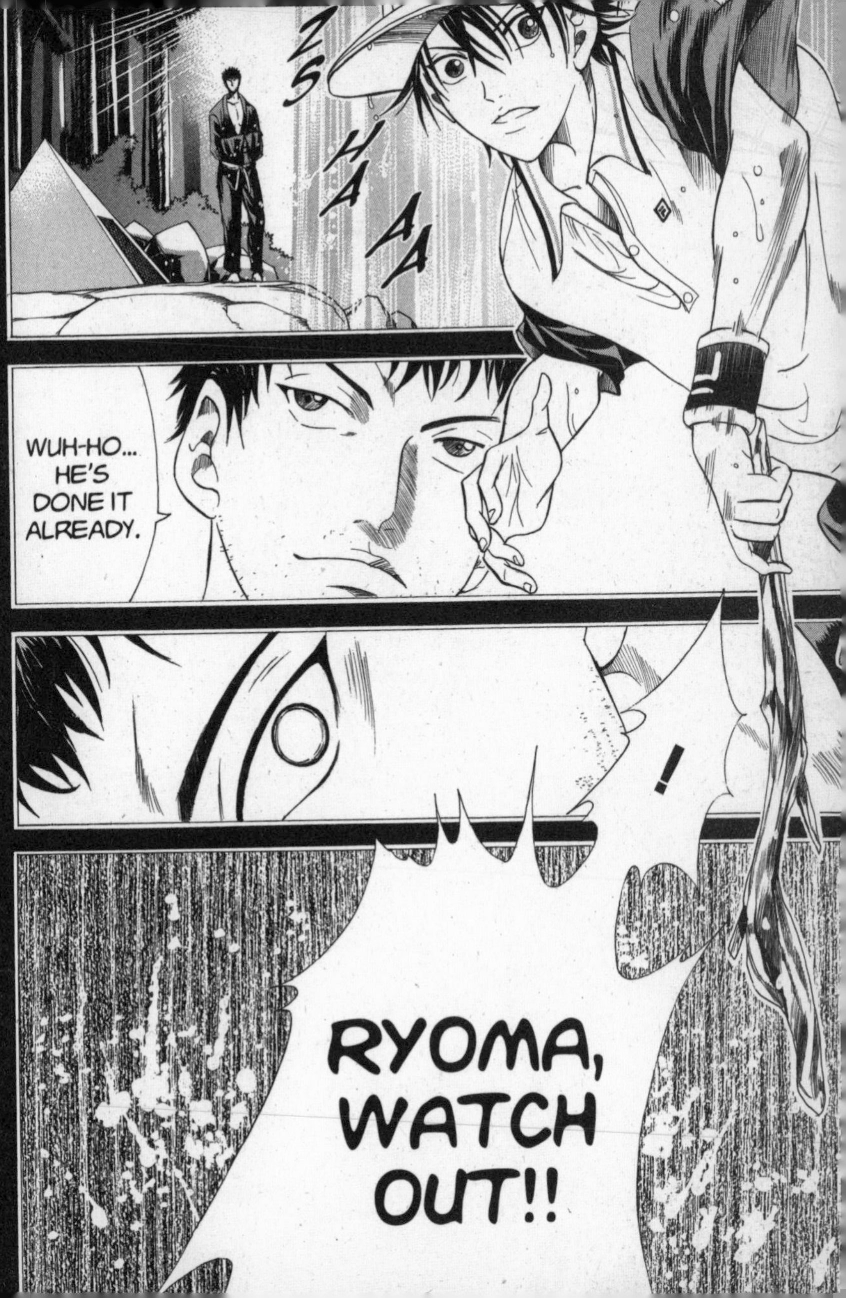
ZSHAAAA
WUH-HO... HE'S DONE IT ALREADY.
!
RYOMA, WATCH OUT!!

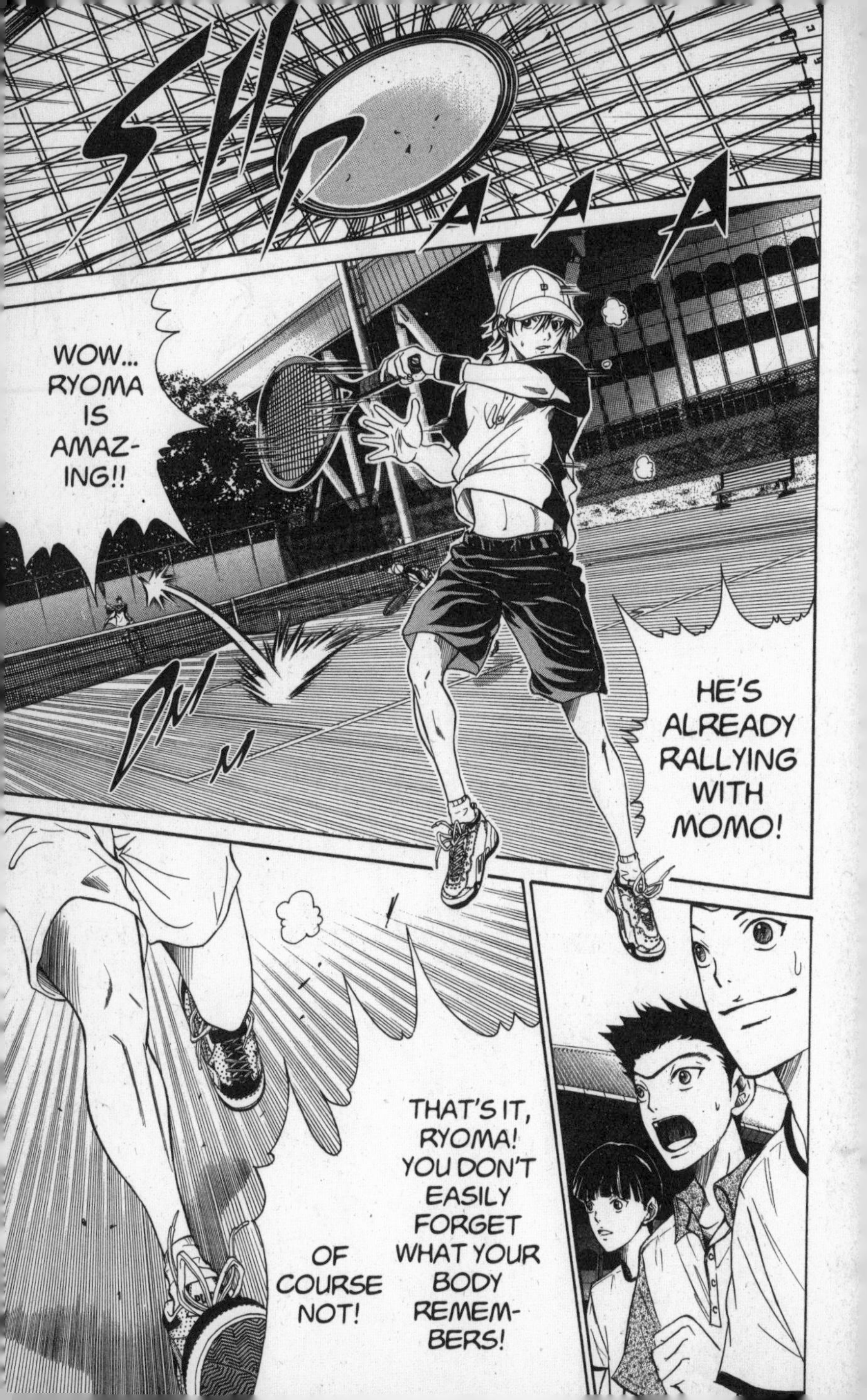
SHPAAAA
WOW... RYOMA IS AMAZ-ING!!
DMM
HE'S ALREADY RALLYING WITH MOMO!
THAT'S IT, RYOMA! YOU DON'T EASILY FORGET WHAT YOUR BODY REMEM-BERS!
OF COURSE NOT!

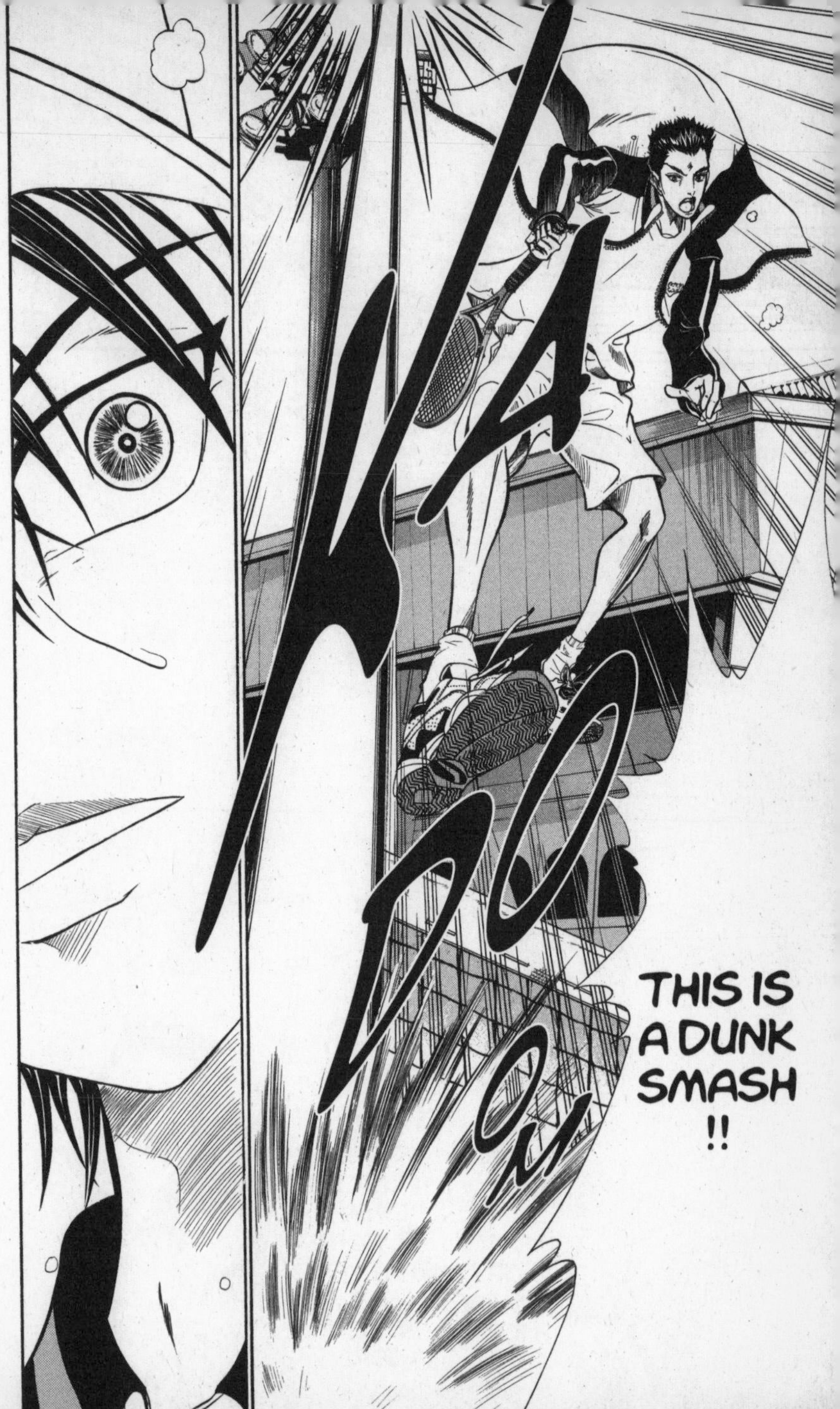
THIS IS A DUNK SMASH !!

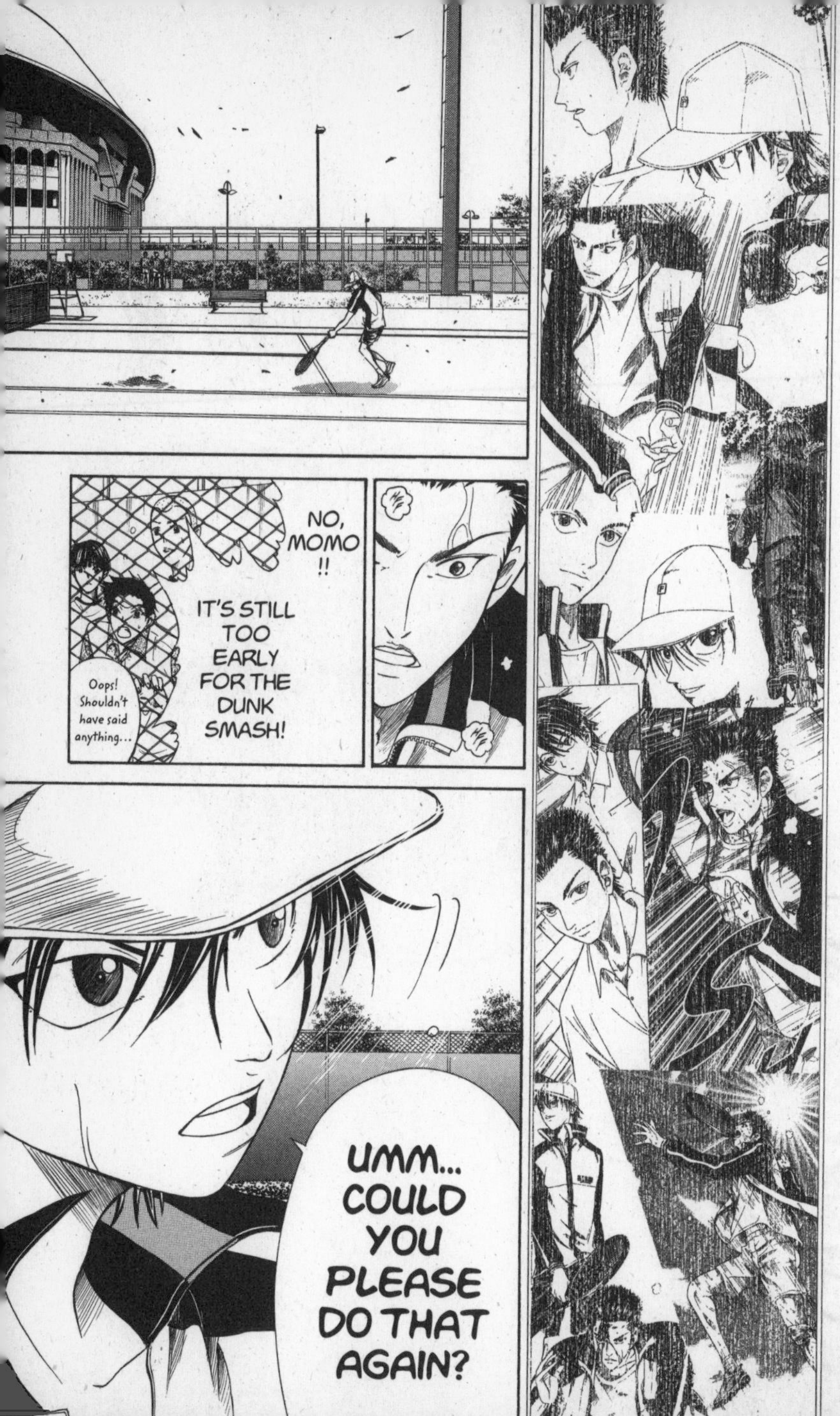
NO, MOMO!!
IT'S STILL TOO EARLY FOR THE DUNK SMASH!
Oops! Shouldn't have said anything...
UMM... COULD YOU PLEASE DO THAT AGAIN?

テニスの王子様

THE PRINCE OF TENNIS

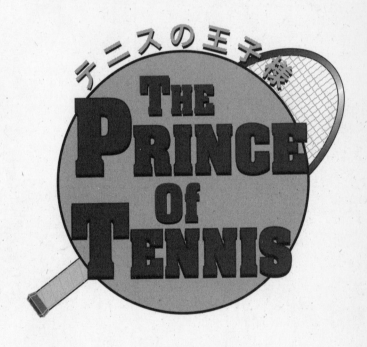

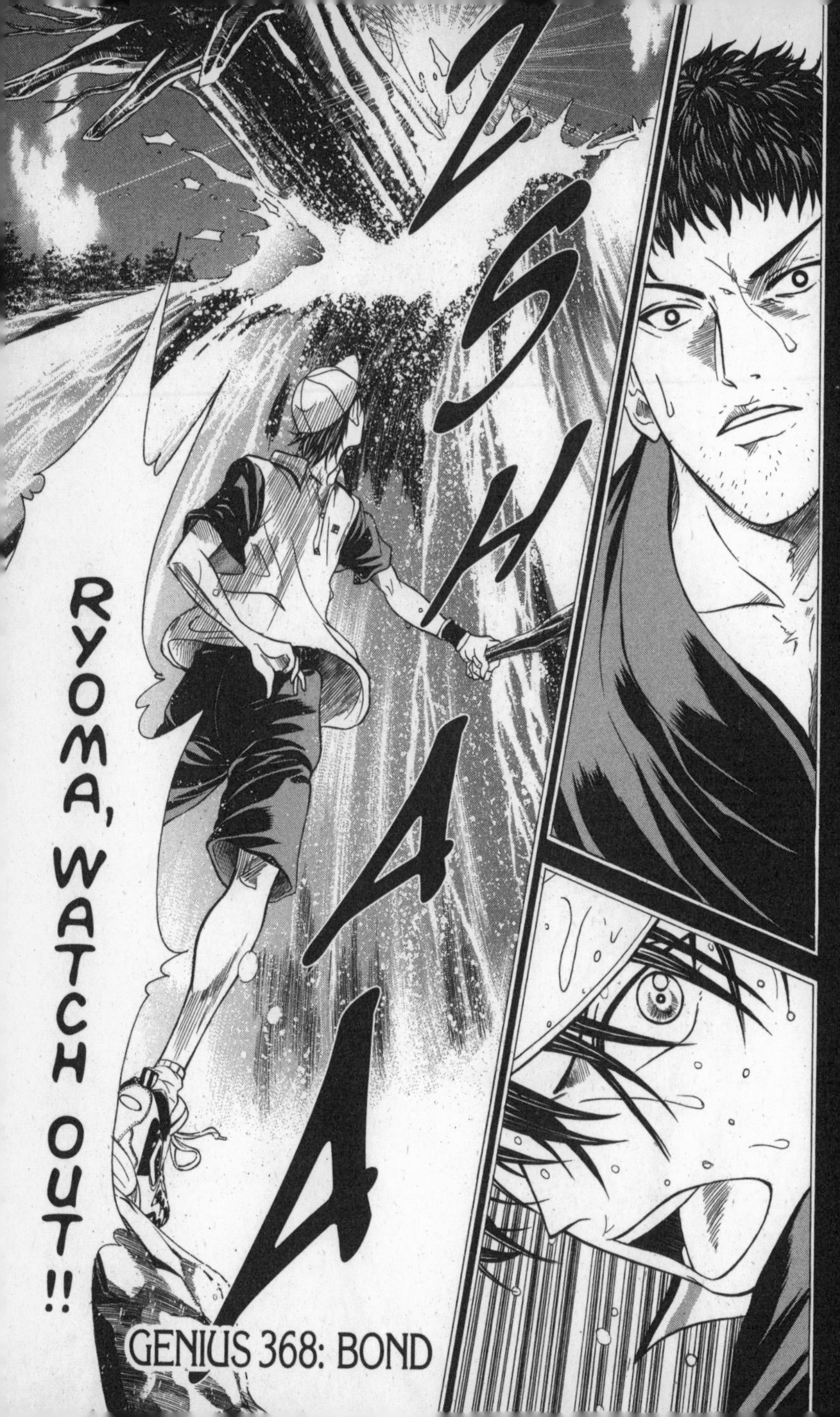
RYOMA, WATCH OUT!!
GENIUS 368: BOND

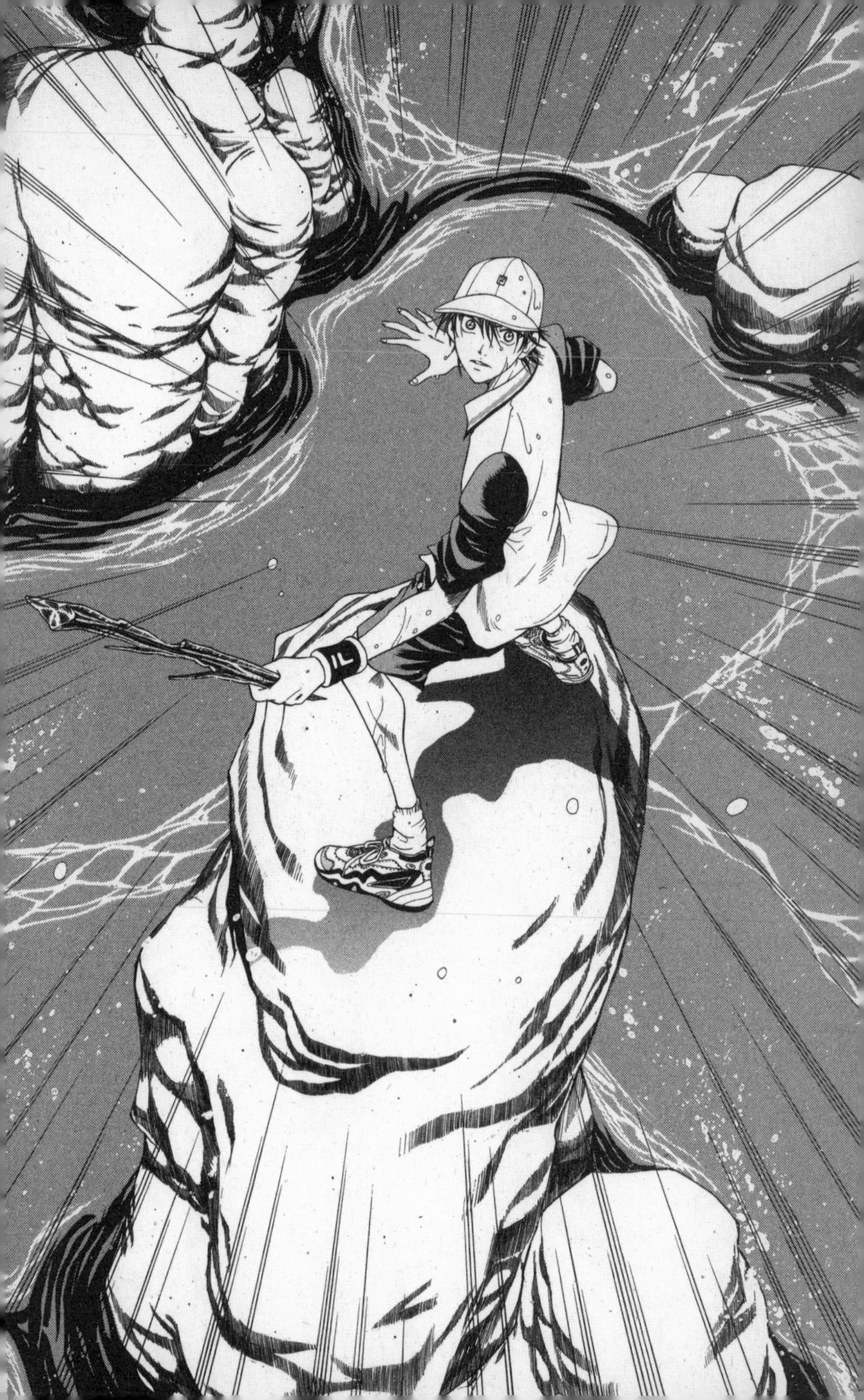

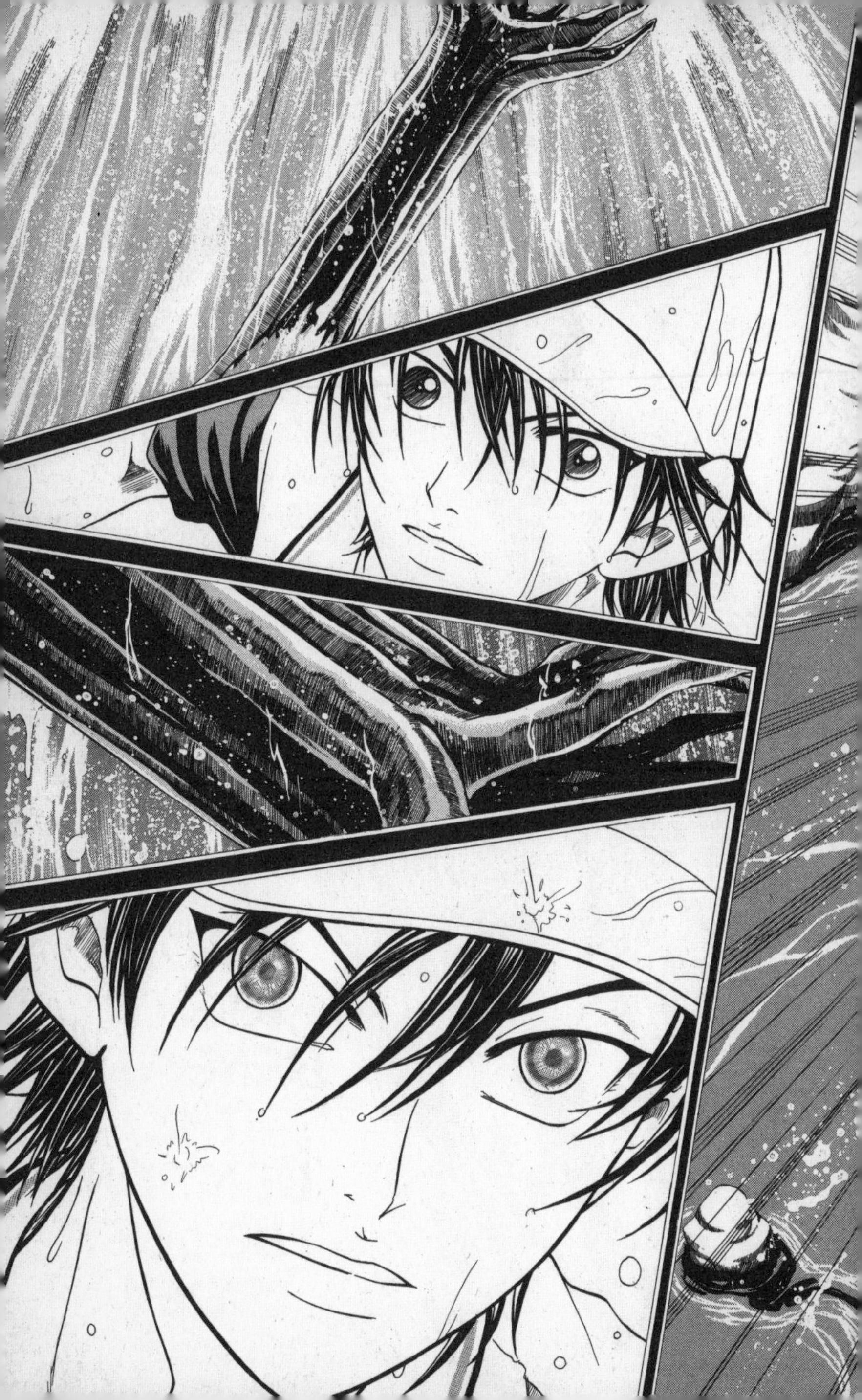

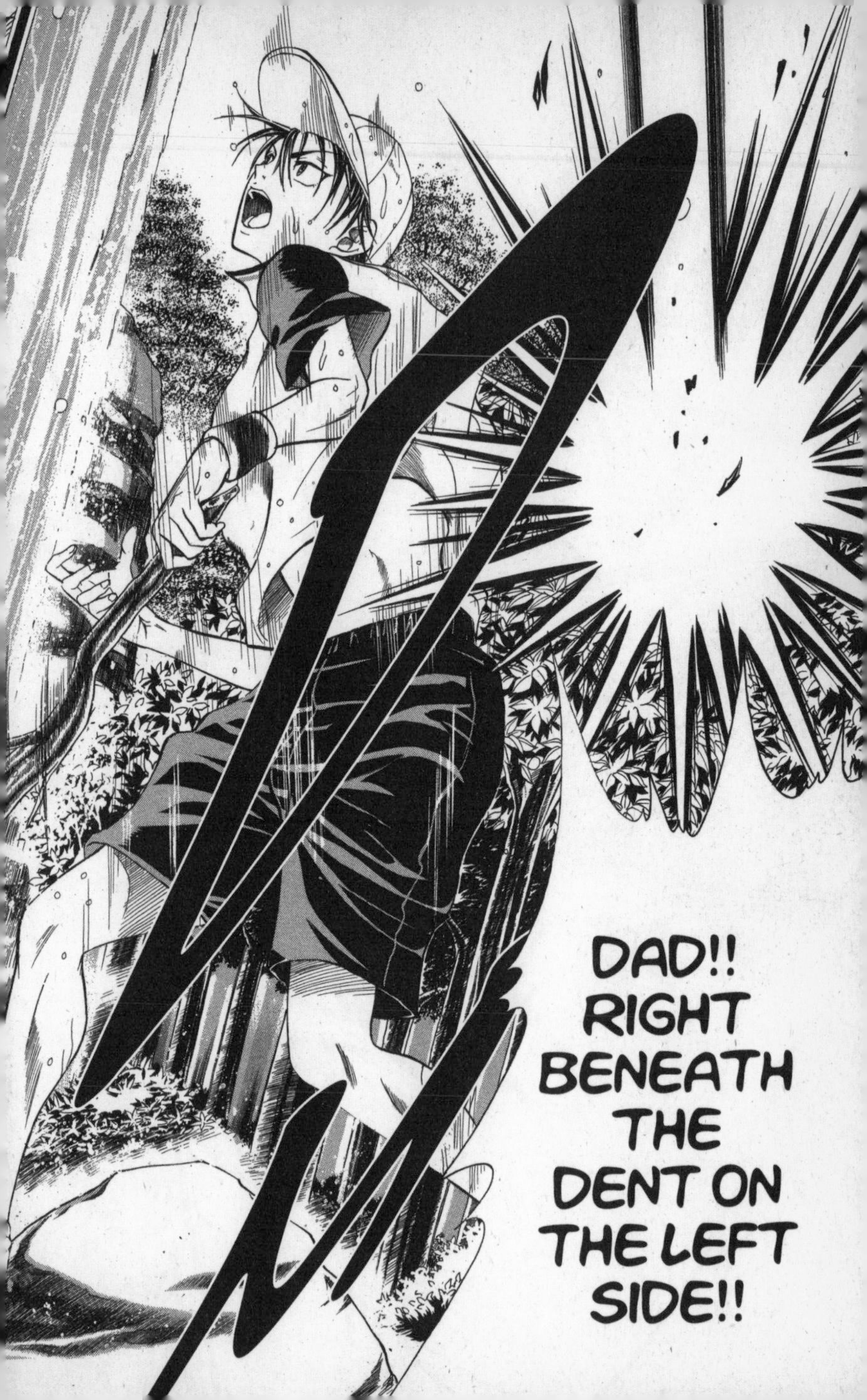
DAD!! RIGHT BENEATH THE DENT ON THE LEFT SIDE!!

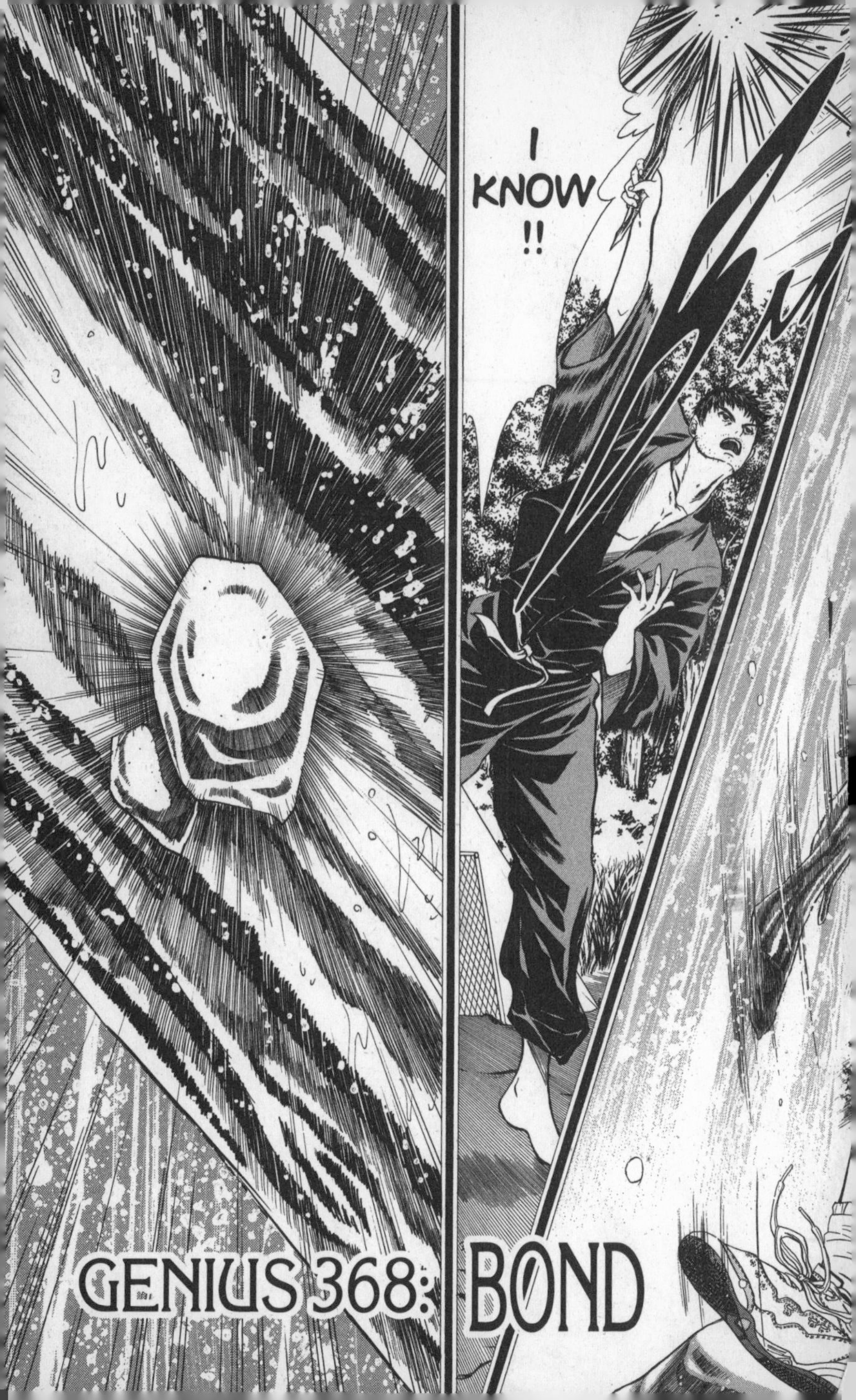
I KNOW !!
GENIUS 368: BOND

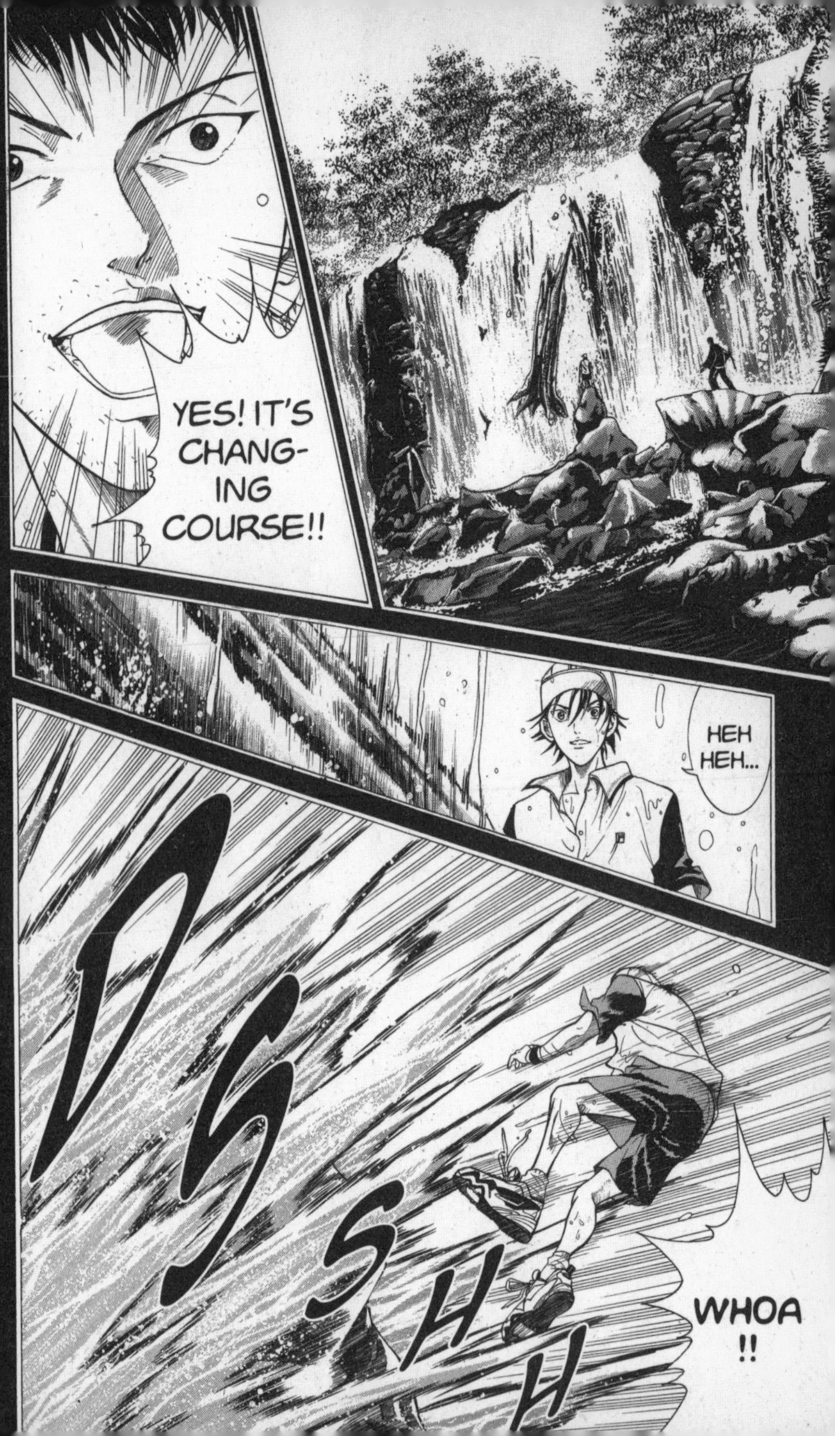
YES! IT'S CHANG-ING COURSE!!
HEH HEH...
DSSHH
WHOA!!

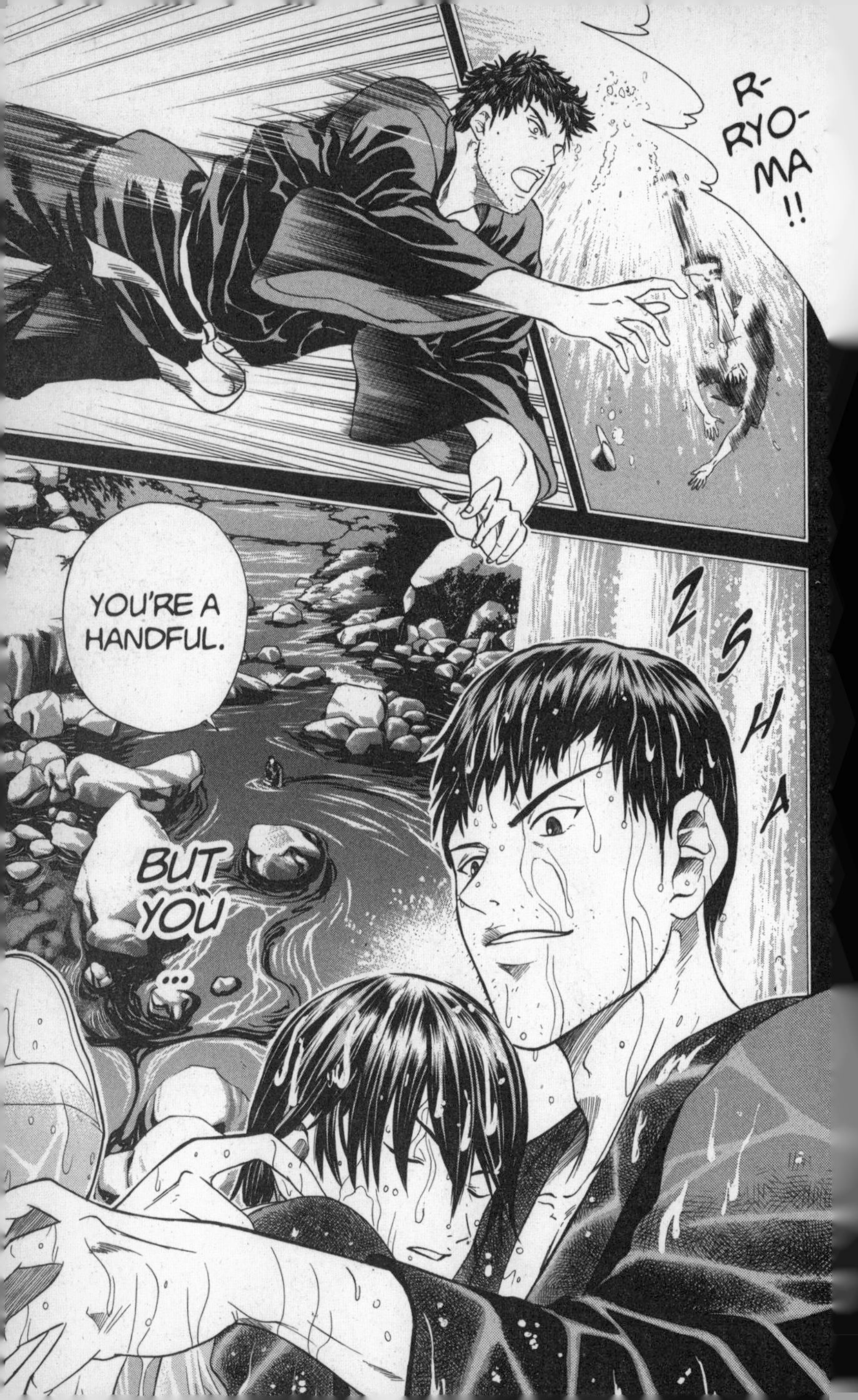
R-RYOMA!!
ZSHA
YOU'RE A HANDFUL.
BUT YOU...

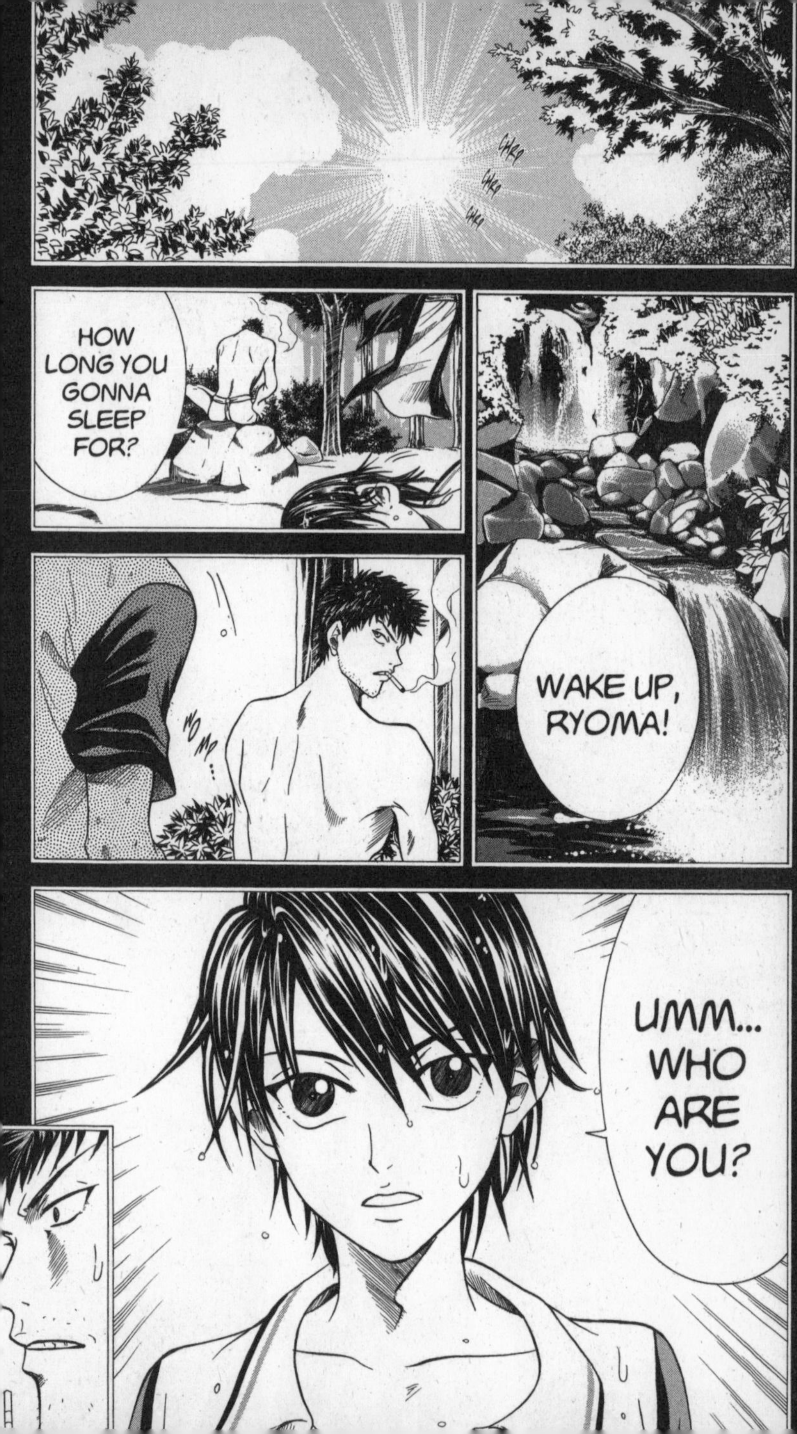
CHRP
CHRP
CHRP
WAKE UP, RYOMA!
HOW LONG YOU GONNA SLEEP FOR?
NOMP...
UMM... WHO ARE YOU?

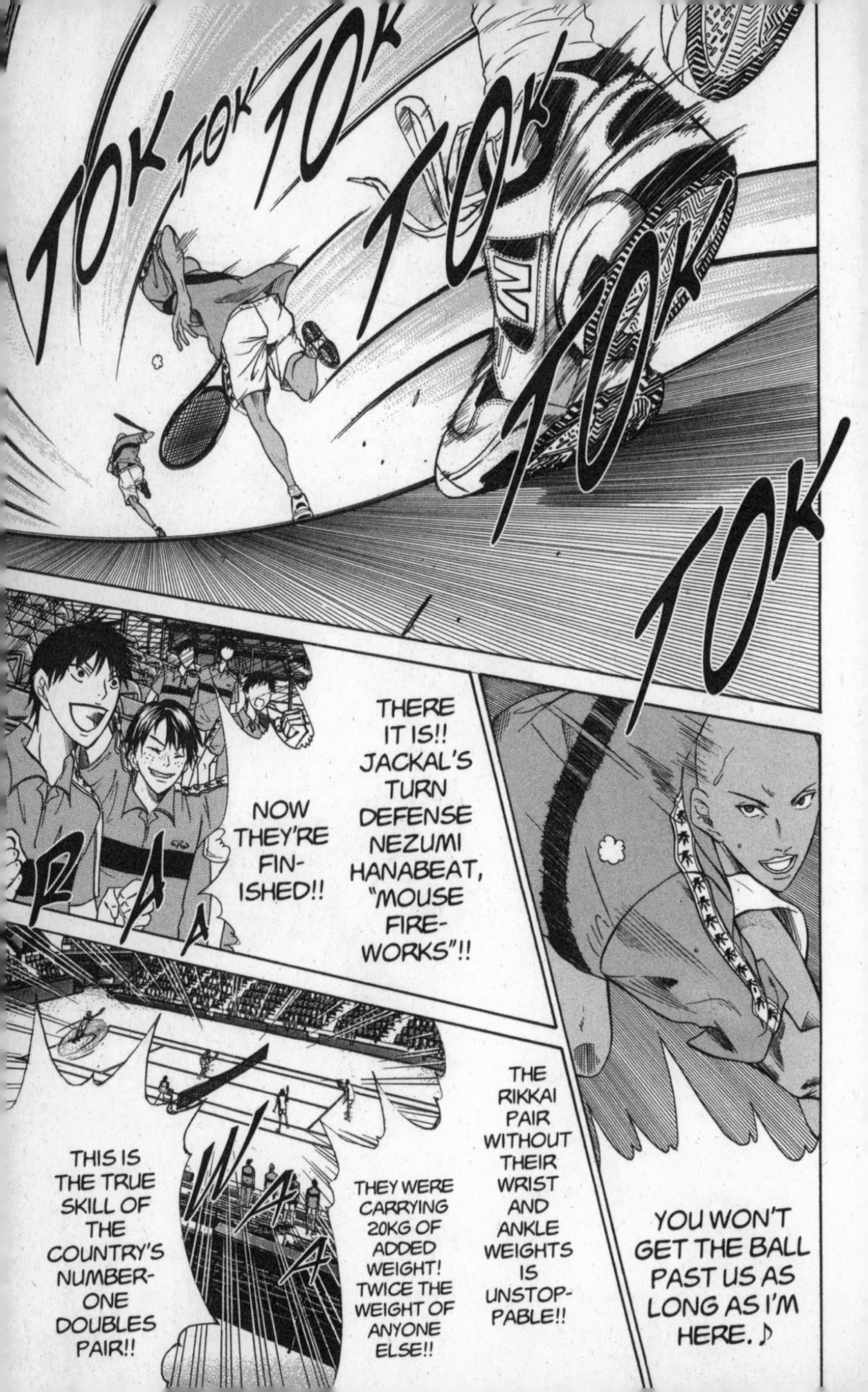
TOK
TOK
TOK
TOK
TOK TOK TOK
YOU WON'T GET THE BALL PAST US AS LONG AS I'M HERE. ♪
THERE IT IS!! JACKAL'S TURN DEFENSE NEZUMI HANABEAT, "MOUSE FIRE-WORKS"!!
NOW THEY'RE FIN-ISHED!!
RAA
THE RIKKAI PAIR WITHOUT THEIR WRIST AND ANKLE WEIGHTS IS UNSTOP-PABLE!!
THEY WERE CARRYING 20KG OF ADDED WEIGHT! TWICE THE WEIGHT OF ANYONE ELSE!!
THIS IS THE TRUE SKILL OF THE COUNTRY'S NUMBER-ONE DOUBLES PAIR!!
WAA

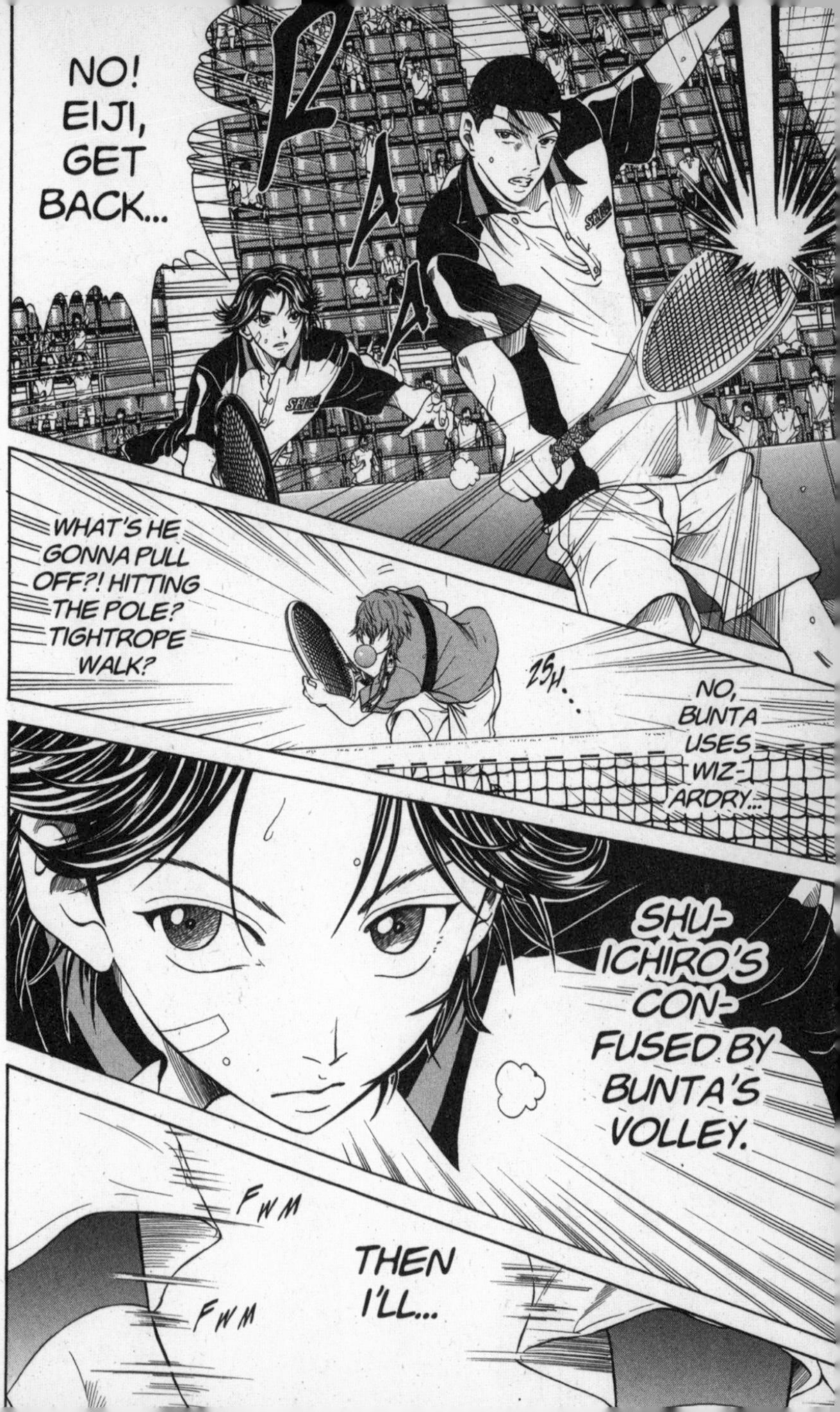
NO! EIJI, GET BACK...
WHAT'S HE GONNA PULL OFF?! HITTING THE POLE? TIGHTROPE WALK?
ZSH...
NO, BUNTA USES WIZ-ARDRY...
SHU-ICHIRO'S CON-FUSED BY BUNTA'S VOLLEY.
THEN I'LL...
FWM
FWM

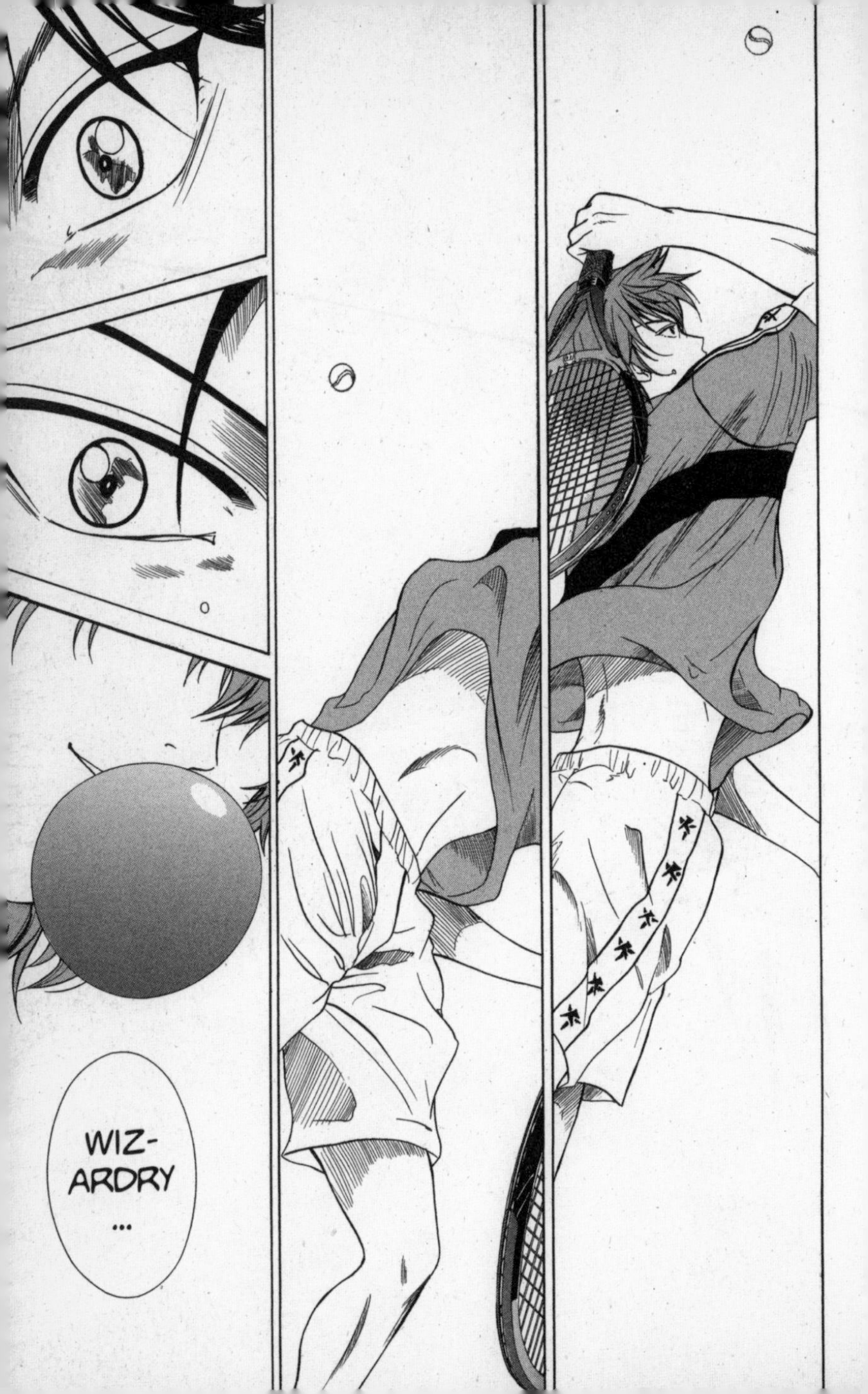
WIZ-ARDRY ...

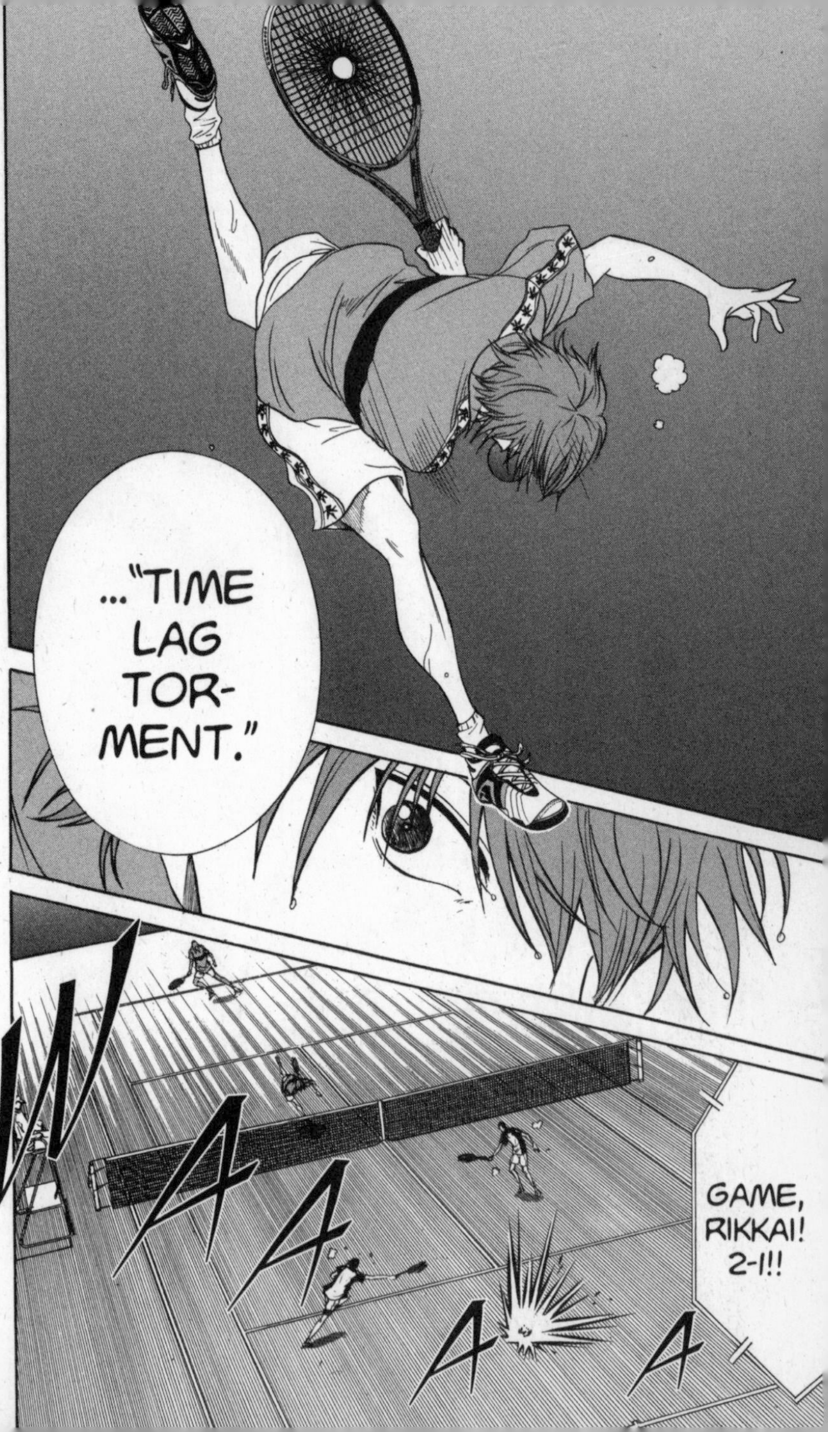
..."TIME LAG TOR-MENT."
GAME, RIKKAI! 2-1!!
WAAAAA

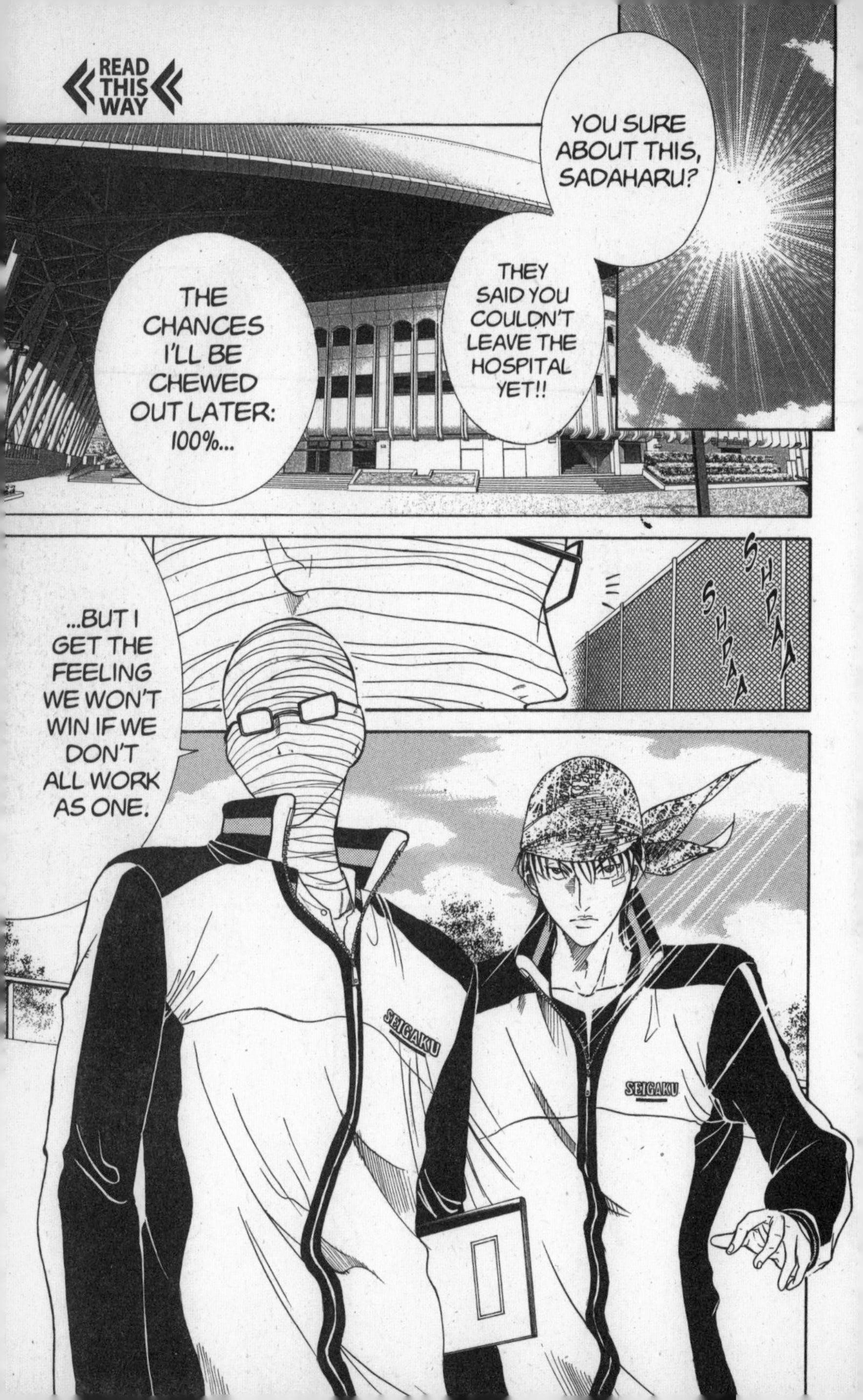
READ THIS WAY
YOU SURE ABOUT THIS, SADAHARU?
THEY SAID YOU COULDN'T LEAVE THE HOSPITAL YET!!
THE CHANCES I'LL BE CHEWED OUT LATER: 100%...
SHPAA SHPAA
...BUT I GET THE FEELING WE WON'T WIN IF WE DON'T ALL WORK AS ONE.

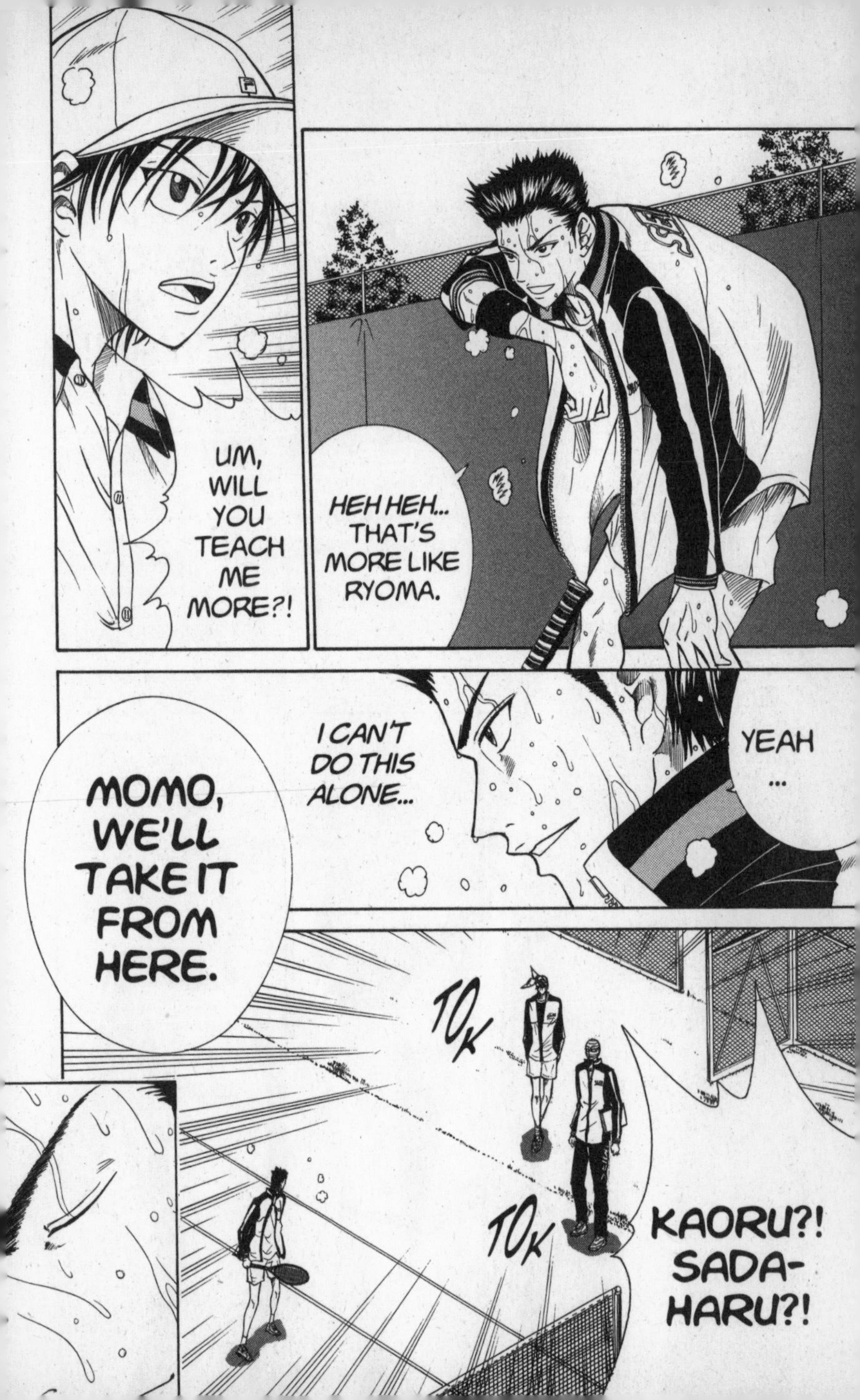
UM, WILL YOU TEACH ME MORE?!
HEH HEH... THAT'S MORE LIKE RYOMA.
YEAH ...
I CAN'T DO THIS ALONE...
MOMO, WE'LL TAKE IT FROM HERE.
TOK
TOK
KAORU?! SADA-HARU?!

READ THIS WAY

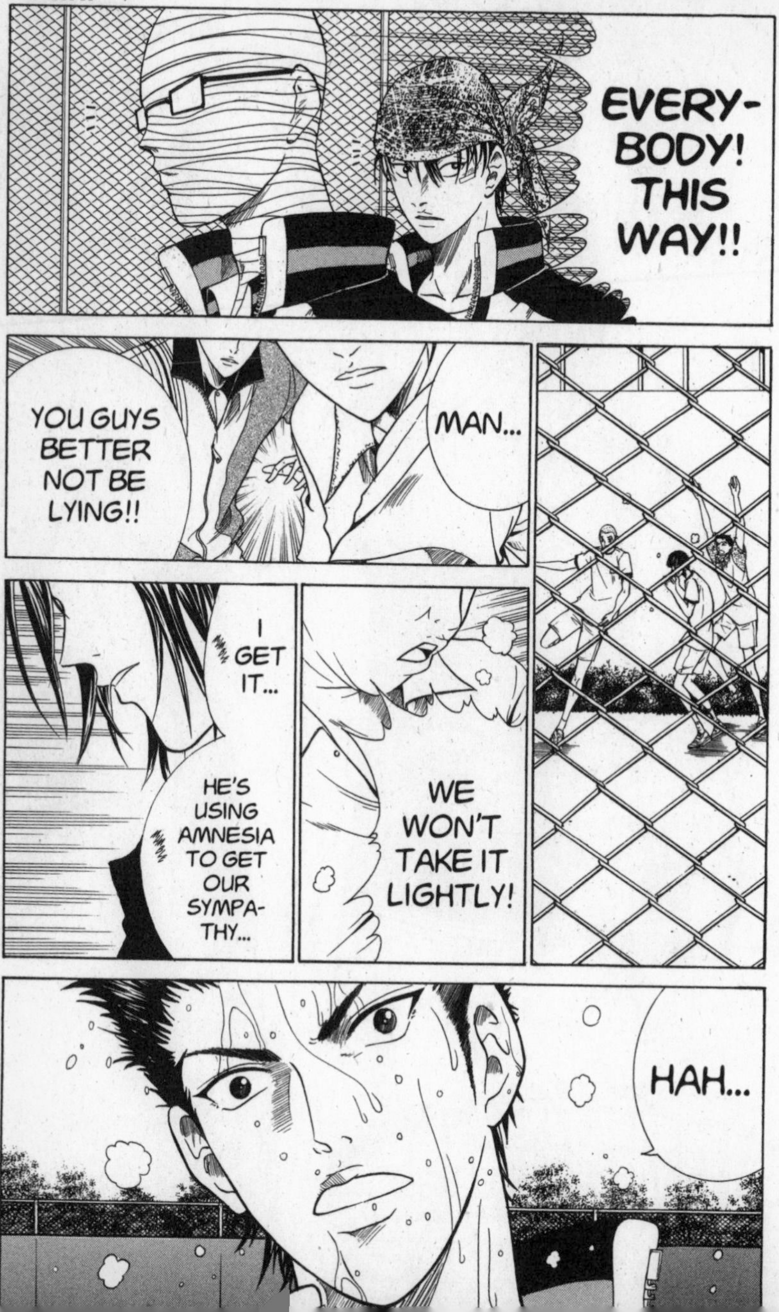
EVERY-BODY! THIS WAY!!
MAN...
YOU GUYS BETTER NOT BE LYING!!
WE WON'T TAKE IT LIGHTLY!
I GET IT...
HE'S USING AMNESIA TO GET OUR SYMPA-THY...
HAH...

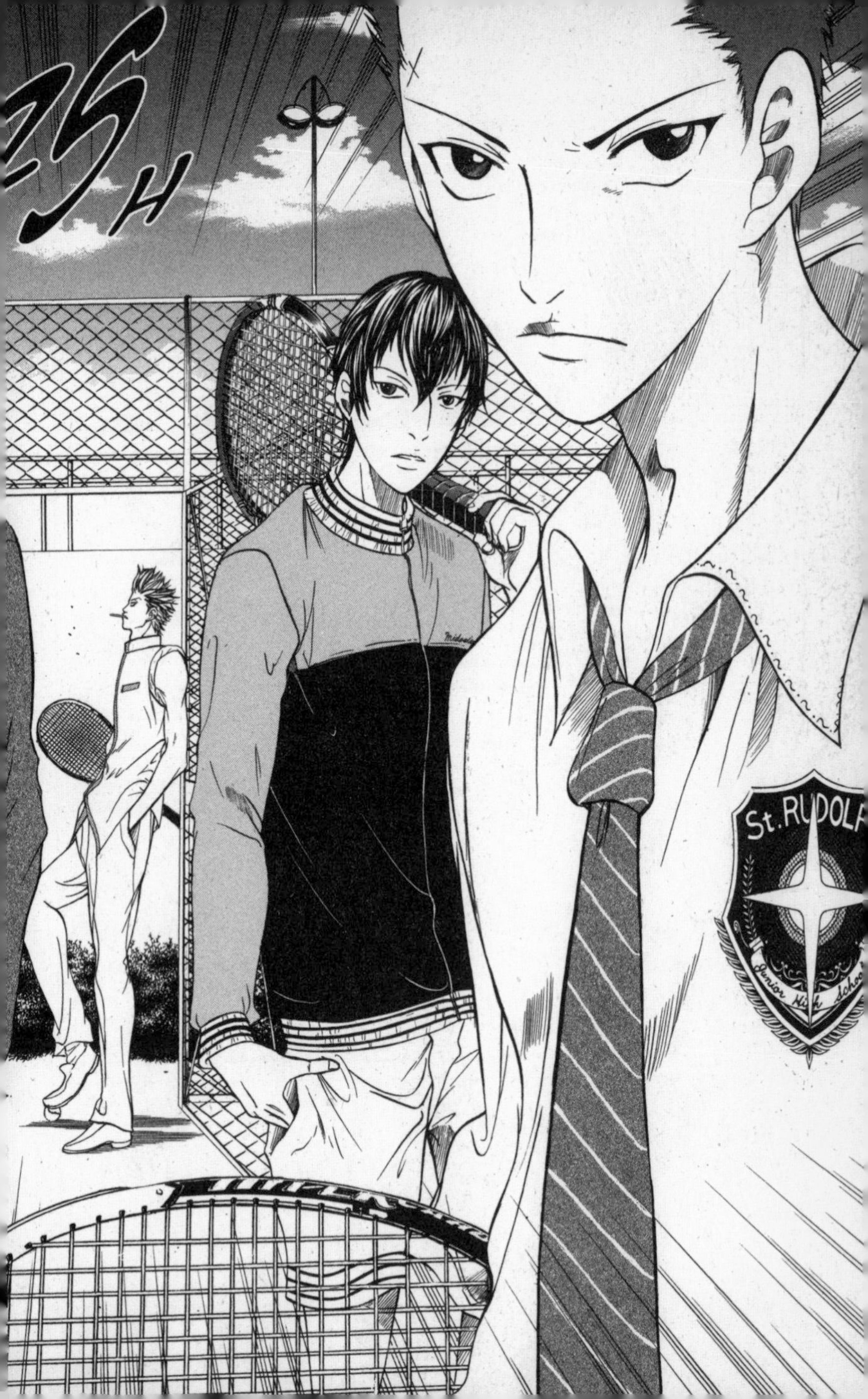
St.RUDOLF

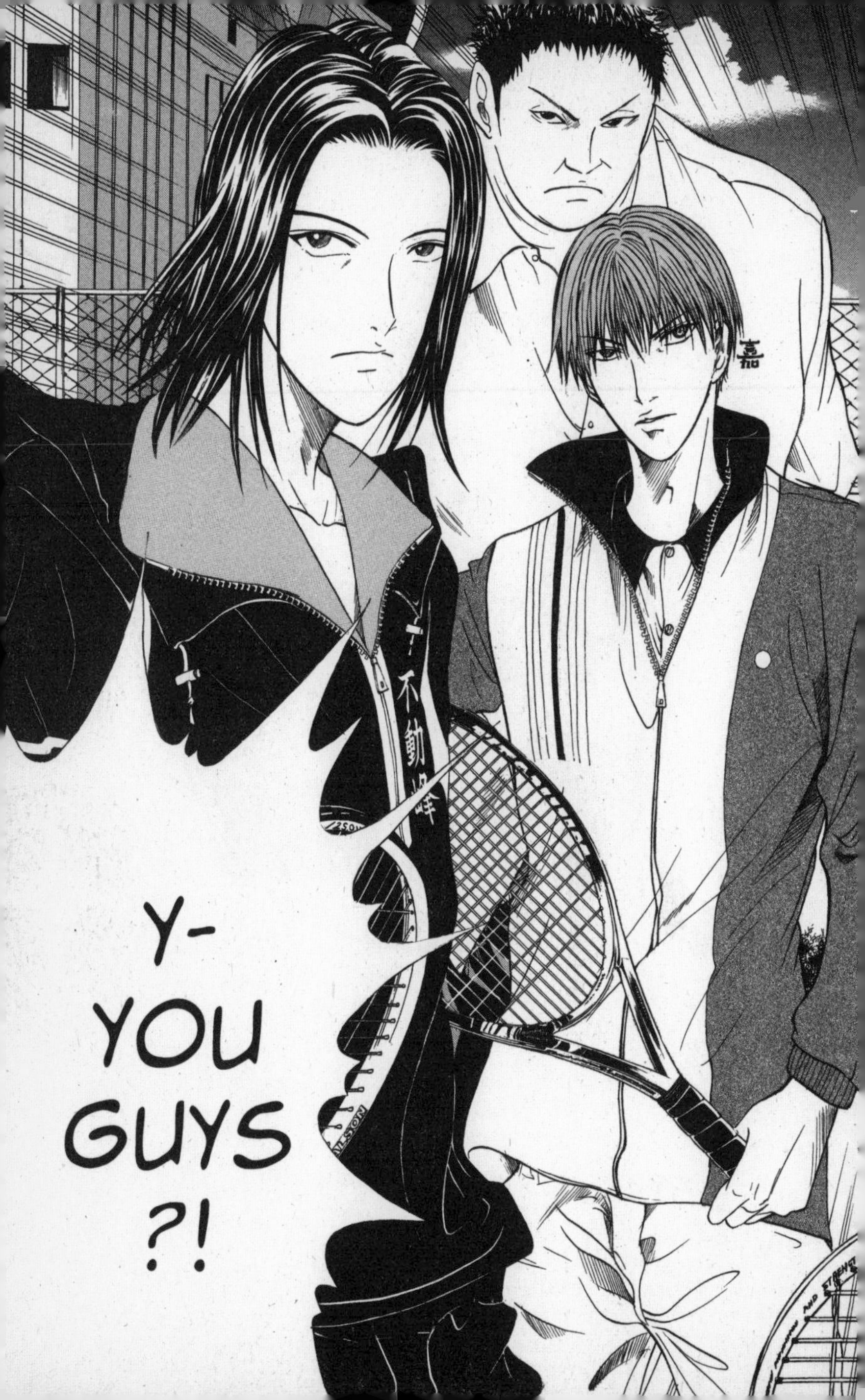
Y-YOU GUYS?!
不動峰

テニスの王子様

THE PRINCE OF TENNIS

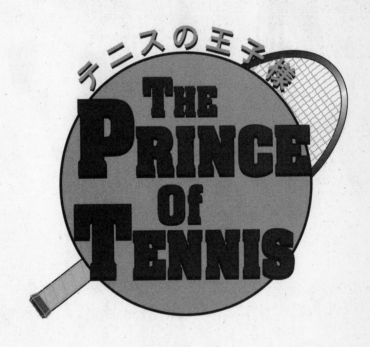

GENIUS 369: CONNECT TO RYOMA

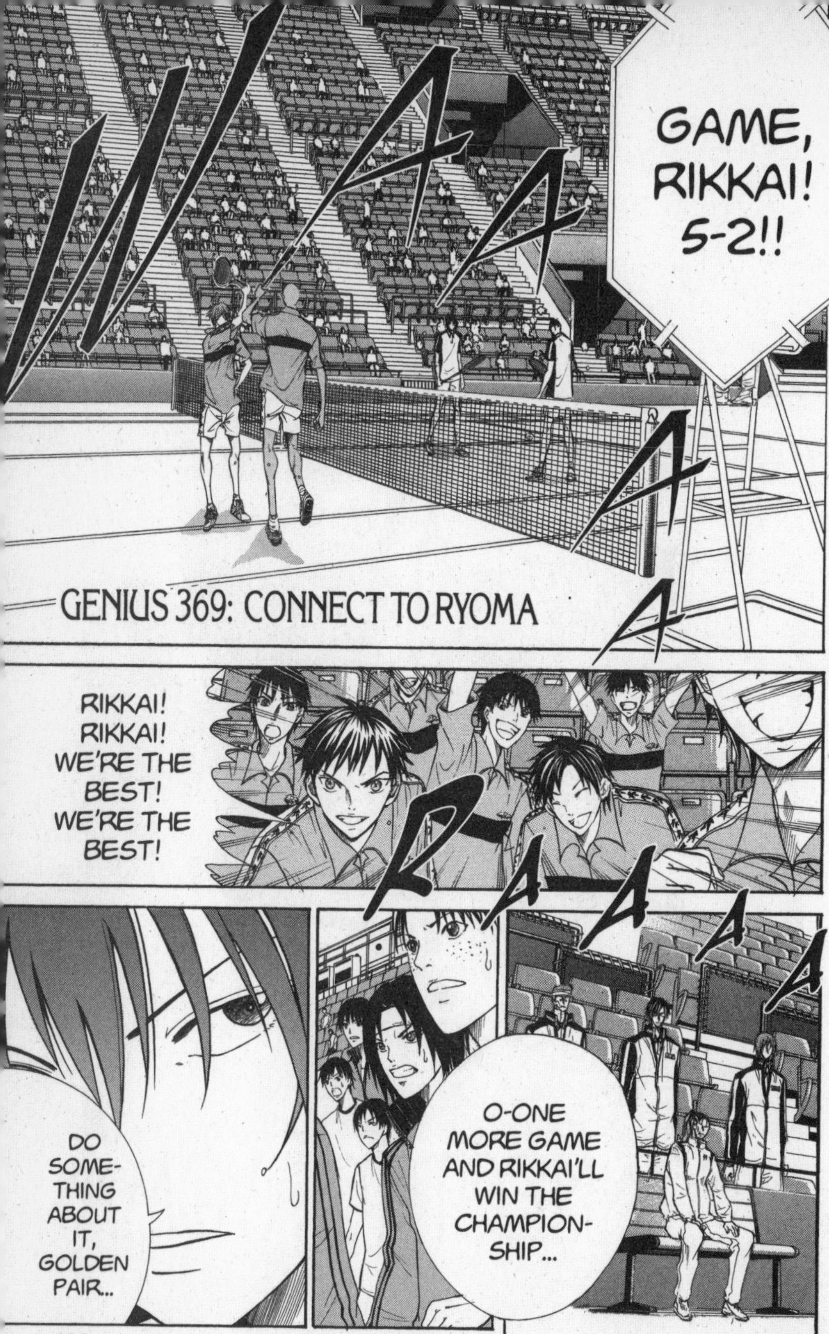
WAAAAAA
GAME, RIKKAI! 5-2!!
GENIUS 369: CONNECT TO RYOMA
RIKKAI! RIKKAI! WE'RE THE BEST! WE'RE THE BEST!
RAAAAAA
O-ONE MORE GAME AND RIKKAI'LL WIN THE CHAMPION-SHIP...
DO SOME-THING ABOUT IT, GOLDEN PAIR...

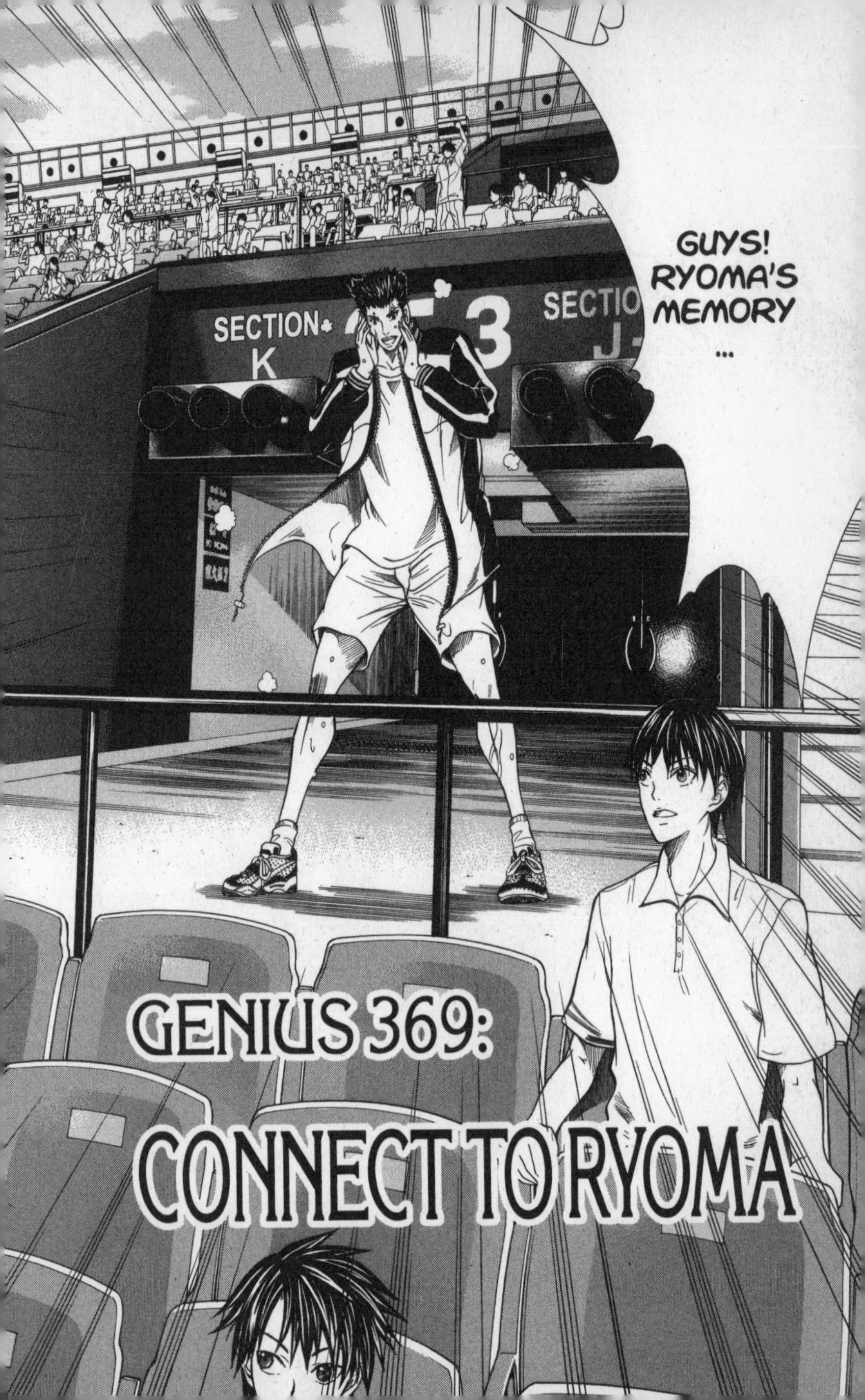
GUYS! RYOMA'S MEMORY ...
SECTION K
SECTION J
3
GENIUS 369:
CONNECT TO RYOMA

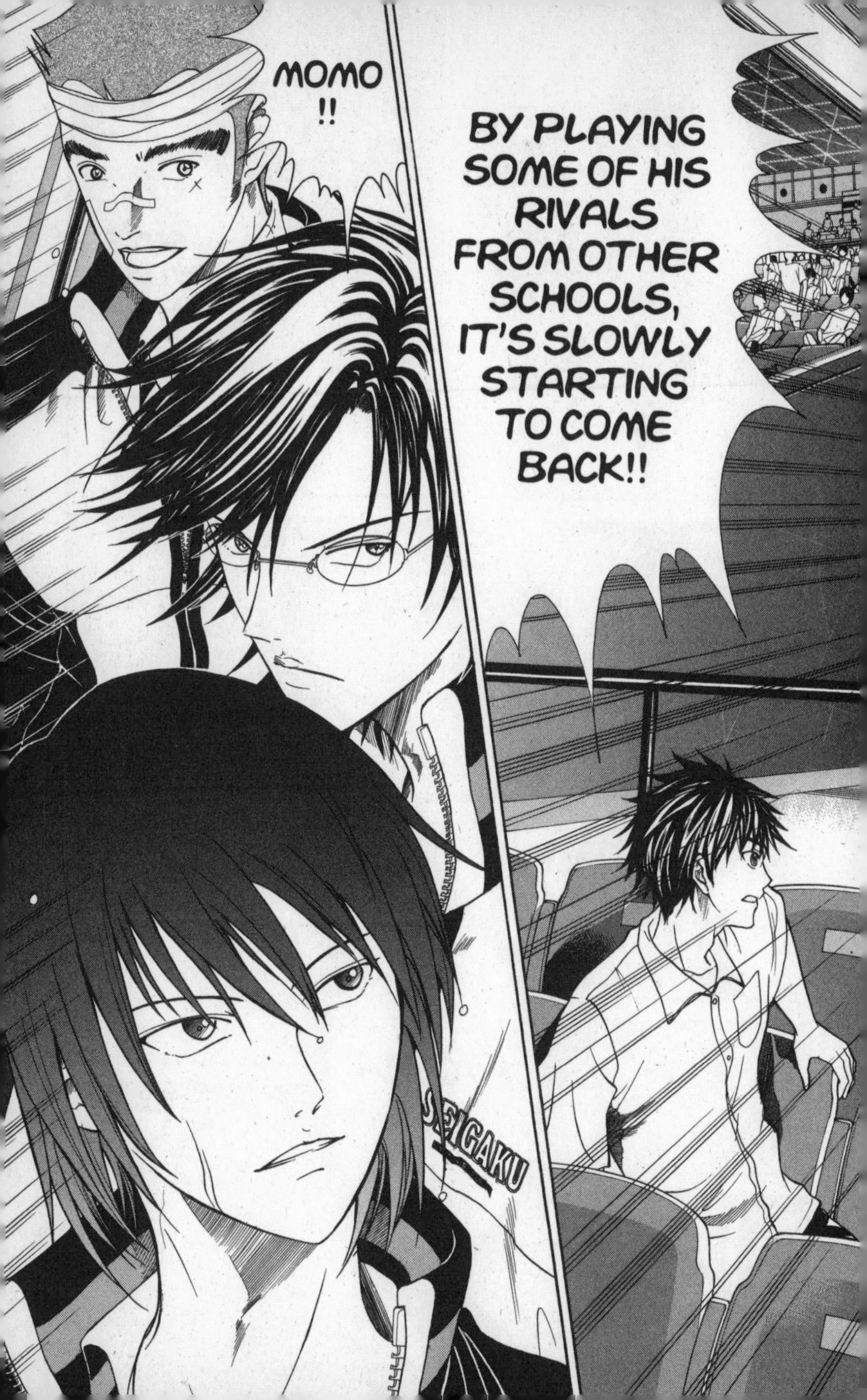
BY PLAYING SOME OF HIS RIVALS FROM OTHER SCHOOLS, IT'S SLOWLY STARTING TO COME BACK!!
MOMO !!
SEIGAKU

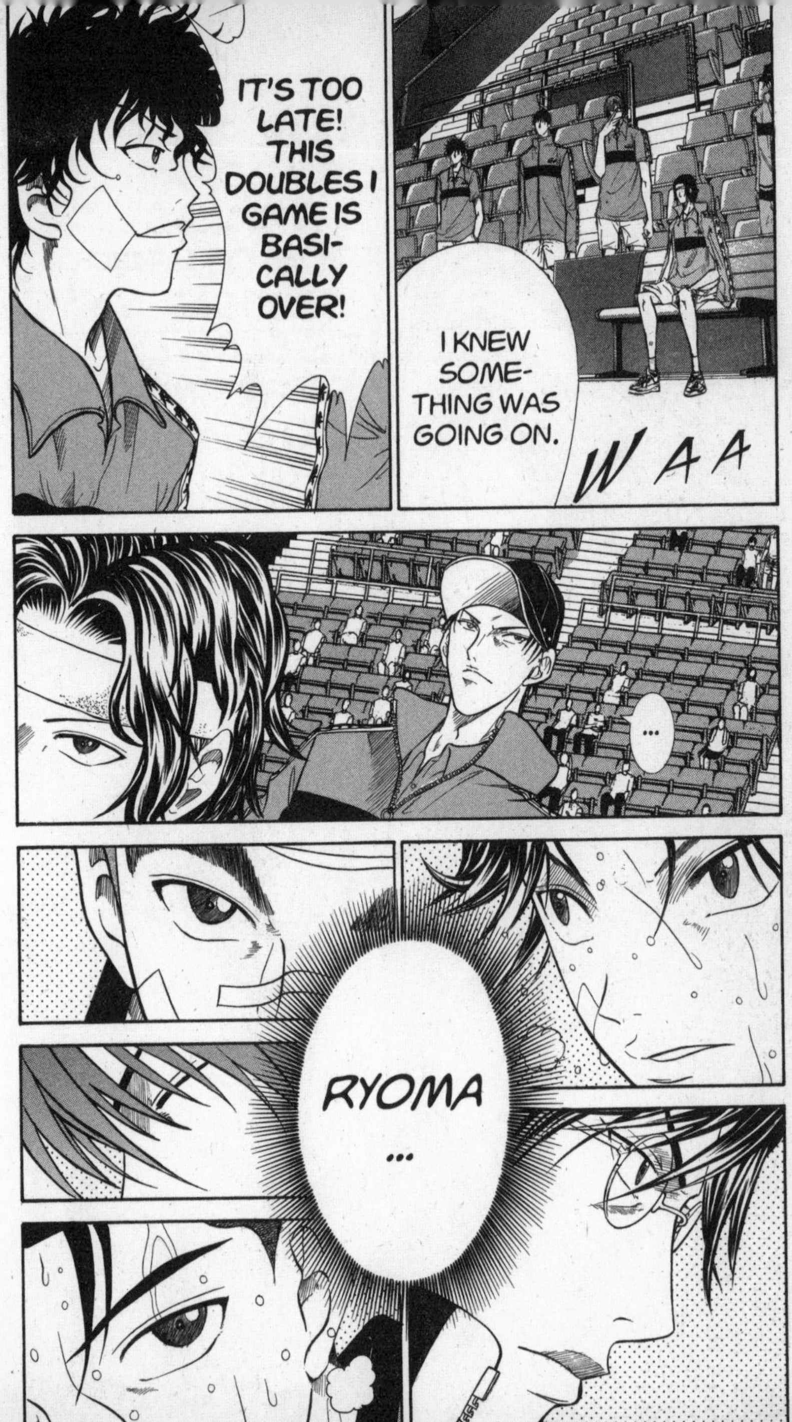
I KNEW SOME-THING WAS GOING ON.
WAA
IT'S TOO LATE! THIS DOUBLES I GAME IS BASI-CALLY OVER!
...
RYOMA ...

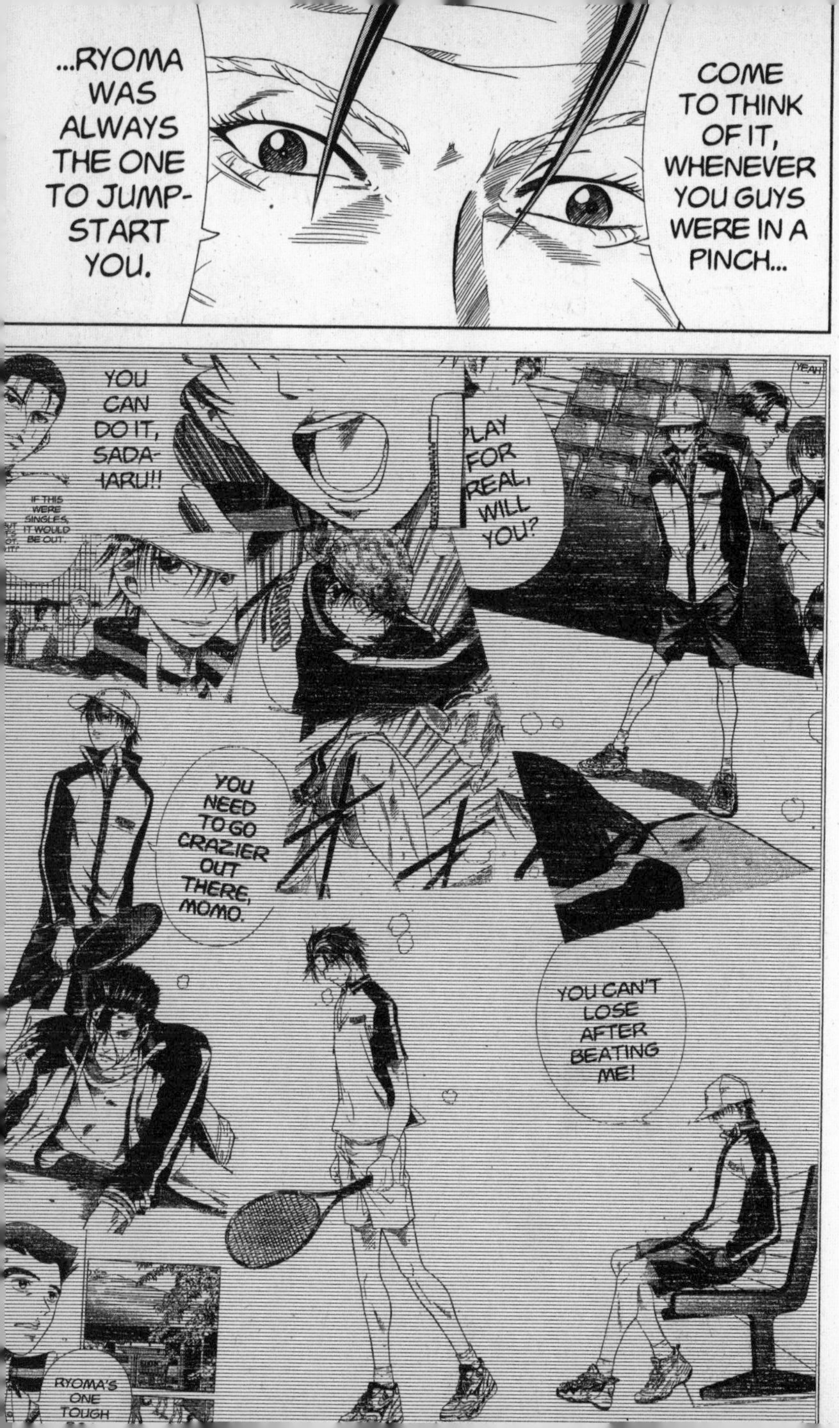
COME TO THINK OF IT, WHENEVER YOU GUYS WERE IN A PINCH...
...RYOMA WAS ALWAYS THE ONE TO JUMP-START YOU.
YEAH
PLAY FOR REAL, WILL YOU?
YOU CAN DO IT, SADAHARU!!
IF THIS WERE SINGLES, IT WOULD BE OUT.
YOU CAN'T LOSE AFTER BEATING ME!
YOU NEED TO GO CRAZIER OUT THERE, MOMO.
RYOMA'S ONE TOUGH

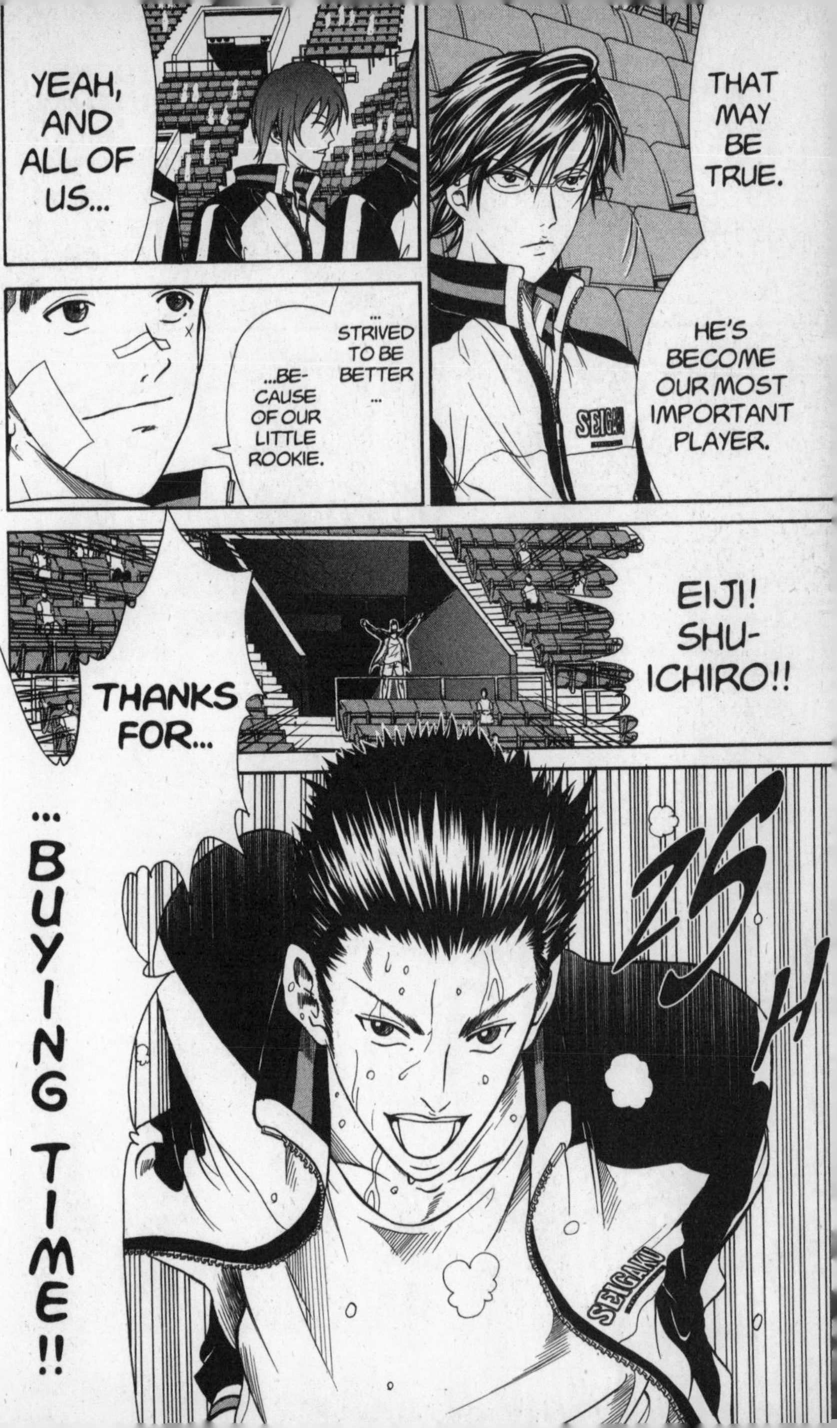
THAT MAY BE TRUE.
HE'S BECOME OUR MOST IMPORTANT PLAYER.
YEAH, AND ALL OF US...
...STRIVED TO BE BETTER...
...BECAUSE OF OUR LITTLE ROOKIE.
SEIGAKU
EIJI! SHUICHIRO!!
THANKS FOR...
...BUYING TIME!!
ZSSH
SEIGAKU

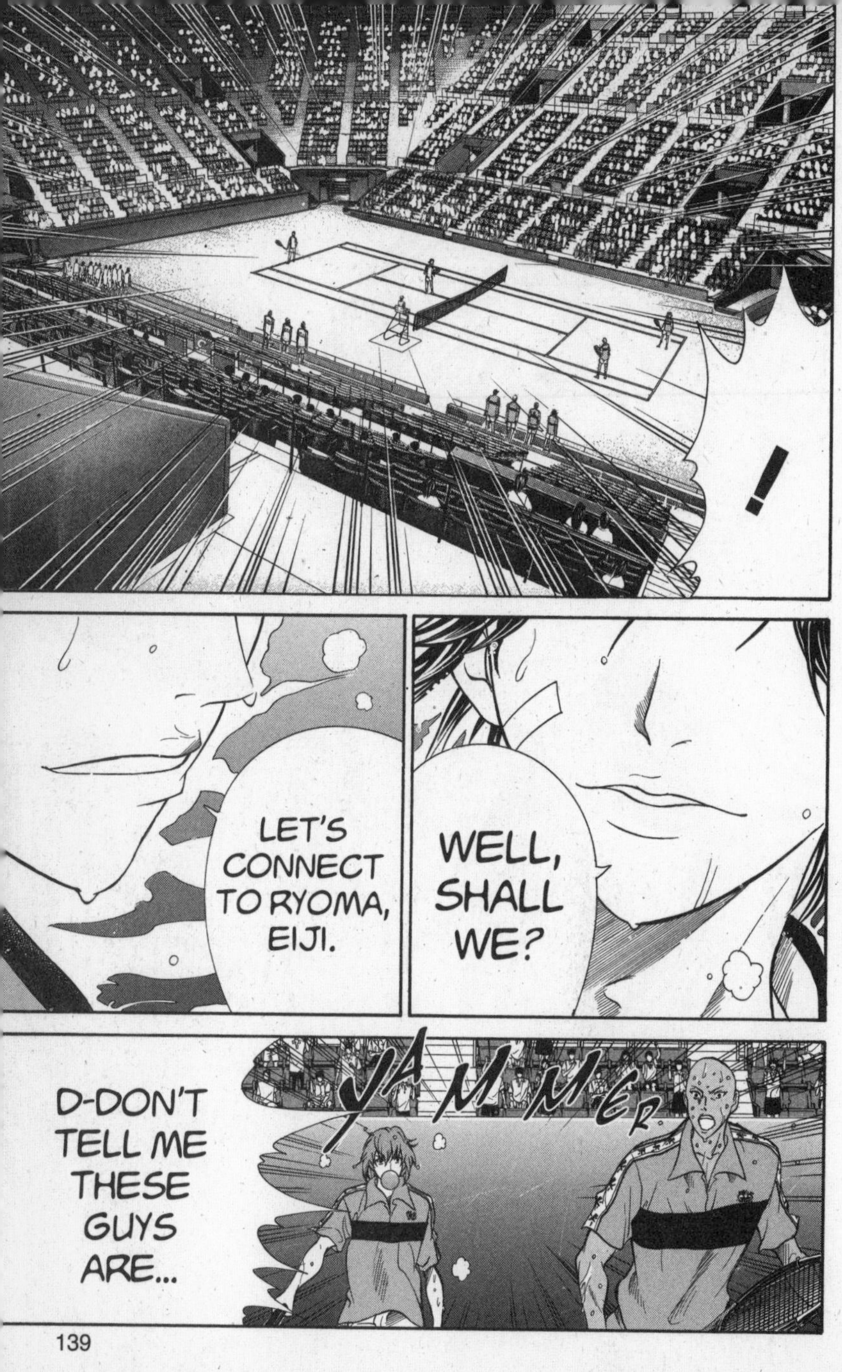
!
WELL, SHALL WE?
LET'S CONNECT TO RYOMA, EIJI.
YAMMER
D-DON'T TELL ME THESE GUYS ARE...

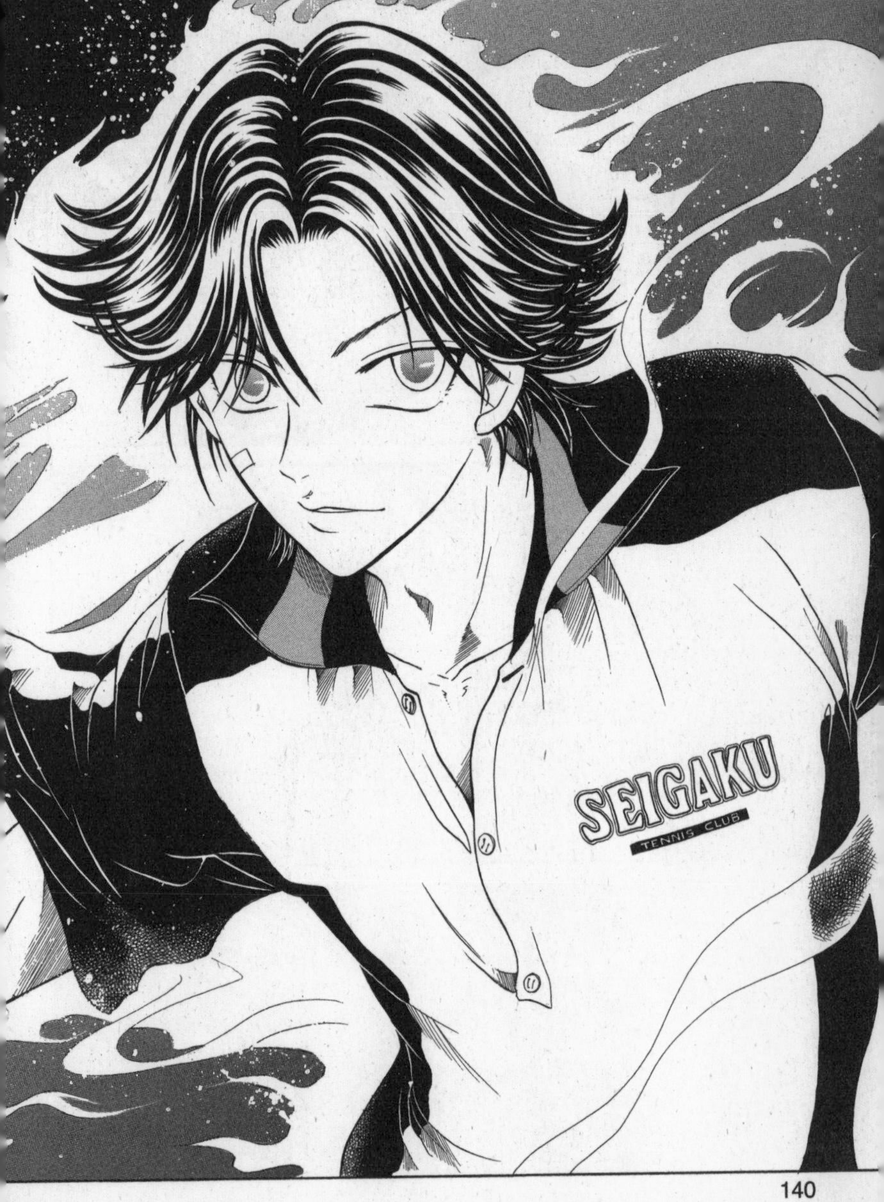
SEIGAKU
TENNIS CLUB

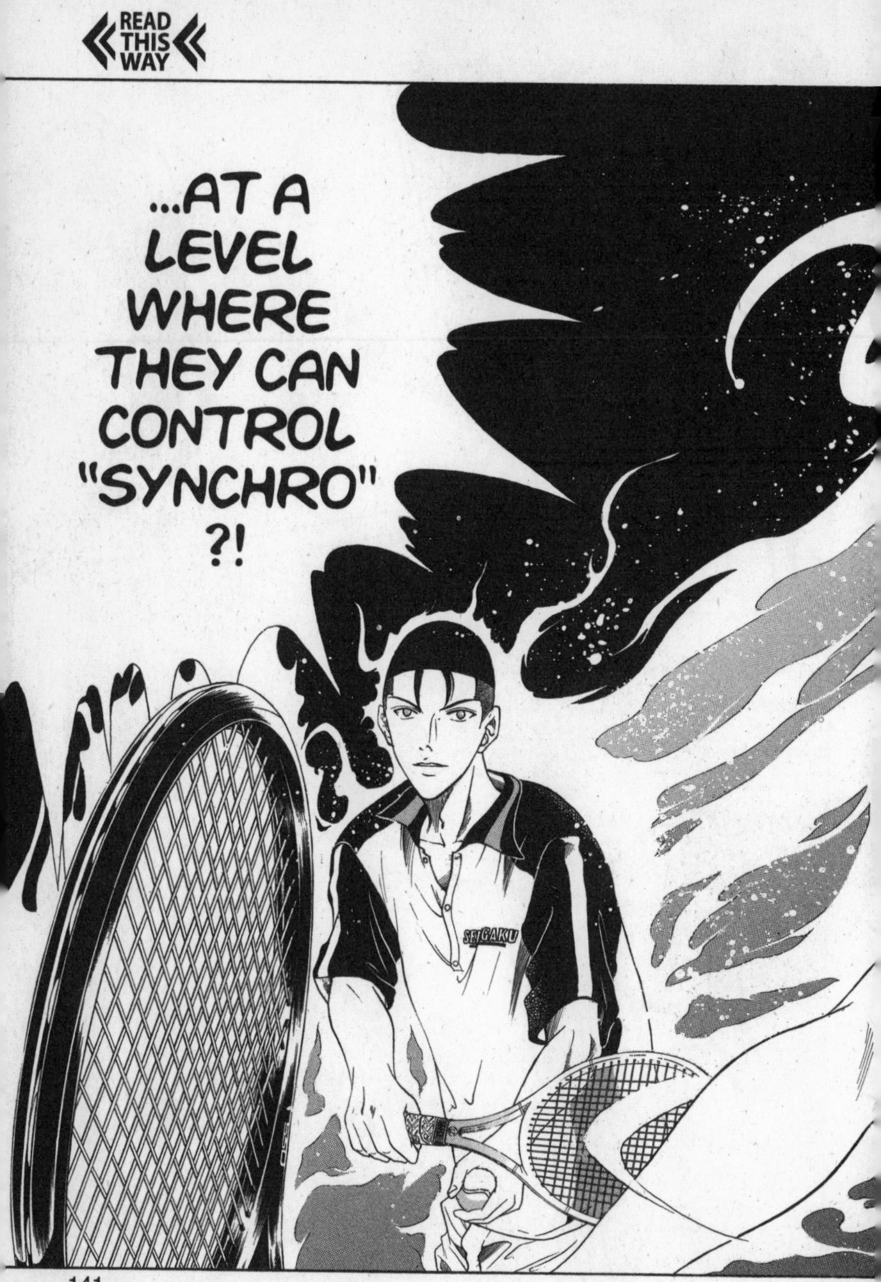
READ THIS WAY
...AT A LEVEL WHERE THEY CAN CONTROL "SYNCHRO" ?!
SEIGAKU

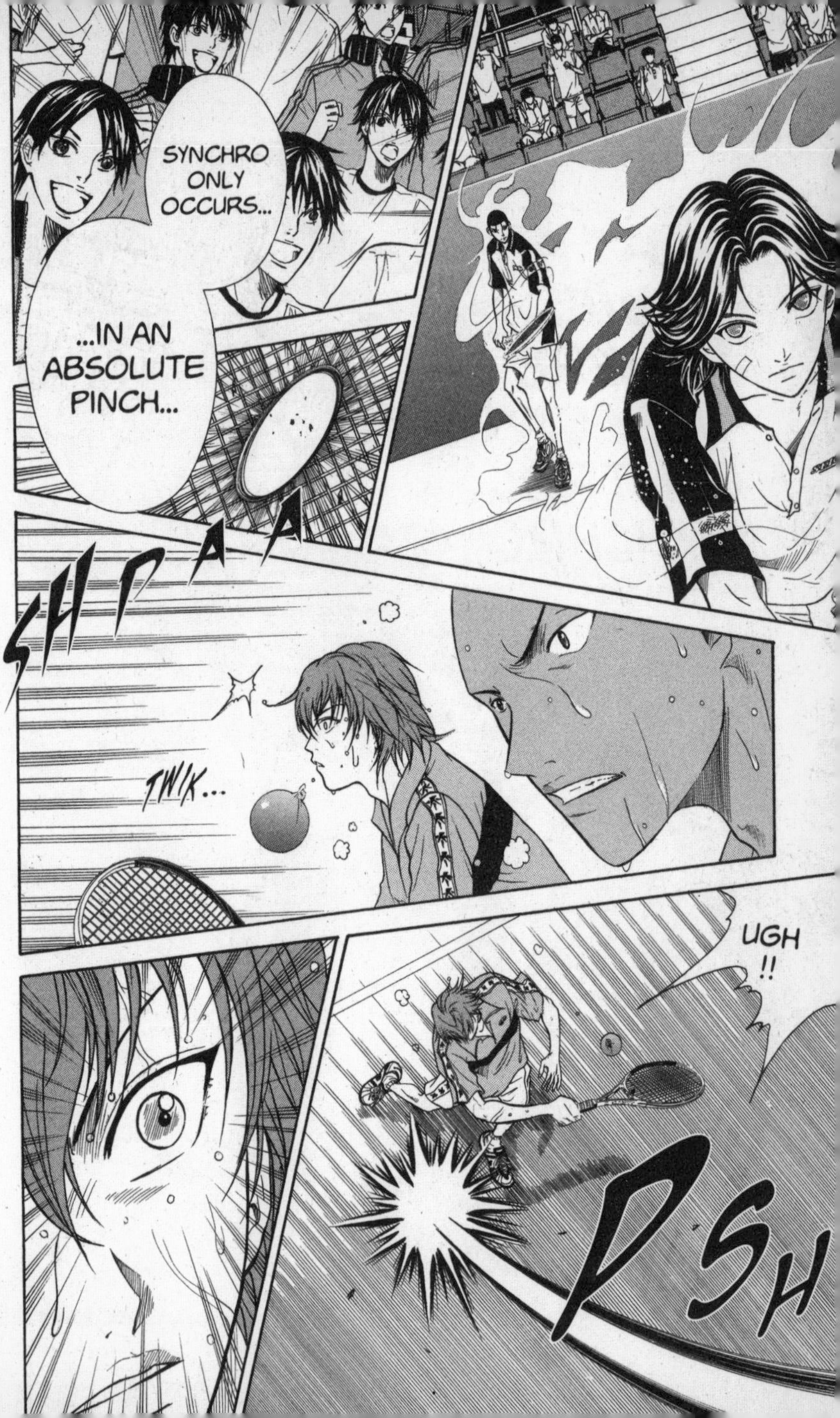
SYNCHRO ONLY OCCURS...
...IN AN ABSOLUTE PINCH...
SHPAAA
TWIK...
UGH !!
DSH

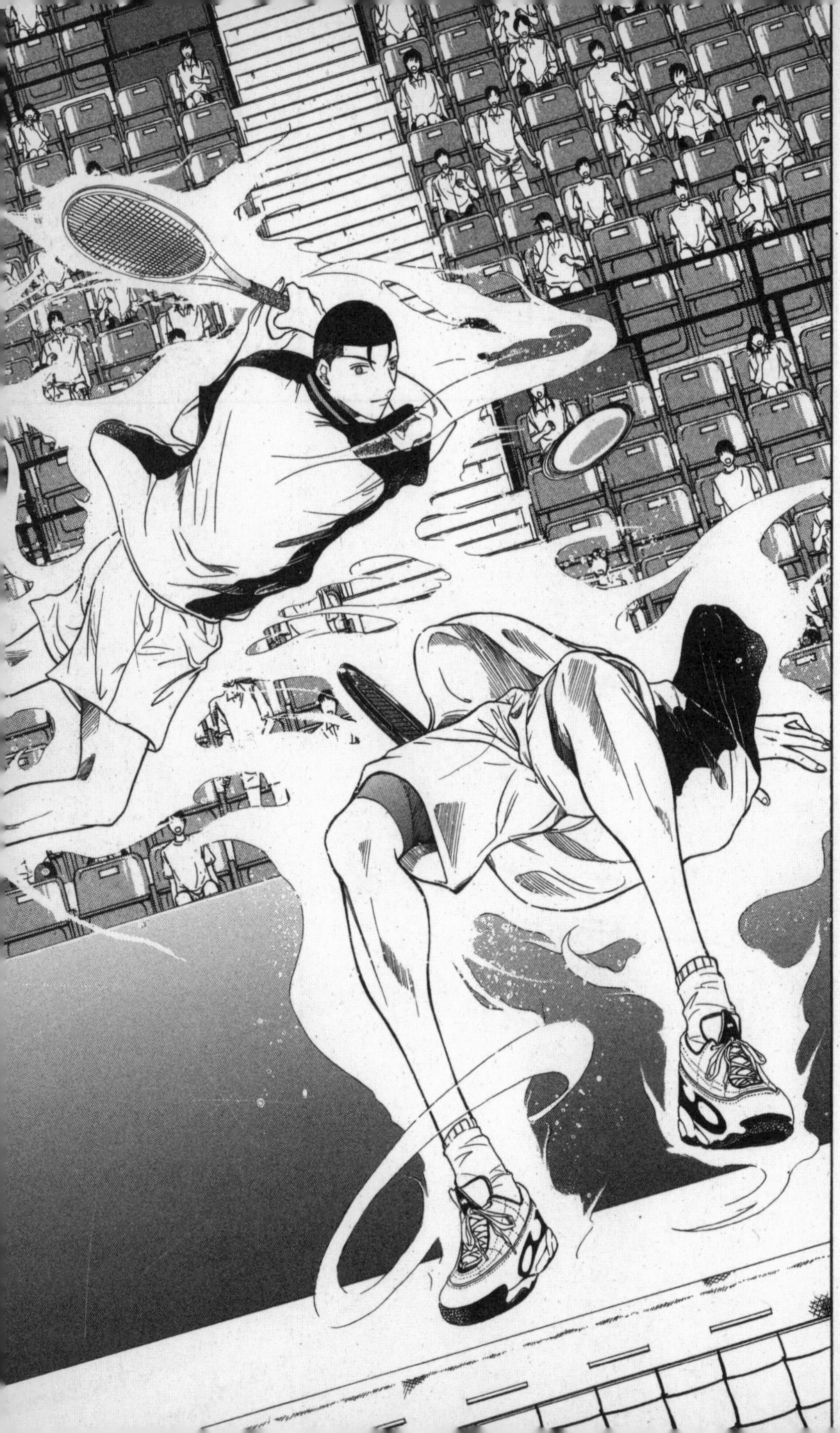

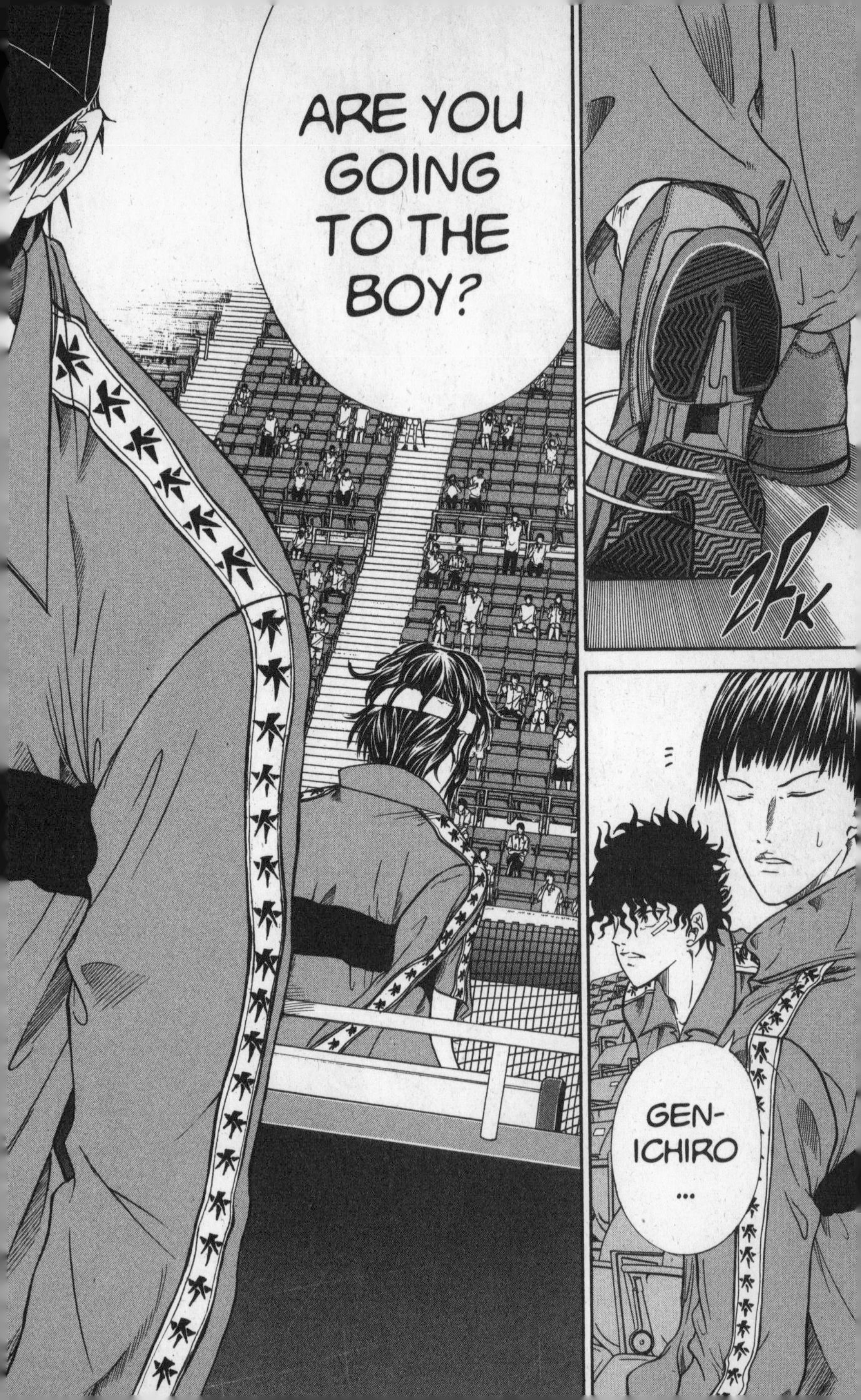
GEN-ICHIRO ...
ARE YOU GOING TO THE BOY?

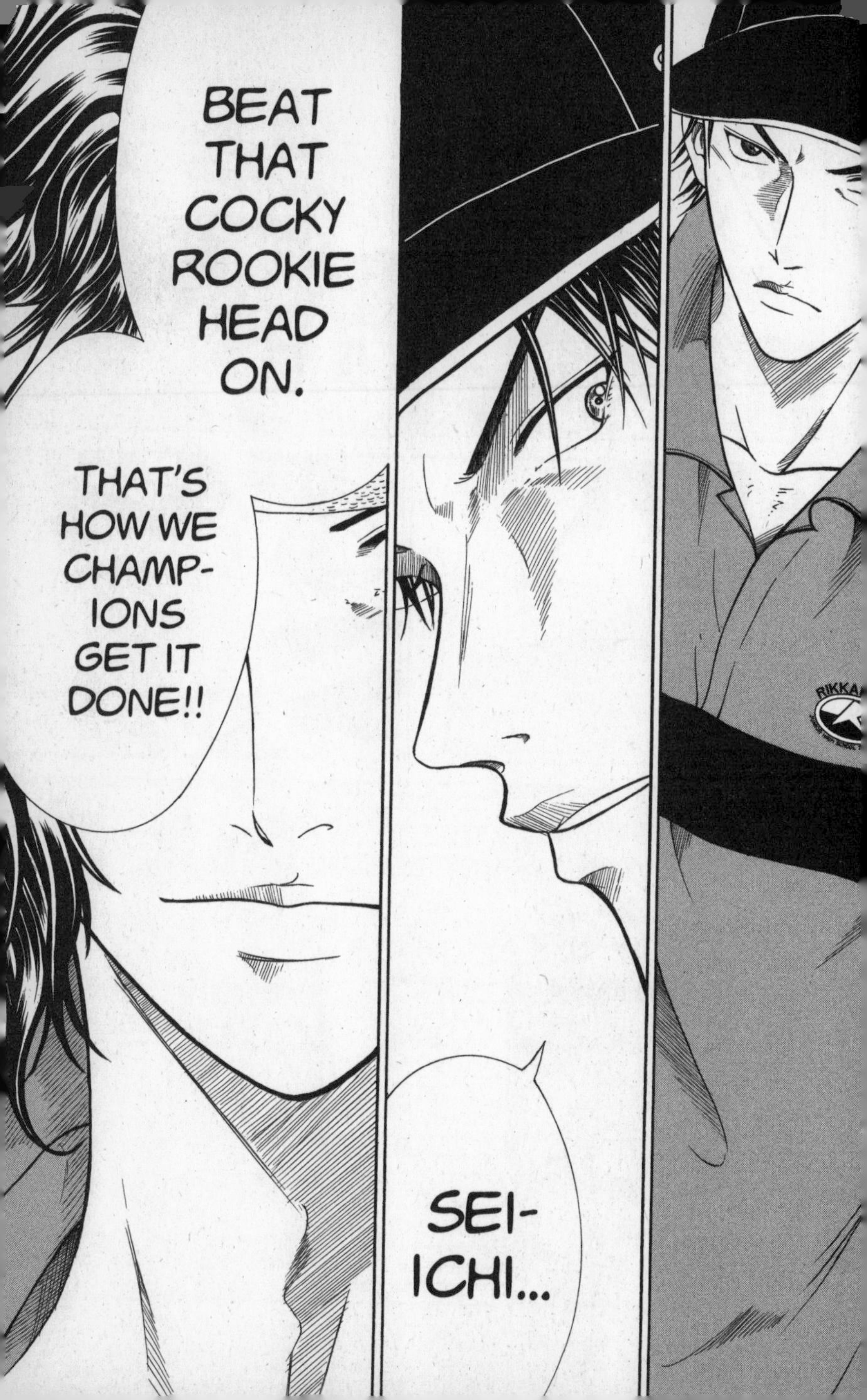
SEI-ICHI...
BEAT THAT COCKY ROOKIE HEAD ON.
THAT'S HOW WE CHAMPIONS GET IT DONE!!

WAAAA
TUD
TUD

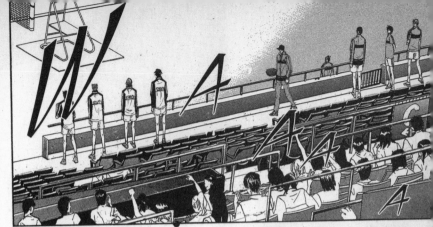

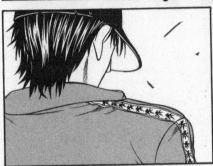

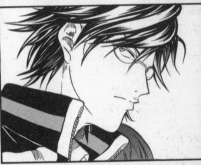

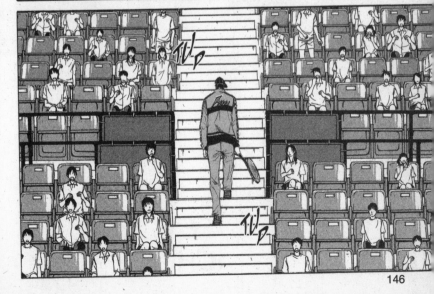

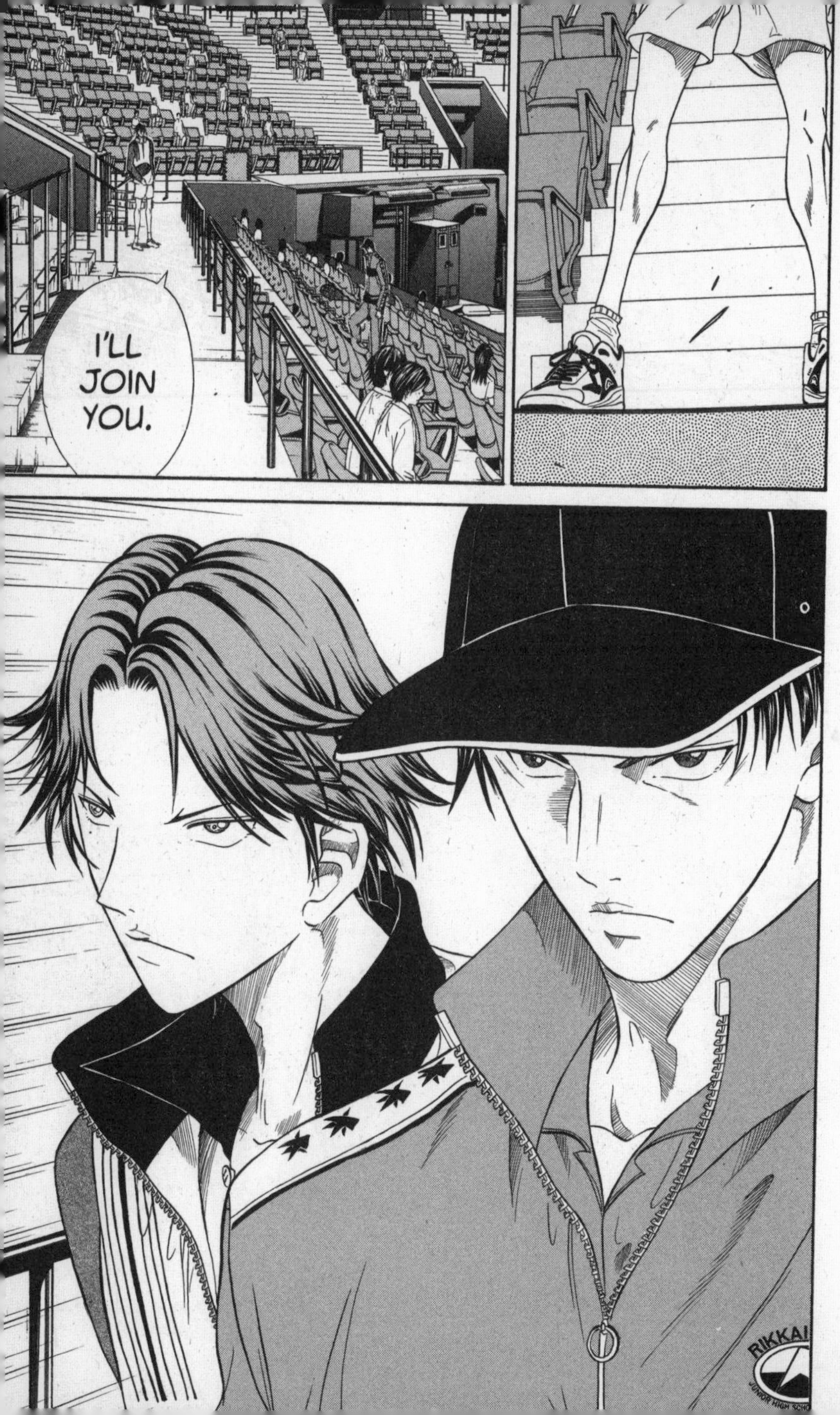
I'LL JOIN YOU.
RIKKAI

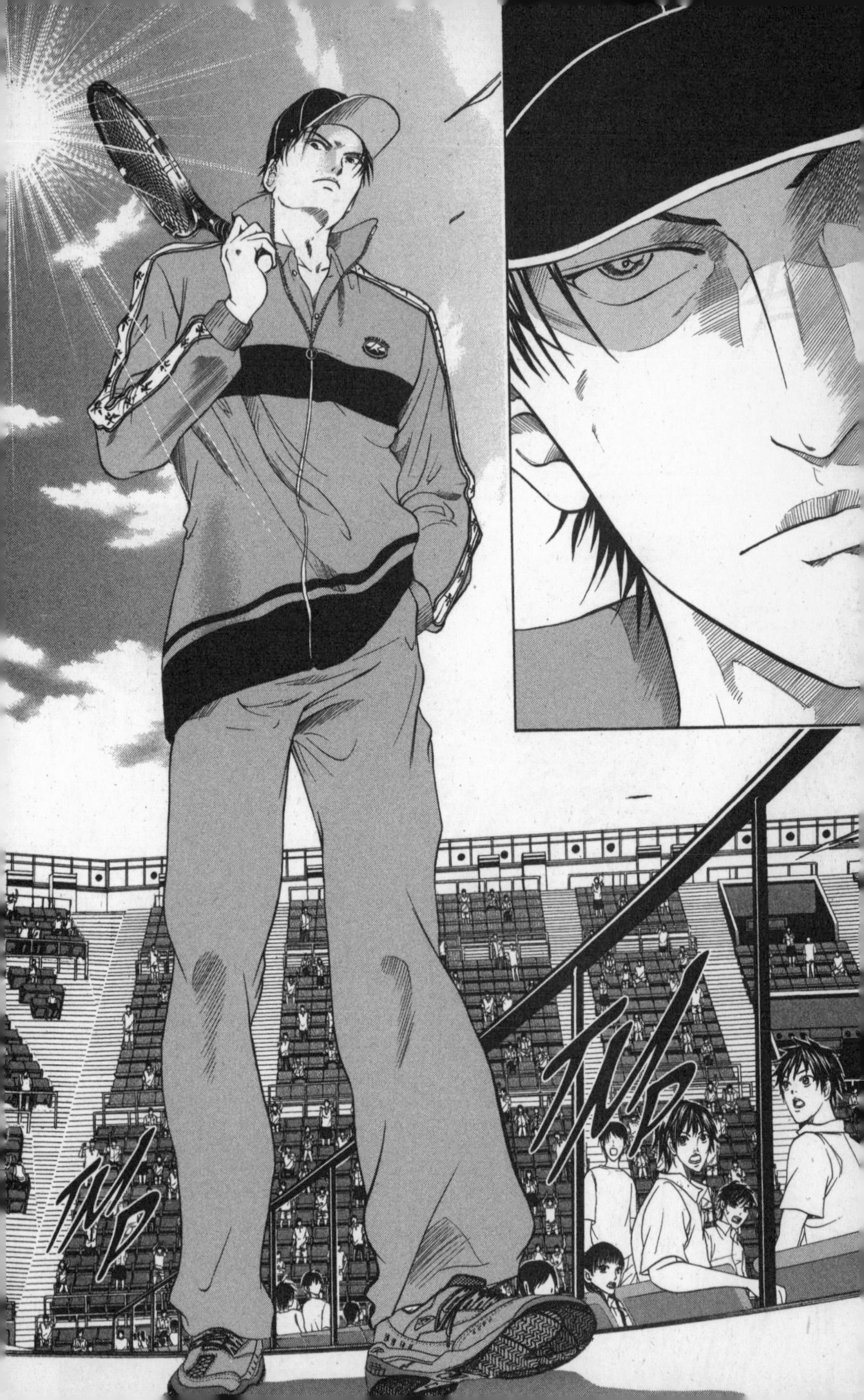

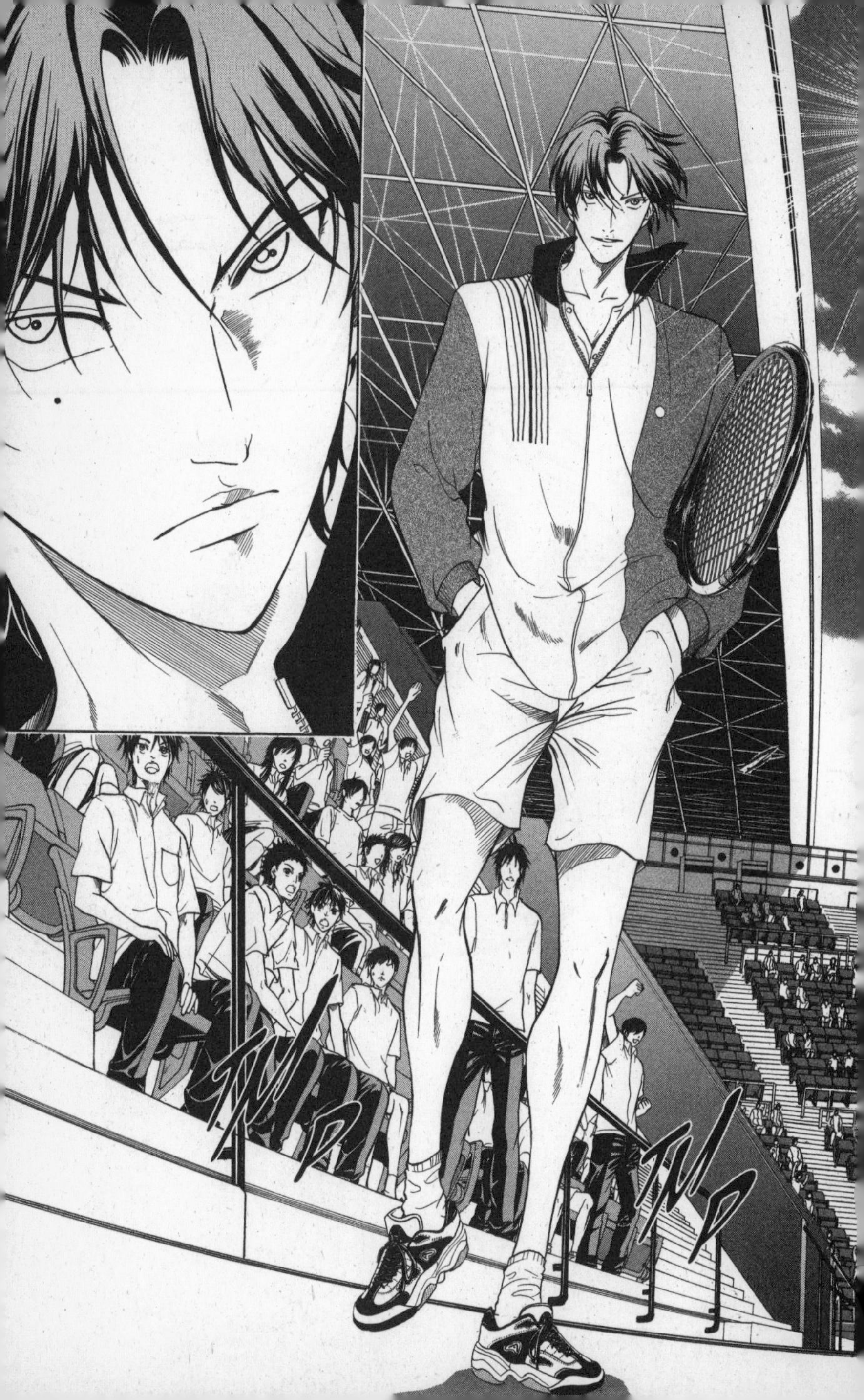
TMP
TMP

テニスの王子様

THE PRINCE OF TENNIS

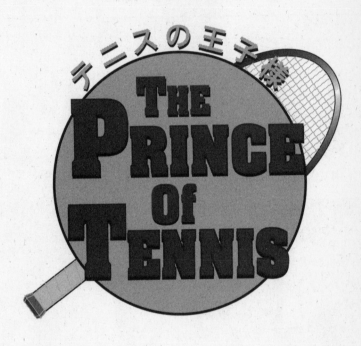

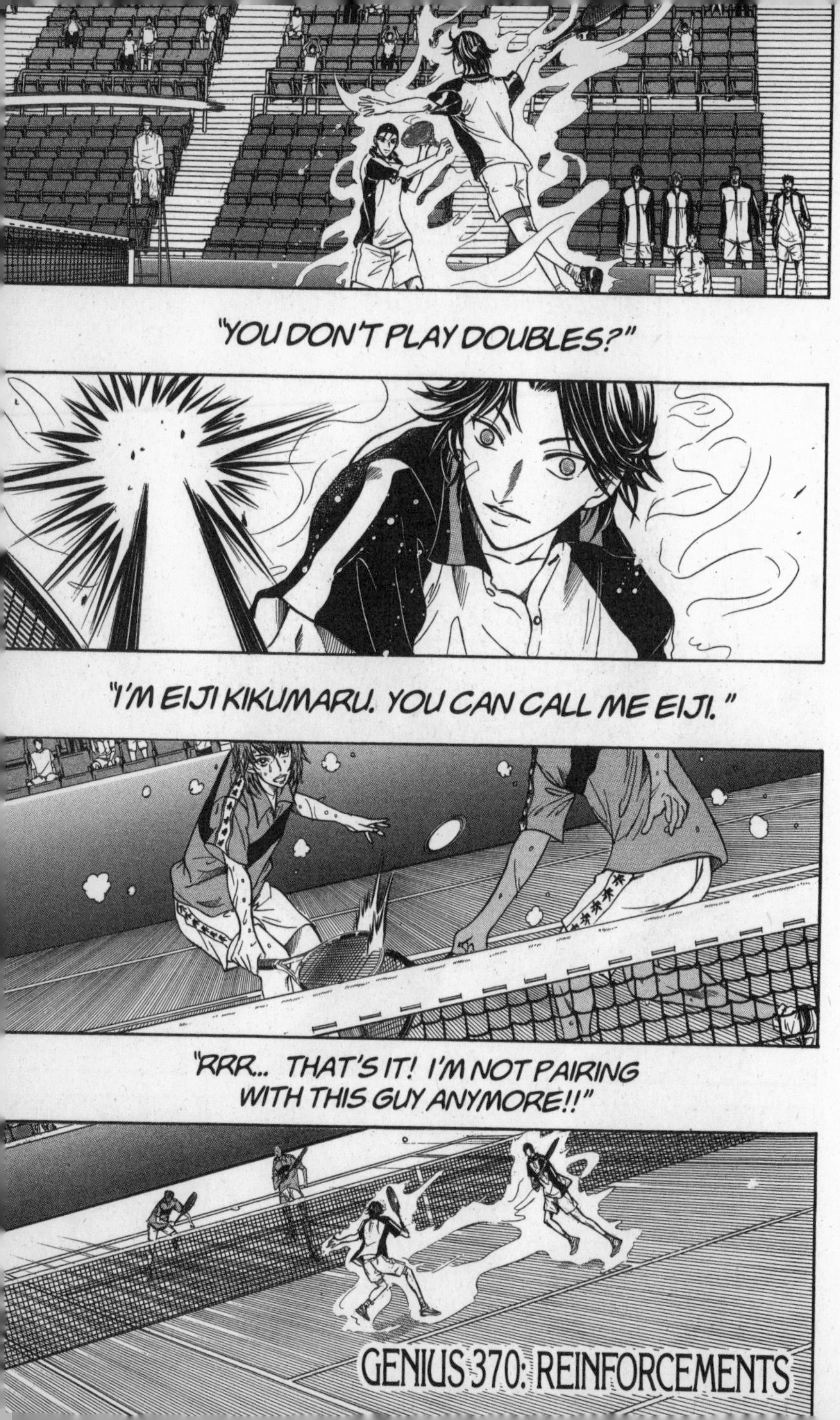
"YOU DON'T PLAY DOUBLES?"
"I'M EIJI KIKUMARU. YOU CAN CALL ME EIJI."
"RRR... THAT'S IT! I'M NOT PAIRING WITH THIS GUY ANYMORE!!"
GENIUS 370: REINFORCEMENTS

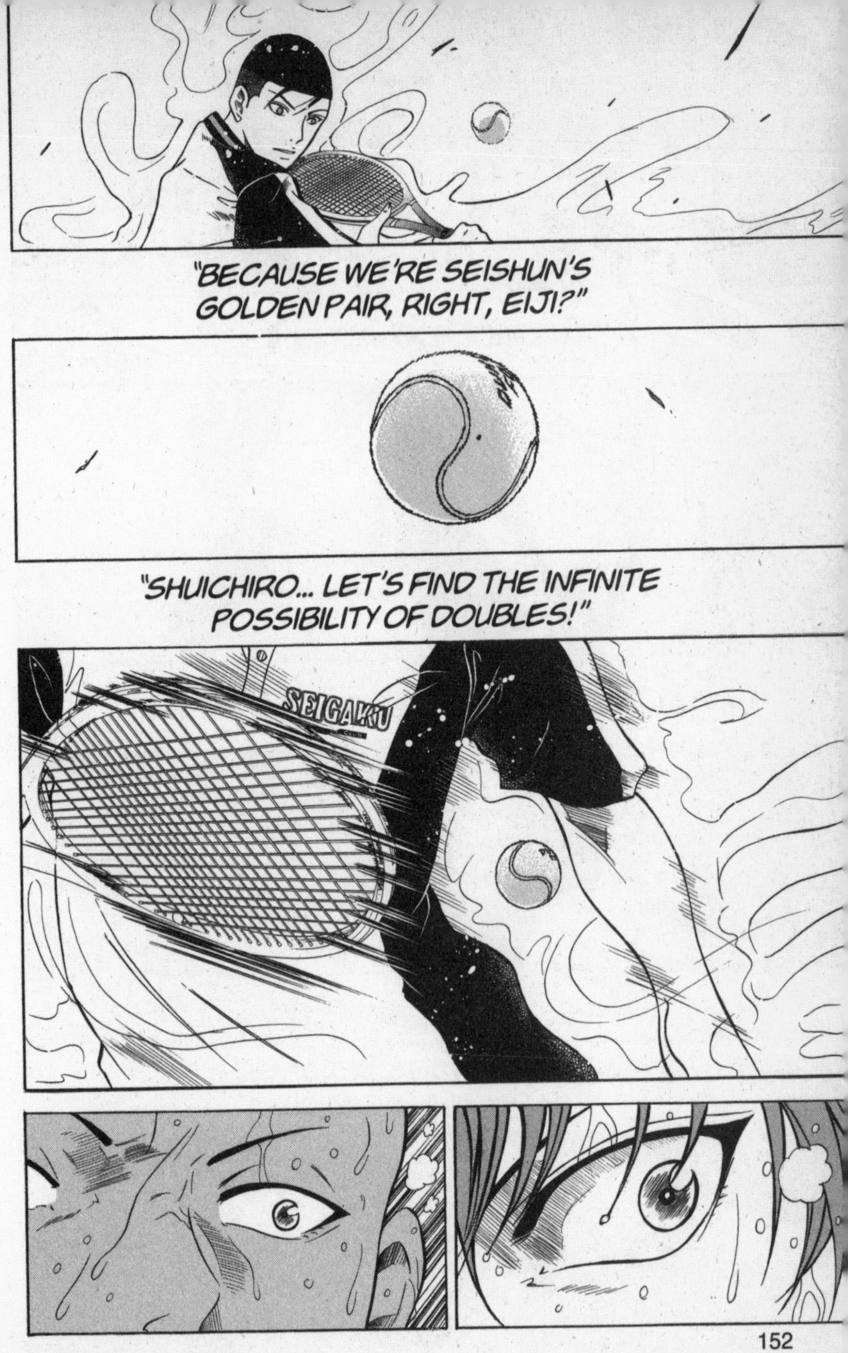
"BECAUSE WE'RE SEISHUN'S GOLDEN PAIR, RIGHT, EIJI?"
"SHUICHIRO... LET'S FIND THE INFINITE POSSIBILITY OF DOUBLES!"
SEIGAKU

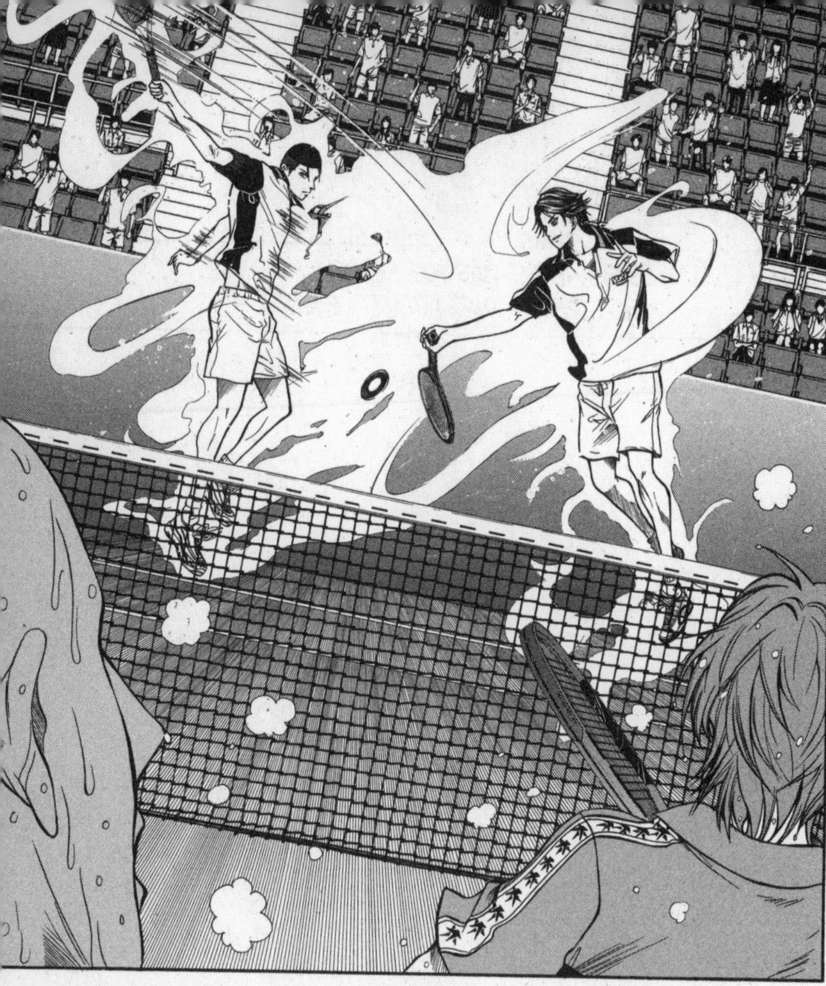

"...AND THEN ON TO THE NATIONALS!!"

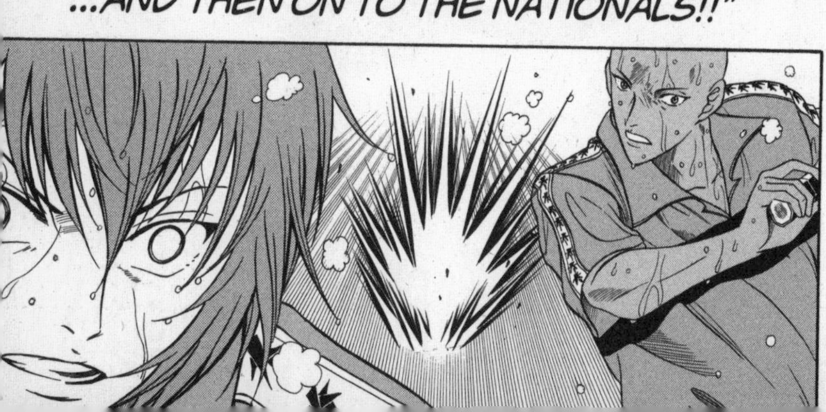

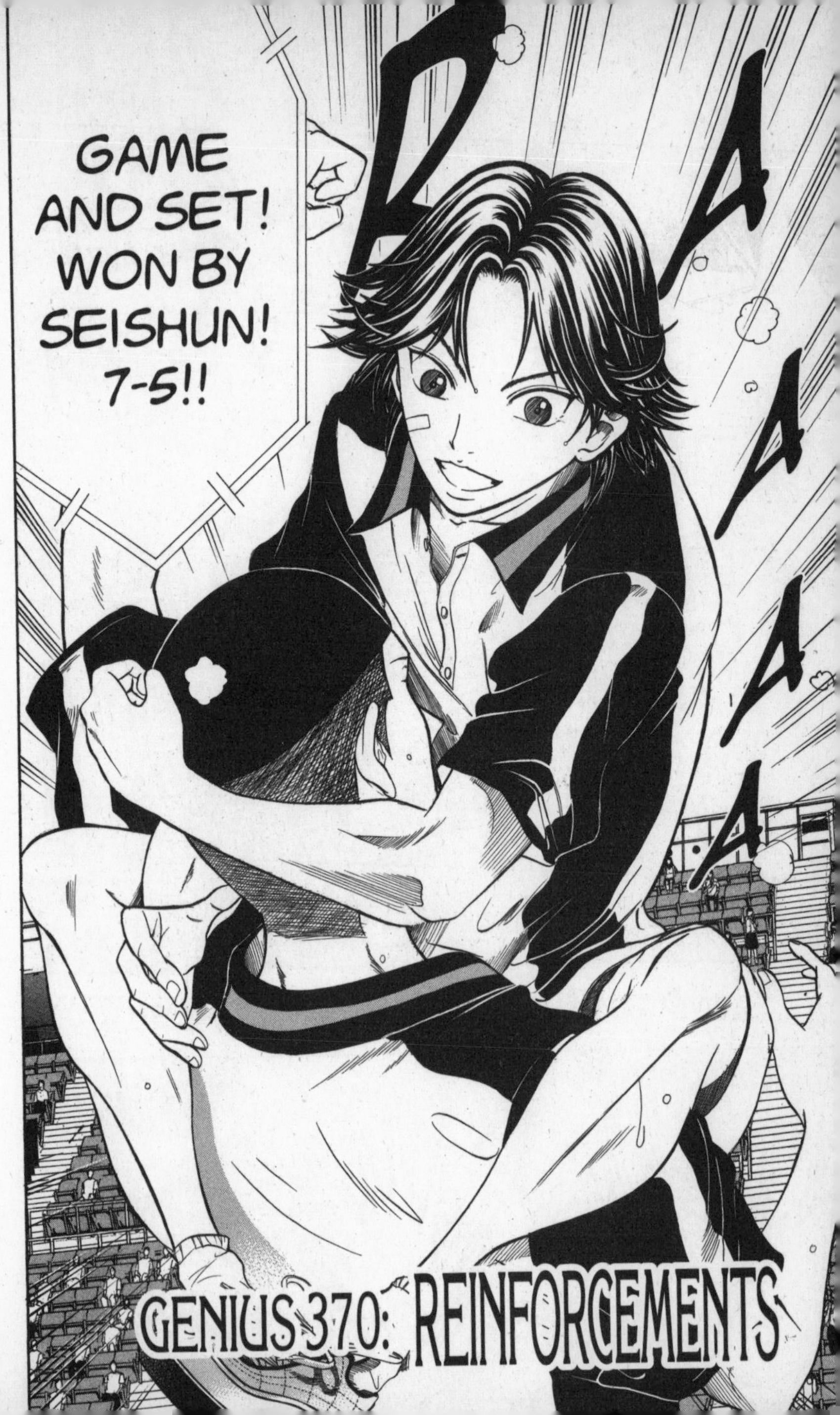
GAME AND SET! WON BY SEISHUN! 7-5!!

GENIUS 370: REINFORCEMENTS

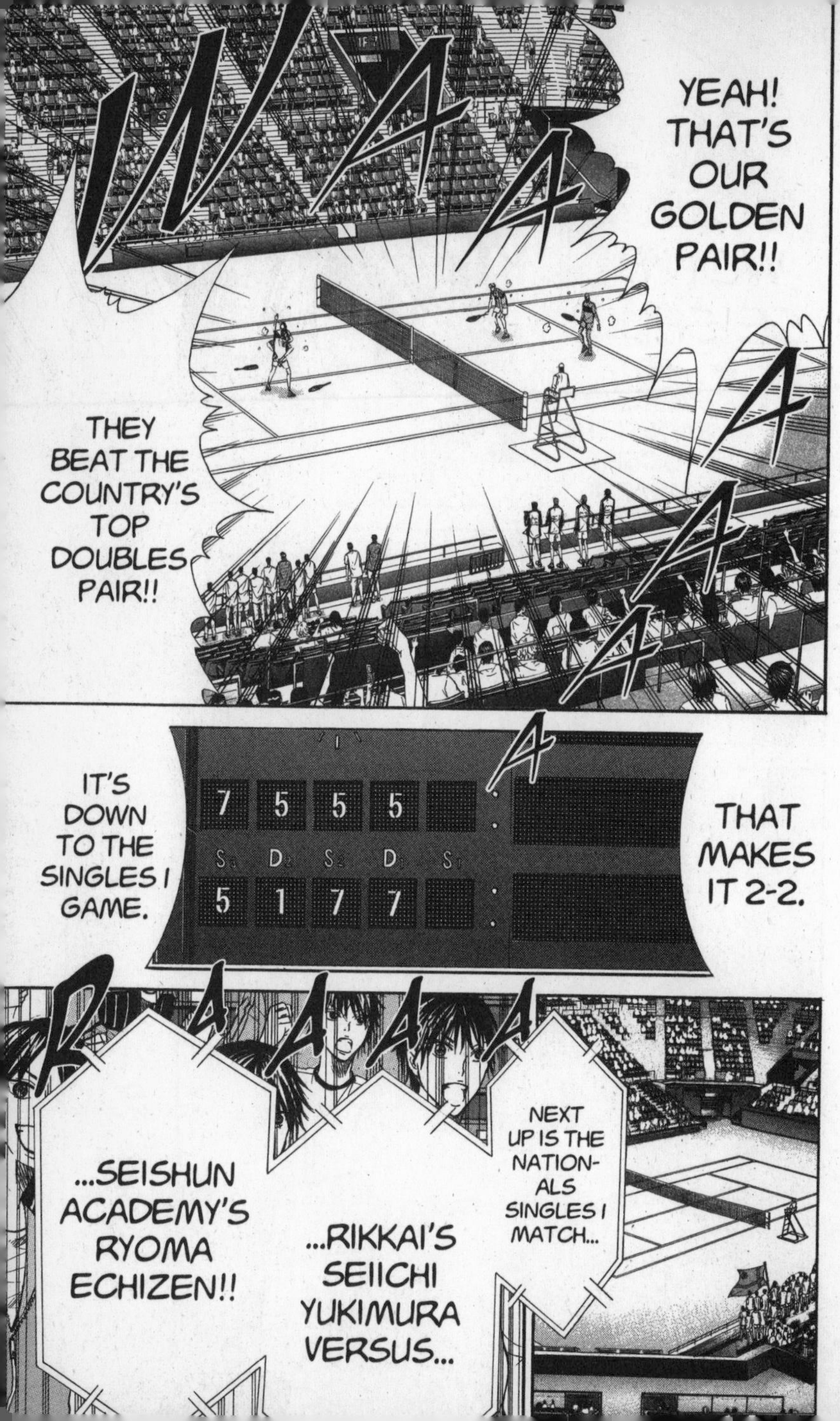
YEAH! THAT'S OUR GOLDEN PAIR!!
WAAAAAAA
THEY BEAT THE COUNTRY'S TOP DOUBLES PAIR!!
THAT MAKES IT 2-2.
7 5 5 5
S3 D2 S2 D1 S1
5 1 7 7
IT'S DOWN TO THE SINGLES 1 GAME.
RAAAA
NEXT UP IS THE NATION-ALS SINGLES 1 MATCH...
...RIKKAI'S SEIICHI YUKIMURA VERSUS...
...SEISHUN ACADEMY'S RYOMA ECHIZEN!!

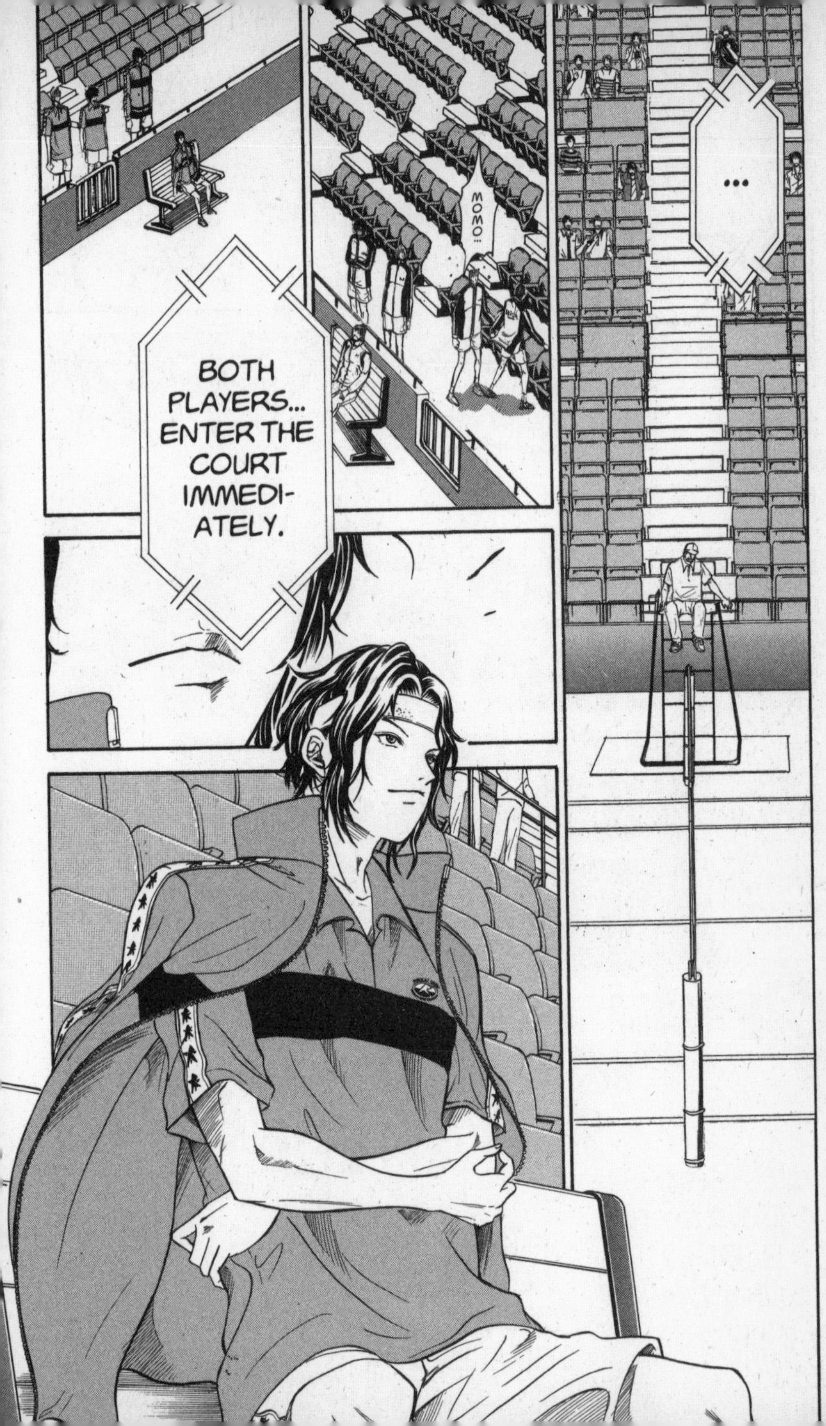
...
MOMO!!
BOTH PLAYERS... ENTER THE COURT IMMEDIATELY.

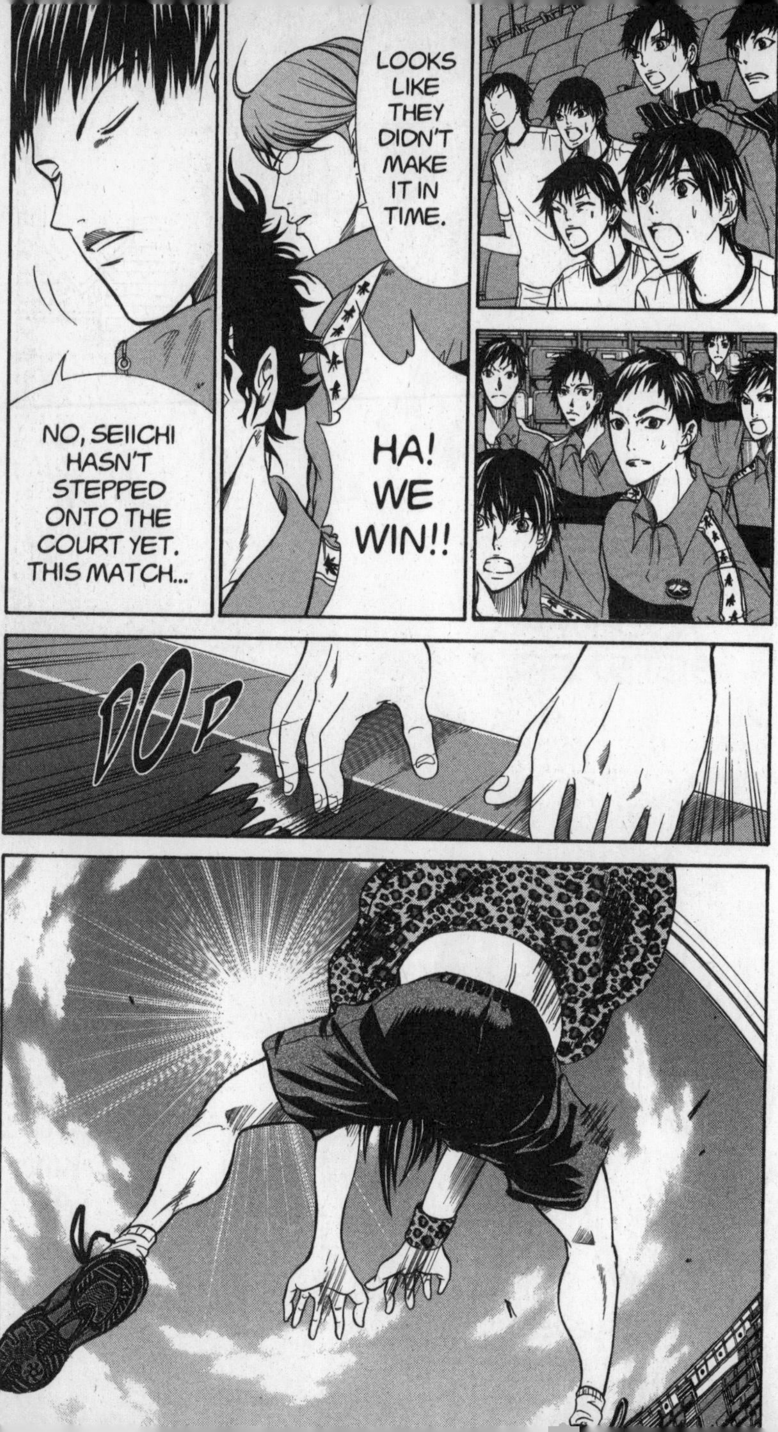
LOOKS LIKE THEY DIDN'T MAKE IT IN TIME.
HA! WE WIN!!
NO, SEIICHI HASN'T STEPPED ONTO THE COURT YET. THIS MATCH...
DOP

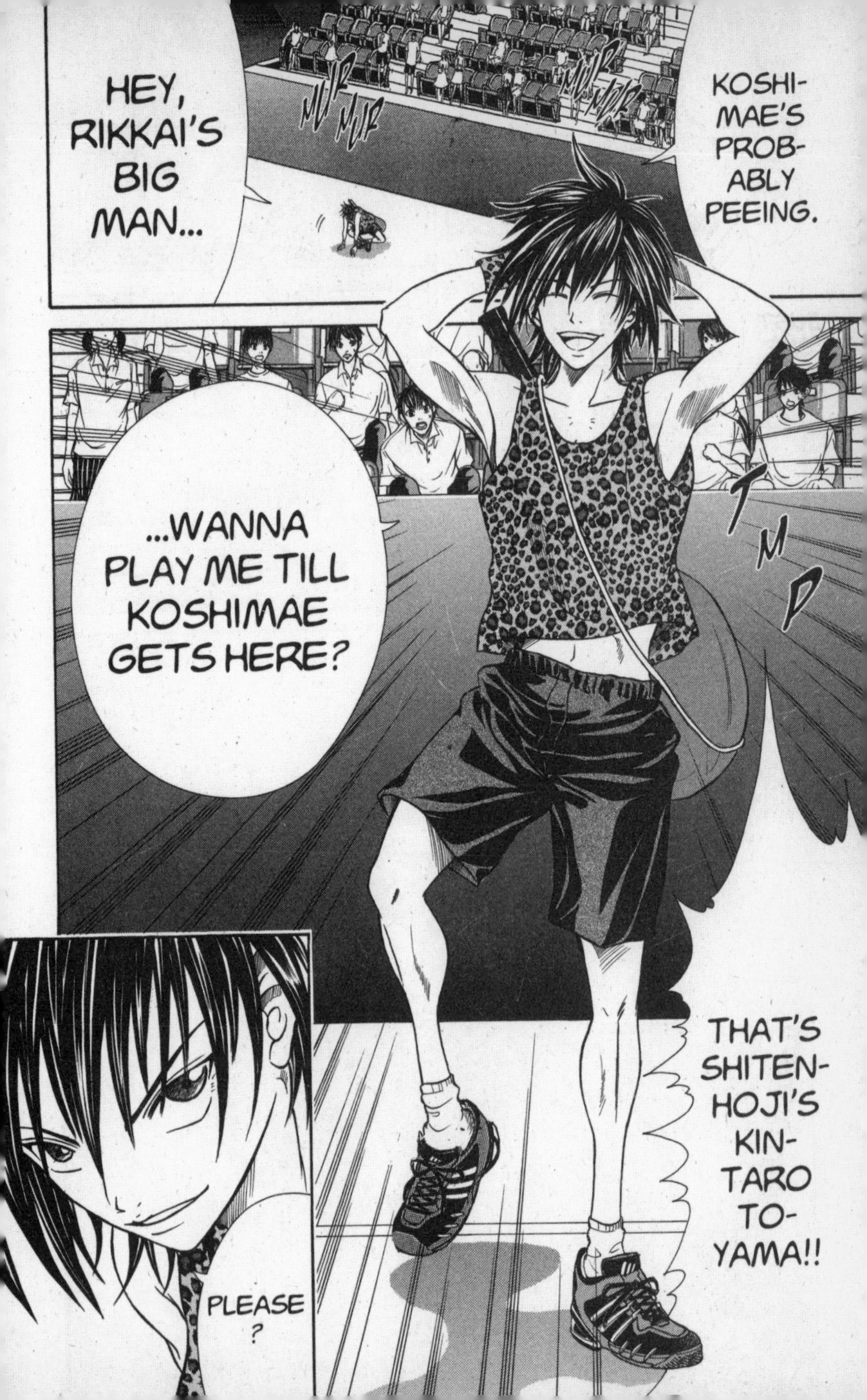
MUR MUR
MUR MUR
KOSHIMAE'S PROBABLY PEEING.
HEY, RIKKAI'S BIG MAN...
TMP
...WANNA PLAY ME TILL KOSHIMAE GETS HERE?
THAT'S SHITENHOJI'S KINTARO TOYAMA!!
PLEASE?

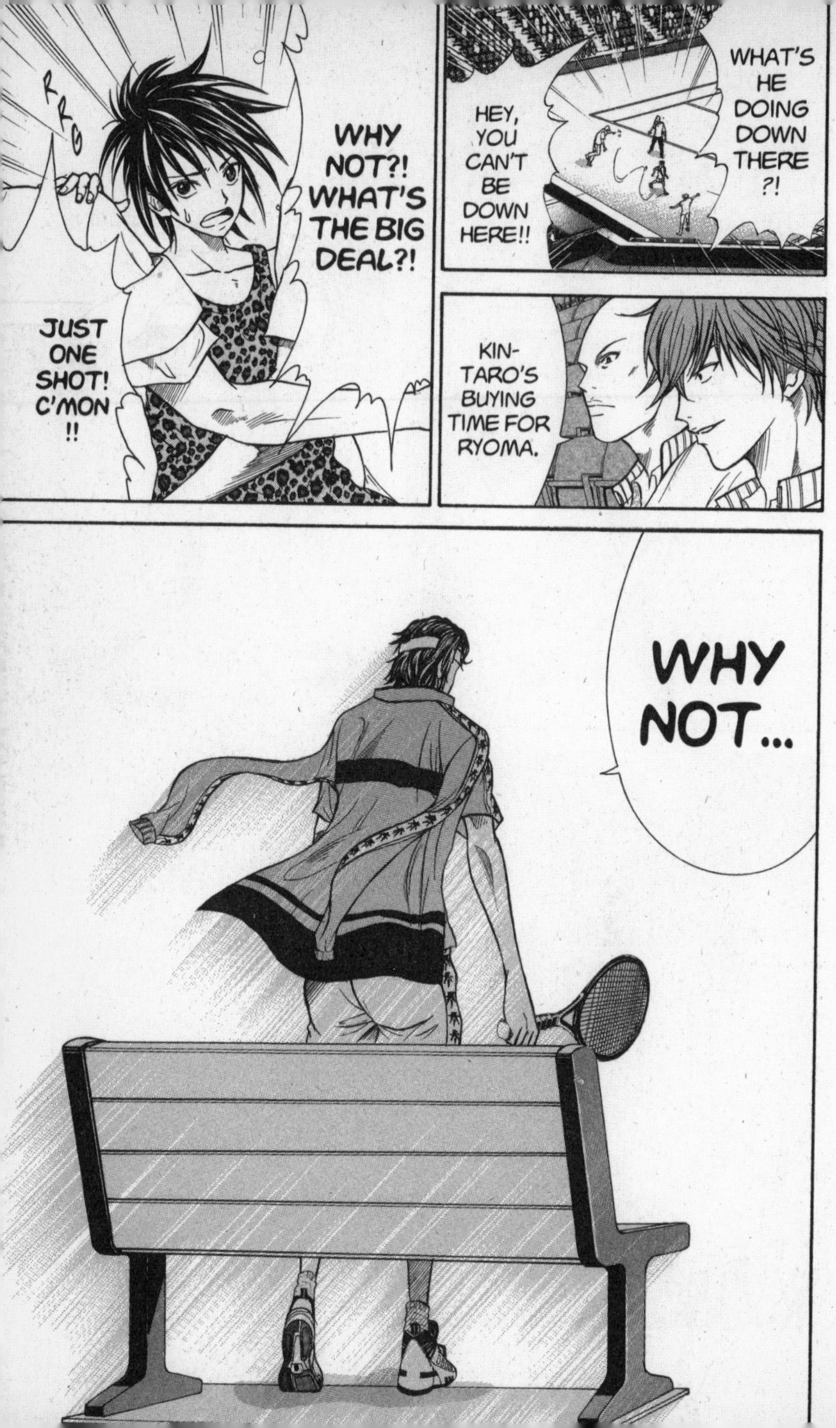
WHAT'S HE DOING DOWN THERE?!
HEY, YOU CAN'T BE DOWN HERE!!
KIN-TARO'S BUYING TIME FOR RYOMA.
WHY NOT?! WHAT'S THE BIG DEAL?!
RRG
JUST ONE SHOT! C'MON!!
WHY NOT...

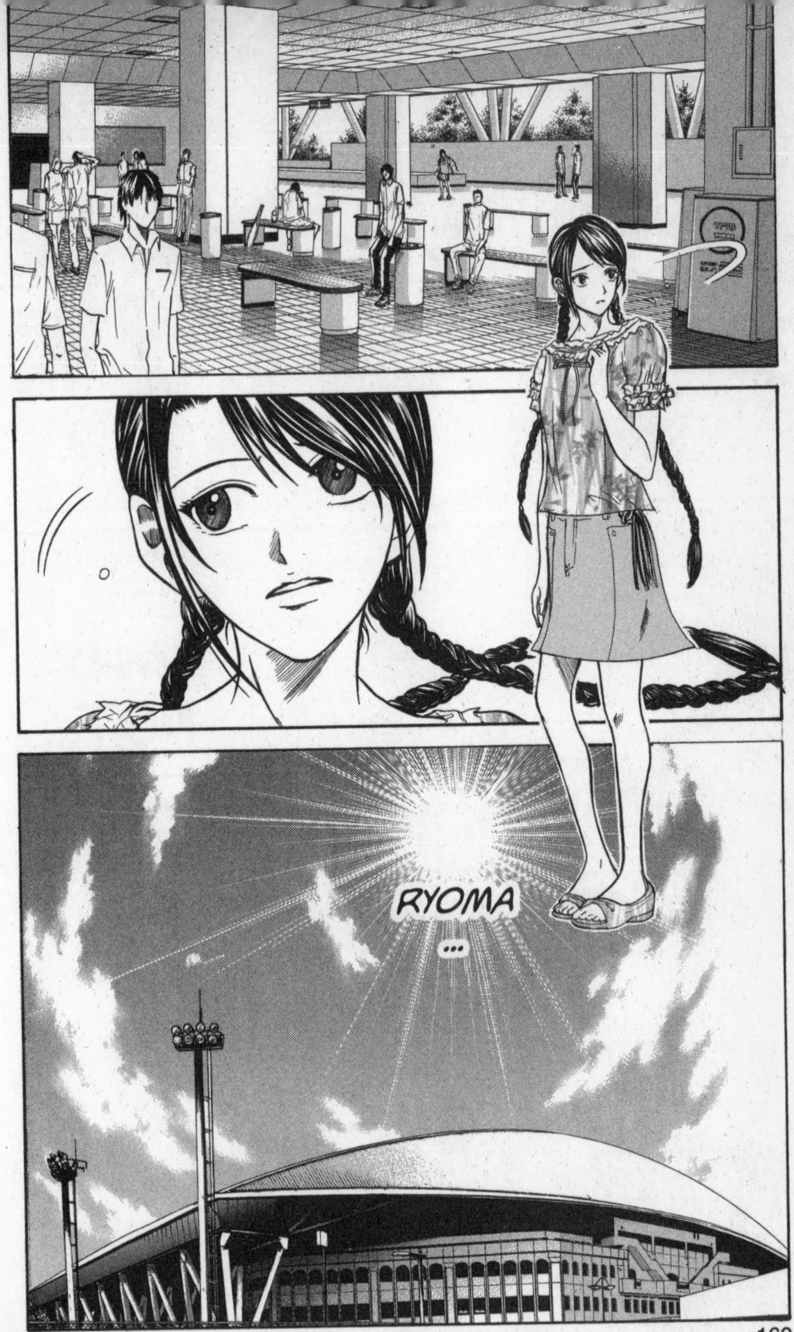
RYOMA
...

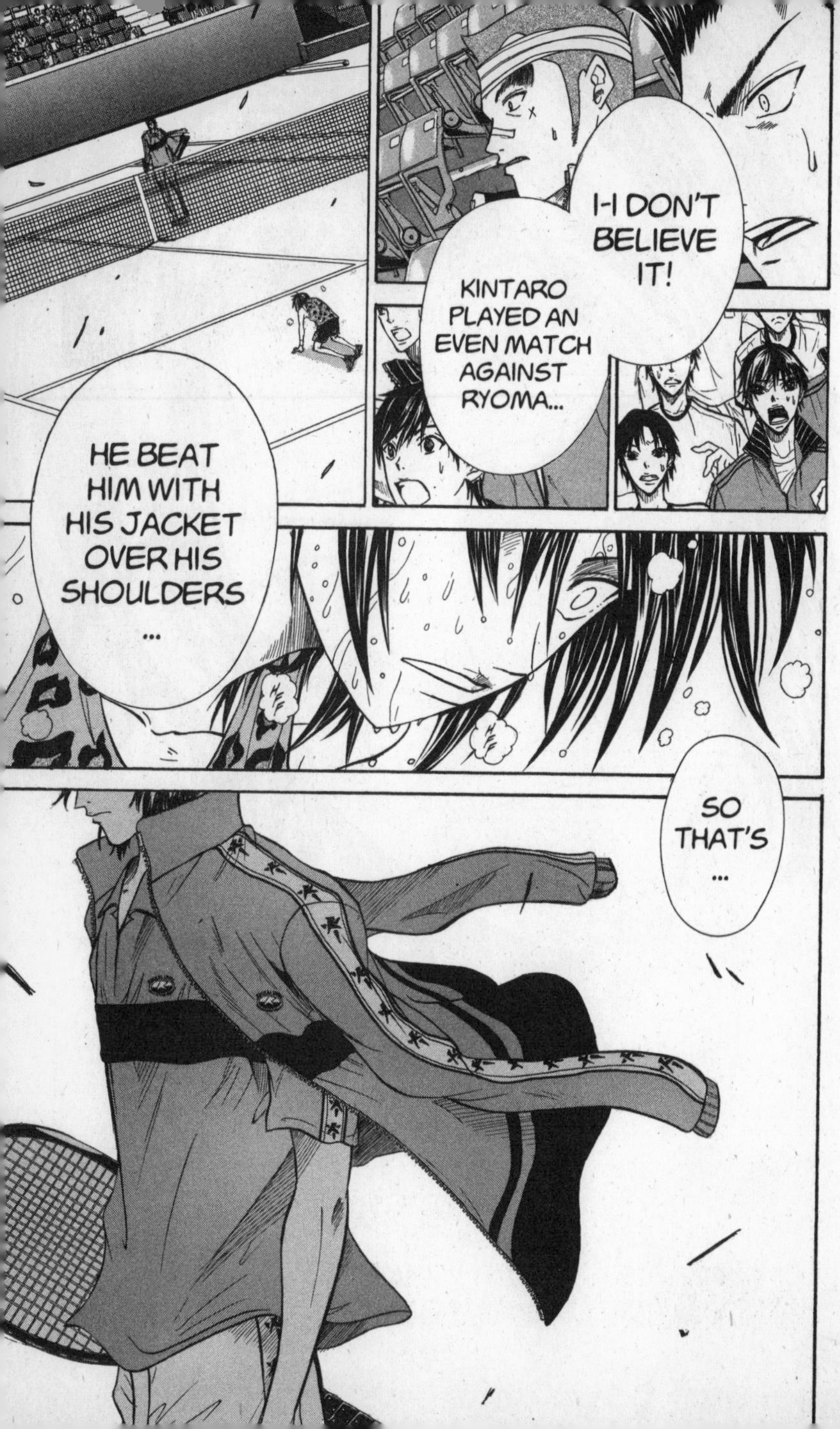
I-I DON'T BELIEVE IT!
KINTARO PLAYED AN EVEN MATCH AGAINST RYOMA...
HE BEAT HIM WITH HIS JACKET OVER HIS SHOULDERS ...
SO THAT'S ...

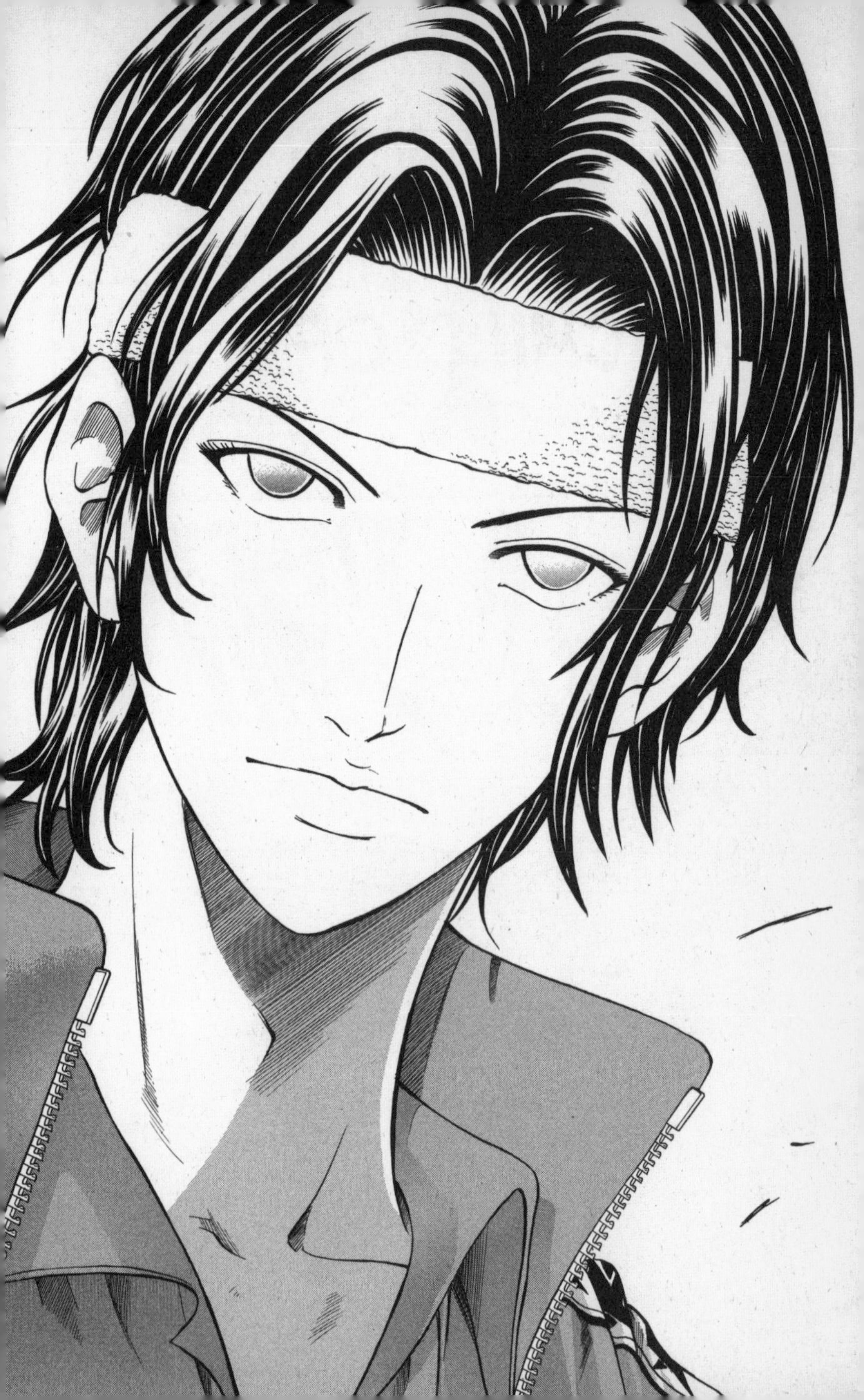

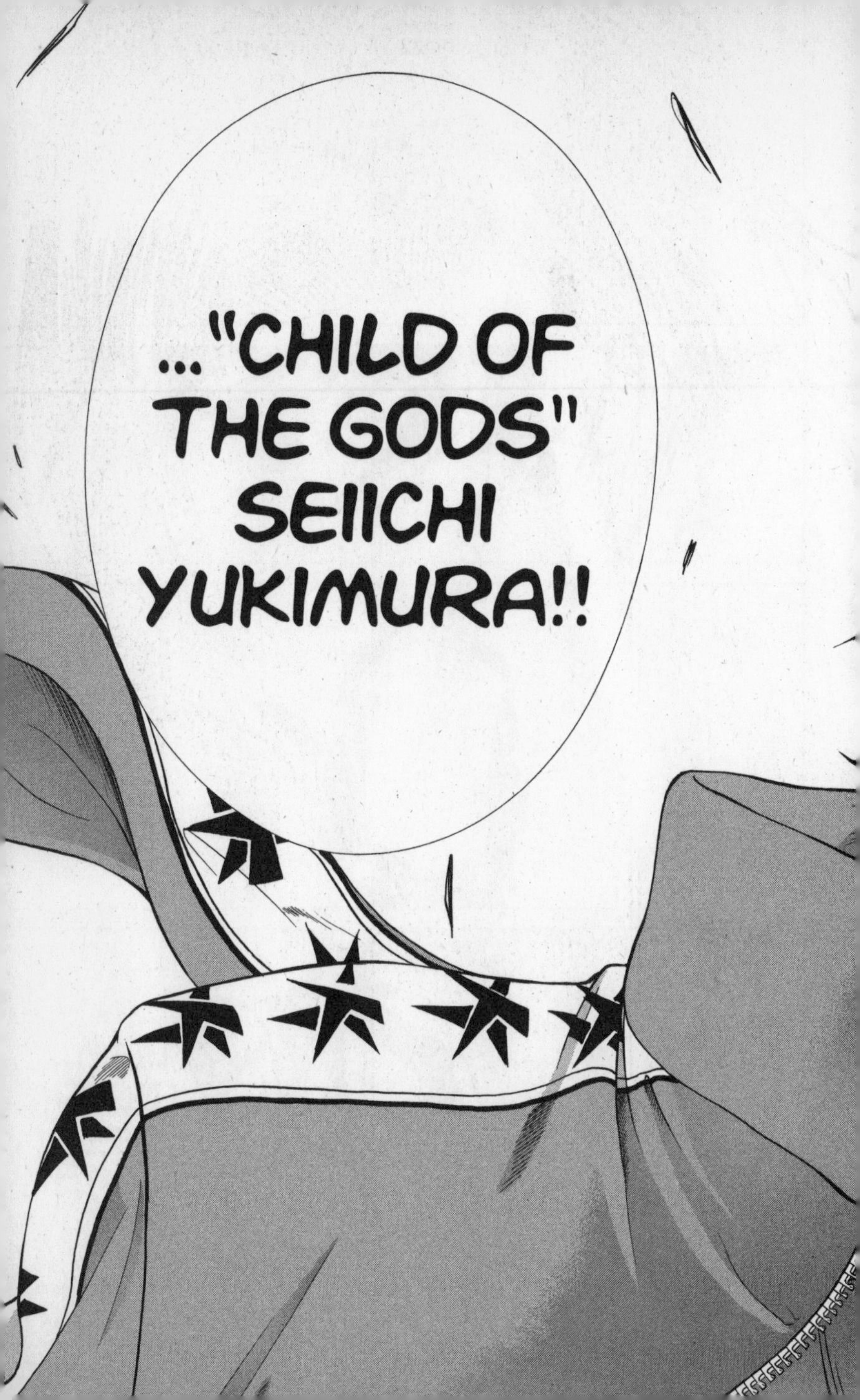
..."CHILD OF THE GODS" SEIICHI YUKIMURA!!

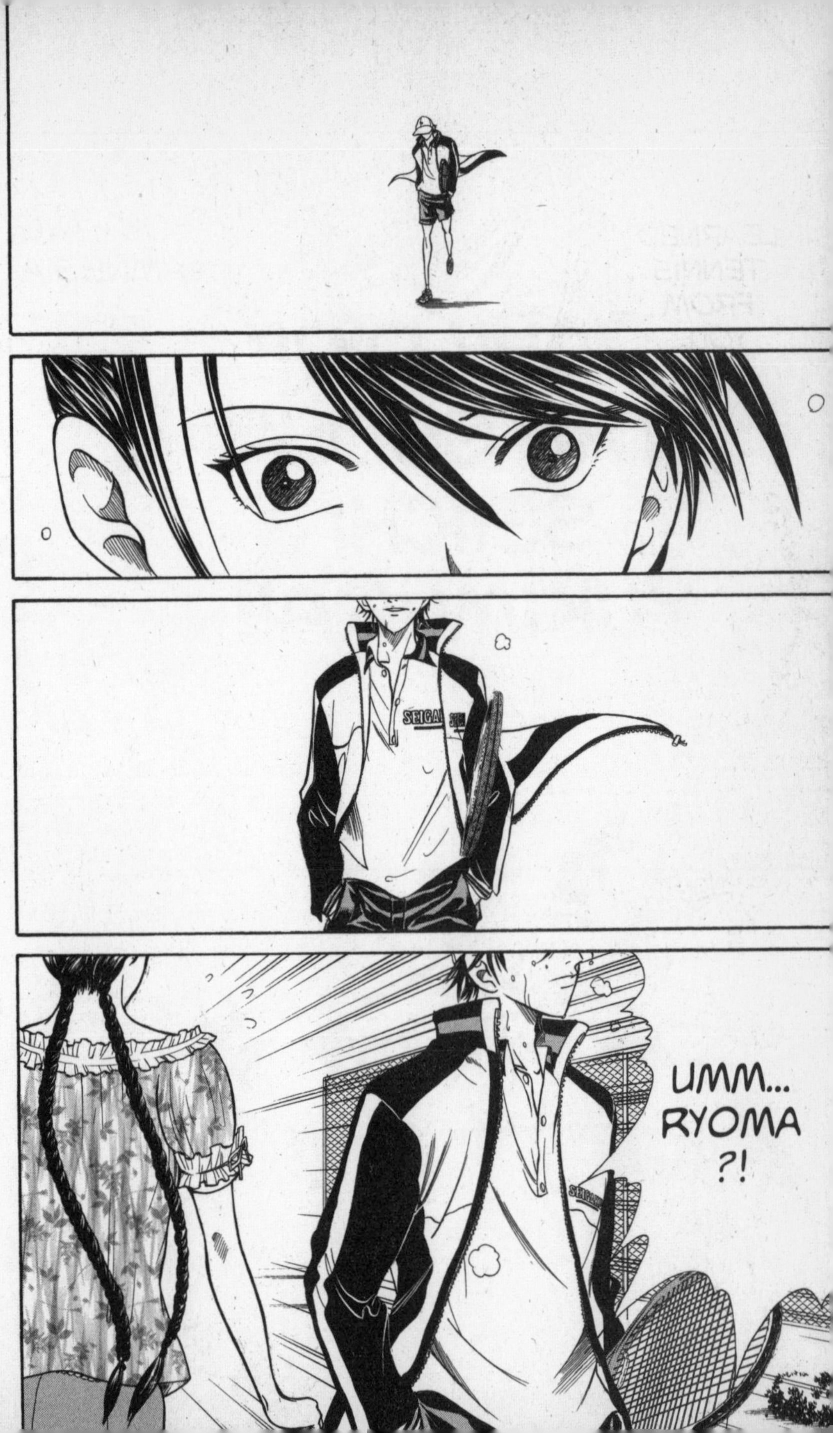
UMM... RYOMA ?!

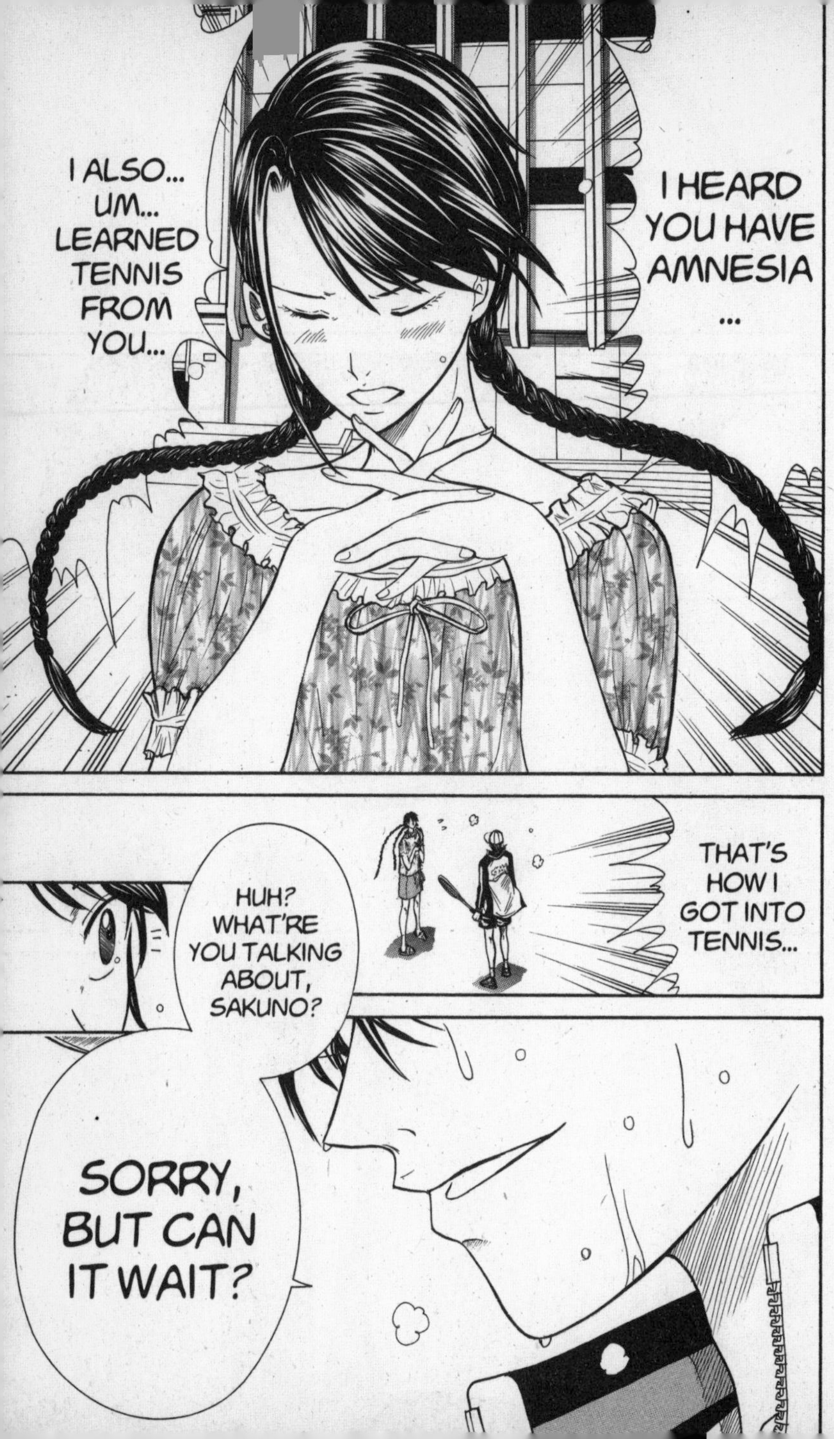
I HEARD YOU HAVE AMNESIA ...
I ALSO... UM... LEARNED TENNIS FROM YOU...
THAT'S HOW I GOT INTO TENNIS...
HUH? WHAT'RE YOU TALKING ABOUT, SAKUNO?
SORRY, BUT CAN IT WAIT?

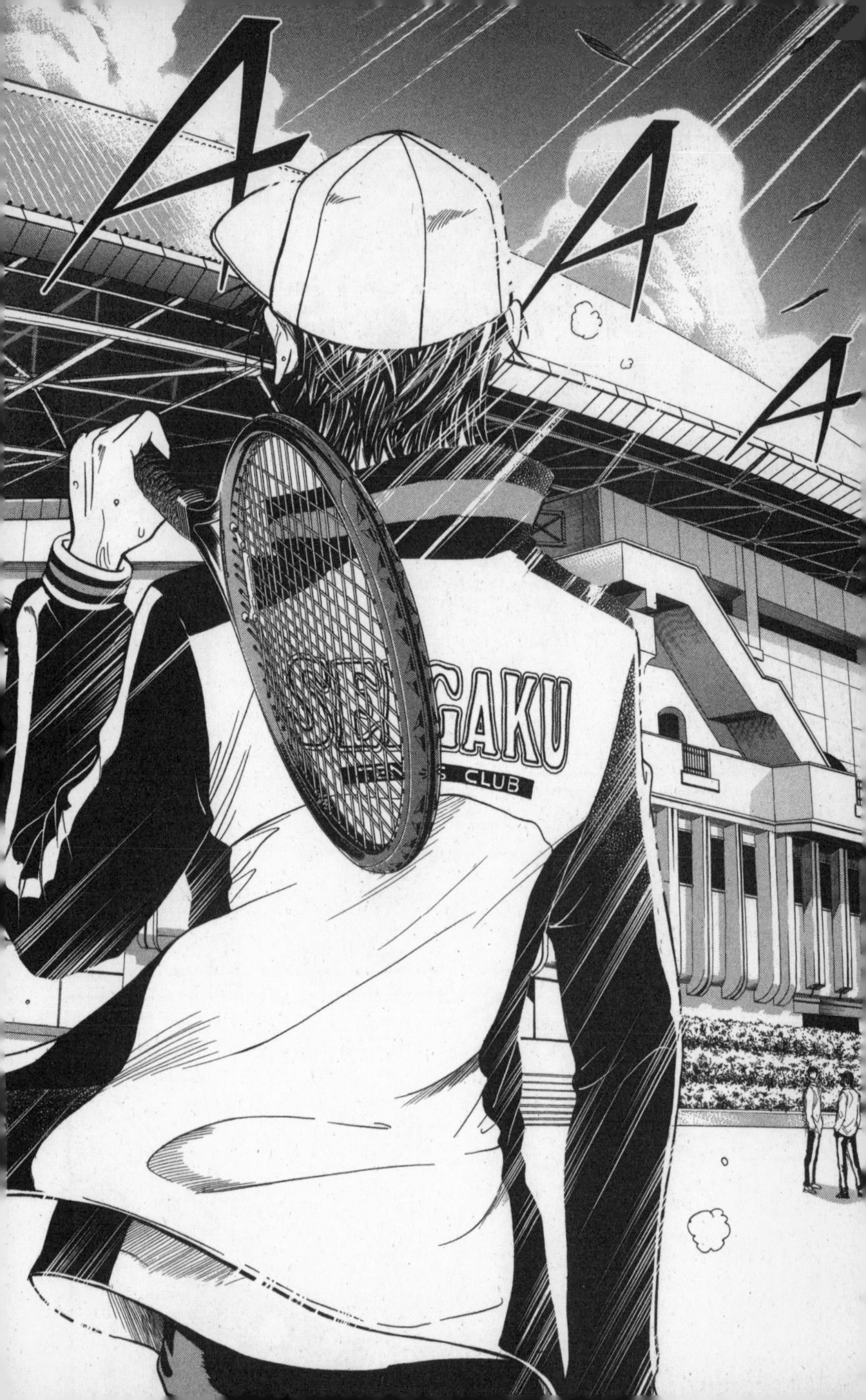
AAAA
CLUB

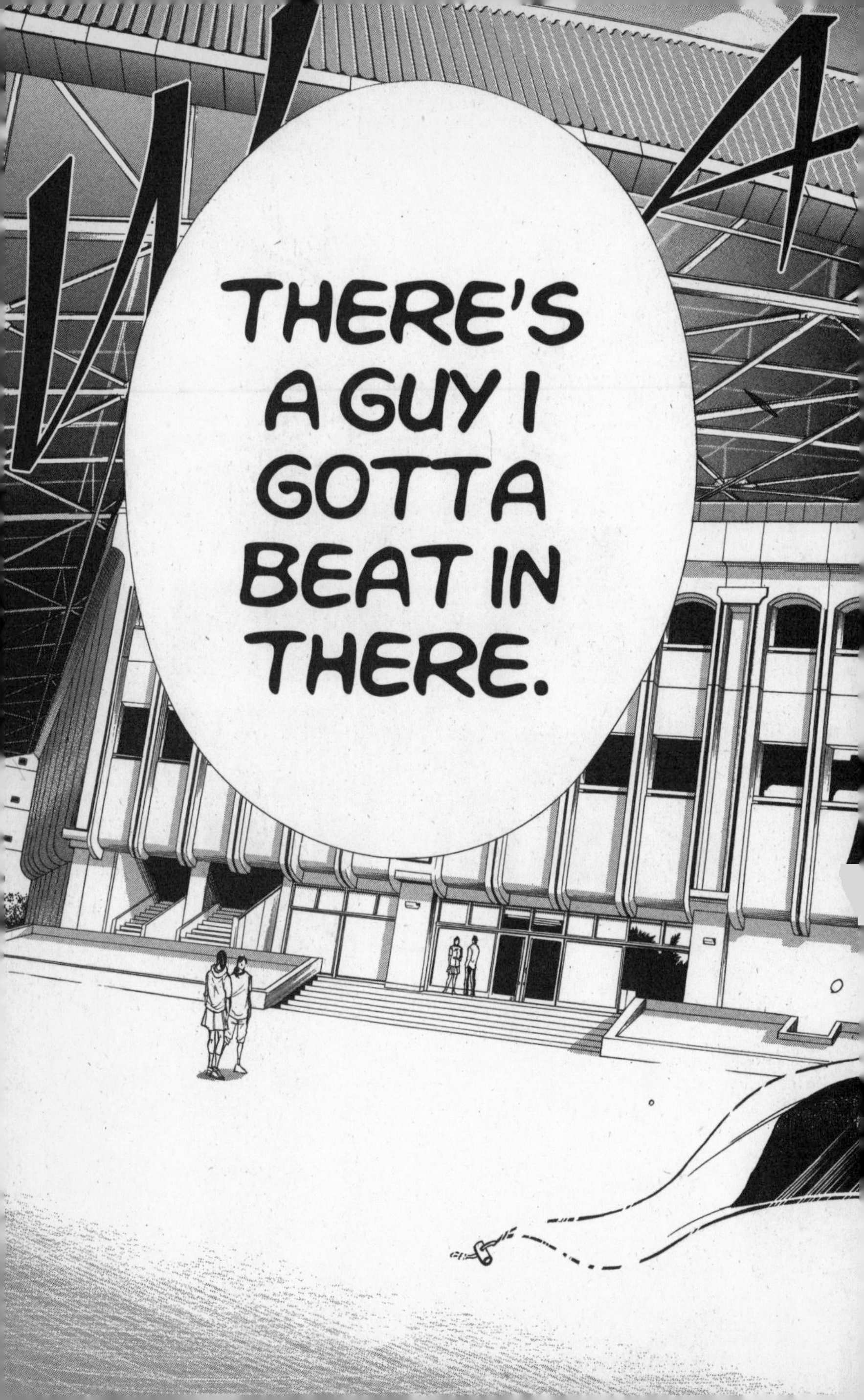
THERE'S A GUY I GOTTA BEAT IN THERE.

テニスの王子様

THE PRINCE OF TENNIS

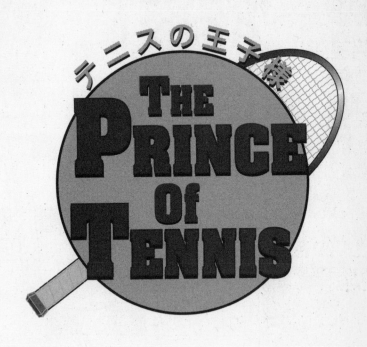

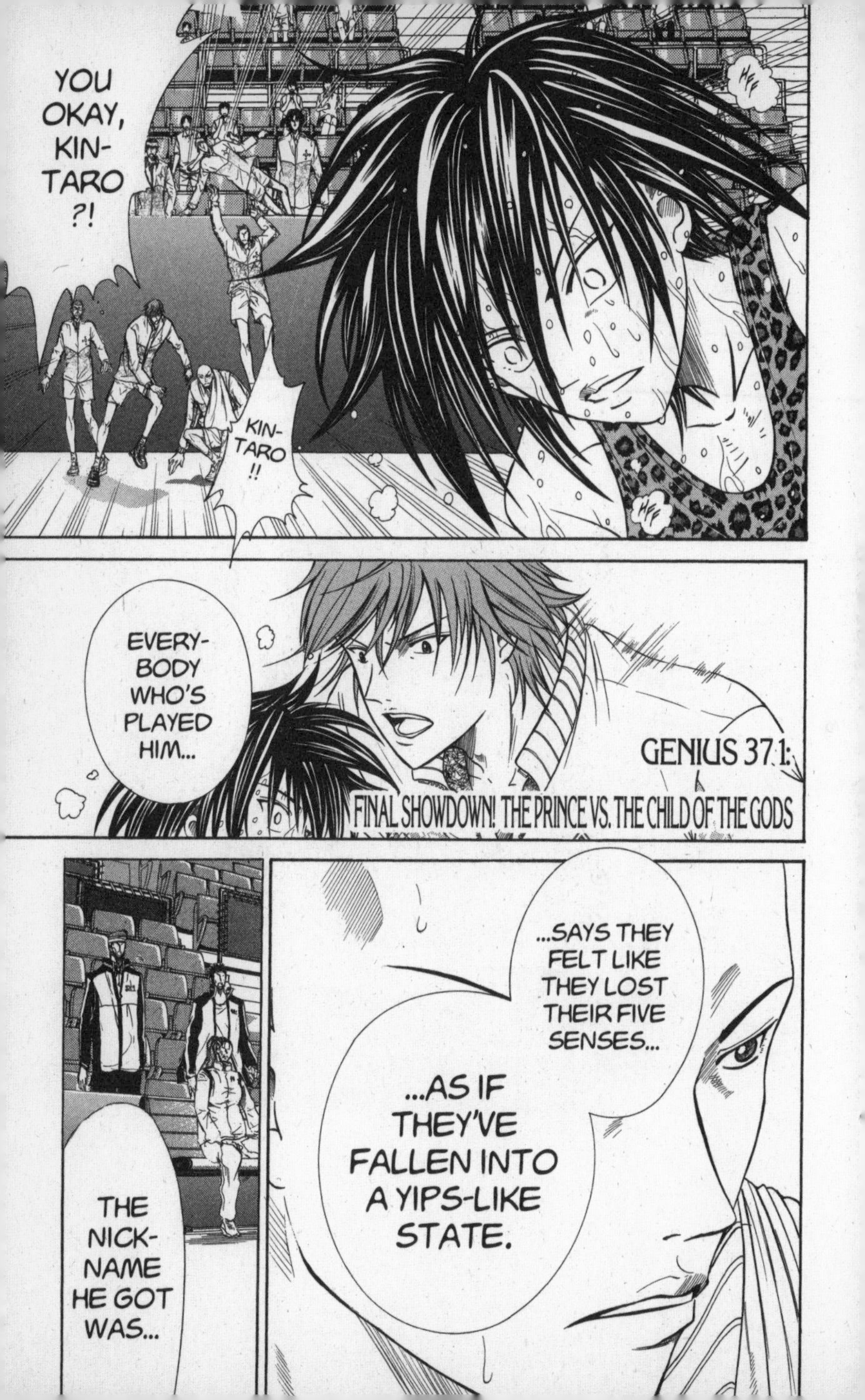
HFF
YOU OKAY, KIN-TARO?!
KIN-TARO!!
HFF
GENIUS 37.1:
FINAL SHOWDOWN! THE PRINCE VS. THE CHILD OF THE GODS
EVERYBODY WHO'S PLAYED HIM...
...SAYS THEY FELT LIKE THEY LOST THEIR FIVE SENSES...
...AS IF THEY'VE FALLEN INTO A YIPS-LIKE STATE.
THE NICKNAME HE GOT WAS...

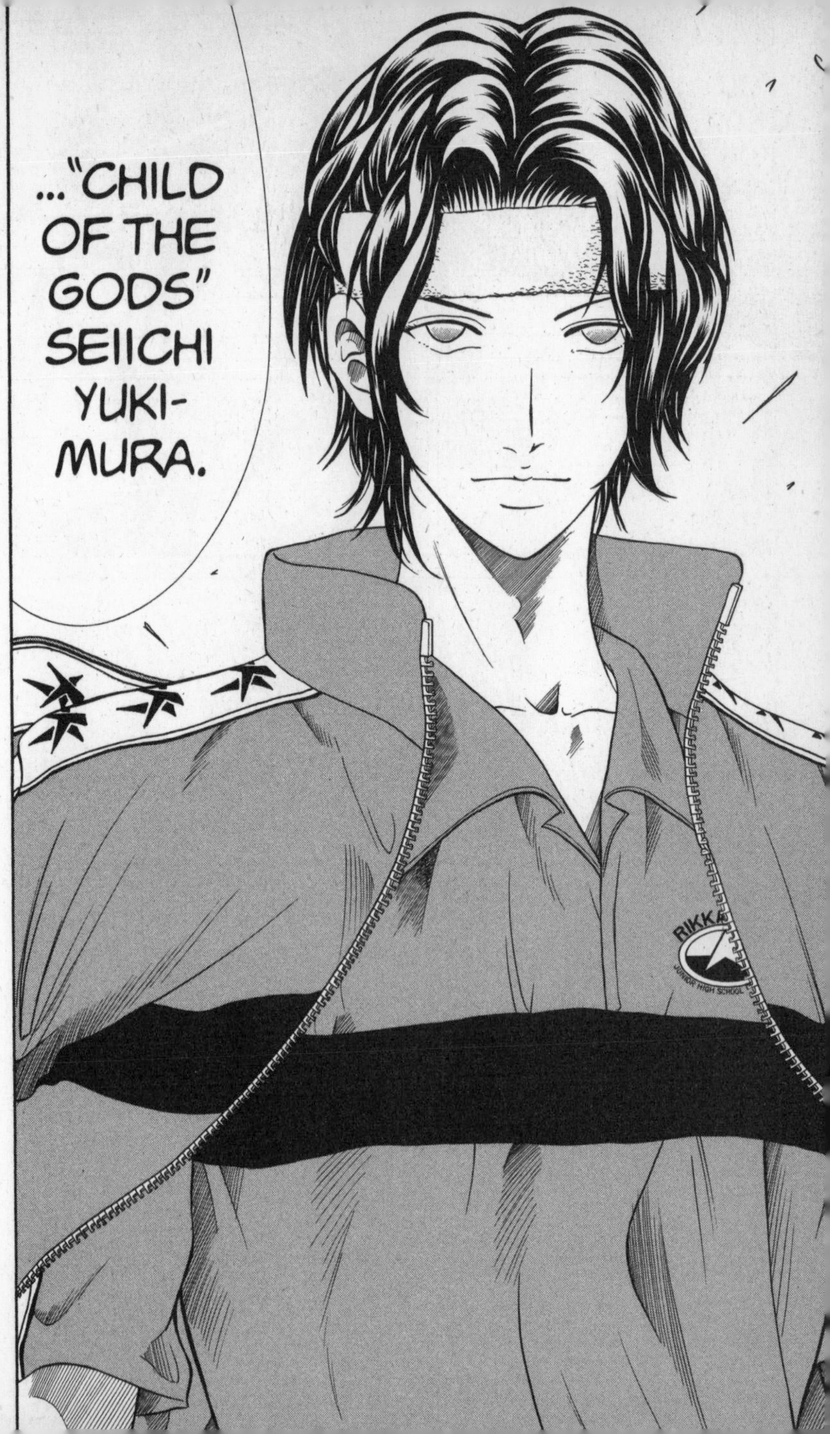
..."CHILD OF THE GODS" SEIICHI YUKI-MURA.
RIKKAI
JUNIOR HIGH SCHOOL

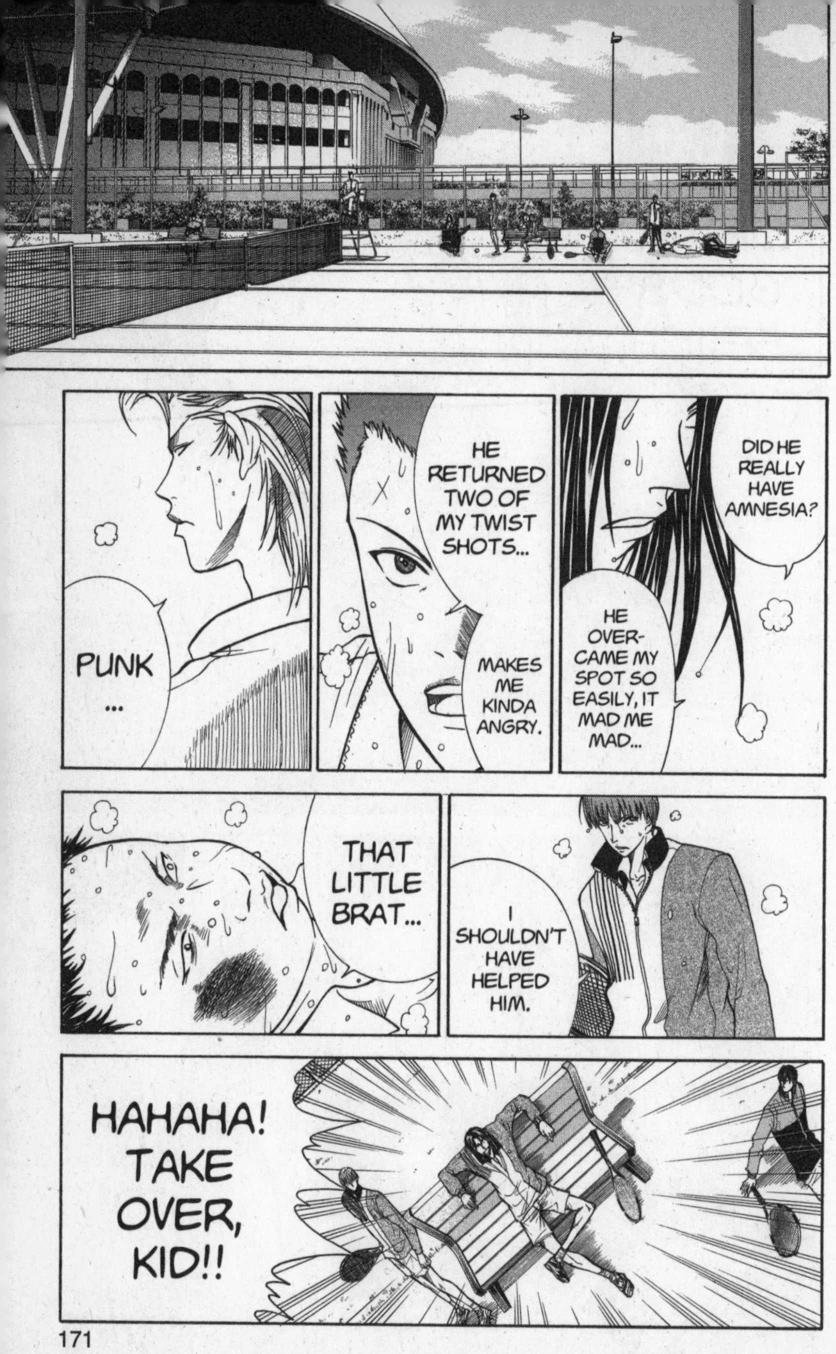
DID HE REALLY HAVE AMNESIA?
HE OVER-CAME MY SPOT SO EASILY, IT MAD ME MAD...
HE RETURNED TWO OF MY TWIST SHOTS...
MAKES ME KINDA ANGRY.
PUNK ...
I SHOULDN'T HAVE HELPED HIM.
THAT LITTLE BRAT...
HAHAHA! TAKE OVER, KID!!

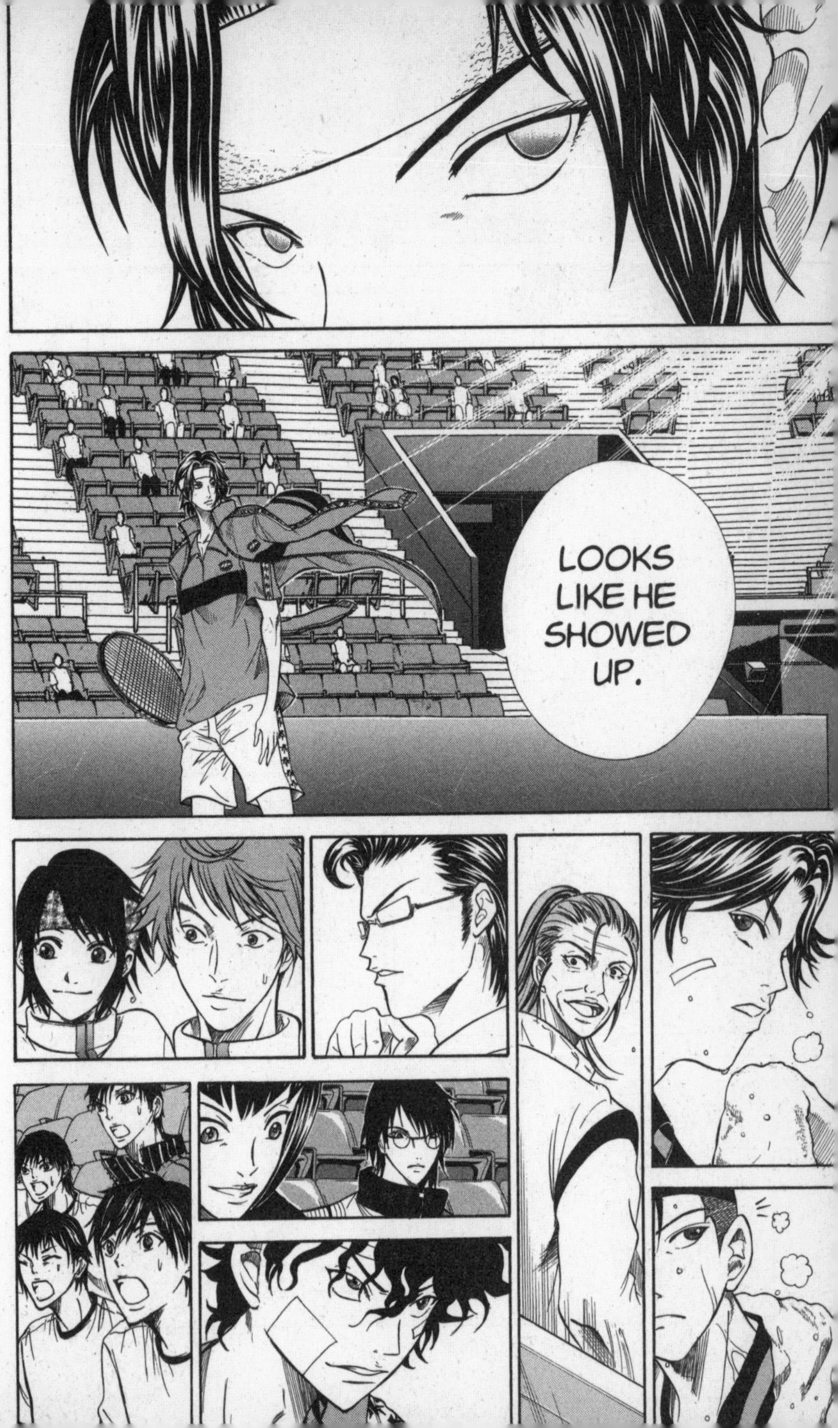
LOOKS LIKE HE SHOWED UP.

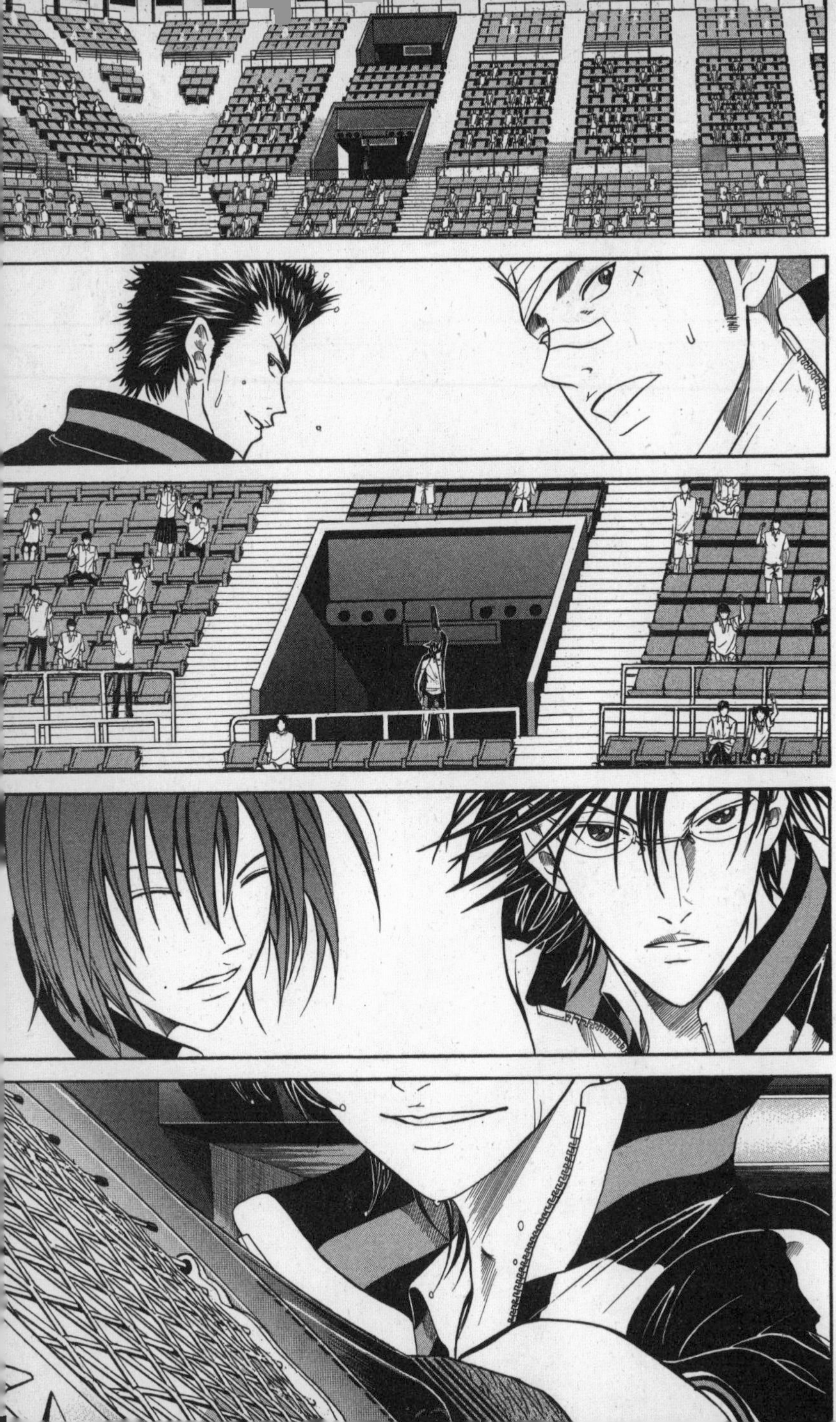

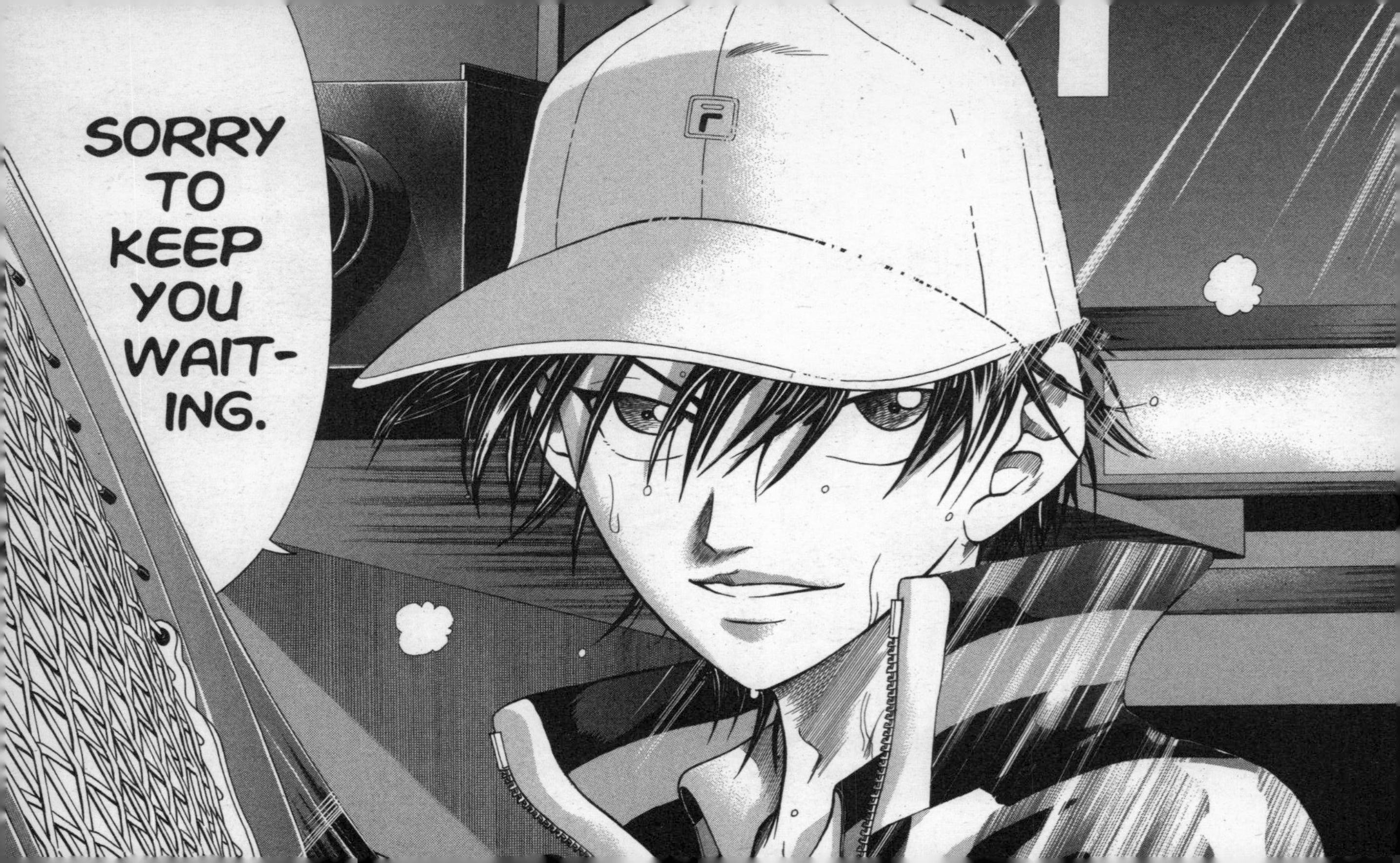
SORRY TO KEEP YOU WAIT-ING.

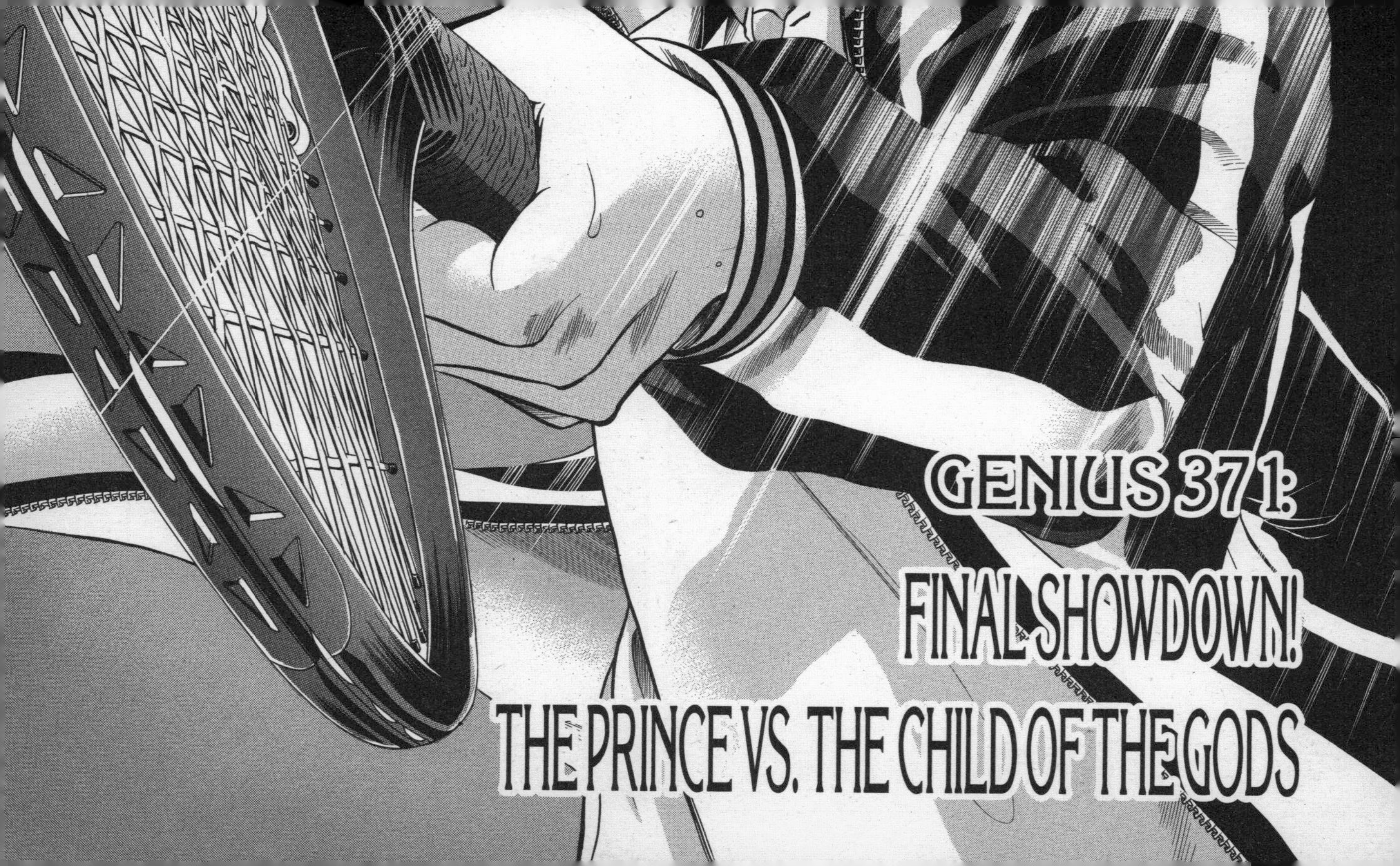
GENIUS 371:
FINAL SHOWDOWN!
THE PRINCE VS. THE CHILD OF THE GODS

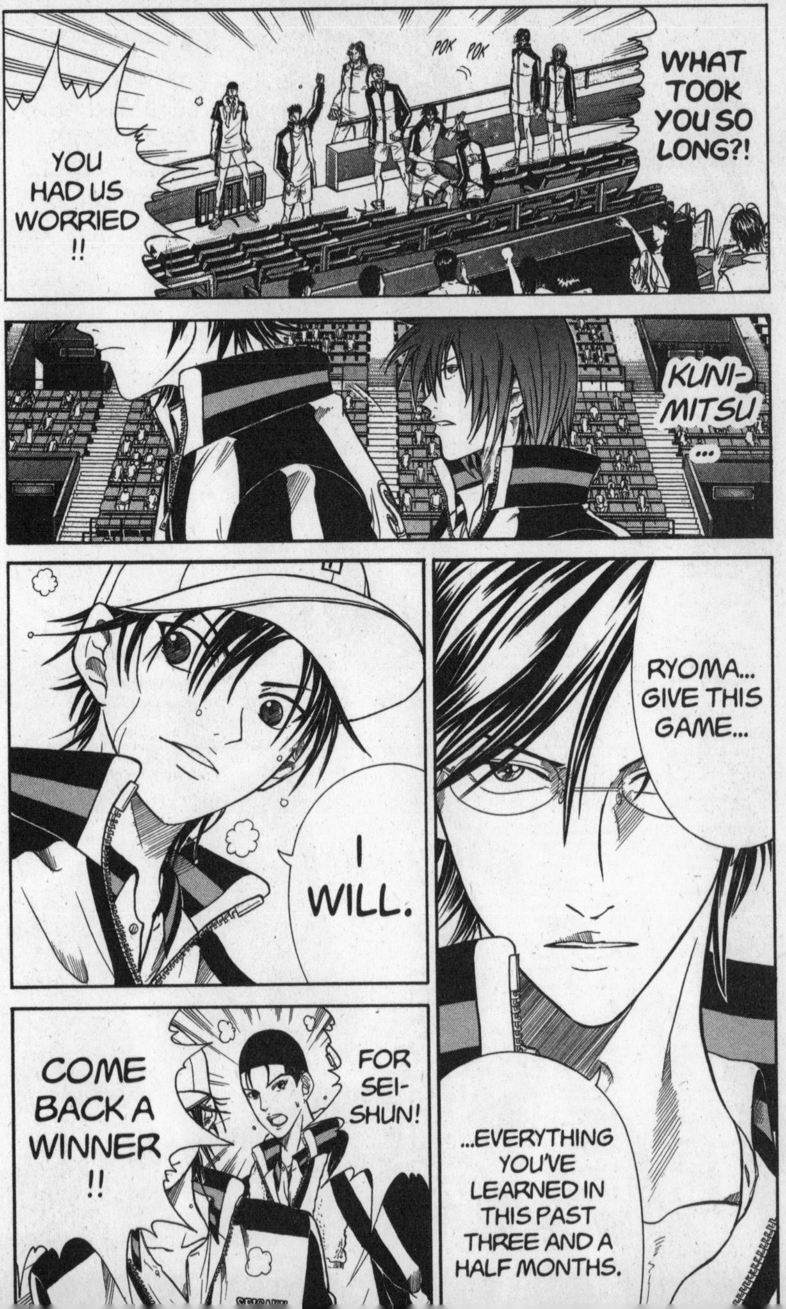
WHAT TOOK YOU SO LONG?!
POK POK
YOU HAD US WORRIED !!
KUNI-MITSU ...
RYOMA... GIVE THIS GAME...
...EVERYTHING YOU'VE LEARNED IN THIS PAST THREE AND A HALF MONTHS.
I WILL.
FOR SEI-SHUN!
COME BACK A WINNER !!

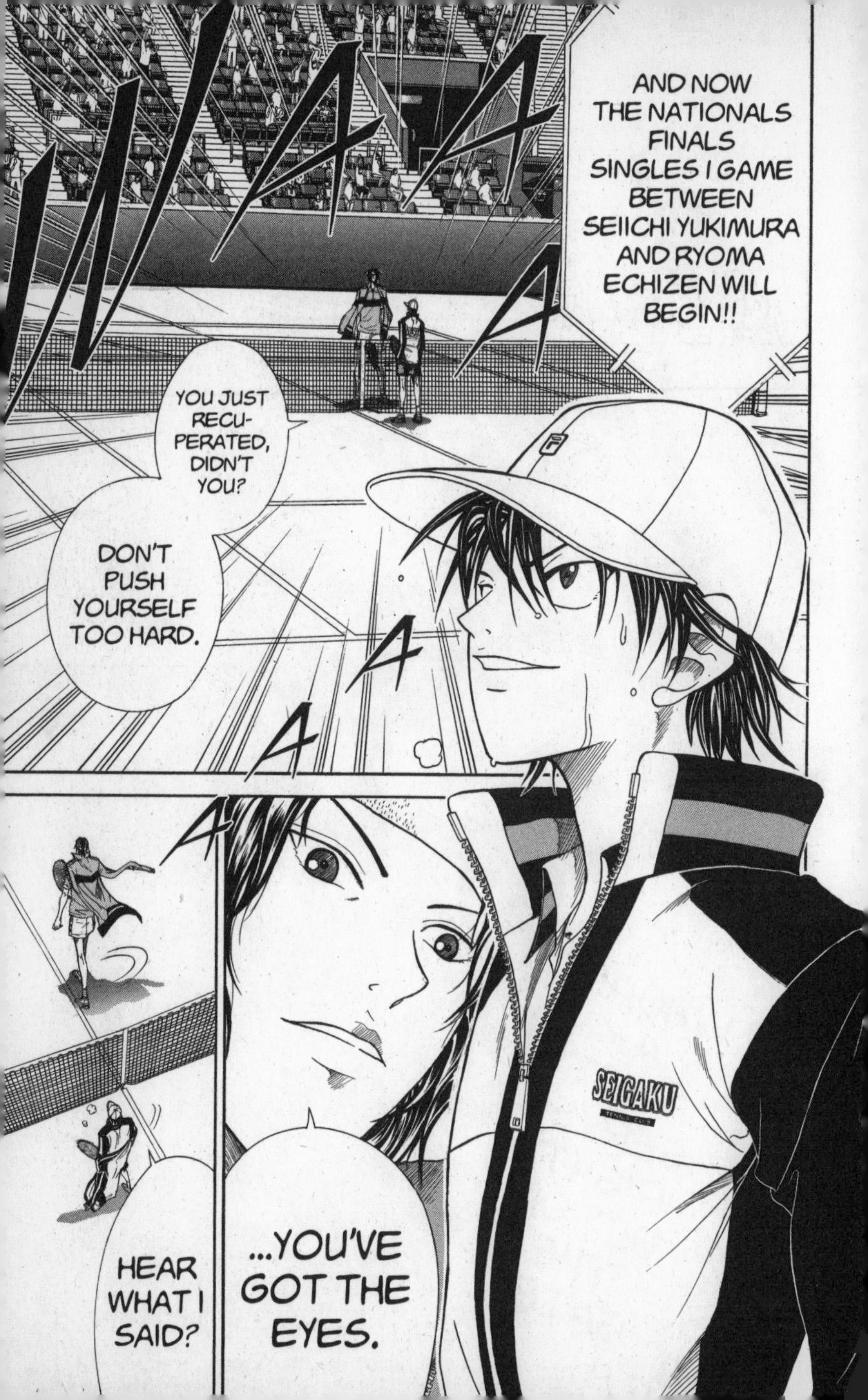
AND NOW THE NATIONALS FINALS SINGLES 1 GAME BETWEEN SEIICHI YUKIMURA AND RYOMA ECHIZEN WILL BEGIN!!
WAAAAAA
YOU JUST RECUPERATED, DIDN'T YOU?
DON'T PUSH YOURSELF TOO HARD.
SEIGAKU
...YOU'VE GOT THE EYES.
HEAR WHAT I SAID?

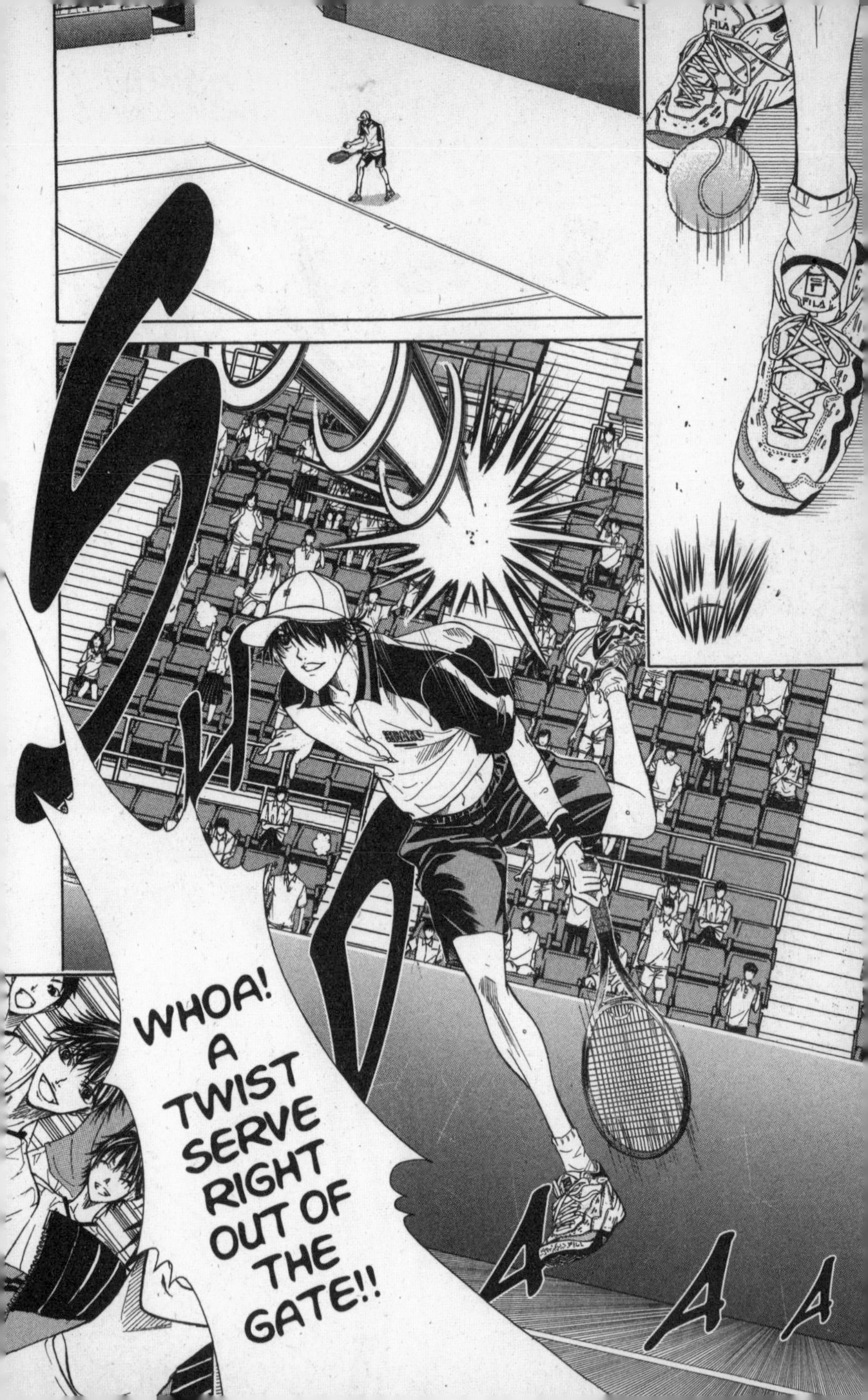
WHOA! A TWIST SERVE RIGHT OUT OF THE GATE!!

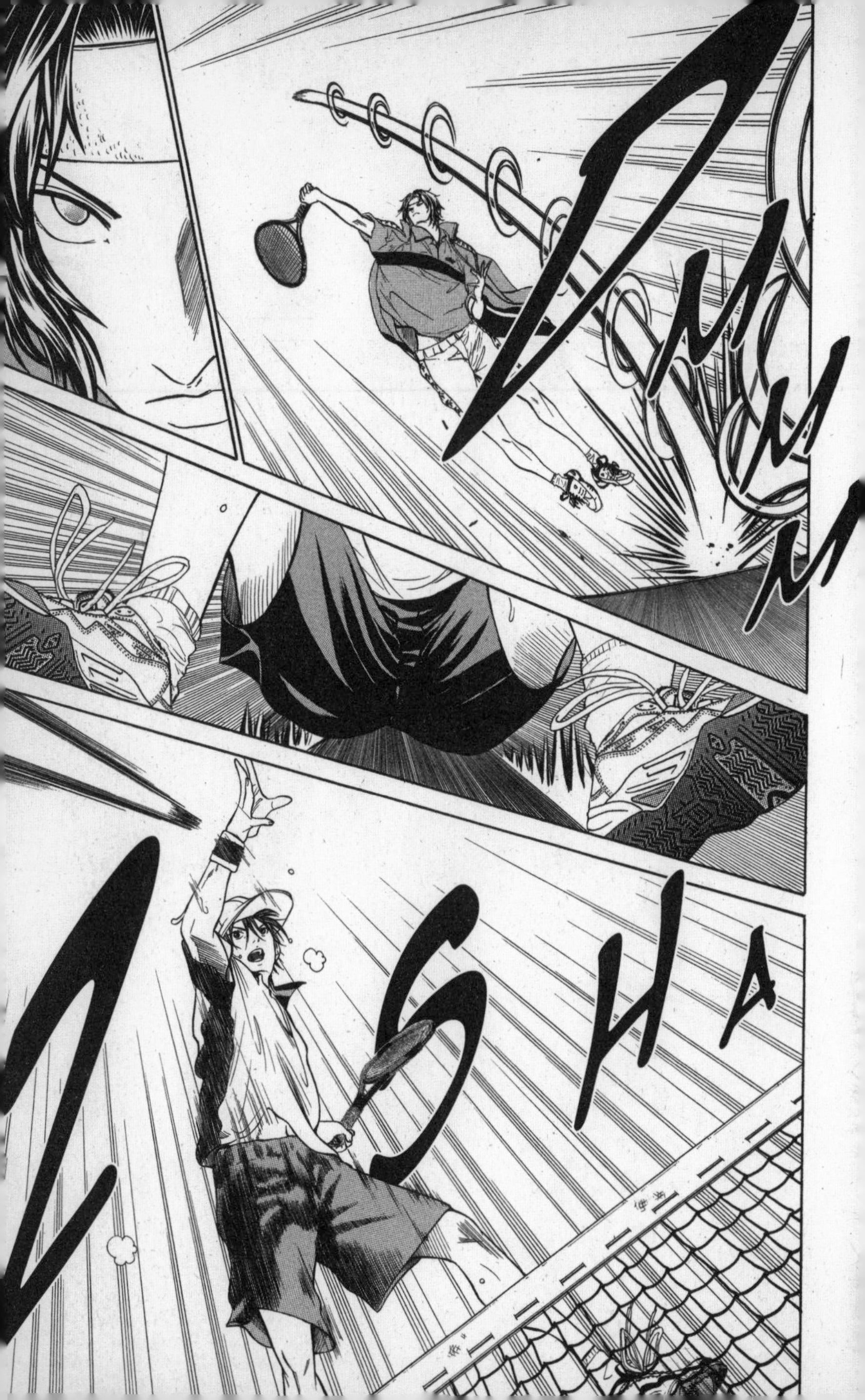
ZSHA

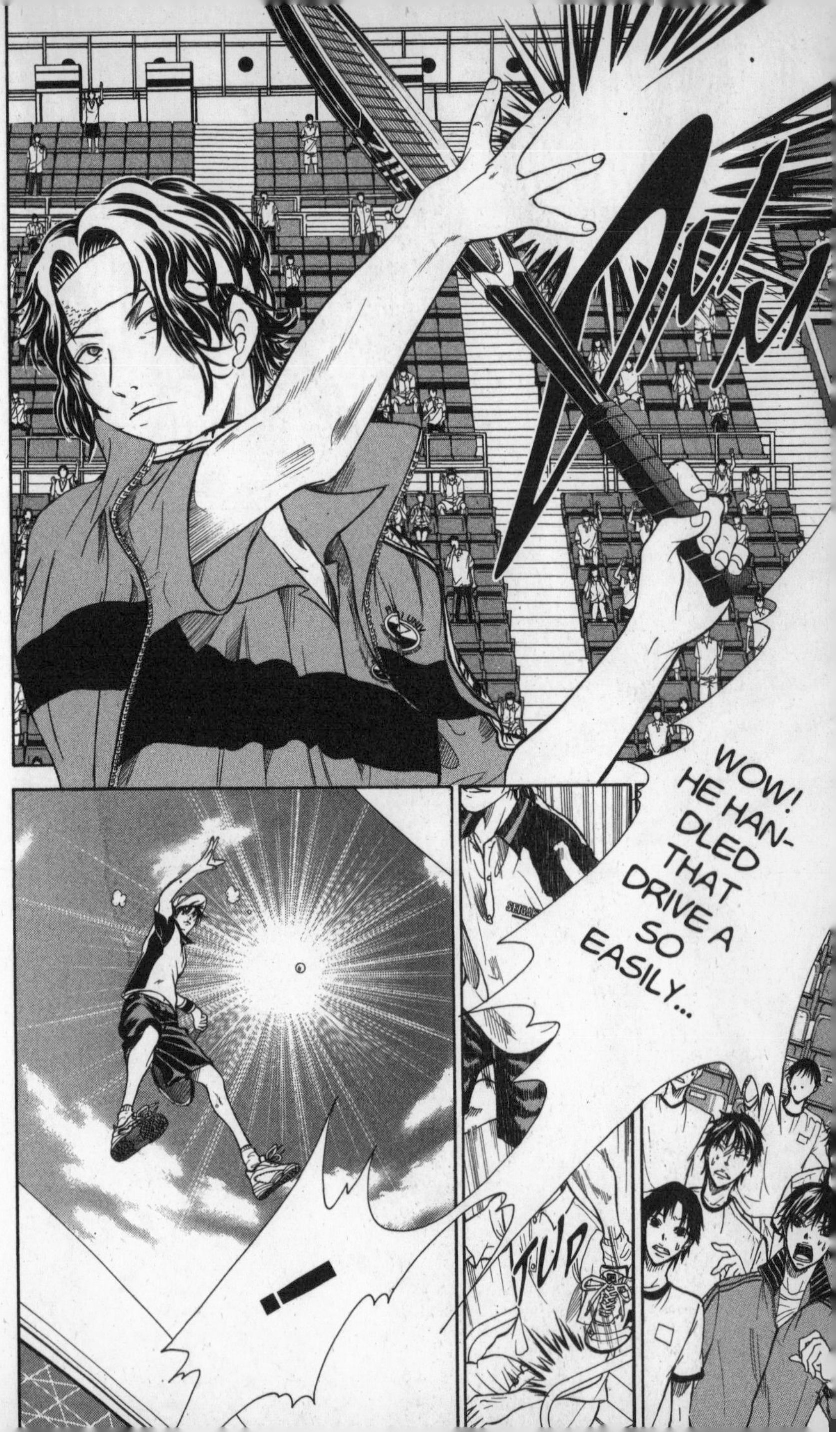
WOW! HE HANDLED THAT DRIVE A SO EASILY...
TUD

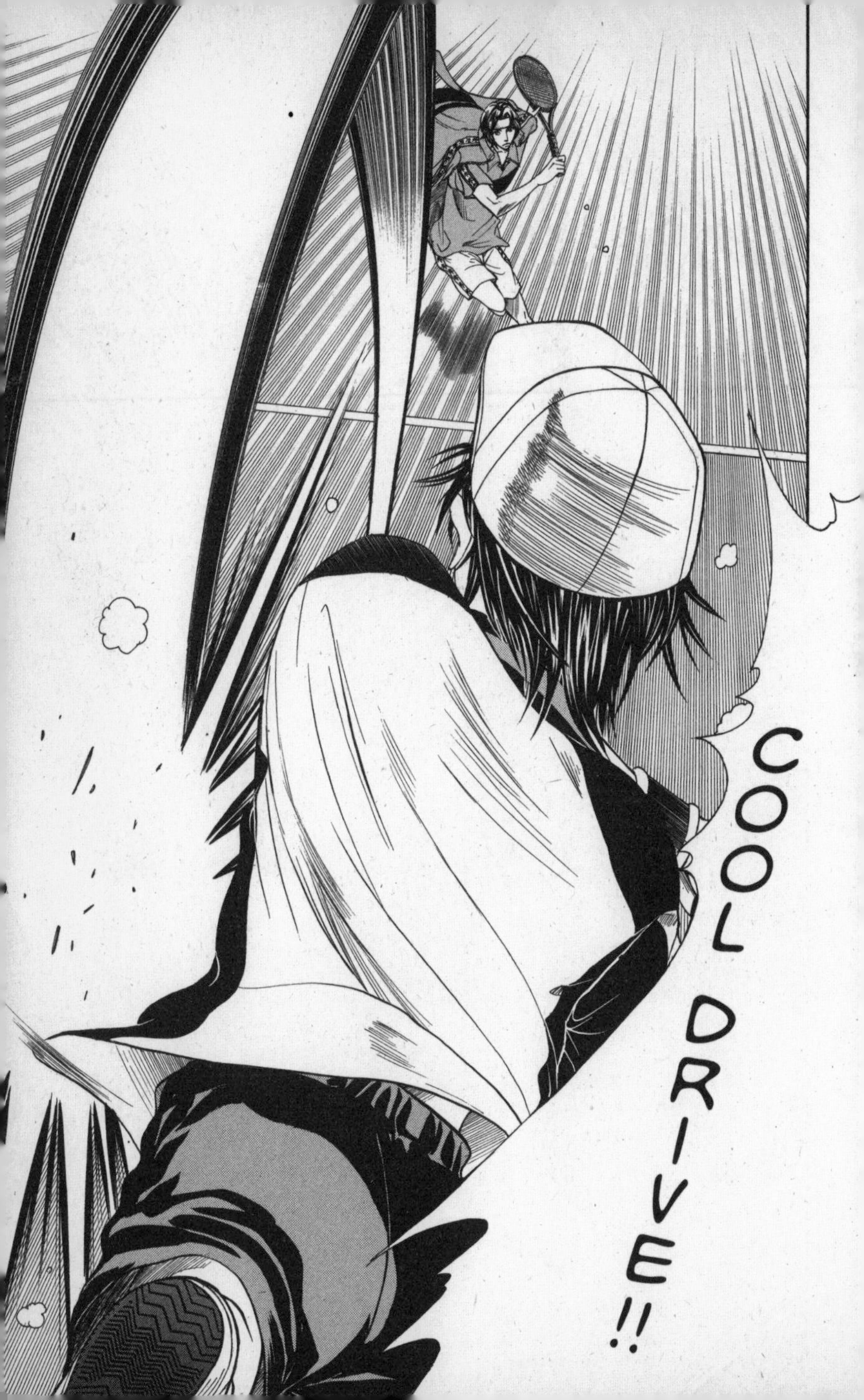
COOL DRIVE!!

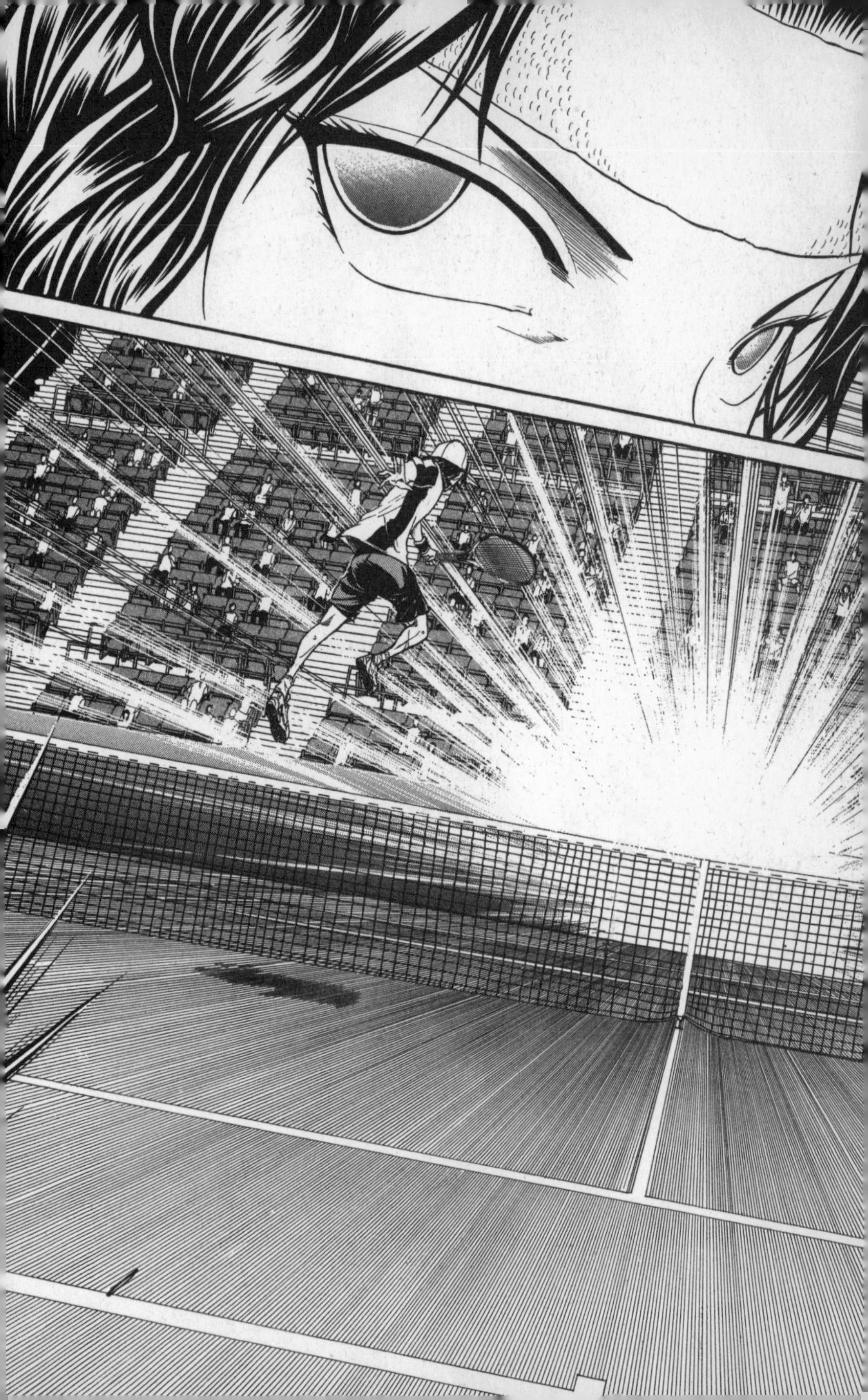

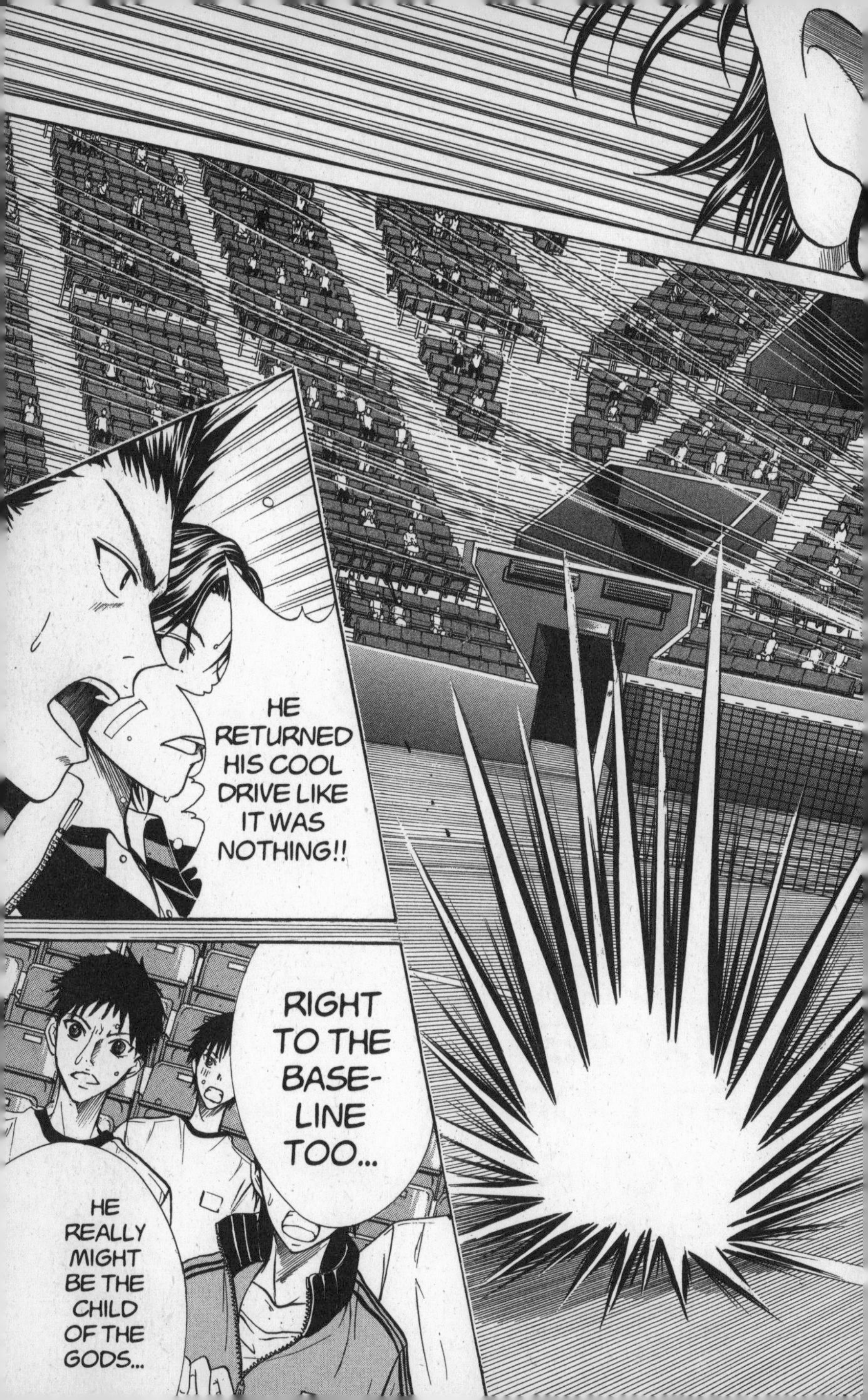
HE RETURNED HIS COOL DRIVE LIKE IT WAS NOTHING!!
RIGHT TO THE BASE-LINE TOO...
HE REALLY MIGHT BE THE CHILD OF THE GODS...

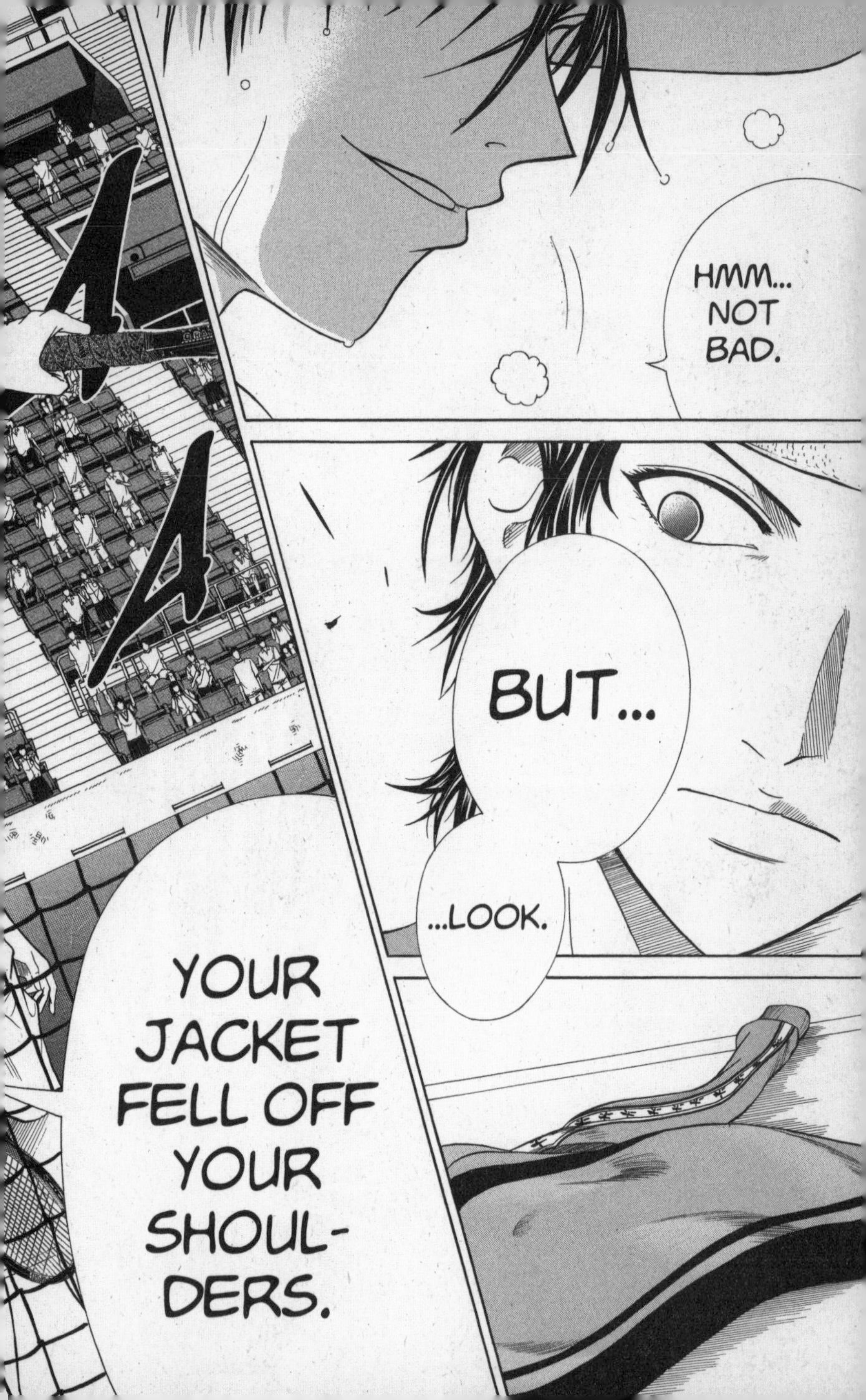
HMM... NOT BAD.
BUT...
...LOOK.
YOUR JACKET FELL OFF YOUR SHOUL-DERS.

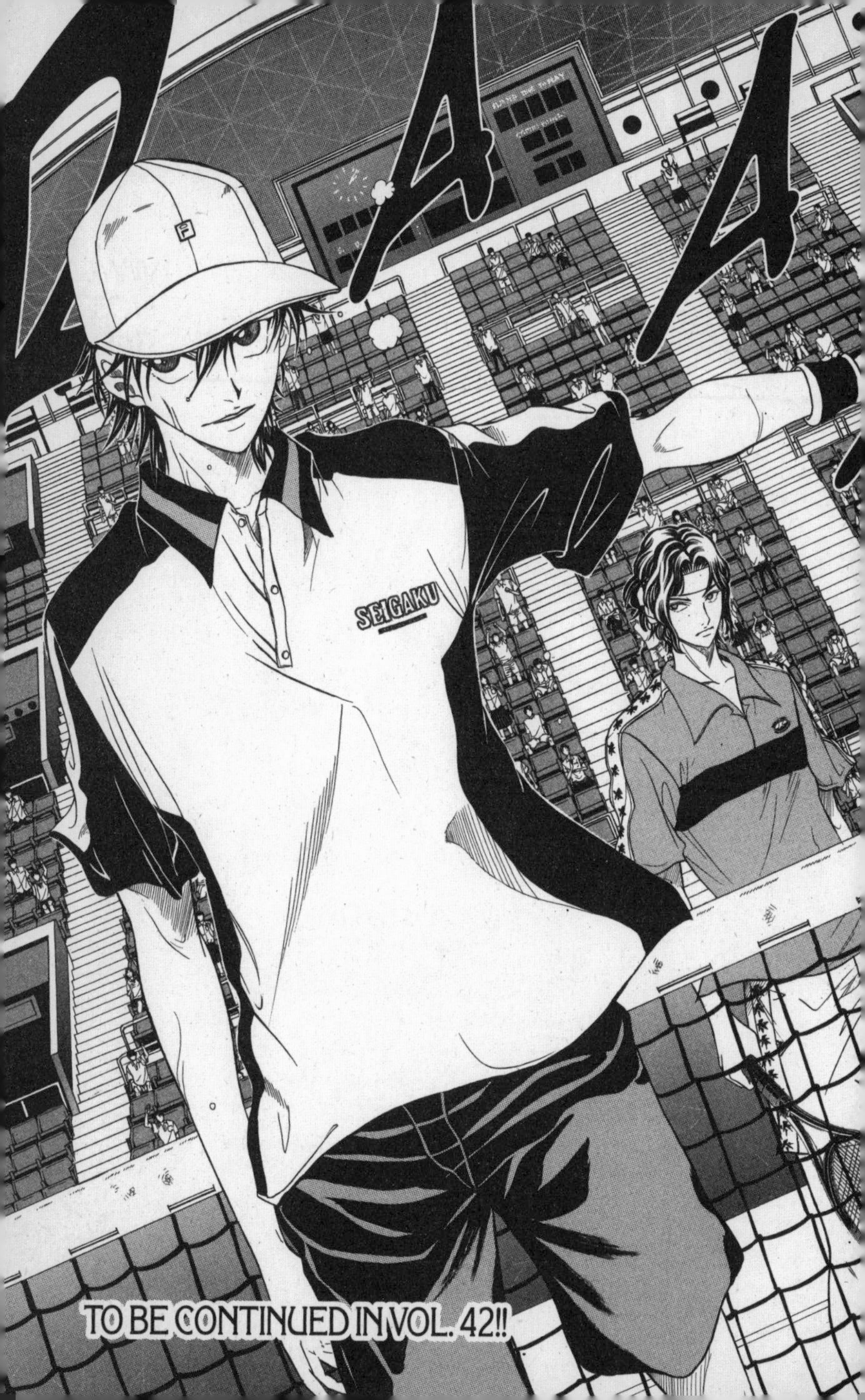
SEIGAKU
TO BE CONTINUED IN VOL. 42!!

FINAL VOLUME!

Dear Prince

The Seishun boys are just one match away from the national title! Ryoma brings out every shot he knows against Seiichi "Child of the Gods" Yukimura. But Yukimura's strange powers cause Ryoma to lose his sense of touch, then his sight. Swinging blindly, his hearing even begins to fail. Can Ryoma come back to win the Nationals for Seishun, or does he "still have a ways to go"?!

Available July 2011!

BAKUMAN。

STORY BY TSUGUMI OHBA
ART BY TAKESHI OBATA

From the creators of *Death Note*

The mystery behind manga making REVEALED!

Average student Moritaka Mashiro enjoys drawing for fun. When his classmate and aspiring writer Akito Takagi discovers his talent, he begs to team up. But what exactly does it take to make it in the manga-publishing world?

Bakuman。, Vol. 1
ISBN: 978-1-4215-3513-5
$9.99 US / $12.99 CAN *

Manga on sale at store.viz.com
Also available at your local bookstore or comic store

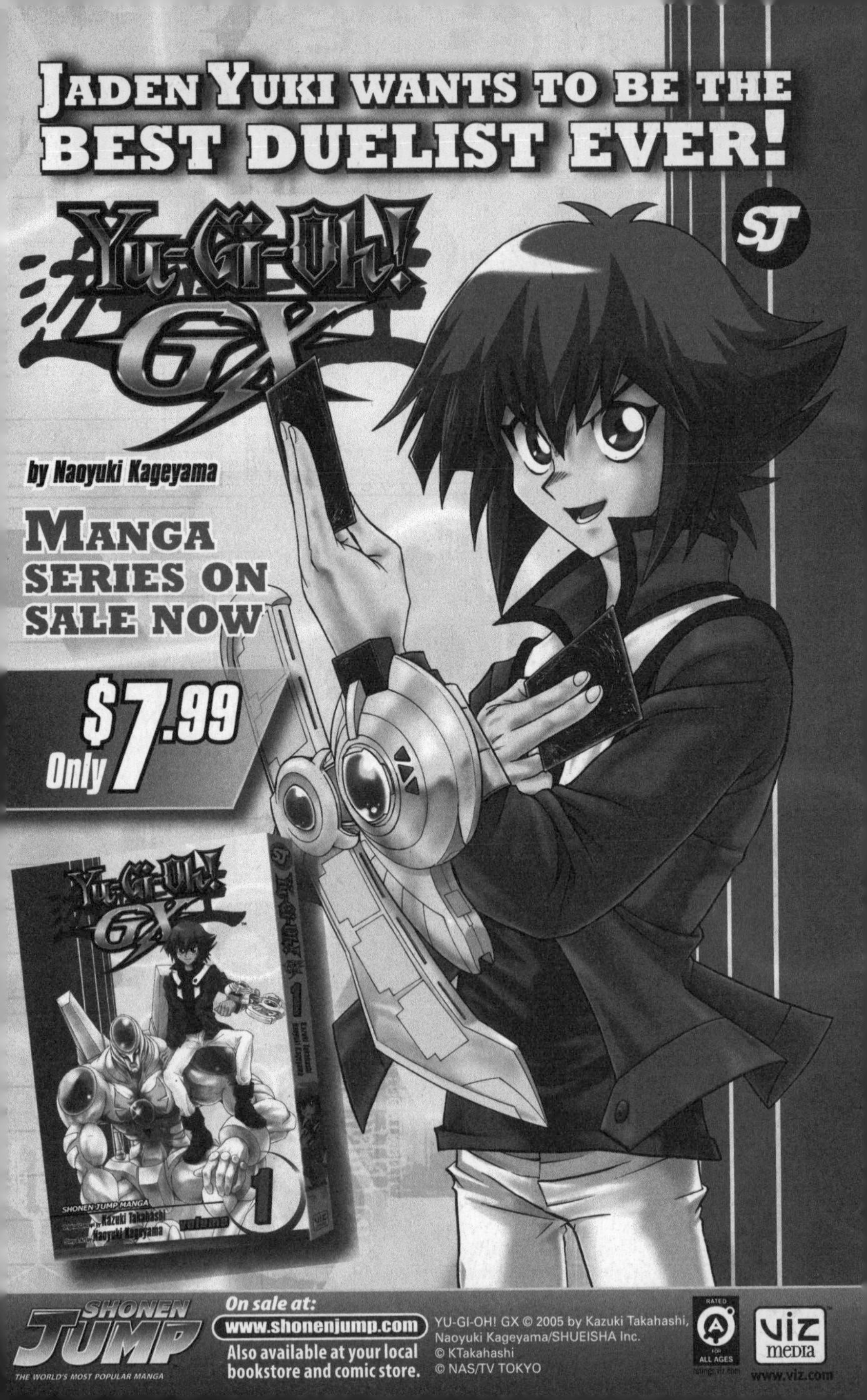
JADEN YUKI WANTS TO BE THE BEST DUELIST EVER!
SJ
YU-GI-OH! GX
by Naoyuki Kageyama
MANGA SERIES ON SALE NOW
Only $7.99
YU-GI-OH! GX
SHONEN JUMP MANGA
Kazuki Takahashi
Naoyuki Kageyama
1
SHONEN JUMP
THE WORLD'S MOST POPULAR MANGA
On sale at:
www.shonenjump.com
Also available at your local bookstore and comic store.
YU-GI-OH! GX © 2005 by Kazuki Takahashi, Naoyuki Kageyama/SHUEISHA Inc.
© KTakahashi
© NAS/TV TOKYO
RATED A FOR ALL AGES
VIZ media
www.viz.com

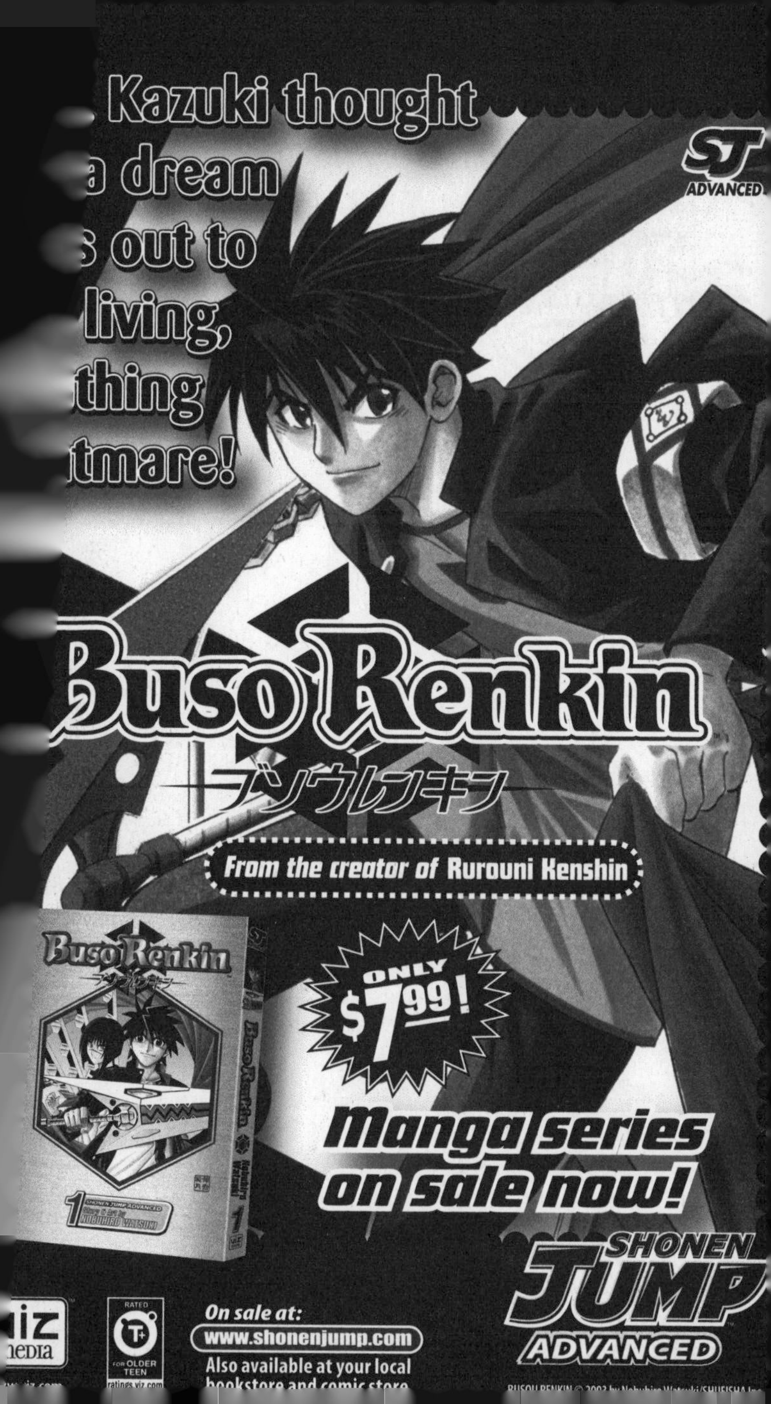

Kazuki thought
a dream
s out to
living,
thing
tmare!
SJ ADVANCED
Buso Renkin
ブソウレンキン
From the creator of Rurouni Kenshin
ONLY $7.99!
Manga series on sale now!
SHONEN JUMP ADVANCED
RATED T+ FOR OLDER TEEN
ratings.viz.com
On sale at:
www.shonenjump.com
Also available at your local

SHONEN JUMP

THE WORLD'S MOST POPULAR MANGA

BLEACH

STORY AND ART BY
TITE KUBO

ONE PIECE

STORY AND ART BY
EIICHIRO ODA

Tegami Bachi

STORY AND ART BY
HIROYUKI ASADA

JUMP INTO THE ACTION BY TELLING US WHAT YOU LOVE (AND WHAT YOU DON'T)

LET YOUR VOICE BE HEARD!

SHONENJUMP.VIZ.COM/MANGASURVEY

HELP US MAKE MORE OF THE WORLD'S MOST POPULAR MANGA!